THE CHEMNITZER CONCERTINA

A History and an Accolade

LaVern J. Rippley

St. Olaf College Press
Northfield, Minnesota
2006

This book is available from:
St. Olaf College Press
LaVern J. Rippley
Northfield, Minnesota 55057-1098
(507) 646-3233
Fax 646-3732
rippleyl@stolaf.edu

Copyright @ 2006 LaVern J. Rippley, St. Olaf College Press, 55057-1098
All rights reserved
Library of Congress Cataloging-in-Publication Data
Rippley, LaVern J.
Library of Congress Electronic Preassigned Control Number: 2005902910
The Chemnitzer Concertina: A History and an Accolade
ISBN 1-929321-01-5

~ Dedications ~

Jerry James Minar

This book is dedicated to Jerry Minar of New Prague, Minnesota, undoubtedly the most knowledgeable individual alive concerning the Chemnitzer concertina. Without his sharing of in-depth, hands-on information about the instrument, this project would have foundered. To write a book about a musical instrument you must look to the masters—Händel for the sublime, Mozart for the ethereal, Beethoven for passion, Schubert for lyric intensity, Haydn for richness. Minar put at my disposal his own mastery in his special field of supremacy. Through the Minar prism of inestimable skill was cast for me a mystery of twilight in an opaline haze that lends the concertinas seen in this book an unfailing illusion of loveliness.

– Dedications –

Kimberly Ann Eul

On a parallel plain, this book is dedicated to Kimberly Ann Paquette Eul [wife of Gary Scott Eul], mother of Nathan Werner Eul and Tyler Dale Eul, whose magic with computer design and layout imbued this volume with beauty. After study at Winona State University and Faribault Technical College, Eul worked at the *Faribault Daily News* creating ad compositions, then became graphic designer for Modern Printers in Faribault, Minnesota. "Eul" comes from German *Eule* (owl), emblematic of a wise, visually brilliant, perspicacious, sagacious and erudite gleaming star, one whose enlightening talent breathed into this book its spirit of loveliness.

Table of Contents

Introduction ....i-iii

Chapter 1   The Origin of the German Chemnitzer Concertina..............................1

Chapter 2   The Concertina comes to America 41

Chapter 3   The Concertina in Minnesota. The Hengel Story 77

Chapter 4   The Concertina Arrives in New Prague. The Jerry Minar Story...............107

Chapter 5   Promotion and Distribution of the Chemnitzer Concertina....................131

Chapter 6   How the Concertina is Played..175

Chapter 7   Entertainment and the Concertina 197

Appendix I   The World Concertina Congress Hall of Fame....................................239

Appendix II   Album Covers Depict the Concertina 257

Index 273

Appendix III   A Photographic History of the Chemnitzer Concertina 287

Introduction

All of my adult life I have been engrossed with immigration from Germany, primarily the passage of people, sometimes of toys, tools or technologies. Frequently, as in the instance of the Chemnitzer concertina, I chronicle cultural transfer. For all practical purposes, the Chemnitzer concertina no longer exists in Germany, thus this is my account of an "immigrant"—a genuine transfer. From 1893 in the United States the Chemnitzer has procreated generations of itself, first and foremost in Chicago, later and primarily, in Minnesota. Like the immigrants, the instrument has now moved west, first to Wisconsin, then to southern Minnesota. Here it remains embedded — as to playing it, building it, and distributing it. From the isolated site of its origin in the city of Chemnitz (Saxony) Germany, the concertina abides in these two states though it is randomly played in others, notably Michigan, western New York, and where the former send vacationers.

When Johann Sebastian Bach died in Leipzig in 1750, Saxony had witnessed its greatest cultural achievement. A generous arts patron until his death in 1733, Elector August the Strong, King of both Saxony and Poland, endowed Saxony with a luxurious, harvest of musical talent. Building forward from this great harvest 100 years, the Chemnitzer concertina would be conceived. Chemnitz was no musical Dresden, Leipzig, or Zwickau (Schumann). In the collage of Saxon cities, however, it breathed the sumptuous musical air that wafted far beyond all the boundaries of Saxony.

When Wolfgang Amadeus Mozart's body was dumped in a potter's ditch in 1756, Central Europe had reached a musical zenith that blanketed the lands extending from Leipzig to Prague, to Vienna, west to Salzburg and north to Bach's Leipzig. A century later, the concertina would acquire Scheffler keyboarding for international standardization. When Ludwig van Beethoven died in Vienna at the age of 57 in 1827, the three-state triumvirate [Saxony, Bohemia, Austria] glowed with achievements in music that have not been exceeded. When Johannes Brahms would be born in Hamburg in 1833, his birth would parallel the invention of the concertina by Carl Uhlig in Chemnitz. Situated deep in the southeastern province of Saxony, Chemnitz lay a mere 40 kilometers from the *Erzgebirge* [Ore Mountain range] that forms the boundary between Germany and Bohemia. In this isolated, mountainous hermitage, the Chemnitzer concertina was not only born but reached maturity.

A German instrument in every respect — inventor, builders, marketers, players — the concertina had little access into Germany proper. It crossed the German border neither to Poland nor into Bohemia except where German speakers [*Deutsch-Böhmen* — in modern times called Sudeten Germans after the name of the mountain range] long had settled. Occasionally and in limited ways, the concertina drifted southward into eastern Bavaria, territory that stretches from Hof toward Bayreuth and Regensburg, but not as far south as Munich. These three cities lie near the *Bayrischerwald* [Bavarian forest] located west from the *Böhmerwald* [Bohemian Forest], a provincial district of the Austrian Empire from which many of the German-speaking settlers in New Ulm, Minnesota had departed. In the *Böhmerwald*'s typical farming communities, e. g. in Bischofteinitz county, German-speaking residents developed an affection for the Chemnitzer concertina.

For the first few decades after its invention in 1834, the concertina was primarily at home in Chemnitz [from 1945-1990, called Karl Marx Stadt]. By the 1850s, high-volume production of the concertina had shifted southward to the *Oberes Vogtland*, the name given to the southwestern corner of Saxony [*Vogt* – advocate, man-in-charge, duke – a word related to English "volt"]. Here talented woodcarvers made the Christmas pyramids, nutcrackers, and related folk art. A folk instrument at heart, the Chemnitzer concertina attained its greatest production in three small, border towns peopled by the wood craftsmen in the *Oberes Vogtland*. These include in particular Carlsfeld, Klingenthal and adjacent villages of Zwota and Brunndöbra, along with Markneukirchen. The latter town has long been famous for its production of string and wind instruments, those requiring specialty woodworking and reed making. Several companies in Markneukirchen date back to the Thirty Years War [1618-

1648] when Protestants [with family names like Berthold and Fürstenau] fled persecution in their Catholic Bohemia to continue freely across the border in Saxony. Important museums in Markneukirchen exhibit the history of this town's instrument production.

Klingenthal, too, received Protestant refugees from Catholic Bohemia, many of whom produced string and woodwind instruments. The final resting place of concertina production in Germany, Klingenthal is today refocused on its musical heritage. Calling their community the *Musikstadt* [city of music], townsmen support a symphony orchestra and an annual accordion competition in May, which was initiated in 1948 for East bloc participants. In 1999, they began another tradition—annual meetings in September of harmonica performers, billed as "Mundharmonika-Live," which draws participants from around the world. However, it was neither in Markneukirchen nor in Klingenthal but in Carlsfeld, several kilometers to the north, where large numbers of concertinas were built. Initiated by Carl Zimmermann, production continued for generations by the Arnold families. Today, however, there is virtually no concertina production anywhere in Germany.

Except for the concertinas and bandonions of the Arnold families, Carlsfeld was little known throughout history. Only a few cottage industries crafting the wooden artifacts noted above keep the town alive. Until the end of the World War II, the Ernst Louis Arnold and the Alfred Arnold Companies exported concertinas and bandonions all over the world. But in 1952 their efforts were incorporated into the Klingenthal Harmonica Works; by 1964 all vestiges of production in Carlsfeld had ceased. In the late 1990s, the Paul Fischer KG Company, a musical instrument manufacturer with traditions dating back to 1887 in Carlsfeld, re-started manufacturing bandonions—not in Carlsfeld but in Zwota [a suburb of Klingenthal]. Mandated by the Russian occupiers in Klingenthal from 1948 onward, the once famous Arnold concertina builders of Carlsfeld [ELA and AA] fabricated the *Weltmeister* accordion in the Klingenthal factory. Since the reunification of Germany in 1990, the *Weltmeister* has become a reputable, German-made accordion, sold worldwide.

Prior to 1893 the concertina made no serious inroads into the American marketplace. Attempts in the 1870s in Philadelphia failed. Following its arrival in Chicago, however, the concertina gradually became not just a visitor, but an "immigrant," an article that, much like a person, departed from its homeland. Over time it was acculturated. Today it qualifies as an American cultural icon—no longer a German artifact—a genuine cultural transfer.

Cultural transfers cross borders. From its French origins, the enlightenment drifted eastward through Germany to Russia. Baroque architecture was born in Spain but spread to Austria, Bavaria and Bohemia. With the French Revolution, *liberté*, *fraternité* and *egalité* mushroomed across continental Europe. German culture after 1815 found its national identity, discarded the French ideal, and thrust its musical and technological ethos into France, Italy and America. Like a pendulum responding to the forces of gravity, the Chemnitzer concertina fits the pattern of 'cultural transfer.'

Unlike the baroque or the enlightenment, the concertina never penetrated the upscale plateaus of European culture. It remained unknown but to the common man. No symphonies, no string orchestras, no choirs considered the concertina despite its folk designation as a "poor man's organ." It persists as a folk instrument crafted by and played by, ordinary people, enduring incognito among higher echelons of the musical world. The *New Grove Dictionary of Music* barely mentions it as "the English, the Anglo and the Duet concertina." Grove states "a bellows-blown, hexagonal—or octagonal—shaped, free reed instrument with buttons parallel to the bellows, thus different from the accordion." It notes, further, that in Italy, the instrument is called a *piccola fisarmonica*, in Germany, a *Konzertina*, unaware that in the 1840s Germans also called it the *Physharmonika*]. Correctly, Grove adds, "ironically, the original German Konzertina on which the Anglo was modeled, enjoyed its greatest success in North and South America—in the polka bands of the mid-western United States and, as the bandonion, in the Tango-music bands of South America." Fair enough! The Arnold factory in Carlsfeld reportedly shipped thousands of concertinas to Chicago and thousands upon thousands of bandonions to Argentina. Friedrich Lange, the entrepreneur who initiated concertina sales in the United States, also shipped thousands of concertinas to Chicago.

Men who build, tune, play and repair the concertina demonstrate common qualities. In conjunction with dazzling musical instincts, they exhibit a mechanical bent. Throughout their history, most held jobs outside their concertina business. Quite a few were tool and die makers. Frequently they worked on the railroad or in jobs that offered access to rail transport, which carried them cross-country—mainly to Chicago, that powerful center of concertina life for a century. Initially and today, concertina people have extremely refined hearing. More often than not they play by ear and cannot read notes. One player explained – "I can't read notes – they go by too fast!" Other performers do read notes, more specifically, they push buttons indicated by numbers that correspond to notes on a clef. All the builders and players are decidedly dexterous. Fingers and arms perform in symphony. They not only play, they also craft the instrument—by hand. No concertina was ever built by a machine; each is the product of resourceful hands, which explains why no two concertinas look or sound alike. Each has its variants: to the touch, in the sound, to a given feel—individual qualities, which are gamely detected by skilful players.

In Germany the concertina became and remained popular at home, in rural villages, as a poor man's folk gadget in working class neighborhoods, and as an instrument popular for concertina club members performing in unison. Miners, farmers and members of the labor unions liked its bonding force. When the concertina arrived in Chicago in 1893 it burgeoned among workers in the packing plants and steel mills of Chicago. At times it rallied poorly-paid employees in the Stockyards to demand better working conditions. It reminded immigrants from eastern Germany and central Europe of their homelands by wafting tunes, melodies and folksongs that abated their homesickness. As the 1930s turned into the Great Depression, the concertina brought solace and comfort to peasant classes on the land and to immigrants in the working neighborhoods of Chicago and Milwaukee. Chicago's Germans and Bohemians were concertina pioneers. By the mid-1920s, however, Polish builders and players latched on to it. Since then, concertina construction has died out in Chicago. The once-exclusive concertina preeminence of Chicago has migrated to Minnesota. Here it remains in the hands of German-Bohemian and Czech producers, ironically resembling the geographic proximity the concertina enjoyed with its origins in Chemnitz in Saxony and Carlsfeld on the Czech border. In its new homeland of New Ulm and New Prague it lives and promises to endure.

Methodology

Recognizing that the audience for this book will be multidimensional, I present my material using a three-tiered approach. Primarily, there is the narrative! My objective is to tell the full story of the Chemnitzer concertina in chronological order as it stretches from Chemnitz to Chicago and thence to Minnesota. However, within the volume's linear history, I have knit each chapter into a story that stands alone. Inevitably, in such a plan, there is repetition of particulars, necessary so that each chapter enjoys entirety. On a secondary level, above and beyond the verbal account, I chronicle the concertina and its people with pictures. Scattered throughout the text, therefore, are photographs with relatively detailed captions in the hope that perusers can garner an accurate impression of the concertina's history by viewing the intra-textual pictures and studying their captions. Thirdly, I have appended a colored section in which the reader can monitor pictorially the concertina's unbroken history from 1834 to the present. Here I include meticulous descriptions so that, in a manner of speaking, this segment "tells" the concertina story visually.

Acknowledgements

No book is ever produced by the author alone. Hundreds deserve to be acknowledged. Inasmuch as thanking everyone is thanking no one, I limit myself to a minimum, without explanation of their contribution and without significance as to their sequence: Jennifer Bothun, Robert Novak, Kim Eul, Peer Ehmke, Jerry and Beverly Minar, Dan and Sue Gruetzmacher, Dan Miller, Christy Hengel, Hank Jacobs, John Bernhardt, Gerald Krzmarzick and the ten investors who raised the capital to publish this book: David Czaja, Eugene Gieszler, Glenn Gieszler, Christy Hengel, William Hlavac, Ambrose Kodet, Jerry Minar, James Morris, Erwin Suess, Jerome Then, Jack Zimmerman.

LaVern J. Rippley
Northfield, Minnesota
September 20, 2005

The Origin of the German Chemnitzer Concertina

When the desire for a new musical sound began sweeping Europe in the early 19th century, instrumental experimentation abounded. Musicians mimicked inventors in search of the fuller, richer sound that would outstrip existing, more traditional instruments. At the same time, peasants were gradually moving from lower to middle-class status even as orchestral and symphonic composers were taking an interest in the dances and folk music of the peasantry. Thus, the hand-held bellows boxed by squares holding reeds grew popular in regions of Central Europe.[1]

Because of this sudden interest in the ever-growing, free-reed family, it is often difficult to trace the history of these instruments. To be sure, the reed is an old device for producing a tone, exemplified in the reed organs of old, the mouth organ, and, for that matter, most wood instruments like the clarinet and saxophone. Bagpipe music, common especially to the Scots, typically results from wind moving against the reed, a device that spread rapidly to Central Europe early in the 19th century. Especially noteworthy were the successes of the wind instrument early in the 1800s. Such names as the Aeoline [1810], the Aeol-Harmonica, and then the names like *Blasebalg-Harmonika* [windbag harmonica or bagpipe] came to life around 1830. Furthermore, in many regions following 1829, there was the accordion, which spread like wildfire across Central Europe. Already in 1827, Christian Messner started hand carving harmonicas at Trossingen where, in 1855, Christian Weiss initiated manufacturing accordions and, two years later, handed the business over to Mathias Hohner [1833-1902] from whom the Hohner production of harmonicas and accordions derives.

In the Klingenthal region of Germany near the Czech border and in the *Erzgebirge* [Erz or Ore Mountain Range], J. W. Glier in 1829 established his Harmonica industry at nearly the same time as Wheatstone in England. Sir Charles Wheatstone devised an octagonal bellows-driven reed system on which he took a patent for his kind of concertina in 1844.[2] However, this contrivance had a single-tone reed system, regardless whether it was pushed or pulled [chromatic vs. diatonic].[3] The man who gets credit for the invention of the German concertina, and the instrument about which this book will focus, is Carl Friedrich Uhlig, who created his first concertina in 1834 at Chemnitz in the State of *Sachsen* [Saxony]. With button-activated melody reeds

Carl Friedrich Uhlig (1789-1874) invented the concertina in 1834. The Uhlig company was founded in 1819 possibly to manufacture stockings but soon evolved into the music business.

on the right-hand side and the same button system with bass reeds for the left hand, Uhlig's company built square reed ends on square bellows. In honor of the place where it was first constructed, this concertina bears the name "Chemnitzer Concertina." Whether Uhlig knew about Wheatstone's concertina or not is unknown, but whatever the truth, the development of both types of concertinas is considered, while parallel, to be completely independent, one of each other.[4]

Born at Bernsdorf near Chemnitz in April, 1789, Carl Friedrich Uhlig began his career as an apprentice to learn the manufacture of stockings. By 1819 he became bored with this occupation and struck out in a new direction to found his own business, no longer that of making stockings but producing musical instruments. At first he sold drums, guitars, violins and their accouterments—strings for example—promising in his advertisements to deliver good equipment at inexpensive prices for high quality goods and services. In his spare time, Uhlig played the clarinet for a Chemnitz orchestra until the construction of instruments consumed all of his available time. Gradually he turned his full attention to reed instruments, taking out patents not only for the concertina but also for Uhlig phisharmonikas and harmoniums.[5]

From his establishment at the address Am Anger No. 902, he boasted his "Store which housed musical instruments, including a beautiful selection of flutes, clarinets, trumpets, and more, for the first time he also offers to the public 'an accordion that is new and for which we have instructions available.'"[6] It is an instrument for which Uhlig has not yet devised a new name and hence refers to it as a new kind of accordion. In his advertisements of 1838, under the title of "Handlung *Musikalischer* Insrumente von C. F. Uhlig at 902," [dealership of musical instruments of Carl F. Uhlig at No. 902] he is asserting that his new accordions and *Mundharmonikas* [mouth harmonicas] come from his very own factory.[7] Again in 1843 his advertisements accentuate that his accordions and *Phisharmonikas* of all kinds come from his own factory.[8] By 1845 he advertises somewhat more boldly the entire *musikalische Instrumenten Magazin von C. F. Uhlig* [Uhlig Instruments store] including among the pieces the accordions of all styles and the *Phisharmonika mit ganz neuer Construction* [the concertina completely revamped and designed].[9]

As early as the 1840s, Uhlig had already developed international orders for his musical equipment and in 1847 arrived in Leipzig as the first Saxon producer of concertinas to appear at the international fair held in that city.[10] Inspired by the overnight success Uhlig enjoyed, other competitors opened up production facilities of their own. Soon the building of concertinas expanded centrifugally from Chemnitz, in particular to Waldheim, on a limited basis to Leipzig, and on a grand scale to Carlsfeld. Within a circumference of 100 kilometers from Chemnitz, the concertina industry in the Klingenthal Vogtland region that thrived for a century rested on the shoulders of Uhlig. Beginning in 1850, Uhlig presented himself as a "Harmonika-Fabrikant" — builder of Harmonikas – though, indeed, he was as much the inventor and dealer of the concertina as anything else. During the period from 1834 to about 1860, the word "Harmonika" is used with such great fluidity, even today, that no one can be certain when it includes the concertina and when it is restricted to the harmonica.

In Chemnitz at an address then known as "Am Anger 902," a site which is today named Brückenstraße, Uhlig established his primary construction site. To be sure, many of the concertina parts were created by a cottage industry scattered around that address with the parts arriving daily at Uhlig's factory for final assembly. A thoroughly successful businessman, Uhlig died in 1874, after which the family carried the firm forward with operations continuing at Am Anger 902. In recognition of his successful career, the local community provided C. F. Uhlig a first-class funeral ceremony in 1874, following which he was buried in the then-new municipal cemetery. Today in Chemnitz, his countrymen and city dwellers have totally forgotten his identity.[11] Not until 1895 did Uhlig's successors depart from Am Anger 902 and construct a new factory with living quarters on the second floor, positioned now in a building at the address of "Am Rosenplatz, No. 2."

Supposedly inspired by a bisonoric (also called "diatonic") instrument created by Cyrillus Demian (1772-1847) of Vienna in 1829, Uhlig's creation was a square mechanism with five buttons on each side, each button capable of producing two different sounds, depending on whether the instrument's bellows were "pushed" or "pulled." In his initial years of production, the instrument is named the *Physharmonica*, a name that appears in none of the dictionaries available at the time or since, not even in the Jakob and Wilhelm Grimm series. By naming his contrivance in subsequent years a "conzertina," Uhlig may have unconsciously created the group of free-reed instruments that would later be joined by the English, Anglo and Duet concertinas. However, today the Chemnitzer concertina is often considered one of the instruments in the overall concertina family only by virtue of its original name. Indeed, in much of the world the word "Chemnitzer" is left unspoken, whereas the general term "concertina" refers to the English or Irish artifice as well as to the Chemnitzer concertina, our primary focus for this book.

Although closely related to several other free-reed instruments (especially the bandonion, developed by Heinrich Band in the 1840s), the Chemnitzer has several features that distinguish it from those other free-reed devices, even those bearing the same name of "concertina." James P. Leary points out in his "German Concertina in the Upper Midwest," that although it shares partial designation with the better known English concertina, the German concertina's shape, diatonic scale, and two-notes-to-a-key distinguish it radically from its nominal counterpart in the British Isles. The English version is hexagonal, chromatic, and fitted with reeds that offer a uniform tone, be it on the push or the pull, while the Chemnitzer renders notes that differ when pushed from those sounded when pulled.[12] Finally, the reeds of the German Chemnitzer are not organized sequentially as tonal steps in musical scales; rather, they are scattered about like letters on a typewriter keyboard in accordance with the frequency of use. Today the Chemnitzer concertina usually contains 52 buttons and can create 104 tones, although Chemnitzers have been fashioned that can produce up to 130 tones.[13]

Even as the English-Irish instrument with imitation from the button box accordions of the day was expanding into the English countryside and Ireland, a reed

Heinrich Band (1821-1860) of Krefeld, west of the Rhine River near Düsseldorf, the inventor of the Bandonion around 1843.

organ maker in Paris in 1838 also called his air pressure instrument a concertina. Possibly for protection of his invention, Charles Wheatstone garnered a new patent for his modified "Improved Concertina." It now offered greater detail and design, somewhat like the English instruments of today. Soon thereafter in 1840, Heinrich Band (1821-1860) in Krefeld near the Rhine River introduced the Uhlig concertina to his town orchestra. A musician in the city orchestra and the owner of a music store in Krefeld, Band became a business partner of Uhlig.[14] By 1846, Band was marketing a version of Uhlig's concertina with 50 buttons, calling it the Band-Union. Some theorize he spun this name from the word Accordion. Others believe he was a working man strongly imbued with the word for a workers' union, although the German word for such an organization is the

From a promotional brochure of the Lange-Uhlig Concertina Company in Chemnitz, Saxony. Note that the company claims a presence on the market in Munich, Chemnitz, Dresden and Chicago.

Max Scheffler (1864-1930), the man who standardized the keyboard of the concertina.

Gewerkschaft, not Union.

Whatever the fate of the bandonion, the inventor of the concertina, Carl Friedrich Uhlig, in 1863 turned his company over to his co-worker and longtime master craftsman in the firm, Friedrich Anton Lange. However, he retained certain rights of determination until his death in 1874. Years thereafter, F. A. Lange conducted the Uhlig business with a new designation which capitalized on the Uhlig reputation, "Lange vorm. Uhlig" [Lange, previously known as Uhlig].[15] In 1895, Lange moved the company from the original Brückenstraße site to a new building on Rosenplatz in Chemnitz-Bernsdorf. By this time, his work force had expanded from 10 to over 20 employees. Under the tutelage of Lange, the concertina evolved into a 78-tone instrument, which enjoyed great success on the export markets. Advertisments in German papers from around the turn of the century read, "F. Lange vorm. C. F. Uhlig" in Chemnitz, Saxony "Am Rosenplatz 2" Telephone 3842 as having outlets for their products in Munich, Chemnitz, Dresden and Chicago.

Samples of the advertising by the F. Lange-formerly C. F. Uhlig Company have been reproduced in history books with photography of their concertina club of 1913 and their workshops. It was basically this instrument which Max Scheffler (1864-1930) expanded into the 76 key system, known in Germany as the Chemnitz tone. His store and workshop were the same as his dwelling at Adelsberg No. 6 in Chemnitz. A major thrust forward into the United States market was the successful exhibition of the concertina by the Lange Company at the World's Industrial Fair in Chicago in 1893, where Lange was awarded a special medallion.[16] And while his instruments were bought and sold widely in Chicago and the Midwest, Lange also sold concertinas that acquired specialty names either by designated order from Germany or being so named by distributors in the United States, for example, the "Majestic." Definitely a Lange instrument, the Majestic plainly bears an American marketing name. Although the firm of Lange continued well into the 20th century as owned by Arthur Müller, it suffered the economic consequences of World War I, a suppression of the instrument by the Nazi government during the 1930s, and eventually the destruc-

City park in downtown Chemnitz from a postcard showing the location of the Uhlig-Lange factory at Rosenplatz as indicated by the arrow at the left.

Max Scheffler house at Adelsberg No. 6 in Chemnitz.

Advertisements for the Alfred Arnold Concertina factory in Carlsfeld. Bottom line is asking for new dealers.

tion of its buildings on Rosenplatz during the bombings throughout the spring of 1945.

As might be expected, the flow of musical instruments to the United States from the region of Chemnitz in Saxony can hardly be reconstructed a century and a half later. However, a cursory review of tables of contents for the German journal for the construction of musical instruments reveals that there was indeed considerable traffic.[17] Many of the articles report difficulties dealing with South America, notably Brazil and Argentina. However, a few samples do concern the United States, e. g. export from the city of Gera (October 10, 1883). The following year the discussion is about export from Saxony to the United States (November 11, 1884), and in the following week (November 21, 1884), specifically about American orders for concertinas. A few years later (August 18, 1886, No. 33, p. 475) the article discusses problems of demand, especially as it concerns steel reeds for the concertina. But in 1887 things seem to improve (August 21, 1887, p. 416), when the report is that there is no lack of orders from America to the Saxon Vogtland [the region of Saxony including the towns of Carlsfeld, Klingenthal, etc.], although the buyers were trying to hold to last year's listing and even reduce them through competitive shopping among suppliers.[18]

As to the values of musical instrument export to the United States, there is an article (January 1, 1888, p. 123) reporting to the U. S. Consulate filing of export values from Saxony. For the year 1887 the following cities were listed in thousands of dollars: Chemnitz $125, Dresden $22, Leipzig $208, Plauen $66 and from Annaberg a whopping $834. Annaberg is centrally located in the Vogtland in close proximity to Carlsfeld, Klingenthal, Johanngeorgenstadt and others. Of course these values included all instruments, not just the concertina.

In the same year 1888, there arose a major problem for German exporters of the concertina. It took shape from the Merchandise Act of August 23, 1887 according to which the English government demanded explicit marking of all manufactured goods coming into the English economy and including any product that would be shipped to British colonies or in British ships. For practical purposes, this meant the need for adequate labeling "Made in Germany" stamped in English on all export production. Taking effect on January 1, 1888, the concertina [and other musical instruments] builders began the interesting practice of constructing for American wholesalers in Germany but labeled as if produced by an American or English firm in Germany.[19]

As a result of the British law, a number of concertina dealers rushed to register their brands. Karl-Ernst Louis Rockhausen in Waldheim registered his key stop valves (acknowledged January 21, 1889), while G. Grimm registered his concertina brand name in Klingenthal. The company also registered its wooden shell, the button bases with drilled holes, and the hammer lasts [Hammerleisten] for concertinas. On December 12, 1892, the journal reports that the company of C. G. Schuster, Jr. in Markneukirchen had registered its brand name for its concertina and reed instruments. The next year on September 9, 1893, the city of Markneukirchen was granted special United States Consular services for the region of the Vogtland under Oskar Gottschalk, a vice consul from the primary American Consulate in Plauen.

The reason cited for the consular substation was the export of musical instruments in 1892 valued at $897,079 plus another $23,857 for mother of pearl products. Meanwhile, varying reports and journal entries stated that the concertina industry, while not thriving, was surviving under the new rules.

In 1894, the Leipzig Journal reported briefly about the Columbian Exposition in Chicago at which H. Hohner, Christian Weiß and Christian Meßner, all from the town of Trossingen exhibited. Prizes were awarded at the exhibition to F. Lange, Chemnitz for Concertina and Bandonions as well as to Christian Meßner & Co. of Trossingen for his mouth harmonicas (Volume 14, No. 3, p. 54). In early 1898 the journal reports the proceedings for bankruptcy of the Friedrich Lange Company in Chemnitz, as of December 31, 1898 by the court administrator (Volume 19, p. 335). For the same year of 1898, an article announces that there were in the Vogtland 21 manufacturers of concertinas employing a total of 379 workers (Volume 19, p. 467). Of interest is the Markneukirchen consular declaration that the value of concertinas and accordions shipped to the United States during the fourth quarter of 1900 amounted to $24,709, a figure that jumped to $31,621 in the fourth quarter of 1901. Meanwhile, the journal reports that the bankruptcy of Friedrich E. Lange had been rescued by commuting the company to his son-in-law, Edward Niemann (Volume 23, p. 401). Surprisingly, there are relatively few entries about the Alfred Arnold factory in Carlsfeld, although from time to time their existence is noted (e. g. Volume 33, 1913, p. 988).

To recapitulate: Carl Friedrich Uhlig in 1834 placed advertisements in the *Chemnitzer Anzeiger* newspaper for his "Accordion neuer Art," [a new styled accordion],

Lange-Uhlig advertisements for the concertina. Here the card reports that the firm was founded in 1835. Pictured above is a bandonion.

Newspaper advertisements for concertinas built in Leipzig. The bottom line offers free catalogs for the years 1911-1912.

The Origin of the German Chemnitzer Concertina

This concertina was built around 1925 by Kurt Jobst at the factory in Brunndöbra. Note that it exemplifies the harp and logo used on the corners, suggesting that it was in some way associated with the Lange-Uhlig firm in Chemnitz. However, the village is located closer to Klingenthal and Carlsfeld.

The Meinel company in Klingenthal in the state of Saxony located on the road to Markneukirchen, today housing one of Germany's most famous museums of musical instruments.

a bit later to be called the concertina. By 1847 Uhlig was appearing regularly at trade fairs, notably at the Leipzig Industrial Fair, then, as now, one of the largest in Europe. His production remained in Chemnitz but competitors and cooperators quickly dispersed to Klingenthal, Waldheim, Johanngeorgenstadt and other villages, especially to Carlsfeld. Beginning in 1850 the harmonica and the button accordion business developed rapidly in the so-called Vogtland, the region immediately southeast of Chemnitz, encompassing Klingenthal and Carlsfeld that sometimes bears the name "Germany's musical corner." In part, production, distribution and sales enjoyed the benefit of improved transportation, rendered by developing waterways, postal roadways and especially the railroad.

Names and towns of the co-producers of the concertina and the year their company was founded include Carl F. Zimmermann in Carlsfeld (1849), Ernst Bässler, Fabrik von Concertinas in Grünberg bei Augustusburg in Saxony (1860), C. Oswald Lenk, Konzertinamacher in Zwickau (1863), Ernst Louis Arnold Konzertina Fabrik in Carlsfeld (1864), Karl Haimerl, Concertinenverfertiger in Haidhausen in Bayern (1869), Gebrüder C. A. Seifert Konzertina-Fabrik in Waldheim in Saxony (1870), Reinhard Windisch in Klingenthal (1870), Otto Weidlich, Akkordeon-Konzertina Fabrik in Brunndöbra (1873), Ernst Leiterd, Concertinenbauer in Brunndöbra im Vogtland (1878), Louis Oswald Herold, Fabrikation von Konzertinas in Georgenthal (1883), Ernst Birnstock, Handzuginstrumentenmacher-Meister in Crimmitschau in Saxony (1886), Bruna Thiele Konzertina-Fabrik in Chemnitz (1890), Leipziger Musikwerke Euphonika A. G. (1895), Friedrich Wilhelm Meinel, Konzertinafabrik in Untersachsenberg im Vogtland (1906), and others. Many new firms came into being during the period from 1900-1930 and then went back out of business thereafter.[20]

In many respects, the next phase in the development of the concertina is owed to Carl Zimmermann. Born in 1817 at Morgenröthe-Rautenkranz about 20 kilometers north of Klingenthal, he grew up in Carlsfeld. But when he turned 16, Zimmermann moved to Chemnitz to work and learn a trade in his uncle Heinrich Rockstroh's iron casting works. Here he came to know Uhlig and started to learn how to play and how to construct the concertina. According to his diary, "ich wußte mich mit der dreiteiligen Harmonika von Uhlig aus Chemnitz beliebt zu machen [I found out how to enjoy myself with the three-row button harmonicas by Uhlig in Chemnitz.] Beginning in 1850-51, Zimmermann took the Uhlig products for demonstration at the Leipzig fair and the World's Fair in London. Soon the Uhlig instrument with 28 buttons (56-tone system), constructed by Carl Zimmermann in Carlsfeld, began to be exported not only to destinations in Europe but even to the United States, probably to New England.[21] According to his autobiography, Zimmermann developed his Carlsfeld business to a point where he employed 76 workers in his factory.[22]

In 1849, Carl Zimmermann published his *Tabelle für Accordion mit 58 Tönen verbesserter Construction* which he demonstrated both at the London exposition in 1854 and at the Munich Industrial Fair in 1854.[23] At this juncture, there were three main types of concertinas under construction in Germany: the Uhlig or Chemnitzer, the Band [bandonion] called the Rheinische, and the Zimmermann called the Carlsfelder, each with its own style of fingering. Following Heinrich Band's death in

1860 [born 1821], his brothers continued the business until his son, Alfred Band (1845-1923), took it over and continued until the 1920s. Almost all of Band's instruments derive from the makers of parts in the Saxon Chemnitz and Vogtland regions. In the 1890s, these expanded to a fourth version devised by Max Scheffler, now called the Scheffler arrangement, which still belonged to the Chemnitz version overall. Because of its complicated characteristics, players began arranging their own keyboards according to preference, which required sheet music but slowed down the instrument's popularity with the common folk. Meanwhile, in 1854, Uhlig chaired a meeting of German concertina enthusiasts in Schönheide at which they agreed that the Chemnitzer keyboard should be standardized, possibly adopting an organization devised by Band already in 1846 based now on rows in G and A, instead of the first Uhlig instrument which used G and C.

From this meeting arose the first standardized keyboard which allowed for uniform notation. Ten years later in 1864, Ernst Ludwig [Louis] Arnold [reportedly married to a daughter of Carl Uhlig] took over production of the concertina from Mr. Zimmermann. The reason for this exchange was because Zimmermann, in 1864 at the age of 47 with his wife Sophie and six of their eight children, decided to emigrate to Philadelphia to join his brother who operated a music business in that city. Four months later the brother returned to Germany. In Philadelphia, it appears, Carl Zimmermann at first tried his luck building and selling concertinas, but when that languished due to the ongoing American Civil War, he survived by servicing French accordions. In 1869, precisely five years after his arrival, Zimmermann on September 20, 1869 became an American citizen, declaring as his career his concertina business-residence at 238 North Second Street in

Carl Zimmermann of Carlsfeld who started the concertina business there in 1849, exported concertinas and moved to Philadelphia in 1864. Later he made the autoharp.

Advertisement for the Autoharp from the 1895 book about musical instruments exhibited at the Chicago World's Fair in 1893.

The Origin of the German Chemnitzer Concertina

The Arnold factory in Carlsfeld taken circa 1900.

The building at the center of the letterhead is seen here in a closeup taken by LaVern Rippley during his visit to the site in January 2002.

Letterhead of the Alfred Arnold Concertina factory in Carlsfeld from the year 1939. It first opened in the small circled building at the upper right. Directly below the letterhead is a picture of this original Arnold structure as it looked in January, 2002, taken from nearly the identical angle.

Map of Europe in 2004. Dot shows city of Chemnitz. Carlsfeld, Klingental and Johann/Georgenstadt are south of Chemnitz on the Czech border.

Philadelphia. Believing he had discovered a new tonal note system, which he patented in 1871, Zimmermann soon gave up the concertina and switched to the zither. For this endeavor, he received patent #257,808 on May 9, 1882, now calling himself Charles Frederick Zimmermann, inventor of the "Auto-Harp, which came to be known in Germany as the "Akkord-Zither."[24] It was for this invention that Zimmermann gained recognition at the 1893 Columbian Exhibition.

Building autoharps succeeded for a time until 1892, when Zimmermann sold his manufacture with a reported capital of a hundred thousand dollars and shifted some 150 employees to Alfred Dolge.[25] Dolge by this time had a reputation for his pianos. Of German descent himself, Dolge in 1873 had visited Breslau, Germany, where he acquired the "blue felt" technique for his key hammers. Thus the piano string business dovetailed with the autoharp concept. Seemingly in conflict with Zimmermann's intent, Dolge sought to transfer the autoharp company to his own Dolgeville in upstate New York near Utica. Little Falls, New York papers report an attempt by Zimmermann to reverse the sale but to no avail.

However, the Zimmermann Company name continued strong. In Dolgeville, Alfred Dolge and Son strove for perfection of their piano business and at the Chicago Columbian Exposition in 1893 won eight separate awards for their products. The extent of the awards included the autoharp. "Two awards were granted to the C. F. Zimmermann Company for autoharps and figure music, and the exhibit of this enterprise also belonged to the Dolge interests, as the products of the Zimmermann Company are marketed by Alfred Dolge & Son."[26] Whether Zimmermann himself had anything to do with the effort is doubtful. Why the expansive Dolge Company would continue the Zimmermann name raises a question—was the Zimmermann surname perhaps so prominent and so recognizable that it benefited Dolge to retain this name for better sales? The awards received for the autoharp specifically refer to superior workmanship and tone quality, the originality and simplicity of the system and its educational value. In the context of the explanation for the autoharp awards we read as follows concerning the work of Zimmermann:

> It is only a few years since the genius of C. F. Zimmermann evolved the simple, and yet so marvelous, chord-bar. In a small way the manufacture of the instrument was carried on for a number of years in Philadelphia. In 1892 the C. F. Zimmermann Company was formed, and a large plant erected at Dolgeville, N. Y., thus giving the manufacturers unprecedented facili-

The Origin of the German Chemnitzer Concertina

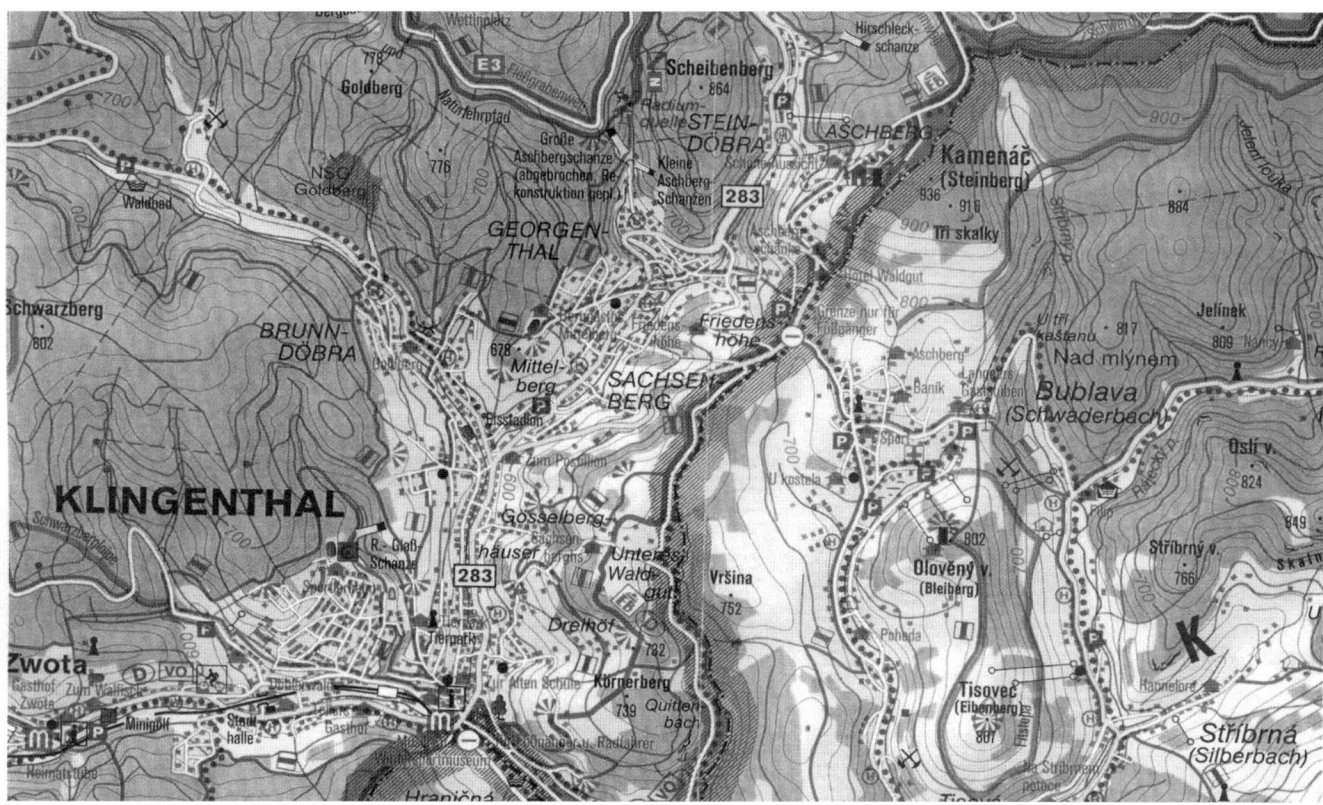

City of Klingenthal with Zwota to the immediate left. Note that the border with the Czech Republic runs vertically through the center of the map. The two circles with a dash inside are border crossing points.

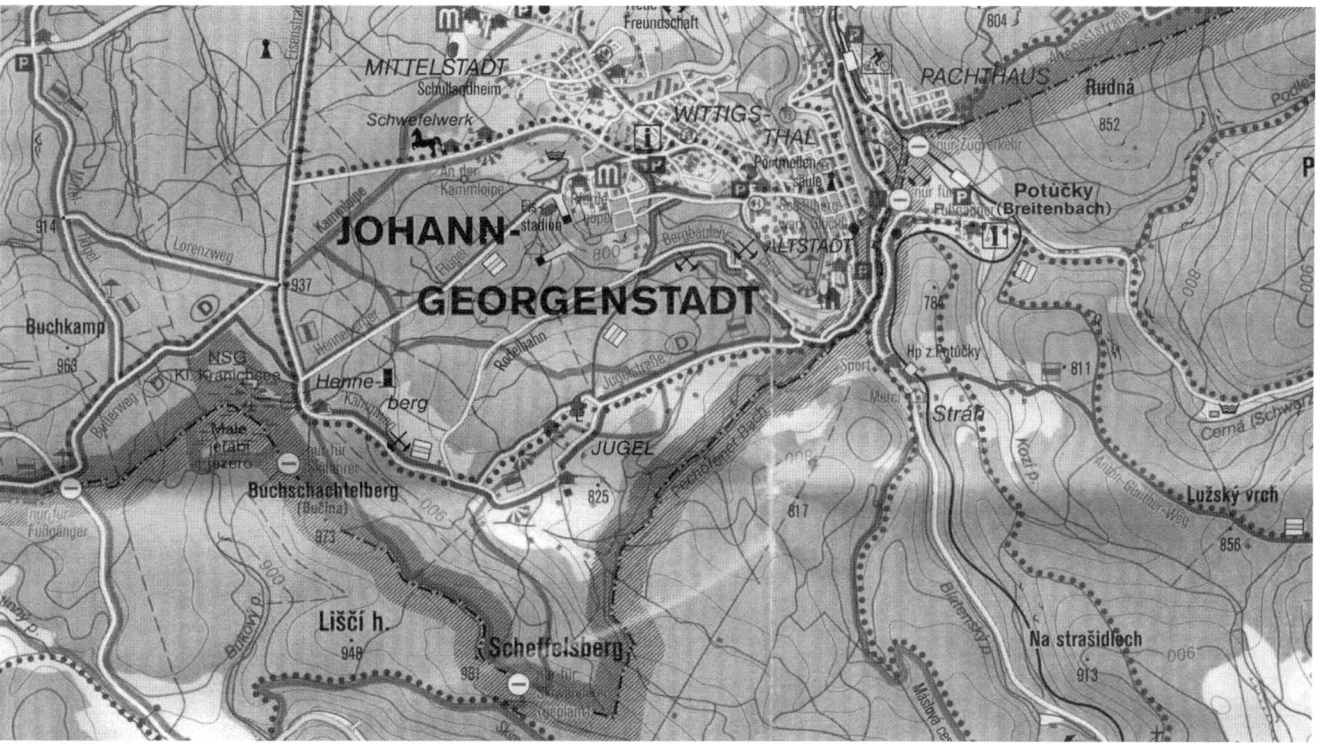

Johann-Georgenstadt. Here the border with the Czech Republic runs in a line with five crossing points signaled by a circle with a dash through its diameter. These circle-dash indicators are border crossings.

ties right at the fountain head of the greatest music supply center in the world.[27]

In addition to the positive description of the talents of Carl Friedrich Zimmermann, the Dolge Company took out a special advertisement in the large tome cataloging the awards presented at the Columbian Exposition, featuring prominently the new C. F. Zimmermann building in Dolgeville.[28] Thus the efforts and achievements of one of the world's most successful builders of the concertina were subsumed into his subsequent successes with the autoharp.[29] What became of the Zimmermann concertina factory brought fame to the Alfred, Ernst Louis and Arno Arnold family. Through the years, this factory sent thousands and thousands of concertinas and bandonions to the New World. Zimmermann's legacy had been diffused and diverted. In 1898 in Philadelphia, Zimmermann met his death as a result of a horse traffic accident and lies buried in the Mt. Vernon cemetery in Philadelphia.

Soon after Zimmermann's 1864 departure for the New World, the son of Ernst Ludwig Arnold became owner and technical manager of the former Zimmermann firm and called it the Ernst Louis Arnold or the Alfred Arnold Concertina and Bandonion works.[30] On many a concertina delivered from the factory are emblazoned the manufacturer's name "ALFRED" down the left side as the listener faces it and "ARNOLD" down the right side. For a time Ernst Louis Arnold used the logo simply "A" but later revised it to read "Marke A" [patented A] and then simply "ELA." But in 1911 when the firm was acquired by his son, the markings changed to Alfred Arnold. Many instruments also appeared with the double AA logo to identify the model. By 1875 the concertina had been expanded to 38 keys and corresponding 76 tones which extended its use to better serve bands as well as individual performances. Next came 47 keys and 94 tones and, by the end of the century, 102 tones from 51 keys. Only in the 20th century were some 122 and 124-tone concertinas being built, while the 102 tone approach advanced to 104 with the addition of one button. Although there are a few 148-tone concertinas

Prospectus for the Arnold Company about 1930. This tango dance band includes Juan Llossas on the left and Walter Pörschmann, then Germany's finest bandonion player.

The Origin of the German Chemnitzer Concertina

A typical concertina from around 1900 buit by the Alfred Arnold Company in Carlsfeld.

known, the most popular concertina in either Germany or America continues to be the 104-tone instrument. Built with the Uhlig-Scheffler keyboard, this instrument remains the authentic Chemnitzer.

As the concertina came fully into its own in the 1870s, clubs and associations for the concertina also were formed in many of the smaller towns of Saxony. In particular in the mining district and by extension in the western German region of the Ruhr mining region, the concertina took hold among the common folk and the workers. Around 1900, within the confines of the harbor culture in Buenos Aires and other South American seaports, the bandonion caught hold for playing the tango. According to some statistics, between

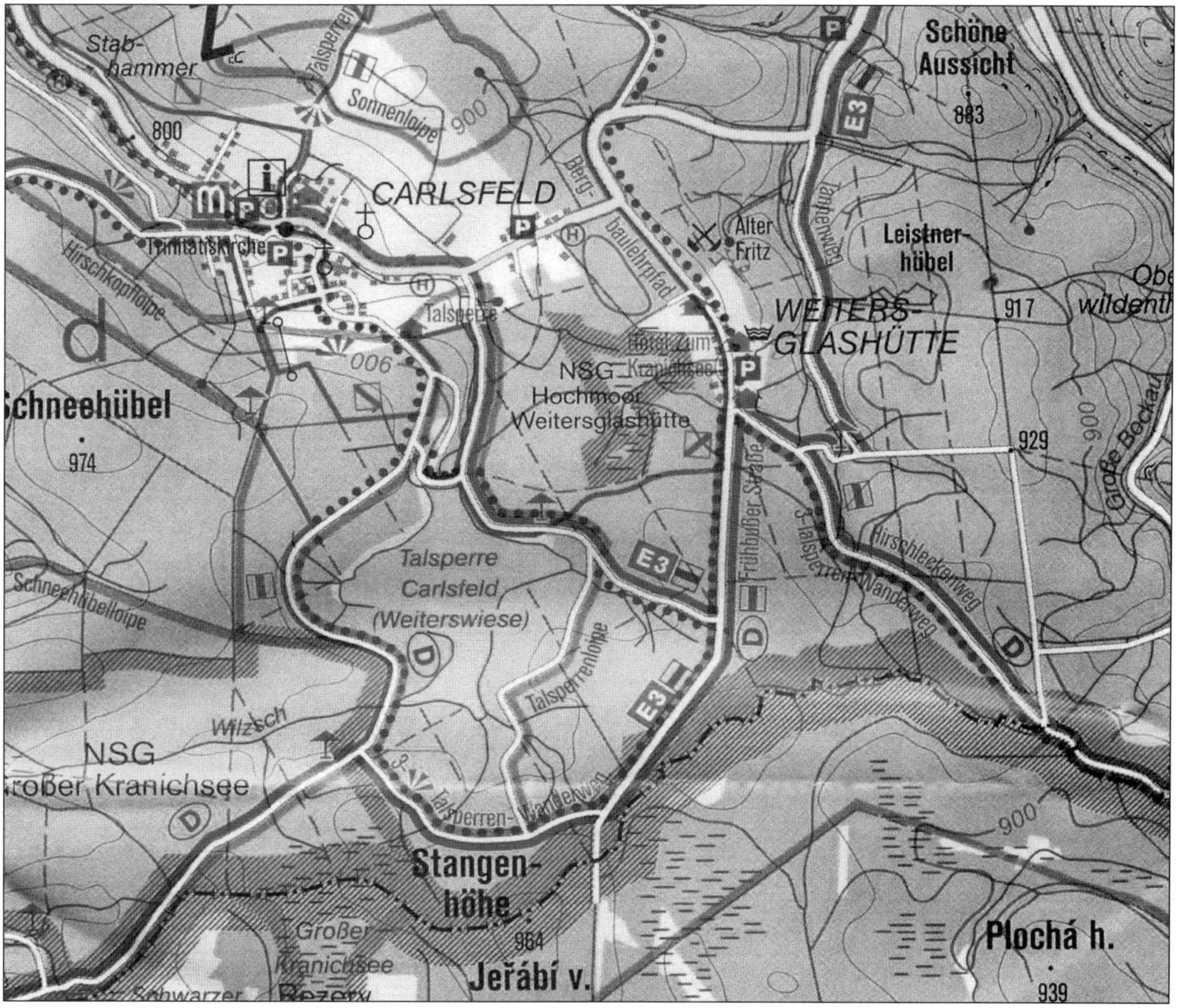

The small town of Carlsfeld home of Karl Zimmerman, Ernst Louis Arnold, the Alfred Arnold and Arno Arnold concertina factory. Note the dot and dash line below the name Stangenhöhe, which demarcates the Czech border.

Early US Patent for an 1856 Concertina
Charles M. Zimmermann - 1856

In 1856 Mr. Zimmermann was issued a patent for this invention from the United States Patent & Trademark Office (USPTO). There are 4 documents included with this patent. A drawing specification sheet from the patent has been reproduced on parchment paper, secured to a quality 8" x 10" Matboard, and is ready to install into a frame. The other 3 sheets reproduced from the USPTO documents, also printed on parchment stock, include 1 additional drawing sheet and 2 pages which describe the scope of this invention in formal terms...

"Be it known that I, Charles Moritz Zimmermann, of the city of Philadelphia and the State of Pennsylvania, have invented certain new and useful Improvements in Accordions, Concertinas, and other Similar Instruments; and I do hereby declare that the following is a full, clear, and exact description of the same, reference being had to the accompanying drawing and to the figures and letters of reference marked thereon. My invention relates to improvements in that class of musical instruments, in which sound is produced by air forced by means of bellows against a series of reeds, such as accordions, concertinas, and melodeons and consists in arranging the valves of the above mentioned instruments in connection with sliding rollers acted upon by the keys, and regulated by stops, in such a manner that by pressing the stops the said sliding rollers may be passed from one valve to another or brought to open two valves together thereby enabling the operator by pressing one key to produce a variety of different notes..."

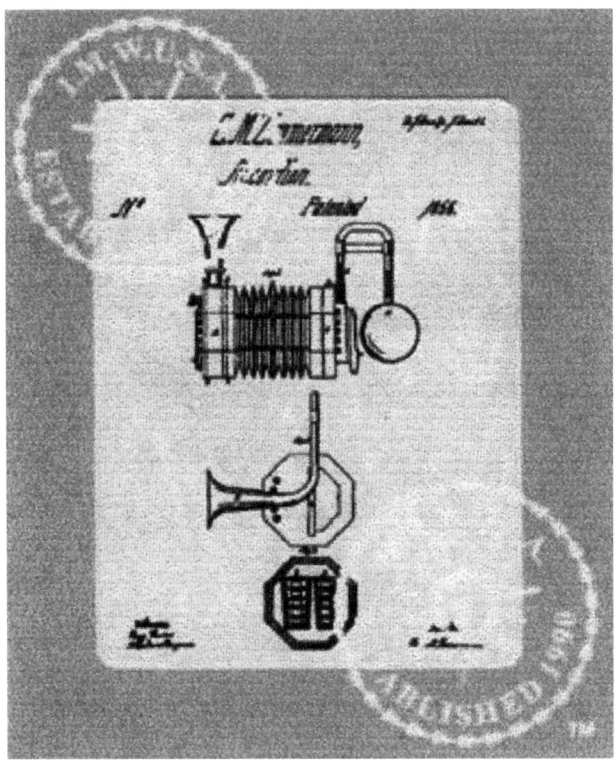 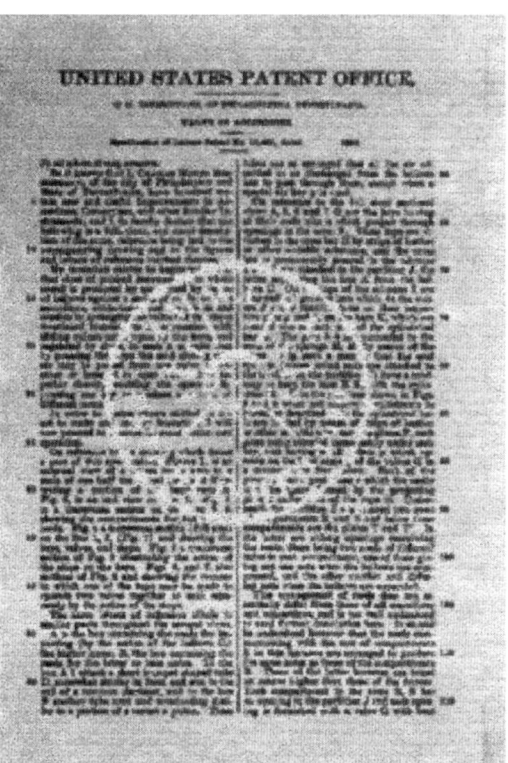

The above patent was offered on eBay during early 2004. The Zimmermann documented as arriving in Philadelphia in 1864, is Carl Friedrich Zimmermann. To date, it has not been possible to determine whether Charles Moritz Zimmermann, also of Philadelphia, might be indeed the same individual.

its founding and its demise after World War II, the Arnold factory alone from its Carlsfeld factory shipped up to 30,000 bandonions and/or concertinas to South America. Meanwhile, orders from the United States for the concertina grew by leaps and bounds from about 1900 to 1930, clearly a significant high point for the concertina industry in Saxony. Sales slowed only when manufacturers in Chicago came fully on stream in the mid to late 1920s and flourished through the 1930s and early 1940s.

When Chemnitz was cut off following World War II, trade to the entire outlet of products to the West ceased. Thus, when Arno Arnold escaped from Carlsfeld to West Germany in the 1950s, he was only temporarily able to resurrect and re-supply the American market, one of his chief outlets being the Watters Distributing Co. of 2219 East 42nd Street in Minneapolis.[31] Arno Arnold concertinas were touted by Watters to have superior styling, were lightweight, having lifetime quality materials, balanced action, and had been tuned by the finest concertina tuners in the world. Furthermore, the marketers claimed the Arno Arnold of this era had a patented three-dimensional sound distribution capacity with stereophonic reed chambers and patented curved hand rails for fast, easy fingering of the keyboard. In the brochures also are photographs of workmen assembling the Arnold "balanced action," while this Arno Arnold himself is seen inspecting the key-action and pieces of the Mountain Alder wood bottoms of the instrument. At this point in time, Watters claims to be the "World's Largest Concertina Handler."[32]

Prior to the end of World War II, the Arnold factory had always been located at Haus am Bach 15b in the tiny town of Carlsfeld, as successor to the Carl Friedrich Zimmermann who left for the United States in 1864. In summary the firm first unfolded under Ernst Ludwig Arnold (1838-1910). Some concertinas bear the lettering ELA, meaning they came from the firm under the leadership of Ernst Ludwig Arnold. Following the death of Ernst Louis, as he was usually called even in German contexts, his sons Hermann, Paul and Alfred took over the business. A short time later, youngest son Alfred (1878-1933) opened a business independent of his brothers, which brother Paul joined in 1914. Concertinas coming from this branch were designated AA as compared to the ELA of the former firm. By means of contacts developed at the Leipzig fairs, the Arnold producers found their best market to be the bandonion in South America, especially in Argentina.

Meanwhile, the bandonion developed rather separately for a somewhat different market. Likewise, in many respects, the bandonion is the result of a waning economy experienced by the miners in the Erzgebirge. Recent investigation indicates that, consequently, the Bandonion and Konzertina Fabrik of Alfred Arnold was the primary exporter of the bandonion to South America, notably Uruguay and Argentina, where it gen-

This elderly couple in Brunndöbra are working at home—he tuning the reeds, she positioning reed leathers onto the reed plates.

erated its popularity by supplying music for dancing the tango. Here the spelling meandered from Bandonion to "Bandoneon" as it is known in South America today. By way of reiteration, it was especially the double AA model, which stands for Alfred Arnold, that still commands a high price.33 The other model in high demand was the original ELA, for Ernst Ludwig [Louis] Arnold, from the earlier production line of Zimmermann followed by Alfred Arnold in Carlsfeld.

Because the bandonion was so massively exported during the early decades of the 20th century, demand drove up production of this instrument to some 7,000 per year in its zenith years. Virtually all of them came from the cottage industry of the Chemnitz / Carlsfeld region. Because a strong market was building from around 1888, the Arnold family expanded into new manufacturing quarters. As already noted, Arnold used the 104-tone system for their concertinas until the death of Ernst Louis in 1910, when youngest son Arnold (Arno), proved unable to take over the main factory. He started a smaller factory of his own across the street while Alfred took over the original enterprise, officially established by him in 1911, placing emphasis on the bandonion. However, Arno kept showing his wares regularly at the Leipzig Messe [trade fair] and other commercial fairs in Germany. Soon the Arnolds established another factory in the nearby town of Johanngeorgenstadt. Here, together with the Carlsfeld factories of Alfred Arnold, by the 1930s, 100 customary workers reportedly were able to construct as many as 600 instruments each month.34 Although Alfred Arnold died in 1933, his brother continued the firm until its demise [or flight of the family to the West] after the Russians arrived in 1945.

However that may be, neither Band nor the Arnolds nor Zimmermann were alone the successors of Uhlig in Chemnitz. Johann Gottlieb Höselbarth and Christian Friedrich Pirner began as co-workers with Uhlig but later went into production on their own. Others who either worked for or were familiar with Uhlig were Johann David Wünsch (1814-1895), who started his own firm called Fabrik und sämtlicher Musikinstrumente: Wünschs weltberühmte Band-oneons. Also prominent at the time was Christian Friedrich Reichel, Accordion-Fabrikant of Chemnitz, who began production in 1854 at Waldheim.35 Sometimes copying and switching labels on instruments, at other times toiling for Uhlig, Lange or Arnold during the day, employees

Here a woman in 1924 delivers bellows created in her home to the concertina assembly point.

Family gathering with a Lange concertina in the foreground, a Christmas tree in the background.

worked on their own in the evening to create their individual concertinas, often with variations in styles to reduce the chance of "Etikettenschwindel," the illegal copy-cating of a product. Thus, there developed other less conspicuous firms like Schönherr and Matthes making what they advertised as the "Praktikal-Bandonion" or the "Chromatiphon" built by Hugo Stark. Apparently the production of Julius Zadamek and Fritz Micklitz in Berlin resulted from their music teacher Ernst Kusserow during the 1920s and got the name "System Kusserow."[36]

As would happen later in 1893, at the Columbian Exposition in Chicago, the trade fair in Europe was an important factor in the development of the market for the Chemnitzer concertina. At the London trade fair in 1851, Carl Zimmermann attended from Carlsfeld as did Wheatstone and Company from London. In 1854 in Munich, Zimmermann came again from Carlsfeld but so did Uhlig and Reichel from Chemnitz, along with the lesser-known Johann Gottlob Höselbarth from there. None of the Chemnitz personnel made it to Paris in 1855 but Heinrich Band showed up from Krefeld with his bandonions along with Wheatstone who came from London. At London again in 1862, Chemnitz lacked representation but Michael Schuster of Markneukirchen in the Vogtland showed up, probably with concertinas. When the trade fair switched to Chemnitz in 1867, naturally Ernst Ludwig Arnold, Carl Reichel and Carl Uhlig all came. In Vienna in 1873 none of the Vogtlanders exhibited.[38] In spite of sales on a multiple continent spread, concertina construction never got far from home. The instrument's chief proponents remained solidly anchored in their Saxon territory near the border with Bohemia. Nor were Saxony's neighbors all too interested in the concertina, with the exception of Bavaria, but only for some decades in the late 1800s.

In the main, concertina production over the decades took on varying styles. In some instances such as Uhlig-Lange and the Arnold companies, it appears that construction occurred in a closed shop. In other instances, this was a typical cottage industry in which parts were cobbled together in homes all across the village, then delivered to the main center for assembly and shipment.

Comparable in importance to Carl Friedrich Uhlig and Friedrich Emil Lange, in addition to the Arnold factories in Carlsfeld and their associates in Johanngeorgenstadt was the town of Waldheim located north of Chemnitz. Here Christian Friedrich Reichel, the stepson of Carl Friedrich Uhlig, began constructing the "harmonika," as he called the concertina in 1856. Born in 1811 in the village of Jahnsdorf, C. F. Reichel initially learned his trade of stockingmaker [as had earlier his co-producer, Carl Uhlig]. This line of work he pursued until 1833, when he switched to constructing instruments. The catalyst for such a move came after he arrived in Chemnitz and was adopted into the home of Carl Friedrich Uhlig. Learning his new trade by working at first for Uhlig, Reichel in 1850 went into production on his own in Spitzgässchen producing harmonicas.[39] But in 1856 he moved to Waldheim where, apparently, he not only built the concertina but, importantly, was quite active as a concertina wholesaler. Reichel hired artists

The H.C. Germania Concertina Club celebrating its 25th anniversary.

and concertina makers from the Erzgebirge and the Vogtland leading to an assessment of some that in the 1860s he was the most successful producer of concertinas in the entire Chemnitz region. Often he traveled for business reasons to Berlin, Vienna, Brussels and even to London. As noted above, likewise active in building concertinas were Johann Gottlieb Höselbarth and Christian Friedrich Pirner, young manufacturers who also began as co-workers with Uhlig but later went into production on their own.

Mysteriously, in 1870, Christian Friedrich Reichel with his entire family departed from Waldheim. As best can be determined, the family emigrated to Milwaukee, Wisconsin. Upon Reichel's departure, the manufacture and procurement of concertinas in Waldheim was assumed by Carl August Seifert and replicated later by his sons. The Seiferts carried on the business of filling many orders from the United States, supplying the Chicago stores with orders from anywhere in Chemnitz or the Vogtland. They ceased production and wholesaling only in 1958. There is even the suggestion that Heinrich Band from Krefeld had sojourned for some time, working at times with Reichel and at other times with Uhlig in Chemnitz. Some even conjecture that his source of Bandonion instruments was, in fact, not his own production at all, but that of Reichel and later the Seiferts in Waldheim. Some theorize in addition that Band constructed nothing and only named the instrument after himself by which the addition of "ion" admits to his "union" with Uhlig or Reichel and the workers there. As mentioned above, others think he wanted to represent the labor union in his instrument's name. Be that as it may, in the course of several decades, Reichel and then the Seifert brothers filled multitudes of orders for concertinas arriving constantly, especially from the Chicago music dealers like Georgi, Patek, Silberhorn and the Vitak-Elsnic Company.[39]

The Chemnitzer's Popularity in Germany and Surrounding Countries.

As mentioned, a push toward the development of instruments "for the masses" had been growing since the beginning of the 19th century. Though the upper classes advocated learning such traditional instruments as the piano and the violin, these were expensive accessories which required all-embracing study in addition to the costly hardware. Therefore, the working classes drifted in search of better options. The development of the *Balginstrumente* (bellows-driven instruments) signified the beginning of a new musical era—an age in which the common man and woman were inclined to partake in music as easily as the aristocrat. Able to stand on its own with melody and bass, the concertina easily became popular among the lower classes. Just as peasants often imitated courtyard clothing only to have it shunned later by the courtiers as "Volk Trachten" [common folk

Concertina Club of Chemnitz-Furth from the 1920s.

clothes or costumes], so too the concertina was mostly shunned by upper-class society, rendering it and its accordion relatives "Volksinstrumente" [instruments of the common folk].

Over time, the concertina became more commonly available near its roots in middle-to-eastern Germany, whereas in the northern, western and southern parts, the bandonion was the more popular instrument. It is also true that in the mining region of the Ruhr and lower Rhine, the bandonion came to be called the *Bergmannsklavier*, "coal miner's piano," a comfort as important to the miner as the *Schrebergärtenkolonie* [small rented garden plots on the edge of large German cities] was for the inhabitant of the Berlin *Mietskaserne* [huge apartment houses erected especially for newly arriving factory workers from rural and foreign lands, expecially Poland]. For example, in the year 1927, the *Deutsches Konzertina und Bandonion Bund* [German umbrella organization for members of concertina and bandonion clubs] reported a tally of several hundred clubs and over 14,000 individual members enrolled in these societies. This, as Hans Luck points out in his *Entwicklung der Balginstrumente*, can most likely be attributed to the geographical locations of their inventors—Uhlig in Chemnitz and Band in Krefeld. Whatever the various forms, it is evident that the squeezebox had taken hold among late 19th and early 20th-century German laymen (and women), at least for the time being.

In order to test the folklore base on which the concertina rested, I have looked at the advertisements appearing in a journal by the name of *Gut Ton Zeitung*.[40] In it can be found promotional entries by such retailers of the concertina as Eduard Haustein in the town of Niederplanitz near Zwickau in Saxony, offering concertinas and bandonions of all kinds. In Dresden there was the H. B. Thiele agency, which boasted its membership in the Concertina Club Edelweiß of Dresden located on Bärensteiner Straße 10. Emphasis on the club connection was to allure fellow members for repair work. His primary claim to service was to repair all concertinas but especially those from the Ernest L. Arnold factory in Carlsfeld. In Klingenthal, Wilhelm Dölling was offering to build any concertina according to the wishes of the customer. At Langensalzer Straße 60 in Gotha was located A. Mühlbauer concentrating on sheet music for

Concertina and Bandonion Club of Chemnitz, the first established in Germany, founded in 1874. This photo is from August 28, 1910.

Employees of the Lange Concertina factory located on Rosenplatz 2 in Chemnitz. The bald man standing in the center is probably Fredrich Emil Lange, son of Fredrich Anton Lange. Circa 1910.

concertinas. The district of Rixdorf in Berlin advertised the construction of concertinas of the highest quality at Rosegger-Straße 12. Ernst Birnstock at Crimmitschau is still manufacturing concertinas and selling used models of all kinds. Karl Bässler at Marbach in Flöhatal, Saxony promoted his concertinas and those of other builders, and there were others.

Among these many smaller producers, the Bässler concertina came most frequently to the United States. Its acceptance was especially noteworthy in Milwaukee where it was marketed principally by the Gustav Forster Music Store. In the appendix of her book Maria Dunkel reports that Ernst Bässler both fabricated and repaired concertinas since 1860 at Grünberg near Augustusburg, a bit east of Chemnitz. In 1880 Karl Bässler took over the operation and reportedly moved to Dresden in 1926. The brothers Max and Georg Bässler succeeded Ernst Bässler about 1926, continuing their operation at Marbach-Flöhatal.

During the same time there were large advertisements for Ernst L. Arnold in Carlsfeld, who offered his bandonions and "concertinas in every tone and quality." Not to be outdistanced by the competition, the firm of F. Lange vormals C. F. Uhlig, gegründet 1835 [established in 1835] continued strongly in Chemnitz on Rosenplatz 2, now claiming to have won prizes at industrial fairs in Munich, Dresden, Chemnitz and Chicago, the only concertina producer making such a claim. In Leipzig, the Saxonia Konzertina Werke claimed in its 1911-1912 catalogs to offer the best concertinas equipped and tuned to either the Chemnitz or the Carlsfeld preference—suggesting that their instruments were being produced by either Lange or Arnold. A similar pattern of promotion continued through the 1920s.

Additional claims by individuals or companies to manufacturing the concertina include names that appear in the *Gut Ton Zeitung*, a few of which are mentioned here alphabetically, followed by city with year of founding in parentheses. Kurt Jobst, Brunndöbra (1920), Max König und Söhne, Zwota (1840), Ludwig Brothers, Zwota (1844), A. L. Meinel and C. H. Meinel, and Meinel Brothers, Klingenthal (1891 & 1919), C. F. Reichel, Chemnitz (1854), Eugen Ross Bandonion-Konzertina-Fabrik in Dortmund (1922), Max Scheffler, Chemnitz (1890), Gustav Schlott, Georgenthal (1925), Seifert Brothers, Waldheim (1870), Wilhelm Späthe, Gera (1859), Hugo Stark, Auerbach/Vogtland (1910), Max Bruno Thiele, Chemnitz (1892), Reinhard Windisch, Klingenthal (1870), C. A. Wunderlich, Siebenbrunn (1854) plus many others.

During the Nazi era, 1933-1945, however, a different fate befell the concertina world in Germany. Due apparently to its popularity with the workers and their socialistic [not to say communist] sympathies, already in 1935 the umbrella organization mentioned above was forbidden, following which its local clubs and subdivisions dissolved on their own. Under suspicion from the Nazi regime, the supply of production and parts also gradually dried up so that even in the United States the concertina as an instrument from Germany seemed doomed. Driven to a degree underground in Buenos Aires and Montevideo because of the partiality these nations were expressing toward Nazi Germany, the bandonion also got shoved into the more hidden corners of the city. Cowering in the small bars where a Creole of immigrants and minority nationalities hovered, the reed mechanism that had been born on the Rhine effectively transplanted itself to the shores of the Rio de la Plata where it crept into the souls of folks who could dance the tango. Yet, although the tango itself has been rehabilitated and integrated back into the finest salons of Europe, the bandonion today is played best by men over 70 years old. Its aging musical artists nowadays work their "old coffins," as the German saying goes, referring usually to the beautiful Arnold instruments brought over from Germany a century earlier. Luckily the story in the American Midwest is quite different, to which we will come back momentarily.

Before turning to the North American scene, however, let us review the fate of the concertina in its pristine homeland. As lower-class musicians stretching across the Central European horizon came together to share their interests in music, they began organizing clubs, resulting in concertina and bandonion musicians playing together in groups. Perhaps the best known among the 20 or so in Chemnitz itself was the Chemnitz-Hilbersdorf Club and the Chemnitz-Borna Club, which offered not only opportunities to play but also to learn the instrument. Naturally, these *Vereine* were limited territorially, but the simple fact that concertina clubs were being formed demonstrates the power that this single instrument had on a people. Playing the concertina enabled thousands to participate as a community in their ever-growing genre of *Volksmusik*.[41] Indeed, not only did these clubs concern themselves with music, they also became centers of culture for those caught between the so-called "ignorant" masses and the exclusive aristocracy, struggling to maintain their own cultural identity. This would later become equally important, if not more so, for German and other European immigrants in America.

Also important in the development of the European concertina market was the publicity for the instrument generated by the F. Lange, formerly C. F. Uhlig Concertina Company in Chemnitz. Playing on their names which appeared on the nameplate of their concertinas with L and U overlapping across a concertina or a harp, F. Lange, as the son-in-law of Uhlig, in his brochures used the following poem in German. Readers recognize the names of the builders in the initial letters of each stanza.

Friedrich Emil Lange, who died January 2, 1933 at the age of 82. He was the son of Friedrich Anton Lange who died Feruary 29, 1892.

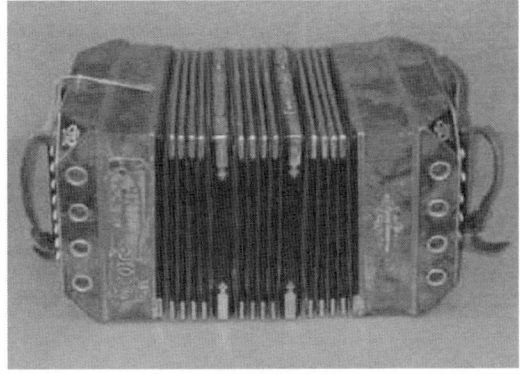

The Uhlig-Lange concertinas in the 1890s bore their harp logo on the corners.

Note the logo with harps on the corners and the L-U run through by a minature concertina on the nameplate.

Newspaper advertisement for the Uhlig-Lange concertina in 1920s. Note the LU logo in circle at the left.

Liebe Firma!
Aus Herzensgründen
Nur Sehnsucht nach der Musik
Gehört aber das Volksmusikempfinden,
Es geht nichts mehr übers Glück.

Und Glück hatten wir trotz schwerer Lasten,

Unverhofft kauften wir uns einen Kasten
Hier haben wir gerade das Richtige gefunden,
Laut Dankschreiben spielen wir ihn tausend von Stunden.
Ist jedem zu raten, hier ist man nicht bange,
Geh hin und kaufe du stets nur bei Lange.[42]

In their brochures at that time, Uhlig-Lange promoters included statements of happy owners, many from the United States. Catchy phrases in German are splashed on the brochures: "Konzertinas hat man lange, deshalb lange, nur nach "Lange!" [Concertinas are instruments you have for a long time, therefore reach — "langen" means seek out or reach for — only for a Lange]. All this activity took place before there were regular dealers for the concertina in places like Chicago, Milwaukee and Buffalo. Sometimes concertinas as well as company promotional material appeared imprinted with the logo L-U displaying a concertina flared through the two letters, and at other times we find advertisements with the words "F. Lange vormals C. F. Uhlig." An overview of the Uhlig-Lange concertina production during this pre-American debut would include the 1863 assumption of the business by Friedrich Anton Lange from Carl Friedrich Uhlig, followed by the death of Uhlig in 1874. Seeking retirement, Friedrich Anton Lange passed the firm to Friedrich Emil Lange in February 1891. The transfer occurred just in time because Friedrich Anton Lange died the following year in 1892. In 1900 his

Newspapers announcing the deaths of the principle figures behind the Chemnitzer Concertina, Uhlig in 1874, F. A. Lange in 1892, and F. E. Lange in 1933.

son Friedrich Emil Lange was listed as the sole owner of the company on Rosenplatz in Chemnitz. However, in 1903 Friedrich Emil added Carl Julius Ludwig Niemann to his staff as "Prokura" [ownership by proxy], who in turn became a substantive owner of the Lange [formerly Uhlig] firm in April, 1910.

By 1926, Niemann became full owner but four years later in 1930, this firm faced bankruptcy for the second time. With a stroke of the pen, however, Niemann avoided the inevitable dissolution of the company by assigning title to Arthur Müller, a master concertina craftsman at that time. Advertisement bills in the 1930s show that Müller continued to use the name of F. Lange vormals C. F. Uhlig, with the L/U logo or trademark [Schutzmarke] prominently in view. He continued to note that his was the oldest continuous Bandonion and Konzertina Fabrik in the world, the establishment reaching back to 1819, though concertinas first began to be produced on a broad scale in 1835. In these 1930s posters, Müller again proudly boasted the company's awards received at Munich, Chemnitz, Dresden and Chicago. No record of the company exists beyond 1949 when, obviously, the Russian occupation dissolved all private property.

Until the concertina arrived in America, however, it spread to other parts of Europe. Polish mine workers temporarily employed in Saxony [the region around Chemnitz and the Ore mountains, of which Dresden is the capital city], enthusiastically brought the concertina back to their homeland. Some publications mention Floryjan Ratajczak (born 1890), one of thousands of Poles who worked in the Rhur district mines of Germany, where he heard and liked the bandonion. He took it back to the Poznan district of Poland and with his brother played for Wielkopolska dances and weddings.[43] At family gatherings, friends and relatives were introduced to the instrument, resulting in exhibitions and public displays which soon made the squeeze box a household word. In this fashion, the popular *Volksinstrument* from Chemnitz made its way throughout Germany and to Central European lands. It became rather popular in Poland, Czechoslovakia, Lithuania, some areas of Belarus, even parts of Ukraine and Western Russia. Unfortunately for German ethnic music, the concertina did not enjoy as lasting a popularity anywhere in Germany as it did in the other countries to which it had been conveyed. Today, however, due to the demand for accordions imposed on the industry by the Russian occupation, most of the eastern European countries mentioned above likewise have forsaken the concertina.[44]

The post-1945 era in Germany brought varying other consequences. The guitar in the hands of young people, the radio, television, record disc player, the tape recorder and finally the CD have wrought havoc on the desirability for the concertina. For the meager market that remained [mostly, it appears, for Bandonions and not the concertina as we know it], production was satisfied from the town of Carlsfeld. When the Russians and East German authorities nationalized the Alfred Arnold

Concertina youth orchestra from the town of Gelnau in the Erzgebirge mountains, circa 1930.

A Tanzbär or Dancing Bear concertina for which the player needed no skills, only enough strength to push the bellows in and out. This one was built in 1938 by Glass-Magister in eastern Germany. JBM Sound has a 1927 Tanzbär.

Above is a newly-built concertina, the work of Paul Fischer K. G. and his small team working in Klingenthal, a short distance from Carlsfeld. Note that he uses the old Uhlig logo on the corners. The current address is Fischer's daughter: Frau Anja Rockstroh, Bandonion & Concertinafabrik Klingenthal GmbH Krummer Weg 1a - 08248 Klingenthal, Germany. Photo by Rippley in 2002.

The concertina construction workshop of Paul Fischer in Klingenthal showing the key mechanism, bellows, long plates and in the bottom right-hand corner, a chart for learners. Taken by Rippley, January, 2002.

Paul Fischer holds a concertina completed in his shop in Klingenthal, Germany, a city located exactly on the border with the Czech Republic. Taken by Rippley, January, 2002.

firm in 1948, the workers and physical production facilities were moved 25 kilometers to the south. Here the entire system of workers and their production were combined with the VEB [*Volkseigene Betrieb,* a company owned by the people, but really owned by the state] Harmonikawerke Klingenthal, which was forced to produce accordions for the vast Russian market. The workers remaining in Carlsfeld in 1964 converted the remaining facilities in the Arnold plant to the production of injector pumps for diesel motors. After the East German authorities subsumed the Arnold building, Arno Arnold [1983-1970] fled in 1949 to Obertshausen in the Frankfurt area of West Germany where he manufactured

The Origin of the German Chemnitzer Concertina

Klaus Wallschläger, Hauptstrasse 7 in Carlsfeld demonstrates a concertina-like instrument called the Symphonetta. German players pump the "end plates" up and down to generate the air for playing each side or end. The symphonetta was first patented in 1898 by Richard Scheller of Zwickau but after 1912 was built mostly by the E. L. Arnold company in Carlsfeld. Taken by Rippley, January, 2002.

the bandonion as well as the concertina until the 1960s.

It should be noted that during World War II not a single bomb fell on Carlsfeld. Therefore, the Arnold company was in no way destroyed by the war. In fact, since the death of Ernst Louis Arnold in 1910, there were actually two Arnold companies operated by his three sons, Ernst Hermann, Paul, and Ernst Alfred Arnold, named respectively the **Ernst Louis Arnold** and the **Alfred Arnold** companies. The Alfred Arnold Company was dissolved by the Russians in 1948, the Ernst Louis Arnold Company first in 1952. Although they were reconciled into Klingenthal accordion builders, they completed their very last concertinas and bandonions in 1957. During the 1920s and 1930s there was an Arnold Bandonion Orchestra and a Konzertina-Verein [Concertina Club] founded in Carlsfeld in 1919 which continued until 1942. During the early years of the 20th century the companies were producing some 10,000 instruments per year, but in part these were crafted for other companies like Hohner, Meinel, Herfeld, Schuster and others. Arnold-named concertina production held stable at around 7,000 per year.

During the 1930s pianos came equipped with self-playing paper rolls which were pumped with foot pedals to actually play the keys. So, too, a few Klingenthaler manufacturers built a concertina that operated from such a roll of paper driven by the bellow air system. One such concertina was called the Tanzbär [dancing bear], manufactured by the company called Glass-Magister which also built accordions and hand-held mouth harmonicas.

A concertina orchestra playing for a raucous Fasching party in Chemnitz during the early 1930s.

Although some of the concertina and bandonion clubs continued in the state of Saxony after the conclusion of World War II, members gradually grew too old to participate regularly. As noted previously, back in 1927 there had been more than 100 concertina and bandonion clubs in Germany. A good example was the Chemnitz Hilbersdorf Verein that was organized in 1890. Another was the Chemnitz-Furth Concertina Verein that flourished in the 1920s as well as the Chemnitz-Borna group. Virtually none survived World War II, although a handful in Saxony struggled to stay alive for a time. By the 1960s in Chemnitz [by then renamed Karl Marx Stadt], only two of the 20-some clubs active during the 1920s continued to limp along.[45] Eventually also, music schools and concertina instruction diminished with accordion lessons taking over from the once popular concertina. During the latter years, the few remaining musicians brought their instruments for repair to Gerhard Birnstock in Crimmitschau, the only repair available in the entire territory of the German Democratic Republic. Continuing in his shop until 1991, he celebrated his 80th birthday in May, 2001.

However, since the disappearance of the German Democratic Republic in 1990, and even a few years prior to its demise, the concertina and bandonion experienced a minor revival. Carlsfeld is today a Mecca for bandonion players who meet there annually for a bandonion festival. Since 1999, the Chemnitz orchestra has a similar encounter annually in the suburban city of Chemnitz-Grüna. Since 1976, Klaus Gutjahr has been producing the bandonion in Berlin and efforts are underway at smaller "Arnold" imitators in Carlsfeld and Klingenthal, e. g., Uwe Harthenhauer. The South American tangos have revived the bandonion to some degree for playing tangos while the North American polka and waltz scene have likewise come to the rescue of the concertina.

In memory of the founding of the concertina club of Chemnitz. Markersdorf 15 years ago, ie. 1909.

The Concertina as Connection to the Homeland.

To understand the importance of an ethnic instrument such as the concertina in America, it is important to examine the mindset of the many immigrants who left their homeland in search of a better life—a life they did not always find. Psychologically speaking, remarkably powerful capabilities have long been attributed to music. Indeed, music therapists point to cases in which Alzheimer's patients, hardly able to remember their own family members, upon hearing a few bars of music can sing a complete song from their youth.[46] Equally appreciated by members of the highest and lowest classes alike is the realization that music contains in its melodies the history, emotion, spirituality and erudition bespeaking the currents and threads that connect human souls to their origins and their cultures. As scientists have shown, if a tune is shifted to another key, even small babies recognize it as the same tune. But if the pitch of a few notes is altered, they instantly recognize that something is wrong, distorted, and out of kilter.[47] Therefore, music can be viewed as one of the greatest expressions of a civilization—transporting in its essence that which has been often embodied in big words: tradition, refinement, manners, breeding, intellectual status, in short, what scholars umbrella under the word enlightenment!

For this reason, many immigrants latched onto the music of their homeland in their search for ethnic identity in the New World—usually old-time polkas and waltzes in the case of immigrant concertina-players. In claiming this old-world music as their own, immigrant musicians in America inadvertently created a new genre of American ethnic music. Polka traditions of several European countries merged into new, specifically American, styles. In this way, new forms of the polka, the old time waltz, the ländler and the schottische took hold in the American Midwest and across a tier of states stretching from Nebraska and the Dakotas to Buffalo and Pittsburgh—a style which effectively characterized the immigrant's struggle to assimilate himself but at the same time to maintain his ethnic identity. In the Polish settlements, of course, the names and styles varied from those used in the German-speaking concentrations. Thus the mazurka, oberek, krakowiak, polonaise, kujawiak and others were easily adapted as polkas, obereks and waltzes on the hybrid Polish-American scene. Over time, too, the styles of concertina playing diverged markedly between the German or Dutchman style and the Polish "fireball" approach, even within the same region.

Though German to the core, the concertina playing style in the pockets where Polish immigrants dominated, developed a distinctly Polish modality. For example, in Wisconsin at Pulaski, Stevens Point and Wausau, not to mention Milwaukee, concertina music is somehow richer, more elaborate and played in various keys not familiar in the German sections of Minnesota and western Wisconsin. In Mosinee was headquartered the International Concertina Association, which permeated the regions more so of western New York State, Pennsylvania and Ohio than the local German areas of western Wisconsin and southern Minnesota. In Minnesota, the Polish of northeast Minneapolis differed markedly in playing format from the concertina players of southern Minnesota. They, with the Slovaks and Croatians on the Iron Range in northern Minnesota, have more in common with their Polish counterparts in eastern Wisconsin than with their neighbors in northern Iowa, southern Minnesota and western Wisconsin, where the simpler German [Dutchman] style prevails.

Concertina Clubs Connect the Old and the New Worlds

Just as the New World affected the music of the Old, however, immigrants affected the musical social organizations of their new homeland. Not only did German, Polish and Czech immigrants bring their music to America, they brought the *Vereine* and *Bünde* [clubs and societies] that had become popular in 19th-century Germany. Driven by the aforementioned desire for cultural identity, immigrants to the Midwest sought out the company of others, who, like themselves, had undergone an experience similar to their own. It is among these circles and settlements that the concertina took hold in the United States.

In Germany there were many concertina clubs, of which some are shown in photographs on these pages. For good reason, the oldest is believed to be the one in Chemnitz, which was established in 1874. Perhaps the second was founded in Hamburg in 1875, the *Melodia*. Not surprisingly, the largest number existed in Saxony, where a principal city after the Capital, Dresden, is Chemnitz, with over 20. At peak times there were an estimated 1000 Vereine [Clubs] in the whole of Germany. In his article "Organisation und Statistik der volksmusik" in *Deutsche Tonkünstler-Zeitung* (October 4, 1934): 49 ff., Max Burghardt mentions that in the early 1930s there were 610 clubs in Germany with 14,000 members at any given time.

The pioneer concertina clubs in the United States grew to maturity in the 1920s. Beginning with the

Chicago Concertina Club (around 1889), the Milwaukee Concertina Circle (1890) and the Czech-American Concertina Club Band (1893), the concertina clubs of the 1920s seem to have sprung up in the select cities across the Midwest. However, concertina clubs have waxed and waned elsewhere in the north central states and continue now a century later, as will be discussed in subsequent chapters.

American concertina clubs were much more than a few regional concertinists coming together to play the songs of their homelands. Unlike many of the *Vereine* in Germany, which limited membership to similar instruments, the American organizations frequently brought together countless musicians. Brass, string and percussion instrumentalists were present in early photographs of the Chicago Concertina Club, one which was clearly interested in mixing the new sound of the concertina with the already popular American "band" sound of the late nineteenth century.

This new take on an old sound brought much local popularity to the clubs and bands of the late 19th and early 20th centuries. Not only were bands hired to play house parties, weddings and other social events, but many also organized their own functions to attract an audience. Dances were held in which members of the community could come together to enjoy polka, waltz, ländler, maybe tango and other ethnic dance music, not to mention the popular songs of the day. Bands often had set audience-pleasing repertoires and were not afraid to pull a few "shenanigans" to get an audience going. Some even drew on the contemporary vaudeville craze to spice up their acts, sporting "gay nineties" garb and using unusual on-stage antics to whip up a crowd. This popularization of traditional polka music not only gave immigrants a way to express and take part in their cultural identity, it significantly changed the face of American music. As Hucker and Spahr write:

> When the polka reached New York in the mid-1840s, it was danced mainly by the upper class. But as waves of Czech and German immigrants brought their own music with them, including the polka, they precipitated a musical democratization that was to have far-reaching and profound effects on the American music business. . . . The music was played by bands in the new, well-lit, family-oriented bars and dance halls that formed the mainstay of social activity in the Midwest where close-knit immigrant communities kept cultural and traditional ties with the "old country" via music.[48]

In this way, the polka (along with the waltz, ländler, schottische) became every man's dance. Its importance for a democratic society has been augmented by performing at a formal dance once reserved for the aristocracy. American peasant groups did not learn the dances of the upper classes, but rather brought lower-class dances to the upper levels of society. Whereas the ordinary, common dance used to be considered vulgar, it now swept the nation.

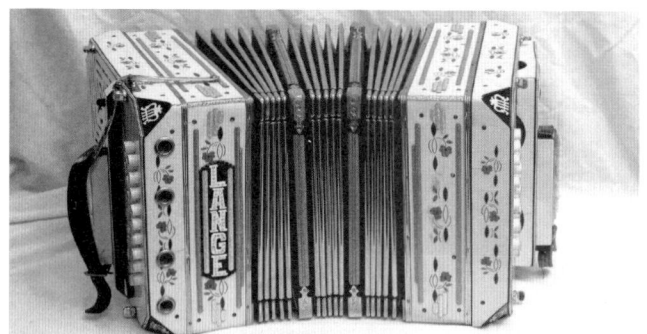

ARNO ARNOLD (104 key / quadruble reed / key of B-Flat) (built in the early 1950s or late 1940s), with the serial number 1350. It bears an "A" on the back side. However, it is really an Arno Arnold concertina with the name John Bolster attached, probably at the request of Pat Watters. Thus it is an Arno Arnold with a Lange nameplate. This concertina is a rare model because it is a B-Flat with long plate reeds, whereas the majority of these concertinas feature individual pinned reeds.

ARNO ARNOLD (104 key / triple reed / key of B-Flat)., built on February 5, 1959 with the serial number 6341. The Arno Arnold factory in Germany produced 17 different models for beginners, learners and professionals, but production ended in the mid-1960s at a time when Pat Watters of Minneapolis was their main distributor in the United States. This one was tuned by John Bolster in Minneapolis. This 1959 model features two-tone colors like the contemporary automobiles.

The Origin of the German Chemnitzer Concertina

A German band with concertina, probably about 1900.

A German concertina club orchestra with mostly Uhlig-Lange instruments.

An outing in Germany with concertina entertainment.

Here the date is reported as 1914. Three Lange concertinas entertain the others holding beer mugs.

The Origin of the German Chemnitzer Concertina

Gentlemen in cylinder hats being entertained by a single concertina player. Clothing suggests a 1910 period.

German members of a ritual dress event are entertained by a concertina player.

The players are members of a Bavarian native costume band from the town of Dachau.

These Bavarians enjoy the name Kerchbaum Truppe—German dialect for the "Cherry Tree Players."

The Origin of the German Chemnitzer Concertina

A "village-sized" group of all ages gather around their drum and three concertinas, probably Lange models.

This 15-piece German band uses six concertinas, apparently Langes.

The History of the Chemnitzer Concertina

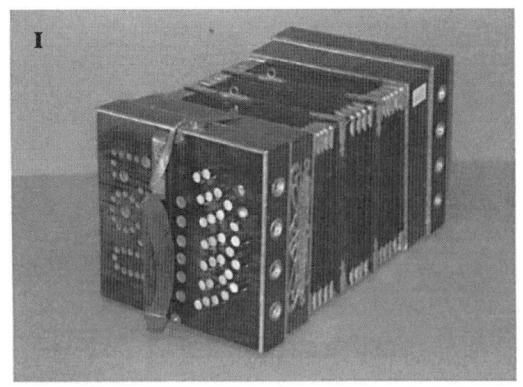
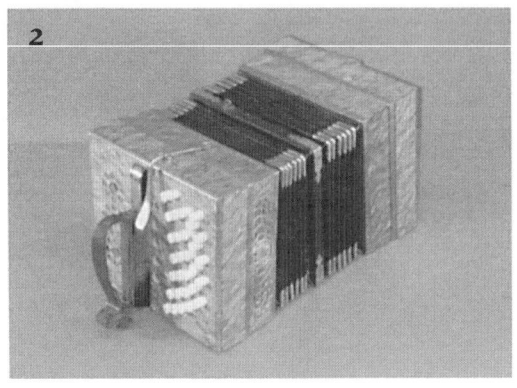

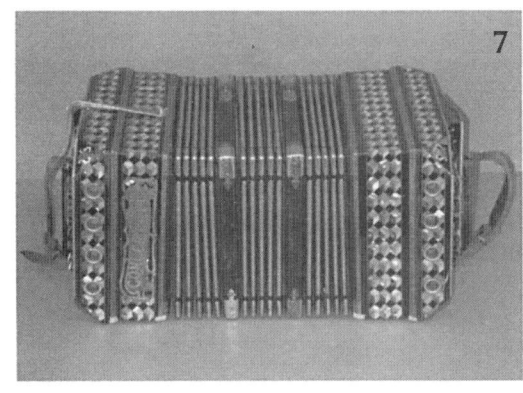

Examples of early German-built concertinas and bandonions built in Chemnitz between 1850 and 1910.

A 76 key Chemnitzer built by the company F. Lange, Chemnitz, Saxony using a neck strap of green and yellow, the Saxony colors.

The Origin of the German Chemnitzer Concertina

This 78-key Lange was under construction from 1890-1930. Max Scheffler expanded the key range to 102.

This 78-key is a Lange-Uhlig with harps on the corners.

This 78-key Chemnitzer is illustrated with mother of pearl flowers and silver bellow plates. It also shows the "LU" Lange-Uhlig logo, built probably in the 1900-1930 period.

Close up view of bellow composite of materials.

This 78-key Lange-Uhlig concertina dates from the 1890s to the 1930s.

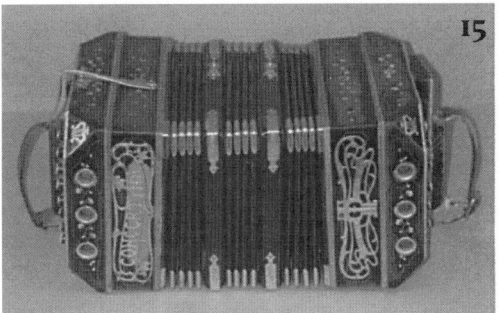

This Lange-Uhlig has only three sound holes.

This 78-key concertina has the familiar logo "LU" for Lange-Uhlig and is noteworthy for its elegant wood, built probably in the 1920s.

An early Lange-Uhlig with square corners.

On the left above is an early concertina signed in lead pencil by C. F. Pirner of Chemnitz. Built probably in the late 1840s or early 1850s, it is a 20-key version with five buttons on each side. The small concertina at the right is probably a 56-key instrument, bearing the initials JGH which could indicate J. G. Höselbarth of Chemnitz in the 1850s.

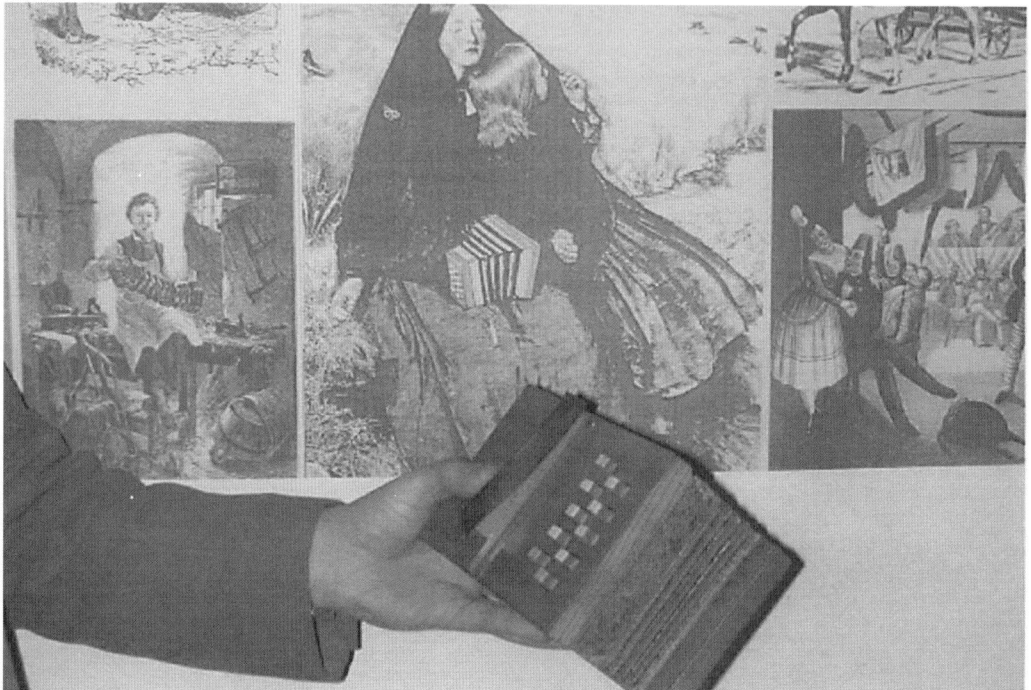

In the background is "Blind Girl," an English painting completed by J. E. Millais (1829-1896) in 1856. Hanging now in the Art Gallery of Birmingham, it forms the centerpiece of a postcard in front of which is held an 1850s 40-key concertina, probably buildt by C. F. Pirner of Chemnitz. England was an early market for the German Chemnitzer, especially following the Continental fair held there in 1851.

This is an Anglo-German concertina built in the Klingenthal area, perhaps for export to England.

This is a 120-key concertina from the 1870s built in the vicinity of Klingenthal. See: http://www.chemnitzconcertina.de/de/dokumentation/html/

The Origin of the German Chemnitzer Concertina

Siegfried Jugel [born 1943] plays a concertina which he helped craft with Gerhard Birnstock during the 1980s. The small Birnstock concertina company got its start in Crimmitschau, a small town straight west of Chemnitz, early in the 20th century. Though founded by Ernst Birnstock, son Gerhard took over the business continuing production on a small scale until the 1990s. When the Arnold factory ceased production at Carlsfeld in 1964, Crimmitschau became the last site in all of Germany still making concertinas. To be sure, much of its activity in later years turned to repair and restoration, the only dealer in the whole of Germany to maintain the necessary skills.

A German youth group playing concertinas, probably in the 1930s. Both the site and the names of the individuals are unknown.

Footnotes

1 Maria Dunkel, *Bandonion und Konzertina: Ein Beitrag zur Darstellung des Instrumententyps* (München-Salzburg: Musikverlag Emil Katzbichler, 1987), p.10 writes in regard to these 19th-century European trends: Nun ist nicht anzunehmen, Instrumentenkonstrukteure konzipierten neue Instrumente für die "Geringsten." Aber sie folgen selbstverständlich latenten Strömungen, und diese verlangen bis zur Jahrhundertmitte[:] Instrumente für neute Käuferschichten, Instrumente mit spezifischer Tonqualität entsprechend dem aktuellen Klangideal, Instrumente mit der Anlage zu harmonisch-akkordischen Wirkungen gemäß dem zeitgenössischen Kompositions-stil. Hier findet nun besonders die Durchschlagzunge ihr adäquates Terrain, denn sie bietet die Möglichkeit, den drei Trends in vielen Variaten zu entsprechen.

[Now it is not to be assumed that instrument-constructors conceptualized new instruments for the "needy masses." However, they followed latent trends, and up until the middle of the century, these trends demanded the following:
Instruments for new consumer groups;
Instruments with a specific tone-quality that reflected the current sound ideal;
  Instruments with a construction that could produce
  harmonic-chordal effects according to the composition style of
  the era.
  Here the free-reed instrument finds its adequate terrain, for it
  allows the possibility of meeting all three demands in many
  variations.]

2 A good overview of this instrument is available in Neil Wayne, "The Wheatstone English concertina," *Galpin Society Journal*, 44 (March, 1991), 117-149.

3 Klaus Kauert, *Der Musikwinkel und die Harmonika* (Schneeberg, Erzgebirge: Sächsische Landesstelle für Volkskultur, 2000) Reihe Weiss-Grün 22, especially Chapter 1, "Das Erbe des Johann Wilhelm Glier," pp. 12 ff. Here we read about Glier's efforts as early as 1810-11 to get to the United States to set up sales offices for the three Glier brothers but, due to the Napoleonic blockades, all exits from the continent were disallowed.

4 Hans Luck, *Die Balginstrumente. Ihre historische Entwicklung bis 1945* (Kamen: Karthause-Schmülling Musikverlag, 1997), Bd. V, Schriften zur Akkordeonistik, Teil 2/ Handbuch der Harmonika-Instrumente), pp. 51 ff.

5 Uhlig placed advertisements in the local newspapers, e. g. the *Chemnitzer Anzeiger* (December 10, 1826), p. 417; *Chemnitzer Anzeiger*, Beilage zu No. 49 (December 8, 1832), p. 651.

6 *Chemnitzer Anzeiger* (July 19, 1834), p. 359. The German text of the ad reads in part: Das Lager musikalischer Instrumente empfiehlt sich bestens mit einer schönen Auswahl . . . große und kleine Violinen, Guitarren . . . Accordion nach neuer Art nebst einem Unterricht und versichert die billigsten Preise. Mein Stand ist zu diesem beforstehenden Markt im Hause des Herrn Weigels am Markte. Carl Fr. Uhlig, Am Anger Nr. 902.

7 *Chemnitzer Anzeiger* No. 58 (July 7, 1838), p. 462.

8 *Chemnitzer Anzeiger* (Jahrmarktsbeilage) (July 22, 1843), p. 382.

9 *Chemnitzer Anzeiger* (1845), p. 418.

10 As noted in the *Addressbücher* for the fairs, in the Stadtarchiv Leipzig for years continuing from 1847 and each succeeding year for a long period.

11 Interviews and discussion with Peer Ehmke and Henriette Schneidewind, "Ausstellungstexte 1. Juli - 28. Okt. 2001," Schloßbergmuseum, Chemnitz, 17-18 January, 2002. The passing of C. F. Uhlig is prominently placed in the *Chemnitzer Anzeiger* (July 9, 1874) by J. A. Rummel, who was in charge of Uhlig's affairs.

12 James P. Leary, "The German Concertina in the Upper Midwest," *Land Without Nightingales: Music in the Making of German America*, ed. Philip Bohlman and Otto Holzapfel (Madison: University of Wisconsin Press, 2002), pp. 191-232, esp. 195.

13 The commonly mentioned concertina with 130 keys was initiated in 1970 by Albert G. (Nicky) Nechanicky in Washington State but has not really caught on with players in the Midwest. Cf. http:// www.polamjournal.com/ polka/nicky.html

14 Hans Luck, *Die Balginstrumente*, p. 52 ff.

15 The business cards of the company in this time frame read: "F. Lange vorm. C. F. Uhlig. Harmonika Fabrik. Chemnitz, Sachsen, Brückenstrasse No. 24. Prämiirt Chicago, 1893. Concertinas, Bandonions bester Qualität."

14 Reproduced in Dunkel, "Tafel 7" p. 175.

16 Frank Abbot et al., eds., *Musical Instruments at the World's Columbian Exposition* (Chicago: Presto Co., 1895), p. 246.

17 *Zeitschrift für Instrumentenbau* (Jahrgang 1, 1880). I have reviewed the tables for the years 1880-1914.

18 Das Geschäft in Concertinas gestaltete sich. . . daß die Nachfrage aus den Kolonien viel geringer war und meist auf die billigen und gewöhnlichen Qualitäten beschränkte, wenn auch feine und solide Waren, namentlich mit Stahlfedern versehene, immer noch einzeln gekauft wurde. [The concertina business is shaping up as a severe lag in demand from the United States and is limited to cheap, low quality products, even though excellent models, namely those with steel reeds, are still being purchased by individual orders.]

19 *Zeitschrift für Instrumentenbau*, Vol. 8 (1888), p. 230, p. 376: Es ist eine selbst von den Engländern zugestandene Thatsache, daß viele deutsche Waren mit englischen Fabrikmarken bestellt und als englische Fabrikate auf den englischen oder den Weltmarkt gebracht worden sind. Ebensowenig ist in Abrede zu stellen, daß englische Bezeichnungen von deutschen Fabrikanten auch ohne ausdrückliche Bestellung für ihre Waren verwendet werden. [It is a fact admitted also by the English that many German products are being ordered marked with English factory production and that they are being brought to market on English and world markets as such. The stipulation has also been made that "made in England" markings are being put on products of German fabrication even when they are not specifically ordered for export in advance.]

20 Listed in Dunkel, op. cit. pp. 156 ff. Taken from address books held by the Music Industry Association.

21 Although most agree that Uhlig invented the Chemnitzer concertina, Henry Silberhorn claims in his magazine, the *Booster*, 1 (1928), 5-

6: "The first German Concertina, consisting of 40 keys and having 10 buttons on each side, was first made by Herr Zimmermann at Carlsfeld, Saxony in 1832. This instrument was received with great favor and from this time the Concertina was gradually improved and modified to its present qualifications. C. F. Uhlig improved the original 38 buttons for 76 keys with a compass of 3-1/2 octaves." For background on Zimmermann, interviews and discussion with Peer Ehmke and Henriette Schneidewind, "Ausstellungstexte (1. Juli - 28. Okt. 2001)," Schloß-bergmuseum Chemnitz, conducted 17-18 January, 2002

22 Unpublished, typed manuscript in possession of the author. Possibly the work of Pat Watters of Watters Distributing Co., 2219 East 42nd St., Minneapolis, October, 1955. See also the advertisements in the *Chemnitzer Anzeiger*, e. g. November 3, 1856, for "Die Harmonika-Fabrik von Gebrüder Zimmermann aus Carlsfeld" with an address located on the Roßmarkt. Also in possession of the author are flyers from 1850 displaying "Praktischer Selbstlehrer für Concertina mit 58 und 74 Tönen" (a practical self-teaching method to play the concertina) by Carl Zimmermann of Carlsfeld in Saxony. The booklet is detailed with notes and numbers in the manner of the Silberhorn method later produced in Chicago.

23 Dunkel, p. 49 and list of trade fairs, p. 163. For pictures of Zimmermann and his factory in Carlsfeld, see Klaus Kauert, *Der Musikwinkel und die Harmonika*, op. cit. p. 18.

24 Ivan Stiles, "The True History of the Autoharp," *Bluegrass Unlimited* (August, 1994), 26-28 disputes whether Zimmermann really invented the Autoharp. Instead, credit should go to Karl August Gütter of Markneukirchen [a city near where Zimmermann was born]. According to Stiles, Zimmermann also never claimed to have invented the instrument, for in his application for a patent he only claims "certain new and useful improvements in harps," which are clearly referred to as "a harp with my improvements."

25 A photograph of Alfred Dolge appears with a description of his extensive display at the 1893 Columbian Exposition in Frank Abbot et al., eds., *Musical Instruments at the World's Columbian Exposition* (Chicago: Presto Co., 1895), p.74. Hence cited as Musical Instruments, WCE.

26 Musical Instruments, WCE, p. 77.

27 Musical Instruments, WCE, p. 83.

28 Musical Instruments, WCE, at the end of the volume, p. iii.

29 Cf. Becky Blackley, *The Autoharp Book* (Brisbane California, 1983).

30 "A Brief History of the Concertina's Development", no writer listed, one page in length, in possession of the author. Probably written in 1972 by Mrs. Pat Watters, formerly of Minneapolis, but then of Music and Dance Industries, Route 3, Box 139, Mosinee, Wisconsin 54455.

31 Pat Watters produced flyers portraying Arno Arnold SONATONE German-made concertinas. According to the printed claims, it had a newly patented action keyboard with lightweight maple wood tone arms and lifetime brass bearings. For a time, the Arno Arnold was also distributed by Tony Wolf in St. Joseph, Minnesota as well as by the George Servatius Music Service of Melrose, Minnesota.

32 Jerry Minar of New Prague, Minnesota, owns an Arno Arnold dated December 13, 1960 and another dated December 9, 1962. The 1960 model was his very first. This 1960 model has the registration number D6571 and uses tapered Hohner reeds, a model which ceased production in 1966. Imprinted inside the bellow chamber are the words "marca registrada," suggesting that this was an Italian production for the former East German Arno Arnold company in Carlsfeld. It could also have come from the West German site near Frankfurt to which some of the Arnold enterprise escaped after 1945, but jobbed in Italy. Marvin Moravec of Montgomery, Minnesota, has a pre-World War II Alfred Arnold from Carlsfeld which bears the date of June 23, 1939. It uses zinc plates and steel reeds, the same as the Pearl Queen and Patek instruments sold during the 1920s and 1930s in Chicago. Having no reed blocks, the plates lie flat, directly on the action box.

33 Here and below see the article by Sabine Krömer, "Der Mann, der das Bandoneon rettem will," in *Frankfurter Allgemeine Zeitung*, Nr. 99 (Saturday April 28, 2001), p. 15. See also *Minneapolis Star Tribune* (Sunday August 26, 2001), travel section.

34 See the photographs of the Arno Arnold factory, the concertina, and the pictures of players exhibiting the AA in Klaus Kauert, *Der Musikwinkel und die Harmonika*, op. cit. p. 28. Since these advertisements are in French and Italian, we can assume they were intended for the foreign markets in these countries.

35 Dunkel, pp. 160, 164. See also the brief entry about the Arnold company "Die Bandonion-Firmen ARNOLD," in Karl Oriwohl, *Das Bandonion. Ein Beitrag zur Geschichte der Musikinstrumente mit durschlagenden Zungen*, rev. ed. with Dieter Krickeberg (Berlin: Ralf Jung Musikverlag, 2004), pp. 36 ff.

36 Dunkel, pp. 163-164.

37 Interview with Peer Ehmke January 18, 2002.

38 Ibid. Notes in possession of the author.

39 Interviews and discussion with Peer Ehmke and Henriette Schneidewind, "Ausstellungstexte 1. Juli - 28. Okt. 2001," Schloßbergmuseum, Chemnitz, 17-18 January, 2002.

40 *Gut Ton, Kalender für Spieler sämtlicher Volksinstrumente Deutschlands* (Dresden: Gut Ton Verlag Haupt & Pöhler, 1912).

41 Luck, p. 62 lists the formation dates of regional turn-of-the-century Vereine [clubs]:

    1894 der Verband Niedererzgebirgischer Konzertina-Vereine
    1896 der Hannoversche Konzertina- und Bandonion-Bund
    1897 der Mittelsächsische Konzertina- und Bandonion-Bund
         und der Verband der Bandonion-Klubs Leipzig und
         Umgebung
    1898 der Norddeutsche Bandonion-Bund
    1902 der Bund der Vogtländischen Konzertina-Vereine
    1908 der Rheinisch-Westfälische Bandonion-Bund

Other societies from around the 1890s were the Hallesches Bandonion Orchester, Bandonion Gruppe Taucha, Bandonion Verein Neustadt-Coburg, Bandonion Orchester Dresden and many more.

42 Dear company, from the bottom of our hearts, we long for your music, folk music sensitivity alone belongs to it, it's not any longer just a matter of good fortune. And good luck we did experience in spite of serious problems, not able to hope we yet bought ourselves

a box, and here we found the right thing, according to our fan mail it is played thousands of times, so we can give the advice that here one is never afraid, go ahead and buy yourself one and do so only at Lange.

43 James Kimball, "The Accordion and Concertina: A Historical Perspective," reports his interview with Ratajczak in Bukowiec Gorny, Poland, in 1975.

44 Interviews with Andrzej Fitrzyk in Krakow, Feb. 15, 2002. "Never in my life have I seen a concertina in circumstances other than shanty [sailor songs] choruses. The instrument must have been imported from the U. S. along with the new fashion of young people in sailing—a supposition and not a scientific statement."

45 http://www.chemnitz-concertina.de/de/geschichte/ueberblick.htm

46 For more information on music therapy and Alzheimer's, see "Key to the Past" by Amber Griffioen (1997), http://www.geocities.com/amber_griffs/mtpaper.html.

47 Concerning efforts of neuroscience to define the magnetic signals sent through the mind by music, see "The Musical Mind," *U. S. News & World Report* (August 13, 2001), 131, No. 6: 40-41.

48 Dave Hucker and Wolfgang Spahr, "Polka's influential trip around the world," *Billboard Magazine*, 108 no. 31 (August 3, 1996), p.1.

2

The Concertina Comes to America

Although the time of the concertina's arrival in America is not known for sure, it is easy to speculate that it came in the latter third of the 19th century—along with the many German and Polish immigrants who were disembarking by the thousands and congregating in the large industrial cities of the Midwest, notably Chicago. Clearly they brought these instruments with them in the 1880s when the concertina was still extremely popular in Europe. Because these immigrants from Central Europe were usually those disrupted from their peasant villages and rural land by the industrializing process underway in the newly-formed, post-1870 German Empire, the instrument took hold primarily in the Midwestern states where German, Polish and Czech immigrants had settled. That said, it is a parallel fact that at least four instructional books for the German concertina had been published already well before 1880 in New England—which is to say, before many of the first-known concertina makers and sellers had even settled in the Midwest. Most of these manuals included compilations of concertina songs, including polkas, marches, waltzes and other dances.[1]

By the late 1890s, German immigrant Otto E. Georgi [possibly the son of concertina builder Ernst Georgi of Chemnitz in Germany] seems to have set up shop as one of Chicago's first concertina salesmen. Best indications are that he arrived in 1892 with the intention to sell the Lange concertina. All the concertinas built by Friedrich Lange, Carl Uhlig's son-in-law in Chemnitz, as well as those by Uhlig himself, were tuned in the key of C. Most of their instruments which were imported into the Chicago region came with the patented logo LU to stand for Lange/Uhlig. Lange/Uhlig also offered the added customer appeal of instruction available for their clients to play the instrument. While Georgi was undoubtedly the pioneer importer, it appears that others, and maybe Georgi himself, easily changed the maker's name and added a dealer or local store owner in place of the orig-

It is not clear whether the Ernst Georgi listed here playing a Lange concertina in Chemnitz, Germany might be the father of the man in the lower picture, who is identified by various sources as Otto E. Georgi. Otto is credited with bringing the concertina to the Chicago exhibition in 1893, soon after he started his music business in 1892. Records indicate that he came from Chemnitz and thus it is reasonable to assume that Ernst was his father or possibly a brother.

Scene of the great hall at the World's Columbian Exposition in Chicago in 1893.

MUSICAL INSTRUMENTS
AT THE
WORLD'S COLUMBIAN EXPOSITION.

A REVIEW OF MUSICAL INSTRUMENTS, PUBLICATIONS AND MUSICAL INSTRUMENT SUPPLIES OF ALL KINDS, EXHIBITED AT THE WORLD'S COLUMBIAN EXPOSITION HELD IN CHICAGO, MAY 1 TO OCTOBER 31, 1893, AND THE AWARDS GIVEN FOR THESE EXHIBITS (FROM ALL NATIONS,) WITH THE TEXTS OF THE SAME, FULLY REVISED.

COPIOUSLY ILLUSTRATED.

EDITED AND COMPILED
BY THE
EDITORIAL STAFF
OF
THE PRESTO,
FRANK D. ABBOTT, Managing Editor.

CHICAGO:
PRINTED AND PUBLISHED BY THE PRESTO CO.,
324 DEARBORN ST.

COPYRIGHT, 1895, BY FRANK D. ABBOTT. ALL RIGHTS RESERVED.

PRICES:
Leather Binding, $5.00; Cloth Binding, $3.50; Boards $3.00 Paper Covers, $2.50.

F. LANGE, Chemnitz, Germany.

EXHIBITOR.   Group 158.   Class 935.
  F. Lange, Chemnitz, Saxony,   Exhibit—Concertinas and Bandonions.
    This exhibit deserves an award:
    For excellent tone quality,
    For superior workmanship.
  Approved: K. Buenz.   (Signed) Prosper Lamal.
    President Departmental Committee.   Individual Judge.

Left above is the title page of the volume published in 1895 to document the exhibits and prize winners for instruments displayed at the Chicago Columbian Exposition in 1893. Above is Friedrich Emil Lange, who died in 1933. Friedrich Anton Lange, his father, died February 29, 1892, one year before the Columbian Exposition took place. Below Lange, is the winning citation in the book of "Musical Instruments" reporting the excellent tone quality and the superior workmanship of the Lange concertinas exhibited at the Columbian Exposition. Below that is a ticket for admission to the exhibit valid for June 7th, 1893. One of the superior judges of the overall musical exhibit was a man with the Bohemian name, Hlavac.

A business card for the Friedrich Lange company in 1893 following the success of the concertina's introduction at the Chicago World's Fair that year. Note the words "won prize in Chicago in 1893."

inal brand name. Any kind of patent or brand protection seems to have been lacking or ignored.

Not only that, but already at the World's Fair in 1893, in Chicago Friedrich Lange proudly displayed his Lange concertinas for the entire hemisphere to see.[2] Some have thought it was Otto Georgi alone who arranged for the Chemnitzer concertina to appear in the Columbian Exhibition. Perhaps Lange came personally for the Exhibition. At issue with such a supposition is the fact that Friedrich Anton Lange, who teamed with Uhlig, passed the firm to his son, Friedrich Emil Lange, in 1891. In 1892, the father, Friedrich Anton, passed away.[3] The younger Friedrich Emil Lange might have come from Chemnitz, Germany to exhibit the concertina and the bandonion at the Columbian Exposition of 1893 as is indicated from various facts. For instance, he is listed as one of the foreign exhibitors from Germany for the concertina competition under the overall judgeship for that section of instruments, Prosper Lamal.[4] Among the two dozen exhibits listed on site from Germany is the entry "F. Lange (concertinas, etc.) Chemnitz."

When we turn to the pages declaring the actual exhibitors from Germany, we find entries for many brands of German pianos from Hamburg, Osnabrück, Kassel, etc., mechanical instruments like hand organs and self-playing pianos from Leipzig, Berlin, Freiburg, etc., and many publications of music from Breslau, Mainz, Mannheim, and especially Leipzig. In the category of "miscellaneous" we find instruments like the zither, accordion, brass and wood devices from Munich, the table harp from Markneukirchen, Mathias Hohner with "mouth harmonicas," from Trossingen, and F. Lange, from Chemnitz, Saxony. The Lange exhibit is for concertinas and bandonions which got its award signed by the individual judge, Prosper Lamal. The commentary states that the instrument was singled out for "excellent tone quality" and for "superior workmanship."[5] Was Lange himself really on site? Probably not, but then who arranged for the exhibit? Was Otto Georgi already in the business of bringing over concertinas for

Germany's primary exhibit — a stagecoach at the Chicago Columbian Exposition in 1893 from the World's Columbian Exposition *(Urbana: University of Illinois Press, 2002) p. 88. Note the realistic passengers — a big attraction in the Manufacture and Liberal Arts Building*

the American marketplace and sufficiently embedded in competitive strategy to arrange for such an exhibit? We know only that Georgi began seriously dealing in the import and sale of concertinas after the turn of the century. Meanwhile, it should be noted that Friedrich Emil Lange died on the morning of New Year's Day in January, 1933. His death announcement by his wife, Martha, born Franz, and daughter Martha Lange Niemann states that he was once a Hamonikafabrikant [concertina builder], now 82 years-old and still living at Rosenplatz 2 in Chemnitz.[6]

Beginning in 1902 Georgi partnered with Louis Vitak to form the popular firm of "Georgi and Vitak." Shortly, Georgi was joined by Otto Schlicht, who arrived from Germany to become Georgi's chief repair and service man. Otto Georgi emerges in the Chicago City directories in various contexts and with differing allusions. In the 1893 edition, for instance, he appears simply as Georgi, Otto, carpenter, at 4852 South Page Street. There is such an address two blocks west of Interstate 57 and one block south of 119th Street, which may or may not be the same as the 1893 site. In the 1910

Newspaper announcing the death of Friedrich Emil Lange on New Year's Day in January, 1933 at the age of 83. He is mourned by his wife Martha, neé Franz, as well as Eduard Niemann and his wife, Martha, neé Lange, showing that the last owner of the Uhlig-Lange company was Niemann, but that in fact the same family was involved though marriage had changed names. Note that they are still in residence and in operation in Chemnitz on Rosenplatz No. 2.

Once established in his business on Gross Avenue, Otto Georgi not only imported and sold concertinas but actively promoted the instrument. With his partner, Louis Vitak, Georgi courted the Polish folk music market, here with the "National Songs of Poland," in particular the mazurka, and the galop which were popular among the Polish immigrant workers at the Chicago Stockyards.

Otto Georgi poses at the bottom of the jacket. In the middle is the oft-reprinted picture of the Chicago Concertina Club, initiated presumably by Otto Georgi. The main title says "Galop from H. Silberhorn for Concertina."

Business card of Otto Georgi when he jointly operated the Georgi and Vitak music store at 4663 Gross Avenue, just around the corner from the site at which they later operated their retail store at 4639 South Ashland Avenue in Chicago. Pictured is the Pearl Queen concertina manufactured by Otto Schlicht.

edition of the directory, he is listed as Otto E. Georgi (Georgi & Vitak) 4663 Gross Avenue. My assumption is that there was a Page Street at this roughly identical site in the 1893 time frame. In the same year of 1910, he is listed as Georgi & Vitak (Otto E. Georgi and Louis Vitak musical Instruments, 4663 Gross Avenue and 769 Milwaukee Avenue). By the 1914 edition, Georgi is registered as the Georgi & Vitak Music Co., Louis Vitak president, Antony Raifanda secretary, 1540 West 47th Street. The latter street is intersected by Gross Avenue, now shown on maps as McDowell, as explained below.

According to the Ohio Federal Census of 1900, Louis Vitak was born in October, 1862 in Bohemia [though the official record states "Austria"]. Living in 1900 in Canton, Stark County, Ohio, he had been married for seven years to Augusta E. (also born in "Austria") and had a son, Louis A. (four years old, born in Ohio) and a brother, Anton Vitak (born 1858). In Canton, Ohio, city directories for 1888-92 show him owning a studio at 18 East Fourth Street where he is listed as a music teacher, teacher of violin, orchestral instruments and harmony. By 1890 he is at 13 East Tenth Street in Canton and in 1891 at Room 23, Wernet Block, at 34 Cass Street, now listed as a sales agent dealing in Orchestral Instruments. By 1920, according to the Illinois Federal Census, Louis Vitak is living in Chicago but without a wife, though he has daughters Olga (18, born in Ohio), Albertina (15, born in Illinois) and Maria (13, born in Illinois).[7] But in the mid-1920s the partners of Georgi and Vitak fell into disagreement and separated. However, as late as 1923, this company is still listed as "Georgi & Vitak Music Co., Louis Vitak, Pres.,[8] Joseph P. Elsnic Secretary-Treasurer, having everything in music—mail order house 4639 South Ashland Avenue.[9]

Here it should be noted that the Otto Georgi busi-

Death cerificate of Otto E. Georgi, who was born near Chemnitz and died November 24, 1937 in Chicago. At the time of his death he was a music dealer, having owned his own business longer than 45 years. This tells us that he first started his business in 1892, just prior to the 1893 Columbian Exposition where the concertina won an important prize.

Site of the Rudy Patek Store at 835 Milwaukee Avenue — probably the blank space/parking lot on the left.

ness was intermittently located at 4663 Gross Avenue "at the corner of Ashland and 47th Street" — prominent boulevards in south Chicago. This site, then, was also in the immediate vicinity of the ensuing Vitak and Elsnic Company that dominated the sheet music business for decades to come. Judging from his death certificate, Otto E. Georgi was born on February 4, 1869 in Saxony [Chemnitz is a major city in Saxony but he was not born precisely in that city].[10] Married to Anna S. Georgi, he is reported at the time of death to be a "music dealer" who "owns his own business," in which he was occupied right up to his demise, a total of 45 years. This indicates that he may have arrived in the United States (Chicago) in 1892, though he could have come the following year for the Chicago Exposition of 1893. According to the *Chicago City Directory* of 1923, he is a "music instructor" living at 1738 North California Avenue in Chicago. At this latter address he was within a dozen blocks west of the Patek and Silberhorn establishments on Milwaukee Avenue, the north side of Chicago as opposed to the south side "concertina concentration" at 4639 South Ashland. At the time of Georgi's death on November 24, 1937 he was still living at 1738 North California Avenue. Thus he died just four months before his confrere, Otto Schlicht, about whom, more later.

That there were two neighborhoods in Chicago where the concertina thrived is due to the ethnic mix of population that dominated these two regions: 4800 South Ashland and 735 Milwaukee Avenue in the north. Both were approximate to downtown by our standards, but the Ashland region was in fact more at the heart of the Union Stockyards neighborhood. Up north workers rode trolleys into downtown Chicago, while here in the south they often simply walked to the famous yards, from which the neighborhood got the name "Back of the Yards." These were the people who stood in awe of the concertina and its music. Here were alive all the folk-songs of the simpler folk from eastern Europe—Poles, Czechs, eastern Germans, Lithuanians, a few Jews, many Catholics and, in short, living proof of the heartland that was reflected in each of the local hearths of homes surrounding the music stores. Interestingly, for a time at least, the Georgi and Vitak Music Company operated a branch at 769 Milwaukee Avenue, thus offering services in the nerve centers of both "concertina" districts in Chicago. At this address, 769 Milwaukee Avenue, Rudy Patek owned his first, or at least an earlier retail outlet for the concertina. Some, among them Walter M. Stark who once worked for Patek, believe Patek purchased this store at 769 Milwaukee directly from Georgi. From

LaVern Rippley at the stockyards gate from a 2005 photo.

Bird's-eye view of the Union Stockyards and packing plants in G. L. Howe and O. M. Powers, The Secrets of Success in Business *(Chicago, 1883).*

this particular store, derives a Pearl Queen concertina owned by Jerry Minar with the stamping — Patek, 769 Milwaukee Avenue — and the words "Patek is a dealer of the celebrated Pearl Queen concertinas." Primarily, the Pearl Queen was sold by Vitak-Elsnic, but as noted here, Vitak and Georgi cooperated in various retail ventures and if Patek bought from Georgi, then for a time at least he handled the Pearl Queen, later naming it exclusively the Patek. They also offer advertisements for the Unita Music Store for Concertina, operated by Georgi and Vitak, but its exact location is obscure.

"Back of the Yards" is defined by sociologists today as being bounded on the west by Western Avenue, more specifically Leavitt Street, which is also the route of the CTA Orange Line. Along this perimeter proceeding north to 43rd Street, the "yards" is contained on the north by an eastward straight line to the Stockyards Gate. It then continues southward along Ashland but jogs a few blocks farther eastward to include the whole of Gross Avenue (now McDowell), which runs at a 45 degree angle to 47th. After continuing southward along either Racine or Morgan, the "yard's" southern periphery is determined by the large Garfield Boulevard which stretches straight back to Western. Here, during the period from the 1880s to the closing of the stockyards after World War II, was the absolute dream heaven for the student of ethnic America or for the unfolding of inter-ethnic and-national sociology.[11] For, as the Irish in the 1890s departed on their pathway to prosperity, thousands of Polish immigrants replaced them, especially following the packinghouse strike of 1886. In response to their needs, real estate developer, S. E. Gross, began erecting tenements around 47th and Ashland, which continued through the 1890s. Proud of his cottages offering a kitchen, parlor and two bedrooms, Gross advertised on posters "Where all was darkness, now is light." He named it "New City" and "S. E. Gross Ashland Avenue and 47th Street Subdivision" Branch Office. By the 1920s when the music store retailers thrived in "New City" there were 92,600 residents of the subdivision, 37% foreign born. The foreigners were primarily Poles, Czechs, Germans and Lithuanians, reflecting directly the musical numbers listed in the respective foreign language catalogs the stores issued, e. g. the Vitak-Elsnic Company. As late as 1970, the U. S. Census confirms the decades-old trends, 35% of the residents were Poles, but by this time in place of the Irish and the Germans, 24% were Mexican, the rest a mixture.

Representing the ethnic neighborhood best are the churches, St. Rose of Lima built in 1881 on Ashland and

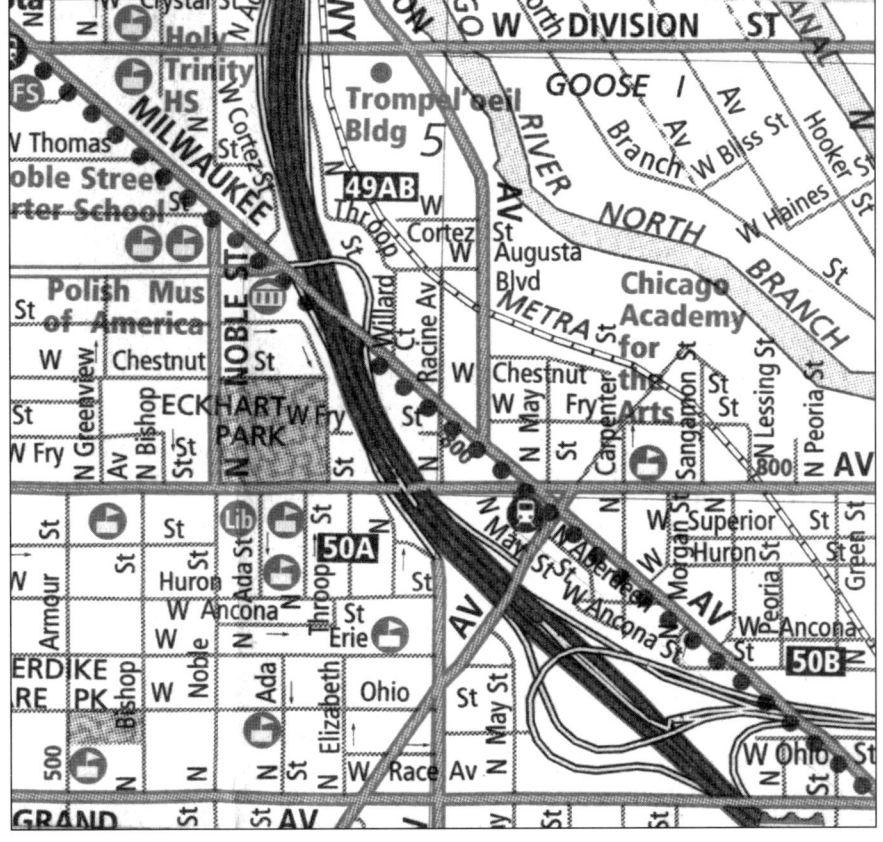

At the left is the core area of Chicago's immediate north side with Milwaukee Avenue cutting diagonally from upper left to lower right with heavy dots. Along Milwaukee Avenue were located the north side concertina dealers, Henry Silberhorn, Otto Georgi, Louis Vitak, and especially Rudy Patek, at 835 North Milwaukee Avenue. Almost at the center of the map running north-south between Chestnut and Milwaukee is North May Street where Otto Schlicht assembled his Patek and Pearl Queen concertinas. Just a bit northwest of Patek's establishment at 835 stands the Polish Roman Catholic Union of America, located at 984 North Milwaukee Avenue, home of their insurance company, museum, and substantial Polish archive. In this Polish ethnic neighborhood, the Chemnitzer concertina was intimately at home.

48th for the Irish, St. Martin Lutheran built in 1884 for the Germans, and St. Augustine Roman Catholic in 1879, also for the Germans. When the Poles arrived in strength, they attended St. Adalbert's Catholic parish in the Pilsen (Bohemia) neighborhood four miles to the north. However, the Poles soon established their own Catholic parish, St. Joseph's, in 1889. But as the number of Poles increased, two additional Polish parishes sprang up, St. John of God in 1907 and Sacred Heart of Jesus in 1910. Out of the eleven Roman Catholic parishes in the "Back of the Yards" district in the mid-

St. Rose of Lima was founded in 1881 for Irish families. A frame church was constructed here already in 1883. In May, 1939, however, during the height of the concertina era, the pastor purchased land at 48th and Justine for a combination church/school/convent building. It was completed in April, 1940 here at 1546 West 48th St. to serve Polish, Lithuanian and Irish families near the Vitak-Elsnic store at 4815 South Ashland.

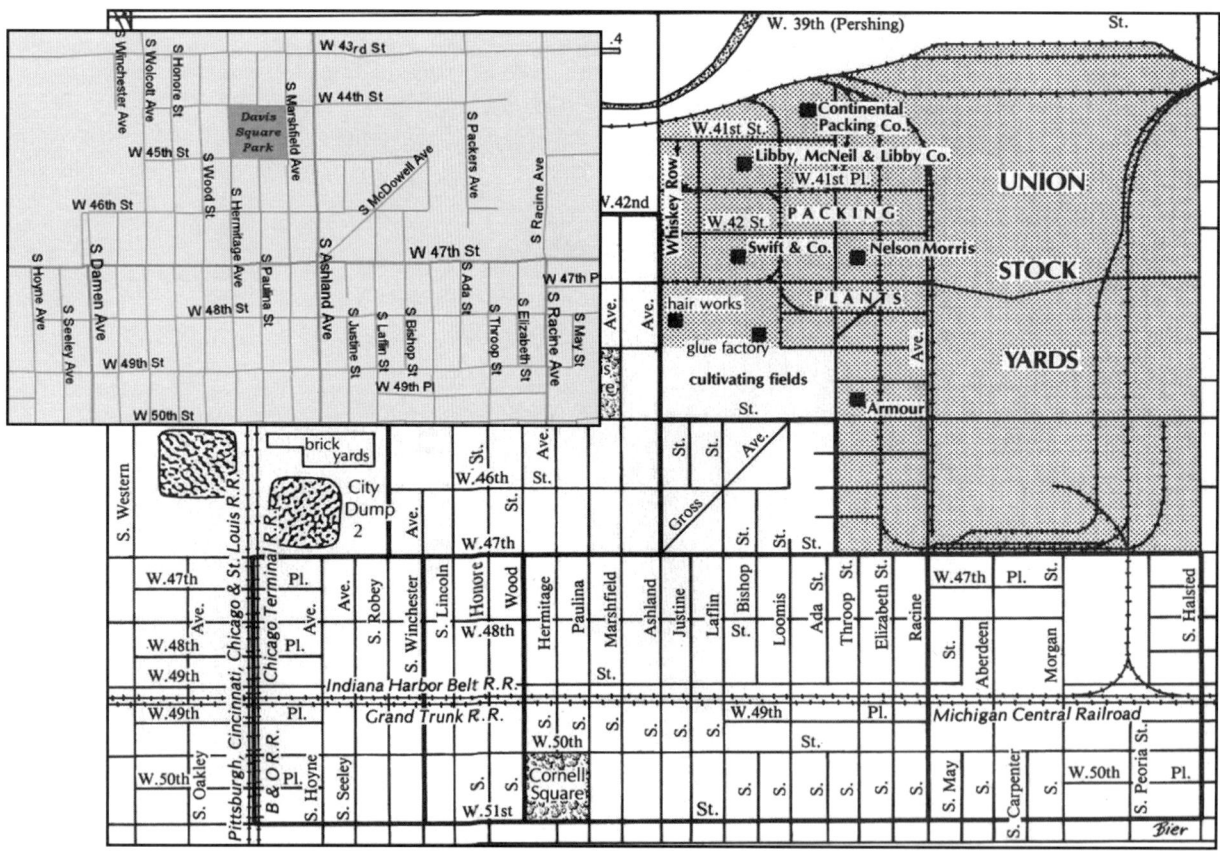

This map of South Chicago depicts the prominent square between Ashland on the left and Halsted on the right, north of 47th Street where once the famous Chicago Stockyards operated. The six corners created by the intersection of Ashland Avenue and 47th Street, where South Gross Avenue intersects on the diagonal, was called Whiskey Point. Note that when Otto Georgi conducted business on that diagonal street, it was called Gross Avenue, which was changed to McDowell Avenue. All the major retail outlets for the concertina on the south side of Chicago were clustered near Whiskey Point, including Vitak-Elsnic. The main map is from 1910, the insert from 2005.

1920s when the Polish music stores were at their height, seven were Slavic and one Lithuanian. A relatively small Jewish community along Ashland Avenue generated a synagogue, which lasted until after World War II. As elsewhere in America, the Polish community here soon also supported a Polish National Catholic Church.

Beginning with Armour and Company in 1867 and continuing through the 1880s, over 30 individual packing houses were established and thrived in what was known as the Union Stockyards. Working and living conditions for those workers who labored not only called for distractions, musical and otherwise, but also became the source of literature like Upton Sinclair's *The Jungle* (1905).[12] Along 47th Street westward to the "yard's" western limit were city and packing house dumps, giving rise to the city's worst neighborhood for tuberculosis and highest for death rates of children.

As noted above, American founder of the concertina, Otto Georgi, conducted his business at 4663 Gross Avenue, the name of which was later changed to McDowell. Named for the first head resident of the University of Chicago area Settlement House, Mary McDowell played a role in the life the of Polish district. She supported not only the Union movement and the effort of Saul Alinski to organize the community, but also helped build Guardian Angel Nursery and Home for Working Women.[13] This institution was positioned in 1913 near the intersection of McDowell, Laflin, and 46th, known previously as Whiskey Point because the six points of the intersection housed six saloons. Called an *ochronka* or shelter, the institution served all the ethnic groups residing in the neighborhood—as did in like manner the concertina and music retail stores on all sides of this interesting complex of churches, taverns and tenements.

It was in this multi-ethnic environment that Vitak later teamed exclusively with his nephew, Joseph P. Elsnic, to create the aptly-named "Vitak-Elsnic Company," which proved to be a long-lasting, rather profitable partnership. Born in Pennsylvania to parents born in Bohemia, Elsnic had learned first the violin and then the piano, the accordion, and several brass instruments including tuba and Sousaphone. Due to this capacity, when he entered military service in 1918, Elsnic went directly to the Great Lakes Training Station as a member of the John Philip Sousa Band, some asserting he was the grand master's top assistant.[14] For most of its business prime, e. g. during its heyday when issuing books for the likes of Whoopee John and other concertina bands in Minnesota, the Vitak-Elsnic Company in the 1950s printed the date on its catalogs and its loca-

Note that the envelope discovered by the author in German archives exhibits a postal marking stamped at the "Chicago Area Stockyards", possibly dated June, 1926.

Running west of the Stockyards was Ashland Avenue, bearing between 40th and 48th Streets South the unsavory moniker, "Whiskey Row" due to its unbroken line of saloons.

An early Lange concertina imported by Georgi & Vitak. This concertina has a German-built frame. The internal action, bellows and buttons were crafted by builders or repairmen in Chicago. Jerry Minar has similar specimens leading to the assumption that certain basic components of the concertina were crafted in Germany and shipped, then assembled in Chicago where separate skills came to bear, showing an interweave of the production sites.

tion at 4815 South Ashland in the southwestern section of Chicago. Then again, it operated at 4639 South Ashland, as noted on its 1924 and 1929 catalogs: "Vitak-Elsnic, Successor to Georgi & Vitak Music Co." In this particular catalog the company boasts that 33 years of experience "in concertinas enables us to advise every admirer of a concertina to make it his aim to own a 'Pearl Queen' concertina." In 1986, William Brown of the Brown Music Store in New Ulm acquired the remaining sheet music and equipment of the Vitak-Elsnic enterprise.

In the very same vicinity of the Vitak-Elsnic firm was not only the Georgi establishment mentioned above, but also the S. S. Gralak Music Store, located at 1532 West 47th Street, within a block's distance from the other concertina promoters. Not only a dealer of the concertina and other instruments, Gralak himself was a renowned concertina player who usually stamped his store's name inside the bellows chamber if his shop sold the product. Worthy of mention in this context was also the sheet music dealer, John Jastnski Music Co., which operated from its site at 4629 South Ashland, again, a few steps away from the many others in the neighborhood. Located here too was one of the music stores owned by W. H. Sajewski, this one called the Polonia Music House at 1532 47th Street., a bit east of Ashland. [Sajewski also operated in the northern concertina district, at 1017 Milwaukee Avenue.] Another retail store was called Lyon and Healy, another operated under the name of Ranier. In addition to publishing ethnic music on a broad front, the Vitak-Elsnic Company sold several makes of concertina.

Often these were used products made in Germany to

This empty envelope discovered in German archives reflects Patek's order for concertinas from the supplier, the Brothers Seifert in Waldheim, a bit northwest of Chemnitz. The date is May 31, 1928.

The former Vitak-Elsnic store at 4815 South Ashland, now a Greek restaurant.

Above are nameplates from the noted "Pearl Queen" concertina. Note that numbers 2 and 3 carry the name Vitak-Elsnic Co., Chicago, Ill. Number 4 above is from a concertina sold by the Brown Music Store after it acquired the Vitak-Elsnic remainder items in 1986. This wooden frame concertina bears a notation that it was made in Europe by an unidentified "Accordion Mfg. Company."

Here the Polish store of S. S. Gralak located at 1532 West 47th Street in Chicago offers a footnote that it stands just one block east of Ashland Avenue—the Concertina Avenue of Vitak-Elsnic. Note that they honor the famous Polish composer-pianist Ignacy Jan Paderewski (1860-1941) and offer mostly Polish language pieces with a few German numbers. During the 1930s, Paderewski was also Prime Minister and Secretary of State in Poland. He died in New York City in 1941.

W. H. Sajewski in his store at 1017 Milwaukee Avenue produced music for the concertina, here an arrangement by Fr. Przybylski, a common Polish surname. This number was marketed through the Patek store at 835 Milwaukee, just three blocks southeast of Sajewski.

Rudy Patek appears to be playing an early Pearl Queen.

Early, rather youthful photographs of concertina player, promoter and retailer, Rudy Patek, after whom the Patek Concertina is named.

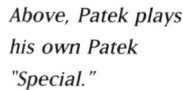

Above, Patek plays his own Patek "Special."

Patek playing a Schlicht-built triple.

Chicago concertina players, Charles J. Blim and Rudy Patek, probably mid 1930s.

specifications and detailed orders from Vitak-Elsnic [Majestic, Wunderlich, Lange products] including, it appears, early versions of the famous "Pearl Queen." A few of these instruments kept coming from Germany, to the best of our scant evidence, and were sold with the new Pearl Queen name even though most were actually built in Chicago by Otto Schlicht, the skilled German immigrant, and his cohorts.

The American-made Pearl Queen first became available about 1911. Serial numbers begin in that year and include the production of about 250 concertinas. In business manufacturing concertinas for himself, Otto Schlicht delivered his products not only under the name of "Pearl Queen" to the Vitak-Elsnic Company but also to the Chicago Patek Music Store under the brand name of "Patek." In addition, Schlicht sold his Chemnitzers under the name of "Peerless" to Kosatka's music store. The T. Kosatka & Co. House of Music was located first at 1425 West 18th Street, but later moved to Berwyn (a suburb adjacent to central Chicago), Illinois.[15] Offering a variety of retail products, Kosatka sometimes advertised its repair service and sometimes taped the store's label inside the instruments, "We do expert tuning and repairing of F. Lange concertinas." In addition to these Chicago outlets, Schlicht supplied concertinas to the St. Paul, Minnesota Kesting Music Store, which retailed them under the name of "Royal." Lending the Pearl Queen, the Peerless and the Patek special tonal quality were the most prized reeds in the industry, produced by German-speaking immigrants John Friedl and his compatriot John Kummer. However, the majority of these Schlicht-built concertinas had German-made reeds, commonly referred to as "machine ground," which bore the commercial trade name of "Dix" reeds. Descriptions of these reeds appear in promotional brochures of the Kesting Music Company of Minneapolis. In the opinion

Rudy Patek in 1953 after leaving Chicago for Wisconsin where he built his own concertinas that bore his Patek brand name. However, he is holding a Schlicht-built Patek with a "Christy" name plate. This was Hengel's Patek Deluxe which Patek used as a demonstrator in the late 1930's.

of Christy Hengel [see Chapter Three], less than 10% of concertinas are fitted with hand-filed reeds made by the likes of Kummer and Friedl in Chicago.

Of special importance in the retail lineup was Rudolph M. Patek, active almost from the day of his birth on September 19, 1896. Born in Chicago, he spent part of his youth in South Dakota but always returned to Chicago. Patek became an expert player, importer, artist, arranger and instructor of the concertina. During the late teens and early 1920s, Patek worked at the Schlicht factory on May Street in Chicago. At first Patek's business was located at 769 Milwaukee Avenue, later at 835, while his residence is listed at 1437 Fletcher, a few miles north of his music studio.[16] In his 1932 catalog Patek tells a bit about his professional self and his promotional policy. Never does he claim to make or to have made the concertina himself. Rather, he reports that he is a leading musician in his own right and that his encouragement, friendship and help has meant much to concertina players far and wide.

The Patek Music Company is the leading exclusive concertina House in the United States. Wherever concertinas are played and discussed you will hear of the unrivaled superiority of the Patek Concertina. You will hear of its great beauty and its glorious ability to produce unequalled tones. You haven't really heard concertina music at its best until you have listened to or played a Patek Concertina. Patek concertinas are so carefully made from such fine materials that we can gladly offer an unusually liberal guarantee—If any Patek concertina experiences trouble because of defective workmanship or material, we will repair it absolutely free of charge if sent to us postage prepaid. In addition to this, all pearl work is fully guaranteed for five years, all woodwork is fully guaranteed for two years, and all reeds for one year. This liberal guarantee is given to you in writing.[17]

With the onset of World War II and the inability of the local concertina makers to secure high quality reeds from Germany, the concertina supply to Rudy Patek diminished. Not only his business but also his marriage declined, ending in his divorce from first wife, Luella. In due time, Rudy Patek married Esther Annerson and in 1962 moved to a small farm near Weyauwega, Wisconsin, where he farmed, mostly raising hogs. Since 1971 he lived inside the city at 202 Second Avenue where, in recognition of his considerable endeavors to promote and perpetuate the concertina, he was inducted into the

The Patek Concertina Club of Chicago. Patek himself was not only an expert concertina player but also a consummate promoter and retailer. One device to enhance sales was the concertina club, of which there were many in the Chicago area during the 1920s and 1930s.

World Concertina Congress Hall of Fame in 1976. At the age of 85, he died on April 1, 1982 and lies buried in Weyauwega's Oakwood Cemetery.[18] Although Patek never built concertinas in his early, highly successful days, he had hundreds of them built to his orders by others, mostly Otto Schlicht. However, he was always self-indulgent enough to install his own Patek name on these subcontracted boxes. Following his move to Wisconsin, Patek did build the waxed reed concertina, completing much of the varied work on his own. In 1966 Anton Wolfe bought Patek's remainder, built the Wolfe concertina and in 1994 sold the majority of his tooling and stocks to Jerry Minar of New Prague, Minnesota. [More about this in a later chapter.]

An undated clipping from the later days of his Chicago career states that the Patek's Music Store is the "Exclusive agent for the Celebrated Pearl Queen Concertinas. [It is] Located on 835 Milwaukee Avenue, Chicago." An advertisement such as this makes it unclear whether the Pearl Queen was now being sold both by Vitak-Elsnic and by Patek or whether Patek

A Pearl King concertina imported by Otto Georgi from the Lange firm in Chemnitz. This concertina has the serial number 29817, completed July 12, 1926.

Otto Georgi moved from southern Chicago at Ashland Avenue to California Avenue after breaking off his relationship with Louis Vitak.

The internal trademark on the Pearl King, which was imported by Otto Georgi from the Lange company, has an eagle abreast a concertina with the words below it, "eingetragene Schutzmarke" / registered trademark.

An early Lange concertina imported from Germany. Note that it does not have the triangular cut corners and thus no display of the harp logo of the Lange-Uhlig manufacturers of Chemnitz. The instrument is owned today by Jerry Minar of New Prague.

perhaps only sold second-hand and used Pearl Queen concertinas, or had made some other arrangement. Stamped on the inside of an early Pearl Queen owned by Jerry Minar is Patek's earlier address of 769, indicating that he was involved with the Pearl Queen and he may have sold this instrument before deciding to market essentially the same instrument with his own "Patek" brand name. He never seems to mention the Peerless, though it was equally representative of the Schlicht factory lineup. Serial number sequences for the Patek and the Pearl Queen concertinas interweave, the Peerless numbers do not. In the year 1930, for example, the serial numbering for Patek and Pearl Queen is 4751 – 5000, indicating that Schlicht had produced his 5000th concertina that year. The last was built in 1946 with the numbers 6152 – 6158, meaning that there were only six crafted in the final year. None of these came from the craftsmanship of Patek himself. However, when living on a farm during his semi-retirement in Wisconsin, Patek did make a few concertinas. Regrettably, he never succeeded in building the light-weight, 15-pound models he sold so vigorously in the 1930s, proof of some substance that he did not actually make any of the Patek, Peerless or Pearl Queen instruments back then, as some have contended.

As mentioned, Patek sold his remaining inventory in 1967 to Anton Wolfe of 2157 Jefferson Street in Stevens Point, Wisconsin. From a farm at Moquah, west of Ashland, where he played concertinas for local parties, Wolfe experienced problems finding replacement parts for his instrument, prompting him to create his own. When Wolfe met Patek in Wisconsin, Patek advised Wolfe to move to Stevens Point because it was a hot spot for concertinas, though everyone knew it was hot only for Star concertinas. He then sold the farm and moved to Stevens Point, where he acquired a former grocery store to house his enterprise. At first Wolfe built concertinas the way the Star builders did in Chicago, namely with waxed reeds exactly as Patek had done when he structured his own concertinas in Wisconsin in the 1960s. However, he came to recognize the higher quality available in the older Patek and Pearl Queen concertinas. With newly inspired initiative, Wolfe then used his own dies, punches and broaches to make reed plates and reeds, so to speak, building his own artistry on the base of the Patek skill, inventory and reputation. In time, he also created his own blocks, action boards, support rails, valves and frames, bellows and hand rails. Some of his early concertinas were sold with the name "Gem," but most were marketed with the

Majestic concertina, imported from the Lange company in Chemnitz and completed the same day as the Pearl King on the previous page. It bears the serial number 29818, one digit off the Pearl King and an identical date of July 12, 1926.

The trademark on the Majestic is composed of two globes with a concertina over the top and the words in English, "Trade Mark." The instrument is identical to the Pearl King, both made in Chemnitz the same day.

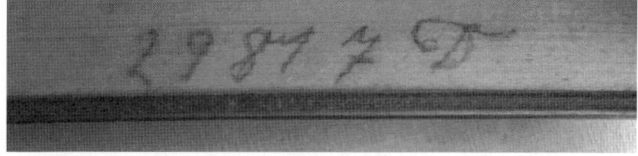

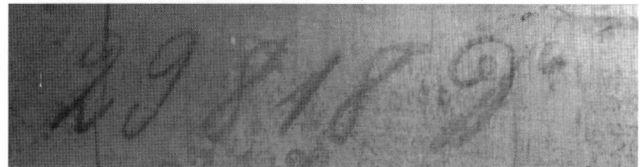

Above are the serial numbers from inside the bellow chambers of the two concertinas, the Pearl King and the Majestic, 29817 and 29818. Both instruments are owned by Jerry Minar of New Prague. The significance of these numbers is that the same instrument was being manufactured to meet differing orders from retailers in the United States.

name Wolfe and eventually as Anton Wolfe, their creator's own name.

Here we must be careful not to confuse the early name Gem with the "Gem Deluxe," which is strictly an Italian-built concertina, one that enjoyed some popularity in the upper Midwest. Eventually the Wolfe inventory was acquired by the capable concertina artist, Jerry Minar, owner of JBM Sound Inc. facilities of New Prague, whose career is described in a separate chapter.

Also of Wisconsin and of equal importance were life-long proponents of the concertina, Pat Watters of Minneapolis and later of Mosinee, as well as Stanley Nowicki and Edward Teikowski, both of Milwaukee. At the same time, large numbers of concertinas were continuously being imported from Germany, expanding the market across the northern tier of the United States. Business boomed throughout the 1920s and undoubtedly there was considerable shifting of nomenclature by the different promoters and sales people, e. g. the Patek, Vitak and Elsnic, Silberhorn and other dealers who thrived until World War II when, abruptly, imports of concertinas, reeds and parts ceased. Edward "Eddie" Lash [Laszczak, of Polish parentage] had been living at 5445 Lieb Street in Chicago until his death in 2002.[19] He was a member of the Chicago Federation of Musicians Local 10.208 and of the World Concertina Congress Hall of Fame. Not only did Lash play the concertina with ample artistry, but recalled with zest his huge success selling second-hand concertinas [especially the Star] in the Milwaukee area during the heydays of Midwest concertina sales. The sales people like Lash, Patek, Silberhorn and many others, however, were not the builders.

At this juncture mention should be made of the move by Otto E. Georgi from the southside Polish community on Ashland to the general vicinity of the northside Polish community where Patek and Silberhorn thrived. Undated flyers list the "Georgi and Vitak Music Co." at 769 Milwaukee Avenue, the facility later acquired and operated by Rudy Patek. While the evidence of Georgi's business now with Vitak, then again independent of the Vitak connection is minimal, there are business cards and a few advertisements also for the Otto E. Georgi "Headquarters for all kinds of Concertinas and Bandonions" on 1738 North California Avenue. Georgi's California store was located between Humboldt Park and the point where it intersects with Milwaukee—in other words, in the immediate proximity of Elston, Armitage, Kedzie and other concertina dealers'

A promotional piece used by Eddie Lash [Laszczak], one of the finest concertina players in his day. During much of his career as a pipe fitter, he was also a preeminent salesman for the Star Concertina and Accordion Mfg. Co. of Chicago. Note that at the time this pamphlet appeared, the Star Company, like Patek and Silberhorn, was also located on Milwaukee Avenue.

Eddie Lash playing a Star concertina in his residence at 5445 Lieb Street, August 9, 2001. The following June, 2002 he passed away. Here he demonstrates the Star for the author.

addresses. On his business card dated September 27, 1923, Georgi claims to be a concertina "Importer, Dealer and Manufacturers' Agent—Wholesale and Retail." Quite likely at this juncture Georgi was an importer of the concertina and possibly without access to the Chicago producers like Otto Schlicht. Thus he imports enthusiastically. We have, for instance, two concertinas quite obviously built in Germany by the Lange company, each with a serial number just one digit apart, the harp logo on the corners, and signed inside with two different trademarks. One shows two globes overarched by an eagle, the other, a concertina on which perches a spread eagle, and both completed the same day in July 12, 1926. Since both concertinas were retailed, it appears that they were on order to the Lange factory where their trade names were attached. One retail shop sold the "Majestic" while the other pushed the "Pearl King," as if to trump the "Pearl Queen" manufactured by Otto Schlicht for Vitak-Elsnic, formerly Georgi-Vitak.[20] Here it needs to be stated that the Pearl King is the only instrument known to have the name of Otto Georgi printed both on the inside and on the outside of the concertina. No doubt Otto Georgi was the primary marketing outlet for the Pearl King.

Early 1930s advertisements for the Patek concertina bear a photograph of Otto Schlicht and of R. M. Patek. Candidly, the text calls Schlicht the American founder and pioneer of the concertina industry, the Master Builder of the World's Finest Concertinas. Checking the fine print we discover that all who have tried to copy Schlicht-built concertinas have been unsuccessful because "there is far more to a concertina than the materials that go into it. It's that mysterious, indefinite ingredient known as CHARACTER." It is the never-ending "attention to the tiniest details, secrets of tones and tone shading, a love for this instrument by OTTO

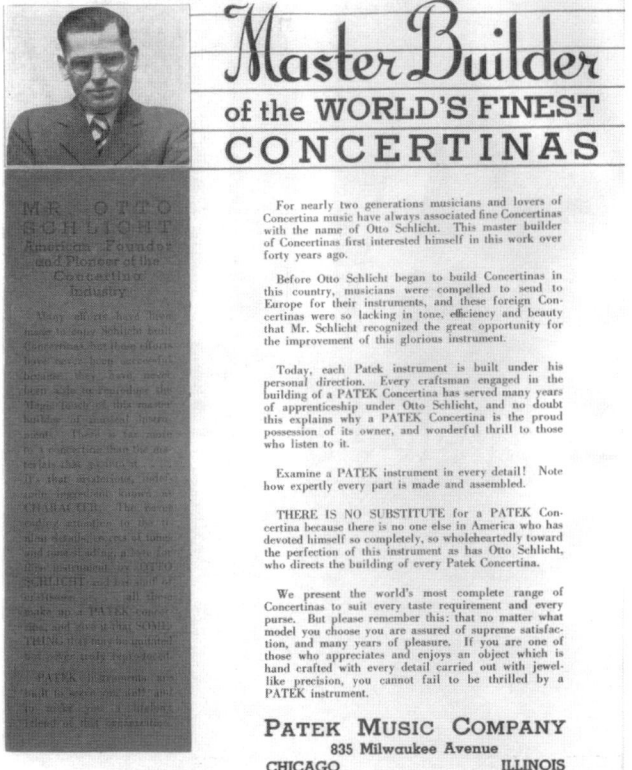

Promotional brochure used by Rudy Patek to sell "his" concertinas, considered the best in the world, because they were the product of the "Master Builder," Otto Schlicht.

Death certificate for Otto Schlicht, 1938. Note that he was born in Danzig, today Gdansk in Poland on the Baltic coast.

SCHLICHT and his staff of craftsmen... all these make up a Patek concertina and give it that something that may be imitated but never reproduced." The advertisement wording goes on to state that "today each Patek instrument is built under Schlicht's personal direction. Every craftsman engaged in the building of a PATEK concertina has served many years of apprenticeship under Otto Schlicht and no doubt explains why a PATEK concertina is the proud possession of its owner, and wonderful thrill to those who listen to it." Continuing, the claim ends "THERE IS NO SUBSTITUTE for a PATEK Concertina because there is no one else in America who has devoted himself so completely, so wholeheartedly, toward the perfection of this instrument as has Otto Schlicht, who directs the building of every Patek Concertina."[21]

Indeed, Otto Schlicht applied for and received several patents for improvements he had made to the concertina. While it is not clear just how many there might have been, one filed June 15, 1932 bears a serial number which was granted as a new patent on December 13, 1932, patent number 1,890,830.[22] This patent was for the Schlicht "Duro Action" base for the internal key mounting on aluminum, which previously was made entirely of wood. Early Star concertinas had aluminum action in the 1920s whereas Patek and Pearl Queen still had wood actions. Also active in the 1920s in Germany under the name of Glass were the companies of Brothers Glass of Brunndöbra (1938), Glass & Schmidt of Klingenthal (1939), Oskar Glass of Klingenthal (1911), and Otto Glass of Klingenthal (1911). One would like to infer that there were connections or relationships to the Chicago Glass brothers, but it is unknown. The Schlict boxes of 1930 started being built with aluminum but were still inferior until the new "Duro Action" was invented and patented. In the view of some, the Star was superior to the "Duro Action" installed by Schlicht on the Patek and Pearl Queen concertinas. The application requests approval for Schlicht's invention to

Trinity Russian Orthodox Cathedral by Sullivan architect at 1121 North Leavitt Street in Chicago. Built in 1903, it stands a few hundred yards from the Patek, Georgi, Schlicht and Silberhorn neighborhood on Milwaukee Avenue. LaVern Rippley is in the foreground. Photo by LaVern Rippley.

improve the action of the inner button and lever action of the concertina. Detailed drawings accompanied the application, prepared by Attorney Axel A. Hofgren for the inventor, Otto A. Schlicht.

Let us recall—Patek was a promoter and salesman only, not a concertina builder—at least not until his removal to Weyauwega, Wisconsin after World War II. According to one of Patek's in-store sales clerks, Walter Stark of Garland, Texas, Patek returned to Chicago empty-handed from a visit to South Dakota. Soon he bought a music store which was going out of business on Milwaukee Avenue — possibly owned by Otto Georgi who, with Louis Vitak for a time, operated a musical instrument retail business located at 769 Milwaukee Avenue. Also in the immediate vicinity were the music stores of W. H. Sajewski at 1011 Milwaukee Avenue and later at 1017 Milwaukee Avenue. A block from there at 835 Milwaukee Avenue, Patek later opened his own store, which he operated during the 1920s and early 1930s. Then about 1940 he moved out to 2847 Milwaukee Avenue, seemingly to escape the near-downtown urban blight near the site where Silberhorn, too, once operated his concertina music store.[23] An excellent contestant on the concertina, Patek performed with big Chicago stars like Benny Ray, Charlie Blim, Joe Stacy, Larry Doost, Frank Schmidt and Eddie Lash.[24] True to his enthusiasm for the instrument, Patek also organized and sustained his own "Patek's Concertina Club," which met regularly at Faikel's Hall at 2128 North Leavitt Street on the corner of Custer, not far from his store.[25]

Otto A. Schlicht, the real artisan and master concertina builder, remained behind the scenes of the Chicago concertinas. Judging from *Germans to America* by Glazier and Filby [which, however, is replete with errors], Otto Schlicht arrived on May 29, 1892 in the United States on board the *Rugia* from Hamburg to New York with an intermediate stop in Le Havre. It appears that he may have immigrated alone, but whether he had spent time in the Chemnitz area before emigrating or whether he came to Chicago directly from Germany is unclear. In the 1930 Federal Census for Chicago, Schlicht was 56-years-old, born in Germany, married to Pauline, who was born in Illinois, and without children. His occupation is listed as being the "manager for musical instruments," presumably a phrase to encompass his supervision of those working for him in his miniature

Otto Schlicht, reproduced from promotional material used by Rudy Patek who claimed Schlicht was the finest concertina craftsman in the world. Schlicht worked on 655-659 May Street in the immediate vicinity of the Patek and Silberhorn establishments. His buildings were removed to construct the Kennedy Expressway.

516/519 Mikwaukee Avenue, site of Henry Silberhorn Building. Note the close proximity to the Sears Tower in downtown Chicago.

factory. According to his death certificate, Otto A. Schlicht was born on March 10, 1873 in the West Prussian City of Danzig to Adolph Schlicht and Bertha nee Waschke. Traveling at the age of 17, Schlicht had listed his destination as Milwaukee and was accompanied by siblings Ernst, 13 years old, and Ida, 10.[26] According to Wally Stark,[27] the Otto Schlicht factory was located at 655 May Street, close to the Patek store, on a side street between the Patek store at 835 Milwaukee and the

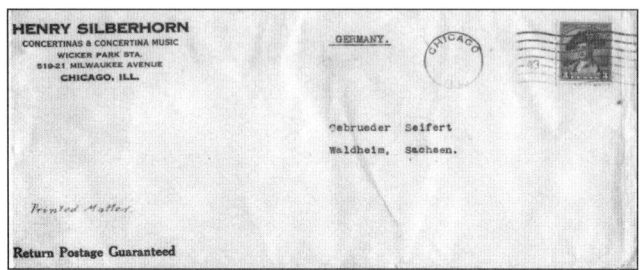

This envelope discovered empty in German archives bears no postal stamp or date, probably because it contained printed matter as noted at the lower left.

Henry Silberhorn store at 519 Milwaukee Avenue in near-downtown Chicago. Today this address would be directly on top of the Kennedy Expressway.

Indeed, the Chicago *City Directory* [Reel 17 1928] calls Otto Schlicht an "instrument manufacturer" located at 655-659 North May Street.[28] Thus his operation was positioned in the immediate vicinity of Patek, Silberhorn and the others, one block east of the point where Elston intersects with Milwaukee Avenue and almost at the juncture with today's main Ogden Street, which runs southwest from the Loop under the Kennedy Expressway. However, Otto Schlicht maintained his home at 4115 North Whipple Street in Chicago, near the junction of Kedzie and Foster along the North Shore Channel, some 30 blocks north of the manufacturing site. According to the *Illinois Death Index*, Otto Schlicht died of an intracranial tumor on March 26, 1938,[29] leaving his wife, Pauline, sisters Hannah Krofl and Olga Knop, and no children. His death certificate states that he remained active as a "maker of musical instruments" in his "own business" for a total of 35 years.[30] He was buried in Mount Olivet Cemetery from a funeral chapel located at 4338 Fullerton Avenue. Meanwhile, Silberhorn had been living privately at 2947 Polk, near its junction with Kedzie, just south of today's I-290, roughly in the vicinity of his competitor friends, Schlicht and Patek. As noted, his business site was at 519 Milwaukee Avenue.

It should be noted that during the first half of the 20th century, this was the heart and soul of Polish Catholic Chicago. Almost next door to Patek stood then, and still stands, the substantial structure of the Polish Roman Catholic Union of America, located at 984 North Milwaukee Avenue, home of their insurance company, museum and substantial Polish archive. While the Germans came first as attested by their St. Boniface Catholic Church at 921 North Noble Street, it was the Polish ethnic community who gave us, in the immediate vicinity of Milwaukee Avenue, Holy Trinity Polish Catholic Church at 1118 North Noble as well as St. Stanislaus Kosta at 1351 West Evergreen. Almost contiguous to the Patek and Silberhorn stores in terms of neighborhood is the Russian Orthodox community, which erected its Louis Sullivan-designed Holy Trinity Orthodox Cathedral at 1121 North Leavitt in 1903. Equally interesting in the surroundings are the two Ukrainian churches, St. Nicholas Ukrainian Catholic Cathedral at 2338 West Rice, and Sts. Volodymyr and Olha Ukrainian Catholic Church at 739 Oakley Street.[31] Apparently Silberhorn, Patek and other concertina promoters were very much at home here in this intensely Slavic, mostly Polish, locale.

But there were others, even if they had trouble measuring up to any one of the three "Ottos," as old timers recall.[32] Even as Pioneer Otto Georgi was setting up his first shop in Chicago, another concertina aficionado was Henry Silberhorn, a Bavarian-born immigrant. As a young man there, he received training in music theory before he came to America at age 18 in 1885. According to the 1920 Federal Census for Chicago, he was born in Bayern [Bavaria] in 1867 and is listed by the census-taker as a "teacher of music." He began not only teaching the concertina, but also publishing instructional texts for Georgi and later for his own pupils and for distribution from his own store. His son, Ernest, helped in the store.

The nameplate on a Silberhorn concertina, most of which were built in Germany.

Soon Silberhorn developed his own line of concertinas called the "Clarion," and supported the formation of concertina clubs and organizations in Chicago. Moreover, in 1927 he started up *Silberhorn's Booster for the Advancement of the Concertina*, a popular magazine for professional and aspiring concertinists alike. About his "Clarion," Silberhorn wrote in his *Booster* in 1930: "through tireless efforts I have succeeded in offering a Concertina which has truly reached the highest point of perfection of the day; viz: a strong and yet mild tone— a real concertina tone—which becomes richer, the longer it is being played; and its name is: the Clarion." Together with Georgi, Silberhorn established a public relations infrastructure which indeed boosted the concertina by means of clubs, teachers, importers, manufacturers and publishers. Not surprisingly, the Silberhorn method is still used today and his method of musical assessment has been utilized to notate sheet music from the era of prohibition to present-day songs.

In a letter from Michael C. Silberhorn, his grandson, we learn that Henry Silberhorn derives from a Rheinland-Pfalz family, who lived at Neustadt near Koblenz [a territory that until 1870 belonged to Bavaria]. Born here on June 29, 1867, Henry immigrated to Chicago in 1885 at the age of 18. Well educated and conversant also in French, Henry Silberhorn, though Lutheran, in 1918 as a mature master of his craft also became a Master of his Masonic Lodge in Chicago. In 1928 when he returned to Germany on a visit, he stopped in Nürnberg where his father told him the Silberhorns had originated. Finding a page and a half of Silberhorns in the telephone directory, he "closed the book, went across the street and had a schnapps and a beer!"[33] According to the same source, Henry married Hedwig Amalie Vogt (Voight) in 1892 and had at least six children. Working initially upon his arrival in Chicago for a wheelwright, Henry always maintained his love for different kinds of music. Thus he soon found a job arranging music, then working for and traveling in the name of a wholesale music house before acquiring his own business on Lincoln Avenue in Chicago.

Reportedly, in the course of his lifetime, Silberhorn published some 8,500 pieces for the concertina, offering some 4,000 of them in a catalog at any one time. His products were offered for sale in some 20 music stores stretching from St. Paul, Minnesota, to Pittsburgh, Pennsylvania, while he also marketed his products through a mailing list that stretched from coast to coast. For 35 years, Silberhorn performed as the conductor of the Chicago Concertina Club, meeting weekly and sang regularly with the Senefelder Liederkranz male chorus in Chicago. Once he also appeared on a radio program with the famous Austrian-born opera singer, Madame Ernestine Schuman-Heink.

Following Henry's retirement, only one son, Ernest, of Park Falls, Wisconsin, carried on the tradition of dealing in fine concertinas. Late in his career as music

2351 Milwaukee Avenue. The Star Concertina Shop began operations in 1926 under the leadership of Walter Kadlubowski, Sr. and Walter Mojsiewicz, as it branched from the International Accordion Company.

Walter Kadlubowski, Sr. and Herman Perkowaki in the Star Concertina Shop in 1953.

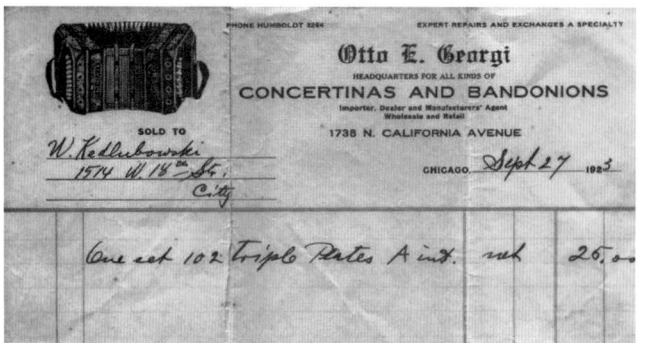

Note that Otto E. Georgi lists himself as the "Head-quarters for all kinds of Concertinas and Bandonions." He is an importer, a dealer, a manufacturer's agent, a wholesaler, and a retail entrepreneur. Here in 1923 he supplies reeds to Kadlubowski who at the time was making accordions but switched soon to building the Star concertina.

Note that there was a Star Concertina Club in Chicago with a president named Edwin A. Hermann, but the name of the secretary is illegible.

salesman and concertina booster, according to his letterhead and brochures, Silberhorn moved his operation to 5942 North Talman Avenue, "just north of Western Avenue." The earliest such letterhead is dated August 22, 1943, but the move could have occurred even earlier.[34] As late as March 4, 1954 he is still at the Talman Avenue address. Much of the Silberhorn collection of sheet music was passed first to Pat Watters and from him to Susan and Dan Gruetzmacher at the address of T 3136 Calico Lane, Wausau, Wisconsin 54403. Even before his death at the age of 94 in 1961, Henry's primary shop and sales office, once located at 519-521 Milwaukee Avenue, Chicago, had been converted into a large warehouse, its current use.

Many other early manufacturers came into their own in the 1920s. One was Ernst Glass, another German immigrant who arrived in the United States on board the ship *Polynesia* from Hamburg at the age of 32, reaching New York July 19, 1886 with the occupation of "laborer."[35] With him on board were his wife, Auguste 28, and his children Otto 9, Paul 6, Elsa 3 and Friedrich, an infant of six months. Just when the Glass family arrived in Chicago is unclear. Nor is it known whether there was any linkage between the Chicago Glass concertina builders and the Reinhard Glass family of Georgenthal and the Louis Glass family of Berlin-Neu Kölln, both concertina fabricators during the 1920s. By the 1910 Federal Census for Illinois, however, Ernst Glass, now 56, is the head of the household and living at 7150 South Morgan Street with wife "Christine" 59 [born in Germany], and son Otto 33, Paul 30, daughter Elsa 26 (now called Elsie) – all born in Germany, daughter Linda 21 born in Illinois, and nephew William 26, born in Wisconsin. Thus we conclude from the birth of Linda in Illinois that the family proceeded to Chicago almost directly from the New York dock, or soon after 1886. Nephew William stays with the family through the 1920 census, at which time Ernst Glass is the head of household at the age of 65 listed with wife "Christina" 69, Otto 42, Paul 39, Elsie 36, and nephew Willie 36. It seems likely that Auguste was a first wife and Christine a second, given the seven-year variation in their ages (ruling out the possibility that Auguste changed her name to Christina). The 1930 Federal Census lists at the 7150 South Morgan address only Otto, Paul and sister Elsie. Otto and Paul are credited with owning their own business and doing repair on musical instruments. It seems probable that Auguste, Christine and Ernst, the father, died between 1920 and 1930. Paul and Otto also seem to submerge during the 1930s.

The *Chicago Illinois General Directory* for 1910 lists the occupation for both the father, Ernst, and the son,

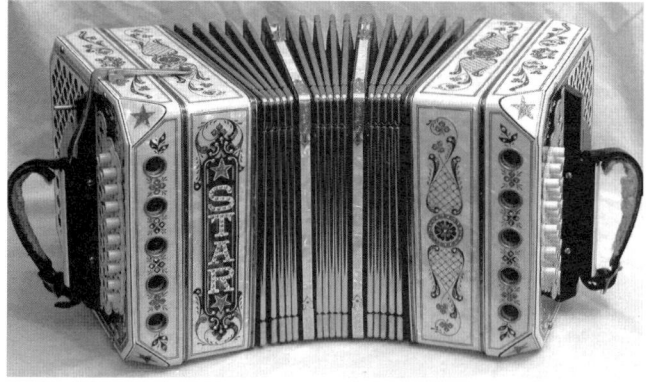

A Star concertina using five ports on the ends. The five-pointed star appears on the eight beveled corners above and below the name plate as well as on the printed material as seen at the top of this page.

Otto, as "instrument repair," while Paul is a "machinist." By the time the directory is published in 1917, both Ernst and Otto are designated as "instrument makers" while Paul is now categorized as "automobile repairman," leading to the conclusion that Ernst and Otto made the concertinas while Paul was more occupied with mechanics. The whole family continues to live at 7150 South Morgan. In the occupational designation on the 1910 Federal Census, we find the same "musical instruments" for the two, "mechanic" for Paul. But in the 1920 Federal Census, all three, Ernst, Otto and Paul, are distinctly listed, each in the occupation column as "Concertina Maker at Home." Still at 7150 Morgan Street, Elsie is unemployed, while Willie is a bookkeeper at a packinghouse. In the 1930 Federal Census, Ernst has disappeared but both Otto and Paul continue as "having their own business" at home, it being music repair.

Thus, it is apparent that the Glass family began constructing concertinas about 1915 as market demand unfurled. With his sons Otto and Paul, who continued production after the death of Ernst, the brand name of "Glass Brothers," manufacturers, importers and distributors lasted until 1951. Using a distinctive reed-block pattern, their balanced button action made Glass concertinas popular with polka players in a wide geographic area. Their primary point of operations continued at 7150 South Morgan Street in Chicago. Although their production reached perhaps no more than 350 concertinas, they became known for their aluminum core, which they cast themselves from their own foundry. As a matter of fact, the Glass concertina had the very first aluminum action lever system in concertina production. For this action, Glass held patent numbers 1,024,771 and 1,737,834 whereas the Schlicht patent for "Duro Action" was 1,890,830. From time to time someone discovers he has a concertina with Glass parts. For example, Jerry Minar of New Prague, Minnesota, owns a Patek concertina fitted with Glass aluminum action though it is not certain whether Schlicht, Patek or some later repairman perhaps fitted the Patek with the Glass action parts. Of the 350 boxes built by the Glass Brothers, Frank Berendt of 6905 West Church Street in Morton Grove, Illinois, is the collector / owner of about 35, ten percent of the total output.[36] In Montgomery, Minnesota, Marvin Moravec is also a proud owner of a Glass concertina.

In a parallel effort at 1511 North Milwaukee Avenue in Chicago, the International Accordion Company manufactured the Chemnitzer concertina under its name of "International" from 1926 to 1930 with Walter Kadlubowski, Sr. as its tuner. Star Concertina manufactured Chemnitzers that were sold by re-sellers under various other brand names, including Royal[37] and Schuckert [Roman Kalina of Lonsdale, Minnesota, owns a Schuckert]. However, almost all the Schuckert

John Zelasko of 4313 Haralson Court SE in Grand Rapids, Michigan, playing a Glass concertina built in the 1950s, at the Pulaski, Wisconsin polka fest on July 24, 2004. Zelasko purchased it from the Dick Rodgers family in Pulaski.

This concertina built by the Glass brothers bears six-pointed stars on each corner, possibly because it rivaled the Star concertina being produced a short distance away. On each end frame are twelve pointed wagon wheels in the port holes, four on each face.

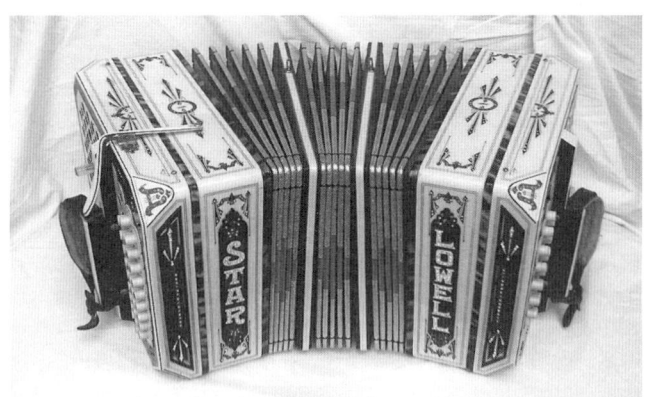

STAR (104 Key / quadruple reed Key of E-Flat). *This 1951 model features decorative grills in place of the usual five sound-hole rings per side. Also, it has Otto Schlicht-built buttons, the same as were used for Patek and Pearl Queen concertinas. Speculation suggests that when the Schlicht builders ceased production about 1946, the new owner, Walles, sold a few remaining sets of buttons to Star before the entire inventory was sold to Christy Hengel in 1953. Lowell Schubert of Delano, Minnesota played this concertina for the Ivan Kahle Band from 1960-1966.*

Walter Kadlubowski, Sr. [with Kajetan Perkowski and Walter Mojsiewicz] founded the Star Concertina Manufacturing Company. Later it was assumed by Walter Kadlubowski, Jr. who operated it for a dozen years between 1960 and 1972. The father and son are shown on the left. The middle and lower pictures show Walter Jr. at different ages. During the 1980s, this Kadlubowski started a new venture, manufacturing the Eagle concertina, which passed upon his death to Richard S. Raclawski of Oak Creek, Wisconsin.

concertinas were in essence the Star for whom Schuckert worked, and were crafted at their production site, 2351 Milwaukee Avenue, just 15 blocks northwest of the Patek, Schlicht and Silberhorn enterprises' musical stores. All of these brands used the original Star Concertina sequence of serial numbers. A few of their products bear the name "Sitek." Although information is scanty, the Sitek concertina may be named after a John Sitek who, in the memory of some, worked at the Star Company. In the 1930 Federal Census for Chicago, John Sitek is listed as immigrating from Poland, 39 years old, born in 1890, having the occupation of "music teacher," and being employed in "music."

With respect to the prime mover at the International Accordion Company during this period, Walter Kadlubowski, Sr. was a 1910 immigrant from the Grodno area, then an eastern city in Poland, but after World War II a city annexed by the Soviet Union, now Belarus. He settled at 24th and Damen in Chicago where he enjoyed playing the Warszawa style of accordion. The 1930 Federal Census lists his profession as "instrument repair shop." At the time he was 39 years old living with wife, Mary, and children named Romona (1916), Stella (1917), Lilian (1919), Teddy (1921) and Walter (1927) Jr.

Among the brands of concertinas manufactured during the 1920s are especially those of the Star Concertina and Accordion Company of Chicago. Masterminded by the Glass brothers and the elder Walter Kadlubowski (1925) as well as the Karpek

A late Star concertina produced during the Bernhardt years.

Accordion Manufacturing Company (1915) of Milwaukee, the Star became a durable mainstay of the concertina industry. Andrew Karpek was a Russian immigrant whose acquaintance with the concertina derives from his Milwaukee contacts, not his Russian heritage. With ample market demand, both plants could manufacture

concertinas and other squeeze boxes for the Midwest, and both also prospered during this heyday of the concertina. Although the International Accordion Company started in 1917 under the tripartite leadership of Walter Mojsiewicz, Walter Kadlubowski, Sr. and Kajetan Perkowski, they at first made only accordions, mainly Varsovien, Russian, Viennese, Italian and Czech. When that market waned, they switched to concertinas, at first importing them primarily from Germany and attaching their trade name "Star." Abandoning the accordions, they decided to go out of business entirely in 1930.

However, Walter Mojsiewicz, formerly a tuner for International, continued building this line of concertina, and persistently used the established name "Star." Mojsiewicz was born September 8, 1892 in Poland, immigrated in 1914 and appears in the 1930 Federal Census as a "cabinet maker." Seemingly this was his primary means of a livelihood until his death in June, 1975. Subsequently in its advertisements, we always find a statement that the company officially began manufacturing the "Star" in the year 1925. However, under the management of Mojsiewicz and his wife Anna, the instrument was assembled locally, even if some parts arrived from abroad. When Kadlubowski, Sr. died in 1937, his son was working as an apprentice to his father. Having learned and honed his skills in the meantime, Walter Kadlubowski, Jr. [born April 20, 1927, the youngest son of Walter, Sr.] assumed production in approximately 1960, and operated the Star Concertina Company with manufacture at 2351 North Milwaukee Avenue in Chicago.

Over the subsequent years, Star experienced a variety of owners. For a period of time in 1964, Kadlubowski employed Gerraldo Carbonari as tuner, who later also became a business partner so that together this joint venture yielded over 1,000 Star concertinas for the American market. Finally in 1974 Walter Kadlubowski, Jr. sold the business to Pompillio Roscianni and his partner, Umberto Carroci, who were the new owners of the Imperial Accordion Company. In the latter part of the 20th century, Larry Dorschner of Menasha, Wisconsin worked for or supplied parts to the Star concertina manufacturing process. Parenthetically,

Star's tuner, Lucio Lorenzetti

in 1965, Larry Dorschner became a residential contractor and constructed a new home for Christy Hengel in New Ulm. During this period Ray Dorschner was the leader of the Rainbow Valley Dutchmen. Larry also made many of the wooden components—frames, reed blocks and valves for the Star Concertina Company, working from his home in Appleton, Wisconsin. During the 1970s and 1980s while living in New Ulm, Larry Dorschner was also employed by the Brown Music Store as a concertina teacher, repairman, frame and reed wood block maker for the Brown concertina.

During a restless retirement, Walter Kadlubowski, Jr. again built a few concertinas, this time around utilizing the name "Eagle" and putting into service his own style of long plates. He continued intermittently until his death on November 25, 1991 at the age of 64. The Eagle concertina exemplified what Walter Kadlubowski, Jr. believed to be a high quality long plate reed system. However, by the 1980s, young Kadlubowski was procuring his reeds from Negrini in Italy, the same steel reed source that supplied Hengel in New Ulm. Often Hengel furnished the Negrini reeds to the Star makers. Having built four Eagle models, Walter met Richard S. Raclawski at Union, Michigan in 1988 and together the twosome built a number of Eagle concertinas, a tradition continued by Raclawski at 11523 Oak Circle, Omaha, Nebraska.[38] Today Raclawski builds his Eagle concertinas and resides at 8340 South Golden Fields Drive, Oak Creek, Wisconsin 53154. Meanwhile, Pompillio Roscianni sold the Star Concertina brand in April, 1989, together with its entire business stock for $52,000.00 to John Bernhardt and Ed Cogana, who subsequently built the Star Concertina as well as managed its sales arena. Star

John Bernhardt in 2005 plays one of his Star products at the The Bohemian American Concertina Association meeting in Chicago.

concertinas continued to be manufactured until John Bernhardt himself ceased operations in September, 2000.

Star's tuner, Lucio Lorenzetti, who had worked for the Star corporation since 1973, continued doing repair work on the instrument at its former manufacturing site. His title appears as Lucio Lorenzetti, Star Concertina Master Craftsman, who died February 13, 2003 at the age of 71 (1932 - 2003). In the 1990s, advertisements for the Star concertina offer tuning and repair by Lorenzetti as well as sales of new and used concertinas. Also available are accordions and button boxes accompanied by accessories and sheet music for concertinists. Expressly highlighted were the new "Star Beauty" concertinas "custom-built to your spec's or buy from stock" retail at $3,500. Showrooms and factory were located at 5808 West 35th Street in Chicago, the southern tip of the city. Sometimes business cards show Cicero, IL 60804.[39] Sales and correspondence inquiries were directed to 60 Martin Lane, Elk Grove Village, Illinois.[40]

An instrument of high quality in all respects, the Star remains popular among concertinists in the Midwest, along with its library of concertina music, which was a secondary, but important, part of the Star business. During his tenure at Star, John Bernhardt headed the Star Concertina Manufacturing Company at 2618 West 59th Street. He built 60 long-plate model concertinas with a redesigned keyboard and sound board switch assembly. Chemnitzer concertinas were for a time created using CAD [computer aided design data] by Sig Manufacturing in Motezuma, Iowa. Jerry Minar was the first to use this methodoligy crafting the new Hengel under his new ownership of the Hengel trademark. During the same 11-year hiatus, Bernhardt also created some 60 standard wax reed Star Beauty concertinas. The last one built has serial number 3995 and remains in Bernhardt's possession. Thus the claim that the Star was produced in numbers approaching 4,000 is no doubt accurate. It is claimed that, during the period from 1940-1960, Star was putting out some three concertinas every week, distributed and sold primarily to the Chicago and Milwaukee Polish markets, but extending as well to the Polish communities in northeast Minneapolis and the Minnesota Iron Range.[41]

Here, as an interlude, we should mention an advertisement on the last page *of Polka & Old Time News* (April 1964) for the Star Concertina from the Star Concertina Mfg. Co. of Chicago. In the words of the text writer, this instrument was

> Special [sic] built with the old-time concertina tone. Engraved exterior. Metal bellow staves and corners. White or black. Moderately priced. Bank financing with small monthly payments. Trades accepted. Delivery four to six weeks. Demonstrator instrument at our office. 78 key concertinas in stock—for rent or purchase. Instructions for concertina available in many areas. Write: United Music Co. Accordion & Concertina Sales and Instructions, 946 Osgood Avenue SW., Hutchinson MN. Leonard Krulikosky, Owner.

Other advertisements indicate the production of a Star-King concertina, presumably as a take-off from the Pearl Queen, being produced for the Vitak-Elsnic Company by the Schlicht group. Others report that the Star-King was created in about 1964 to compete with the Hengel. The promotional quotation below seems to speak directly to this competitive situation. Thus we read on occasion:

> The Star-King Concertina. The Concertina with the Big Concertina Reed. Custom Built. Duro Aluminum Action. Condensed Key-Board. High and Low Switch. Bellows are protected with stainless steel staves and corners. Available in many keys. Colors black or white (as shown). Fully guaranteed. Serviced locally. The Star-King concertina is a new model which is very light in weight. Hand made by the finest concertina craftsmen in the United States. Built by the Star Concertina MFG. Co. of Chicago ILL. The oldest builders of concertinas in the

STAR "SCHUCKERT'S QUEEN" (104 key / quadruple reed / key of B-Flat). The well-known concertina player, Henry Schuckert of Chicago, was also a tuner, music composer and dealer. Much like Silberhorn, he sometimes acquired concertinas from Star or Schlicht, did the reed work and tuning, and put his own name on the instrument for sale. Chicago players were fond of the condensed keyboard and the smaller buttons of these star models.

Henry Schuckert, Sr. at his store in 1948. Below is a Schuckert concertina, essentially a version of the Star, here with rounded corners. Schuckert was an employee of Star Manufacturing, did much of the reed work there, and sometimes crafted his own shells and named the instrument after himself. He was also noted for being a good tuner.

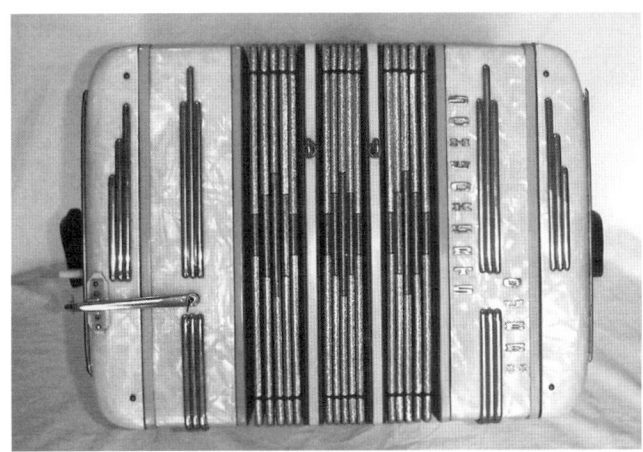

The top side of the Schuckert's Queen showing the name on the far right.

country. Some Dealerships still available. Write Star-King Distributor and Dealer. United Music Company. Leonard Krulikosky, Owner. 946 Osgood Avenue S. W. – Hutchinson, Minnesota. Trades accepted. Bank financing with small monthly payments.

Another Chicago music store owner and sheet music publicist, as mentioned above, was Henry Schuckert. Starting out as a "musician," according to the Chicago *Lakeside Business Directory* of 1917, Schuckert lived and worked at 6318 South Western Avenue, a mile west of the Ashland Avenue concentration of concertina music stores. Soon he realized he had to acquire an outlet adjacent to the Vitak-Elsnic cluster of showrooms and by 1930 he joined that market area. Located at 5451 South Ashland Avenue just a couple blocks from Vitak-Elsnic, S. S. Gralak and other concertina stores, the "Schuckert Music Store" in Chicago imported many concertinas. Henry Schuckert also bought them from the Star producers and named them after himself—the "Schuckert." At times he apparently reconditioned or added his own reeds to build specialty concertinas, one called the "Vibrato Queen." In between times, Henry Schuckert was associated as a freelance composer with the Hollywood Music Publishing Co., RCA Victor and Dot Records. He also arranged various numbers on sheet music for concertina, e. g. "Our Boys March" "composed by Henry Schuckert and played on the concertina in concert by H. Schuckert and Henry W. Schepp." In later years, Schuckert moved his store south to 8222 South Ashland.

Henry Schuckert, Sr. was born September 15, 1887 in Austria[42] and immigrated as a youth to the United States in 1899. By 1930 he is listed in the Federal Census as a naturalized citizen, married to Marie and the father of two children, Henry, Jr., born December 23, 1911 and

Above is George Karpek, the son of Russian immigrant Andrew (at right) who operated the family business for accordions and concertinas at 820 South 16th Street in Milwaukee. Born in Russia on August 20, 1892 Andrew died in Milwaukee in September, 1942.

Albert G. Nechanicky with two of his 130 key concertinas. The concertina itself was built by the Star Company.

The Andrew / George Karpek accordion and concertina manufacturing and sales establishment was located in this building at 820 South 16th Street in Milwaukee. It is now a Mexican restaurant [March 20, 2005].

Marie, born in 1914 in Illinois. According to this 1930 census, he is the "proprietor of a music store." Checking his obituary, we learn that Schuckert engaged in the business of music in Chicago from 1922 to his retirement in 1963. Soon thereafter he moved to Bremerton, Washington, where he died June 18, 1967.[43] Within a few years, his wife, Marie, followed him in death on December 6, 1971, as did his son, Henry, Jr. on November 5, 1985.

Popular as an affordable and yet high quality instrument during the 1930s was the Karpek concertina, manufactured by the Karpek Accordion Manufacturing Company of Milwaukee, Wisconsin. As noted above, the firm, which began in 1915, was operated and from 1917 onward, owned by Andrew Karpek first on Vliet Street and then continuously at 820 South 16th Street in Milwaukee. His top assistant was George Pivnoff, though much later his chief support was son George. The company's retail catalogs from the 1930s illustrate not only button and piano accordions but also concertinas, among them the Karpek, of course, but also other brands like the Pearl Queen. In their years of top production the Karpek firm also produced a few of the so-called Accortina instruments, one that uses a concertina style right-hand button system with a regular accordion bass or left-hand operation and monochromatic instrumentation [same notes on push or pull keys]. For a time during the 1970s, George Karpek built the Karrousel Concertina, called the new slim-line.[44] It was called slim because the body and bellows were narrowed down to look like an accordion and to require less bellow movement so as to give the player better hand and finger placement. Measuring eight by fifteen inches, the Karrousel sold for about $2,000. Begun by Russian immigrant Andrew Karpek, the Karpek firm continued under his son George until his death at the age of 70 in 1988, which led to a final closing by his widow on June 4, 1991.[45]

From neither Chicago nor Milwaukee was the maverick concertina player-builder, Albert G. Nechanicky.

Born February 22, 1909 at Odessa, Washington, Albert soon chose the business name of Nicky. The tenth of fifteen children, Nicky started out playing the button accordion, then switched at the age of nine to the concertina using Henry Silberhorn's instructional method. Out of high school and playing for parties and on Spokane radio stations, Nicky bought a Pearl Queen concertina in 1934, one specially built with 124 keys. Although he played little between the 1930s and the 1970s, he has championed the 130-key system for the concertina and up to the time of his death promoted the arrangement with some success. A number of these concertinas exist with the name of Nicky, although it is unclear whether all the Nicky concertinas were perhaps actually assembled at Star Manufacturing. The Nicky has an extended range 130 key core with four rows versus the usual three rows of buttons. On the bass side there was a more complete chromatic design for bass solo playing. The Nicky concertina is larger, measuring 11 by 11 inches rather than 10 by 11. However, it is more expensive to build and to buy and therefore it has met with only limited success.[46]

There is no record of expert players on the Nicky. Among the luminary players and concertina teachers at the Karpek company was Henry (Hank) Jacobs, a professional tool and die maker, who has played the concertina since 1931 and who taught at the Lincoln Music House and at Polonia Music Store. Jacobs is known across the Midwest for his adaptation of the concertina slide rule, which allows fine players to automatically adjust any concertina into a secondary key just by setting the slide

Hank Jacobs [Jakobowski] of Cudahy, Wisconsin was born in South Milwaukee in 1919. By the age of 11 he was performing on a 76-key Lange concertina when he graduated to a Bässler concertina purchased from the Gustav C. Forster music store. A tool and die maker by trade, Jacobs was associated with the Karpek store since 1936 but after returning from service bought a Star in 1947. He has played far and wide in the Milwaukee area, mostly with the Rush Shumway Band.

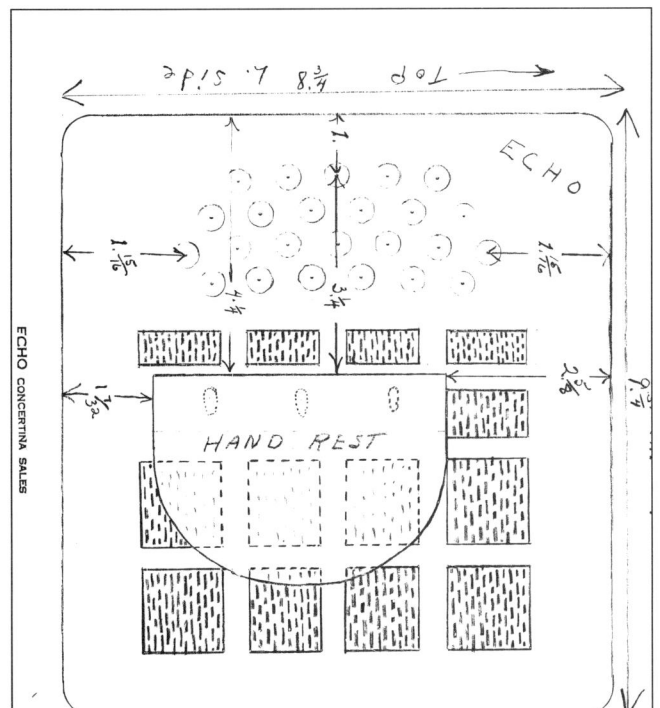
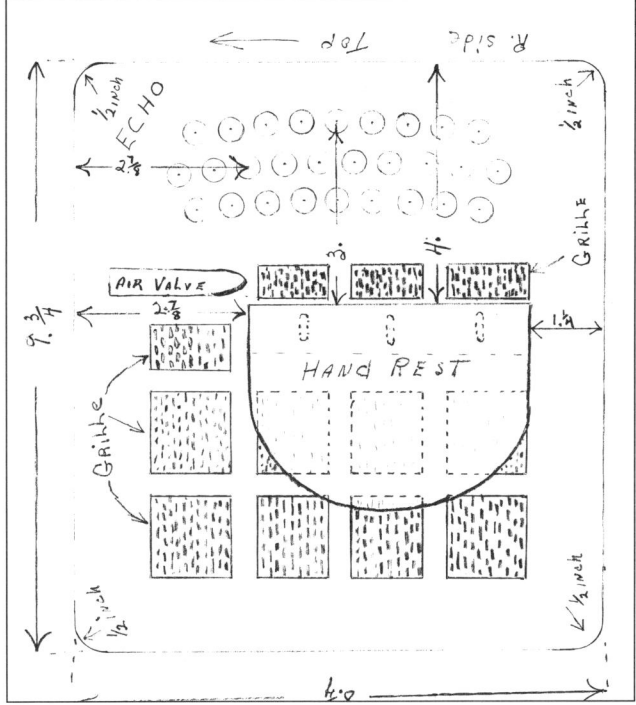

Above are the sketches Stan Uhlir made by hand for Morbidoni to build the Echo double reed concertina. Thus in the 1960s when the production of concertinas waned, Uhlir takes credit for the design but properly acknowledges the Morbidoni Accordion Company of Italy for its construction. Later Uhlir and, subsequently, Robert Novak of Lake Elmo, Minnesota, would build the quadruple reed Echo here in the United States.

rule and equating the different buttons accordingly. Other stellar players from the Karpek sphere of influence include Stanley Nowicki, Edward Teikowski, Max Gajewski, Helmut and Max Peters, Mildred (Concertina Millie) Kaminski, Frank (Pee Wee) and Ervin (Max) King [stage name for Kuczynski, originally from Green Bay], Paul Schroeder, Lester Bondowski, Patti Groshek, "Concertina" Eddie Rickert and John Bondowski.[47]

While the life of the concertina in Buffalo, New York is beyond our pale, it should be mentioned here that the instrument was introduced there by musicians from the Chicago area. Prominent among them was a South Bend, Indiana native, Mathew Pajakowski, who moved to Buffalo at the age of 17. Player, arranger, recording star, Pajakowski managed a 12-piece orchestra and played weekly on WEBR radio in Buffalo for the Rosinski Furniture Music Hour and recorded on Columbia Records. In 1941 he was killed in a car accident. Two of his students, Frank J. Stanczewski and Al Tucholski of Buffalo carried on his tradition and generated a large following of both dancers and players. In the decades after World War II, the concertina tradition in Buffalo, Pittsburgh and other eastern states varied greatly from the Chicago Midwestern pattern.[48]

More or less in parallel with the efforts to continue production of the "Star" and the "Karpek" was the fate of the Patek and the Pearl Queen. Popular during the 1920s and running through about 1945 when reeds ceased to be available, these artistic machines were in a sense duplicated by Stan Uhlir of Minneapolis when he initiated production of the Echo Concertina.

Born in Heidelberg, Minnesota, Uhlir learned the concertina at the age of eight. He played five years with Joe's Young Band, Joe Prchal having taught Uhlir a great deal about the instrument and its music. Stan Uhlir enjoyed a real mentor in the person of Edward Dobes, who played a Pearl Queen and always wanted to build concertinas like it. In 1931 Dobes played with his own Krava-Dobes Orchestra assisted by Uhlir. In the later 1940s Uhlir started rebuilding concertinas.[49] His goal was to produce a light-weight, easy-to-handle instrument. Uhlir designed a double-reed compact concertina featuring free-floating buttons and a new style of hand rest. Perhaps the most important factor for his instrument was his dual-taper reed blocks, which resound in chambers with echo low reeds that produce the concertina tonal quality with a minimum of pressure.

Designed and engineered in Minnesota, the Echo Double-reed Concertina was a closely imitated instrument crafted in Italy by Alberto Morbidoni of

Robert Novak is the successor to Stan Uhlir, concurrently the builder of the Echo concertina, playing here at the Concertina Bowl held Saturday, January 31, 2004 in Blaine, Minnesota. In his primary occupation, Novak is the owner and operator of a retail and bulk oil business.

Michael Smieja, retired St. Cloud truck driver and the inventor of the key mount roller system, is a close associate of Novak making the Echo concertina.

Kolacky Day parade October 1, 1931. On the wagon are members of the Dobes-Krava Band. L-R Frank Krava, clarinet; Edward Dobes, concertina; James Rynda, violin; Frank Wondra, trumpet; George Soulek, drums. The band was headquartered in the Montgomery, Minnesota area.

Castelfidardo (Ancona) in central Italy, the famous accordion builder. For at least a period of time, Uhlir served as the primary contact salesperson in America, running advertisements inviting players to touch base with their Echo dealer or Echo Concertina Sales, 4413 — 31st Avenue South, Minneapolis, Minnesota — Stan Uhlir, sales representative. Although he began by importing some 200 double-reed concertinas from Italy, Uhlir then designed and built the quadruple Echo concertina on his own, completing a total of about 30 in the basement of his home, with output of about two per year. But when he suffered a heart attack in 1974, Uhlir semi-retired and more or less handed over his production to Robert Novak of Lake Elmo, Minnesota. Working with Uhlir was his assistant, Elmer Pearson, who constructed a total of four "Pearson" concertinas under his own tutorship. Honored for the quality of his reed making, Pearson crafted several sets for Uhlir before his unexpected death in the early 1970s.

Uhlir also perfected a method to create high quality concertina buttons, which he installed on his Echo concertinas and, in addition, supplied them to Brown Manufacturing in New Ulm, to the Star factory under Bernhardt and to Jerry Minar when he acquired some equipment from Uhlir in 1993. Subsequently, Minar has used them for his Hengel products. For a time, Minar also made them available to Brown and to Bernhardt for his Star concertina. When Uhlir died in 1996 at the age of 82, his business passed in full to Robert Novak, who continues production on a small scale.[50]

Novak, meanwhile, is anything but a routine builder of the Echo concertina. A mainstay of the North Star Concertina Club, Novak operates out of his basement craftsman shop assisted by Michael Smieja, a St. Cloud retired truck driver, who has invented the key mount roller system upgrading the mechanism to a quality approximating sophisticated bearing gear boxes. Born April 2, 1939 to parents living at 887 East Rose Street, Novak followed his family Polish traditions by attending parochial grade school at St. Casimir Parish in St. Paul.

George Hebaus, tuner, grill craftsman and bass horn player helps build the Echo concertina and remains active with the North Star Concertina Club.

Richard Raclawski, who learned the art of concertina construction from his Chicago mentor and Star builder, Walter Kadlubowski, Jr., is playing his Eagle instrument at the Blaine, Minnesota Concertina Super Bowl on January 28, 2004.

After graduating from Cretin High School in St. Paul, he became a freight handler for the railroad. In search of himself, he then studied at the technical vocational school on Jackson Street near the Capitol to become a tool and die maker—a common early career for concertina builders.

His initial effort at age 25 was founding a small company called Moldcraft which supplied products far and wide. In 1967 he married Jeanne Goerrs, whose father was in the bulk and retail petroleum marketing business. From that date forward, it became Novak's primary source of income. Not until 1962 when he met Stan Uhlir did he become strongly interested in the concertina. Soon he was crafting certain parts for Uhlir. The latter, however, was either having his entire instrument built by Alberto Morbidoni in Italy or was adding the Echo name to instruments procured in the United States, and then again building them from scratch on his own. Simultaneously, George Hebaus, Novak's friend and assistant in tuning, was stamping out grills for Bernhardt, who was making the Star Concertina in Chicago—illustrating just how interwoven the production of this instrument really was/is. However, the stamping machine was actually made by Novak.

Born in St. Paul on April 22, 1938, George G. Hebaus graduated from Cretin High School in 1956. Four years later in 1960 he received a B. S. from the University of Minnesota and was awarded his Ph.D. in Civil Engineering from Colorado State University in 1980. Married in 1960, he is the father of five children. Although his career took him into hydraulic research engineering at the Univerity of Minnesota for the Department of Agriculture, his love and fascination was the concertina on which he did research to develop a mathematical model of the reed system that would incorporate the many variables attendant to the art of sound production. At the Red Wing Technical College, he took courses on concertina repair from Helmi Harrington of Duluth, which he completed in 1993. From 1994 onward, he tuned concertinas for Stan Uhlir, then purchased some of the equipment from Slim Maser in West St. Paul shortly before his death, and continues his work for the Echo instrument in connection with Bob Novak.

In tandem with the Echo is the Eagle concertina, a successor to the Star, now built by Richard Raclawski. A tool and die maker in Milwaukee now at home in the suburb of Oak Creek, Wisconsin, Raclawski has produced just fourteen Eagle brand concertinas to date. However, instead of the waxed reed mounts in the Star, the Eagle has hooked long plates mounted with reeds acquired from Italy. Thus it is a close "relative" of the Echo and in many ways mirrors the standard of the Chemnitzer line in the United States, the Hengel.

Among minor concertina builders in the Jerry Minar purvey was a father-son team in the Roback family. From the polish community in Minneapolis, there was Walter J. Roback (originally Chrobak, born Decembeer 23, 1907) who worked on the railroad and found himself often enjoying a layover in Chicago. There, in due time, he developed close contacts to the builders of Star con-

A younger Don Roback, top, and a more recent photo at right.

Walter Roback, father of Don.

certinas. Inventive and crafty with his hands, Walter's primary responsibility for the railroad was re-tracking derailed cars. In he concertina world, Walter not only made bellows but also created his own specialty press to shape the paper bellows, all at his home located at 3555 Two and a Half Street in Northeast Minneapolis. He also developed a close friendship with Stan Uhlir [builder of the Echo] and made about a dozen concertinas on his own. One of the Roback concertinas is owned by John Filipczak, leader of the Classics Band.

After the death of Walter in 1980, his son, Donald W. Roback, born in 1936, took over bellows construction and concertina repair. An electrical engineer by training, Donald Roback crafted perhaps a dozen concertinas from scratch, mostly doubles, until he experienced difficulty procuring reeds from Italy. Until shortly before his death on February 10, 2004, from his home in New Brighton, Minnesota, Donald Roback produced bellows for Bob Novak. Subsequently, Novak acquired the Roback press to make bellows for his Echo concertinas. Roback's widow, Katherine, dispersed much of his tool supply to Novak and Michael Smieja, and to Jerry Minar. Over the course of time a few other individuals have built a limited number of concertinas. Among them are Doug Dickover in Minnesota calling his the Tyroler, Ed Kreis in Wisconsin calling his the Kreis, plus other products called the Andrew, the Larson and others that connect in name to their makers. At the close of the twentieth century, it is rather obvious that the concertina is a thinly represented musical instrument veiled from the world at large, and nearly absent from its origins in the Ore Mountain region abutting the City of Chemnitz, Germany. True to its origins, however, is its popularity among German immigrants and their descendants in the upper Midwest, where it thrives producing the so-called Dutchman style. Just as clearly, it remains popular within the Polish heritage of Minnesota and Wisconsin. Clearly linking these two traditions are the descendants of the Czech or Bohemian settlers who thrive playing and building the concertina. In that respect, the concertina has held tenaciously to its rebirth place, Chicago. Imported concertinas were played widely among the Polish workers in the Chicago Stockyards and among those in related occupations. Names like Patek, Vitak, Elsnic bespeak loudly the Bohemian ethnic constituency. Just as interesting are prominent Polish names like Kadlubowski, Wydra, and Blazonczyk. And the Sudeten Germans from the peripheral region of today's Czech Republic, notably Christy Hengel in construction and Wilfahrt in performance, have given the instrument a Midwest life that is destined for the ages. To these individuals we turn our attention in the next chapter.

John Bernhardt, last owner of Star concertina, May 5, 2000.

Serial Numbers and Year of Construction of Pearl Queen and Patek Concertinas Crafted by Otto Schlicht and his support personnel.

There were 5,000 Pearl Queen and Patek concertinas manufactured up to 1930, an average of 250 per year.

From 1931-1946 there were 1,158 manufactured, an average of 72 per year.

Bass 3/0 key was added in 1926 or 1928.

The fret plate feature was added in 1928. Fret plates are white grills.

Serial Number 5162 was the first triple equipped with all upright reeds.

Listed below are serial numbers of Schlicht-built and of Star-built concertinas. The serial numbers, however, are rounded to the nearest full year of production.

Patek and Pearl Queen concertinas
Year Built   Serial numbers (approximate)
None before this date
Year	Serial numbers
1911	0 — 250
1912	251 — 500
1913	501 — 750
1914	751 — 1000
1915	1001 — 1250
1916	1251 — 1500
1917	1501 — 1750
1918	1751 — 2000
1919	2001 — 2250
1920	2251 — 2500
1921	2501 — 2750
1922	2751 — 3000
1923	3001 — 3250
1924	3251 — 3500
1925	3501 — 3750
1926	3751 — 4000
1927	4001 — 4250
1928	4251 — 4500
1929	4501 — 4750
1930	4751 — 5000 [Pearl Queen 4909 was completed November 14, 1929 and tuned by J. Vicevich]
1931	5001 — 5200 [Pearl Queen 5122 was completed May 1, 1930 and tuned by J. Vicevich]
1932	5201 — 5423 [Don Klossner owns Pearl Queen #5294]
1933	5424 — 5450 [Jerry Schuft #5424]
1934	5451 — 5500
1935	5501 — 5635
1936	5636 — 5710
1937	5711 — 5854 [Elmer Scheid #5849]
1938	5855 — 5899 [Rodney Ristow owned Pearl Queen Quad #5890]
1939	5900 — 6051 [Jerry Bierschbach owns #5909] [John Wilfahrt owned #6048]
1940	6052 — 6060
1941	6061 — 6100
1942	6101 — 6120
1943	6121 — 6144
1944	6145 — 6149
1945	6150 — 6151
1946	6152 — 6158

The last one built, #6158 is owned by Jerry Minar.

Star Concertinas

The Star concertina was built by the International Accordion Company and its successors in Chicago, such as Star Concertina Manufacturing, which issued instruments with serial numbers continuing from 1926 until 2000. While it has not been possible to link serial numbers to exact years, the following have been discovered inside Star concertinas providing references from which it may be possible to extrapolate years of construction for others within the same ranges.

0000 — 0299 [264, Star International 1930]
[281 Star Beauty 1931]
0300 - 0599
0600 - 0799
0800 - 0999
1000 - 1199 [1149 — 1949 *1949 — The first "Streamline" (waxed reed) model was produced in 1949. Through the years it was extremely popular. The last Streamline was produced approximately in 1979. From then on only the Star "Beauty" was built until the introduction of the "Oldtimer" model in 1994.

1200 - 1399 [1258 — 1950] "Schuckert's Queen" is 1259
1400 - 1499 [1413 — Feb. 13, 1952], [1445 — June 7, 1952]
1500 - 1599 [1502 — 1953], [1523 — Oct. 1953]
1600 - 1799
1800 - 1999
2000 — 2199
2200 — 2399 [2362 Star Special 1968]

2400 — 2599 [2525 Star Double 1969]
2600 — 2799 [2713 Star Quad 1972]
2800 — 2999 [2994 Star Beauty 1981]
3000 — 3199 [3145 Star   1983]
3200 - 3399
3400 - 3599
3600 - 3799
3800 — 3999 [3995 Star ("Oldtimer" model) is the last, and was built by John Bernhardt]

The first Oldtimer model was produced in January, 1994. A definition of the "Oldtimer" might include the structural variation that the reeds are riveted on the long plate. They were hooked in as compared to the waxed-in reed style. When the first Star concertinas were built, the builders used long-plate reed mounts. In the late 1940s Star reverted to the Italian accordion method of mounting reeds with wax. The true Chemnitzer concertina always had long-plates until the mid 1940s. Since the reeds became unavailable from Germany due to the 1945 fall of Chemnitzer to the Russian zone of occupation, Star producers reverted to the wax-mounting method. During the Bernhardt years in the 1990s, there were about 30 concertinas built with waxed reeds and 30 with long plates. The Schlicht-built concertinas for Rudy Patek (Patek) and Vitak-Elsnic (Pearl Queen), as well as the Hengel concertinas, are all equipped with long-plate reeds.

Footnotes

1 In chronological order:
   1857 *Instructions for the German concertina* (New York: W. A. Pond)
   1860 *Howe's new school for the German concertina* (Boston: Elias Howe)
   1869 *Guide for the German concertina* (Winner, Septimus. Boston: Ditson & Co.)
   1869 *Winner's new primer for the German concertina* (Winner, Septimus. New York: W.A. Pond & Co.)
   1879 *Eclectic school for the concertina* (Boston: E. Howe, Chicago: Howe & Grant)
2 Frank Abbot et al., eds., *Musical Instruments at the World's Columbian Exposition* (Chicago: Presto Co., 1895), p. 246. Also cf. Pat Watters, "A Brief History of the Concertina's Development," reprinted in his newsletter from *The Music Trades* (October 1955). Marketing the Arno Arnold Concertina as well as other brands including pre-war used bandonions, Watters operated from his Distributing Company at 2219 East 42nd Street in Minneapolis, Minnesota.
3 Death announcement in the *Chemnitzer Anzeiger* (February 29, 1892), by Henriette, the widow of Lange and his heirs.
4 *Musical Instruments at the World's Columbian Exposition*, p. 163.

5 *Musical Instruments*, p. 246.
6 *Chemnitzer Tageblatt*, Tuesday (January 3, 1933).
7 Information about Louis Vitak from interviews conducted by Victor Greene for his book, *A Passion for Polka* (Berkeley: University of California Press, 1992), p. 54 is clearly in error. Vitak did not reside in Akron and there is no evidence he was ever in Cincinnati.
8 According to the *Chicago Tribune* Death Notices (April 19, 1933), Louis Vitak died April 17, 1933 at his home at 4445 Greenwood Avenue. He was the father of Olga Burge, Albertina Kaelin, Marie Doerr, and Dr. Louis A. Vitak, and the brother of Mary Elsnic. Funeral services were held from the chapel at 4227 Cottage Grove Avenue with interment in the National Bohemian Cemetery. He was a member of the Praha Lodge No. 231, I. O. O. F. Son Louis A. Vitak would die in 1944.
9 *Chicago City Directory*, 1923.
10 County of Cook, City of Chicago, State of Illinois, #6033069.
11 A good beginning reference is by Glen E. Holt and Dominic A. Pacyga, *Chicago: A Historical Guide to the Neighborhoods. The Loop and South Side* (Chicago: Chicago Historical Society, 1979), pp. 121 ff.
12 Holt and Pacyga, p. 122. See also the various web pages for the churches mentioned here, the Stockyards and other items.
13 See the b/w photographs in Holt & Pacyga, p. 130.
14 Among others, Greene, *Passion for Polka*, p. 55 and footnoted in his interview with Dorothy Kommer.
15 Website of Steve Litwin and Mark Kohan of the *Polish American Journal*, http://eee.polsmjoutnsl.vom/ polka/chemnitz.html.
16 *Chicago City Directory*, 1923.
17 Patek Catalog of 1932 in possession of Jerry Minar, New Prague.
18 Obituary in Weyauwega *Chronicle*, April 1, 1982.
19 Edward A. Laszczak [Eddie Lash] died June 27, 2002, preceded in death by his brother Walter, and survived by his nephew, Wayne Laszczak. He was buried from the Kolbus Funeral Home at 6857 West Higgins Road on June 29, 2002 with mass at All Saints Parish, 9201 West Higgins Road in Chicago.
20 Jerry Minar of New Prague owns these two concertinas.
21 The advertisement appears in the early Patek catalogs and was also incorporated into an early advertisement for the Christy Hengel instrument when Hengel lived at 523 East Elm Avenue in Waseca, Minnesota, and later from his home/shop at 403 North Minnesota Street in New Ulm.
22 The text of the application is reproduced, in part. Schlicht requests protection for his invention to improve the action of an "instrument of the concertina type, it being an object of the invention to provide a new and improved action for such an instrument which is simple in construction and fast in operation. Another object is to provide such an action in which the valve actuating bars are pivotally mounted by means which serve as noise insulators between the parts. A further object is to provide an improved action in which the actuating bars are effectively mounted in proper alignment and in which two sets of levers, mounted on adjacent pivot rods, positioned equidistantly from the key-board, are supported so as to permit the use of levers of simple form with straight key-operated arms which may be manufactured and assembled at a low cost. Another object is to provide an action in which a fibre or other non-metallic member is provided intermediate to the bars and their pivot bushing so as to prevent any metallic ring being transmitted therethrough and for the purpose of displacing the bar away from the bushing to provide clearance for a set of long bars having substantially straight key-operated arms."

23 Jerry Minar has Patek sales slips from 1940 on which Patek has taken his regular letterhead and rubber stamped the new address over the former one on Milwaukee Avenue.

24 Correspondence and telephone interviews with Walter Stark, 1405 Dove Drive, Garland, Texas, who worked in the Patek store from 1925 - 1940. Walter's father was a cousin to Luella Patek, Rudy's first wife.

25 A poster for a Saturday evening May 23, 1931 meeting of the club shows about a dozen concertina players, some trumpets and saxophones, drums and bass horn. It also shows a large banner listing Patek's Concertina Club, and identification for members Elmer Wandersee, Eddie Fitzpatrick, Wally Stark, Oscar Geron, Joe Stacy, Ray Schulz, Johnny Roberts and Rudy Patek, among others.

26 Ira A. Glazier and William P. Filby, *Germans to America* (Wilmington, DE: Scholarly Sources), Vol. 64 "January to July" lists Schlicht on p. 263.

27 A set of sheet music numbers are credited to Wally Stark as "arranger" of the various pieces for the concertina, e. g. the Broadway musical "Mame."

28 As noted, Schlicht held a patent for his duro action mechanism in the concertina, the number for which is 1,890,830. It is unclear whether his individual line of concertinas was patented but it does not appear likely. However, as a manufacturer of a sequenced line bearing the two names of Pearl Queen and Patek, an overall patent might have been considered.

29 Cook County, Illinois Death Records — Certificate of Death 8811.

30 This would take Schlicht back to his 1903 days as a repairman for Otto Georgi.

31 See among other sources Ron Grossman, *Guide to Chicago Neighborhoods* (Piscataway, New Jersey: New Century, 1981).

32 Otto Schlicht, Otto Georgi and Otto Glass.

33 The letter is addressed to Jerry Minar of JBM Sound, Inc. of New Prague dated December 15, 2000.

34 A letter from Henry Silberhorn to Roy F. Pleiness in New Orleans can be viewed at http://www.concertinamusic.com/sbox/links.html

35 Ira A. Glazier and William P. Filby, *Germans to America*, Vol. 53, May, 1886-January, 1887 (Wilmington, Delaware: Scholarly Resources), p. 166.

36 Conversations with Frank Berendt of Morton Grove, Illinois and Robert Novak of Lake Elmo, Minnesota.

37 Here it should be noted that the name Royal was also used by Slim Maser and is not to be confused with the earlier "Royal" concertina, which was a Schlicht wholesale product retailed by Kesting Music Store in St. Paul, Minnesota, under the Royal name.

38 http://www.rcrescent.com/eagle_concertina.htm

39 Sample business cards can be viewed at http:// www.concertinamusic.com/sbox/links.html

40 *Entertainment Bits* (October-November, 1990), p. 17, *ibid.* (October-November, 1991), p. 17.

41 Email and telephone conversations with John Bernhardt, builder of Star, in Chicago.

42 Although unconfirmed, he could possibly have been born in Moravian Austria across the border and inland from the Chemnitz region of Germany. The Schuckert name also appears in Welfersdorf in Upper Austria and in Roppertsdorf in Styria.

43 *Bremerton Sun*, Monday, June 19, 1967, p. 14.

44 Featured in advertisements *Music and Dance News*, about 1980. Date missing from scrap newspaper in possession of the author. Jerry Minar owns a Karpek Karrousel quad made of beautiful dark wood, possibly crafted by a German button box manufacturing company. However, its shape is the standard size for a normal quad concertina.

45 *Polka News*, May 8, 1991. See also the interview "Karpek's Fancy: An accordion Revival," *Business Journal* (September, 1988). Jerry Minar owns a Karpek Karrousel quad made of beautiful dark wood, possibly crafted by a German button box manufacturer. However, its shape is the standard size for a normal quad concertina.

46 Steve Litwin, Polish American website.

47 *South Side Spirit* (Milwaukee), November 6-12, 1988.

48 http://www.polamjournal.com/polka/chemnitz.html

49 Stan Uhlir is featured with photographs at different stages of his life in *Entertainment Bits* (February-March, 1980), p. 8. For a supplementary column, see EB (October-November, 1986), p. 7.

50 Interviews with Robert Novak. See also website of Daniel Melander, www.tc.umn.edu/melan005/Concertina/

3

The Concertina in Minnesota. The Hengel Story

John Anthony Wilfahrt, Jr.:
Master, Mentor, Celebrity, Legend

Clearly the one person responsible for the early prominence of the concertina in southern Minnesota was the presence of its early player, showman, radio and later television performer, John A. Wilfahrt, of Sigel Township south of New Ulm, Minnesota. One of eleven children, John Anthony Wilfahrt, Jr., known throughout his career as Whoopee John, was born on May 11, 1893 on a farm at the southwestern edge of Clear Lake in Section 14. Both his paternal and maternal grandparents stem from the western edge of Bohemia [the Czech Republic of today], then a crown colony of the Austrian empire. On his paternal side, the home village was probably Schwarzach, while the mother's side [Portner and Hoffmann] derive from Rindl along the Ronsperg to Schwarzach road in the Bohemian Forest. John Wilfahrt, Sr. was both a farmer and carpenter by trade though he also served on the Sigel Cooperative Creamery board and on the township school board. Wife Barbara [Portner] was the musically inclined parent who, with her husband, moved into New Ulm in later years until her death in 1937, while John, Sr. lived until 1953.[1]

Meanwhile in 1914, John Anthony Wilfahrt, Jr. married Bertha Gertrude Hillesheim [his neighbor from Sigel Township] and farmed. Soon he was conducting a dance band by night, by day a tire shop in New Ulm, and in between ran a music store. As the band business gained prestige, Whoopee John phased out of the tire business, which was subsumed by his brothers, Charles and Ernst, at the same time as the music shop came into the ownership of Brown's Music Store. In 1952 in a radio interview at Menomonie, Wisconsin, Whoopee John tells of his humble beginnings playing the accordion. At about the age of eleven he received a simple accordion from his mother, the one whom he credited with singing and humming all the Old World tunes to the youth. "We did not have a radio or phonograph and I was too young to go to dances. The only music I could pick up was folk songs that my mother [Barbara Portner] used to sing around the house. So I made up original music and played it on the accordion until my father, tired of all that noise, told me to practice somewhere else. I tried the kitchen pantry for a while but that didn't work, so I ended up practicing my button box accordion in the barn." As early as 1908 at the age of 15, John was playing for house dances of his German-Bohemian neighbors, which convinced his father that the boy deserved a better instrument. In 1911, he bought a 76-key concertina from a neighbor, then in 1912 the senior Wilfahrt shelled out $150 for a 104-key concertina.

Demonstrating the close-knit origins of Minnesota ethnic German music, the Wilfahrt band started opera-

Barbara Portner with John Wilfahrt, Sr. (and a daughter), the parents (and a sister) of Whoopee John. Note that despite John's sometimes down playing of his father's appreciation for music, the elder Wilfahrt obviously also played the concertina, a Lange, as shown above.

The Whoopee John Band in 1924. They had played for a golden wedding anniversary and stayed overnight. The next morning they posed with the "golden groom" on his farm in South Dakota.
L-R: Whoopee's cousin Emil Domeier, brother Eddie Wilfahrt, John with his concertina, and cousin Otto Stueber. The "golden groom" on right is unknown.

tions in earnest in 1912 using close relatives. John's brother, Eddie, accompanied Whoopee on the clarinet and his first cousin on a neighboring farm, Edward Kretsch, picked up the trumpet to add a ring of clarity. Joined soon by Otto Stueber, another cousin through the Portner line, the band initially called itself the "Böhmische Dorfmusikanten," Bohemian Village Musicians. What is of special significance here is the geographic proximity between the villages of the Bohemian Forest and the Erzgebirge region with its city of Chemnitz, just across the border and the low ridge of hills to the west. Always German-speaking, this region of Bohemia had been settled after the Thirty Years War by German farmers from the kingdom of Saxony, of which the Chemnitz district is a part. Though situated more directly in line with Franconian Bavaria to the west, this region west of Pilsen clearly connected northward through internationally known spas like Karlsbad and the city of Eger to the German towns of Plauen, Zwickau and Chemnitz. From 1945 to 1990, this area was cut off from the West by its membership in East Germany, the Deutsche Demokratische Republik. In pre-1945 years, this was the primary source for concertina parts.[2]

Although played by many others on the old time music circuit in the Chicago area early in the 20th century, the concertina gained prominence in southern Minnesota, especially from Whoopee John Wilfahrt. By another coincidence, he was long the "folk hero" of Christy Hengel, today's best known builder of the concertina, both men of New Ulm, Minnesota.[3] Likewise coincidental is the fact that when Whoopee John moved into town from the Sigel township farm, he lived at 419 North Minnesota Street, just steps away on the same side of the street from the site of Christy Hengel's house and workshop at 403 North Minnesota. Inspired by Wilfahrt to learn to play the concertina, Hengel later made it his obligation to acquire all the concertinas ever owned by the Wilfahrt master. Wilfahrt's first was a 1906 Majestic, made in Germany by Lange, a small single-reed player, which became available at an auction in St. Peter. Next came John's triple Pearl Queen, which the senior Wilfahrt had bought for his son at the price of $150, as mentioned above. We recall from the previous chapter that the Pearl Queen was built with component parts shipped from the Chemnitz area in Germany and assembled by the Otto Schlicht factory in Chicago. Hengel knows about, but failed to acquire, Wilfahrt's 1918 Pearl Queen triple, also made by Otto Schlicht. But Hengel did succeed in getting the 1929 Pearl Queen model, used by Wilfahrt to make some of his first recordings, among them the "Tinker Polka." This one Hengel acquired from Douglas Dickover who had bought it at an auction previously for $10. At this time during the late 1920s, Wilfahrt himself had become a concertina dealer.

On the one hand, his dance band now advertised with posters boldly promoting "Wilfahrt's Concertina Club Orchestra," being a play on the fact that his chief radio appearances at the time were on WCCO, the clear

Through his early New Ulm period (prior to 1930), John Wilfahrt operated his dance business from his home. Here is the return address from his business envelopes. It covered the entire left side of the envelope and was in use before zip codes and street addresses were needed.

Whoopee John with breast logo WCCO (Wilfahrt's Concertina Club Orchestra), which may have been a disguise for his clever promotion of the orchestra as a Minneapolis radio station WCCO broadcasting orchestra. In reality, the title of the band fit both designations.

channel primary broadcasting point from the Twin Cities of Minneapolis and St. Paul. Even as late as the 1950s when Wilfahrt was appearing every Saturday night at the American House on Rice Street in St. Paul, WCCO carried a half hour on radio from the hall, after radio announcer Clelland Card habitually touted the old master as "the King of the concertina."

On the other hand, however, it demonstrated clearly that Whoopee John Wilfahrt banked his success on a concertina emphasis.[4] In the many photographs of the Whoopee John band, he is always holding a concertina even though, at his feet, at times, is a piano accordion standing on the floor. Judging also from photographs, it is apparent that John's father likewise played the accordion which he passed down to his son. During this time frame Wilfahrt and his concertina orchestra also made their first recordings for the Okeh German series of the 1920s. He later moved to the Vocalion label as "Whoopee John."[5] According to a 1925 advertisement for the sale of used instruments from his music shop at 517 Second Street North in New Ulm, John A. Wilfahrt offered for resale at that time the following brands of concertinas: Majestic, F. Lange (several), Pearl Queen (several), Pearl Queen Beauty [the "Beauty" referred to the diamond-patterned mother of pearl inlay], Diamond Queen, and a Bandonion "having 104 keys with shifting levers on both sides to change from triple to quadruple, German make." With 104 keys, this would have been comparable to any current-day concertina except for button arrangement. However, each of the concertinas he listed is noted as having 102 keys with full triple reeds, except for the Majestic, which has only 78 keys but double octave; the Majestic and Lange instruments are all advertised as "German make."

Wilfahrt in 1934 bought a Pearl Queen quadruple on which was emblazoned an attached plate bearing the name "Whoopee John." After Whoopee's death, this instrument was later sold by his son, Patrick, to Paul Zelenka in St. Paul. Zelenka in turn sold Christy Hengel the "Whoopee John" nameplate for two dollars. By 1936,

The History of the Chemnitzer Concertina

Whoopee John with his Pearl Queen concertina promoting himself and his Decca Records.

Whoopee John had "graduated" to a white Pearl Queen low Triple and, in 1939, to a Pearl Queen Quadruple, now owned by Christy Hengel and in a state of museum quality preservation. Pearl Queen, let us recall, is the concertina which resulted from Otto Schlict in Chicago with Vitak-Elsnic marketing the concertinas. For example, Whoopee John started learning on a button accordion but in 1906 acquired his first concertina, a "Majestic" built by the Lange factory in Germany. Together with his repairman, Otto Schlicht, Georgi paired successively first with Louis Vitak, then with Joseph P. Elsnic and his brother Emil Elsnic to publish music and to market the Pearl Queen as built by and, in part, as imported by Otto Schlicht. The same Schlicht also supplied Rudy Patek at the Patek Music Store, which sold essentially the same concertina in that establishment under the name of "Patek." Thus for all intents and purposes, Pearl Queen and Patek are the same instruments.

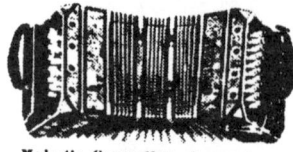

In 1925 Whoopee John Wilfahrt owned his music store at 517 Second Street North in New Ulm and offered instruments "for sale at bargain prices." Note that he was offering concertinas at a "reasonable" price.

Master Craftsman Christy Hengel

Without the person of Christy Hengel, there would be no Minnesota concertina. Born on Christmas Day, December 25, 1922 [and hence the name], Christian D. Hengel first saw daylight on the farm about 17 miles south of Redwood Falls west of Highway 71, northwest of Springfield, in Willow Lake township, near the village of Wanda, Minnesota. The eldest of six children, (Agnes, 1924— married to Michael Grausam, who died in 2000), Isabelle (1926—living in California), Jerome (1930— Korean war veteran killed in 1961 when a truck struck him on a hayrack), Raymond (1932— boiler room foreman for Del Monte in Sleepy Eye) and Mary Ann (1938— married to Sylvester Kotten who operates a large dairy business west of Sleepy Eye). Paternal ancestors include great-grandfather Peter (and Catherine) Hengel from the Bischofteinitz region of German-speaking Bohemia, who arrived first in Dubuque where they married, and then proceeded to begin farming near the Essig Township Hall [formerly a schoolhouse] in Milford township in 1858. Although this farm passed to Anton Hengel [and in 1927 to Otto Wiltscheck], it was George Hengel, Christy's father, who, when he returned from World War I, left New Ulm for the farm near Wanda.

Christy's maternal side stems from Christian Schroeder who arrived from Germany with Michael Brandt and farmed in the Wanda area. Married to Mary Ross in Springfield in 1889, they had a daughter, Anna Schroeder, who was born in April, 1903 and became the reason why the Hengels farmed for several years near Wanda. Anna Schroeder married George Hengel on October 4, 1921 at Wanda. As is typical for the transmission of folklore, and especially folk music, Christy Hengel learned much from his mother.[6] Taking music lessons at Lamberton, Anna Schroeder learned to read notes and eventually played the old pump organ with its bellows and reeds in the farmhouse. Within the family she also played, often when her parents, especially her mother, sang German folk songs, thus offering the opportunity for Christy to develop an ear for the tunes—because he never learned to read notes. As has been noted in the previous chapter, music can be as instinctive to the brain as language. As Mark Tramo, a neurologist at Harvard University reports, "Much of the information that is transmitted during speech is transmitted by pitch and timing," two crucial elements of music. Brain-imaging studies indicate that the right brain is

The parents of Christy Hengel, George and Anna (Schroeder) holding the year-old Christy at their home in rural Wanda.

On the right, Christy with sisters Agnes and Isabelle in 1929.

Christy in 1936 with sister Isabelle and brothers Jerome and Ray Hengel.

Christy Hengel mounted a gasoline motor on his balloon-tired bicycle.

sensitive to pitch in music or speech while the left brain is sensitive to split-second differences in timing.7 Thus at a very early age, already in his pre-memory stages, Hengel's ear developed for his future precocious work as a musician and craftsman for the concertina.

In Christy's own words, his first ear-driven contact with the concertina occurred in 1934 (then 12 years old) while staying with his Schroeder grandparents. One evening cousin Lawrence Turbes and Christy went into town as young teenagers to spy out the ballroom in Springfield. Playing for the dance that evening was Whoopee John, wearing a Tyrolean hat, playing his 1929 Pearl Queen triple concertina (now owned by Hengel himself). Afraid he would get a spanking, Lawrence beat it for home at 9 P.M., but Christy, too fascinated to "obey" his grandmother's demand, stayed on until 11 P.M. There he was, the concertina master player of the Midwest, the star of WCCO radio and popular bandmaster all over Minnesota, skillfully but instinctively by ear, rendering all the popular tunes Christy had heard from his mother on the organ. "When he'd finish a piece he'd throw the concertina up into the air and then catch it on the way down."8 Actually, grandmother Schroeder was a second cousin to Whoopee John's wife, Bertha, but nevertheless, Christy caught a severe scolding. Typical for his age and circumstance, he claimed he had been playing all along in the alley with Lawrence.

Boarding now for the school year 1934-35 at his Schroeder grandparents in Springfield, Christy was to prepare for his solemn communion, which he did, but also discovered in the house a button accordion, single

1941. L-R The Hengel siblings with friends: Raymond, Jerome Primesberger, Christy on motorbike at the age of 19, Arnold Sawaty, Jerome, Mary Ann (Kotten).

row, double reed with two pull stops. Since nobody in the house knew how to play it, the Schroeders gladly let Christy toy with it and when he learned some early German tunes like "Du, Du liegst mir im Herzen," they were so gratified they gave him the instrument. When the elder Schroeder occasionally went two doors down to play cards with the Paschger old maids, he sometimes invited Christy along to play a few German tunes on the button accordion. So appreciative were the women, they each gave him 50 cents every time he played—banker's wages to the youthful Christy—at the site where today an actual bank has replaced the women's former domicile. Inspired and confident, Christy raised his entrepreneurial sights to a new instrument for which he trapped weasels and skunks. At the age of 14 in 1936 he acquired his first real Hohner button accordion, ordered from the Montgomery Ward Catalog for $14.95, plus shipping.

On January 7, 1938 a fateful injury put Hengel into a long period of recovery. Having poured water on the sled run in the yard to make the downhill skid speedy, his traction failed one time when it came time to duck the oak post near the bottom—he tipped, his leg hit the post and shattered. Fifteen and still in the eighth grade, Hengel never returned to school after his recovery. Because his birthday fell on Christmas in December, he was naturally older than his classmates. Compounded by blood poisoning from a toe injury inflicted when picking up angle worms as a young boy while his father was plowing, Christy left school at the age of 15 without having finished the 8th grade. Christy's formal education had come to an end. Bored and confined nearly four months with a plaster cast, the inquisitive Christy found amusement playing the button accordion, which he had bought in 1936. Fascinated by the sound and the chance to compound it, he rigged a harmonica on a rack around his neck so that he played both instruments at once. Later when his uncle left for South Dakota, his brother-in-law gave him his trumpet, which Christy learned also. Holding the trumpet on his left elbow he could render the melody on it keeping also his left hand for the bass and right hand for the melody on the accordion—two hands and his mouth. Christy never learned to read music, he did it all by ear, —always by ear, "I can tell you the note count but I can't read a note. . . just fouls me all up. I have to hear the tune with them to make any sense out of the notes." Due to his break and subsequent flat foot, he was rejected for military service during World War II.

Recovered and back on the farm near Wanda, Christy Hengel played tunes in the evening, but during the day he grew fascinated by the then intricate mechanisms of the gasoline engine, used principally for small farm jobs like pumping water, running the milking machine, sometimes for the home washing machine, then again to elevate grain, occasionally to saw wood and related farmstead chores. In addition to tinkering and repairing the gasoline engines, Christy one day carved his name "Christ D. Hengel" in the large board that closed the gable end access for the hay fork to lift hay into the barn. For some reason, the tools felt fine to his hands and the wood responded to his artistry. Before that barn fell victim to a fire, Christy rescued the board from its moorings and retains it to this day in his basement. As was typical for farm youth in German immigrant families, Christy worked for his father until he was 22, after which rite of passage he was permitted to keep his own earned money.9 Without his own transportation except for his bicycle, the young 17-year-old Hengel improvised by mounting a gasoline engine on his bicycle, calling it his "Harley-Davidson," a project that took him about two years to complete. From the age of 19 until he was 31, Hengel logged more than 5,000 miles on that improvised motor bike. His interest in manual skill on the increase, the 22-year-old Christy bought himself a 1935 Ford.

Not to leap too suddenly from gasoline engines and '35 Fords, Hengel gradually weaned himself from the button accordion and switched to the concertina. That occurred when his uncle, Michael Macht, the husband of his father's sister, played the concertina for family gatherings. When the family got together and the "official" music had stopped, Christy drifted back into the bedroom, picked up the double reed, 76-key Lange (104

Mike Turbes at Hengel's home playing a Pearl Queen Diamond De Luxe, September 24, 1971. Turbes died in 1972. On the floor at the left is a Patek De Luxe.

on the full key models) and eked out a few tunes. Then Uncle Mike offered to sell it to Christy for $25, but he had no money and his father George would not kick in a penny, so the offer expired. Meanwhile his cousin Michael Turbes was playing the concertina not far from the Hengel farm so that Christy could jump on the motor bicycle and head over to listen. Then in August, 1939 at the age of 16-1/2 with $15 financial assistance from his grandmother Schroeder, Christy got his own first concertina from Mike Turbes for $55—paying the balance by installments as he successfully trapped more weasels and skunks. Christy's 17 year-old contemporary, Elmer Scheid, had already acquired his own new Patek concertina purchased for him by his father at a cost of $425 and was known to play it on Willmar radio station KWLM 35 miles to the north.

Under pressure now to compete with Scheid, Christy bought his second concertina—on the Feast of the Immaculate Conception, 1941—a Catholic holiday, the day after Pearl Harbor—when he drove the motor bike to put $70 down on the 1918 Pearl Queen Triple in the Key of C. It was not an expensive new Patek but rather a well-used instrument, the very same Pearl Queen that had been owned by Whoopee John. So addicted was Christy now that he would sneak away from farm work to catch the 4 P. M. radio broadcast from Willmar. More than once he confesses to defying his mother when behind the thick grove he would tie up the team of horses hitched for cultivating corn, and trail up to the back bedroom window where his sister had positioned the radio so he could clandestinely hear the half-hour show without his mother knowing. Until he told her decades later, his mother never found out what he and his sister had conspired in doing.

Before settling into concertina repair, Hengel exercised his gasoline engine and motor bike talents by rebuilding some parts of the 1918 Pearl Queen. Then one day Alvin Runck, from a farm west of Springfield, heard about Hengel's craftsmanship and asked for service on some keys of a concertina owned today by Ambrose Kodet. Thereafter in 1943 came Orville Wog of Sanborn a bit to the south of the Hengel farm with a double reed Patek which Christy repaired. After tinkering and tuning for others during the next months, in 1944 Christy began to remodel his 1918 Pearl Queen Triple. First he added a fourth set of reeds and an octave switch. Judging that to be a fairly simple procedure, Christy got the notion he could make his own concertina. First he dismantled the entire keyboard of the Whoopee John 1918 triple. Next he had to make longer valve covers for extended holes to take it from a triple to a quad. That concertina had two medium sets of reeds upright (perpendicular) and a set of piccolo reeds lying flat on the keyboard. By removing the piccolo reeds he made room for three additional upright reed blocks, which made it possible for him to add a set of medium and low reed plates. The reeds he purchased from Henry Schuckert in Chicago. Four years later in 1948, Hengel did the same reconfiguration to another concertina. This time he reworked a 1929 Pearl Queen Triple C by stripping down everything in order to add four reeds to make it a quadruple. This time to get the needed extra reeds, he bought a 1930 E-flat Patek from William Helget which came with an extra set of medium reed plates. In this instance, Hengel cut down the medium reed plates to pitch them higher, blocked the holes with metal plates, and added the E flat reed plates again from Henry Schuckert in Chicago.

Tuning concertinas was another skill Hengel had to learn. Using first a reference guide to set medium reeds at A:440 pitch, he later acquired a tuning machine he got from Mrs. August Schnittker, the daughter of John Friedl,

John Kummer holding a chromatic button box in his basement workshop.

The Concertina in Minnesota. The Hengel Story

Hengel plays a Bässler concertina, made in Germany. This was his first concertina, purchased in August 1939. Taken in 1940 at the George Hengel house near Wanda.

Hengel plays a Pearl Queen owned by Mike Turbes who sold it to Wenzel Fischer.

In May 1951 Hengel started playing with the Six Fat Dutchmen on a 1937 Patek, which he had purchased from Alfred Menge.

The Patek Deluxe with 1937 Friedl reeds, taken in May 1951.

→ 85

a fine reed maker, along with John Kummer, for Otto Schlicht in Chicago. Then came Christy's breakthrough when in 1953 he tuned a 1945 model Pearl Queen for Melvin Krzmarzick. At the time, some concertinas were coming from the factory tuned at A:435 pitch, as was the case with the 1937 Patek owned by Elmer Scheid. When members of the Scheid band started complaining that Scheid's concertina was too low, he had trouble agreeing with them. He had used the 1945 Peal Queen to make the first recording with the Babe Wagner Band and was confident of its tuning. Finally in 1953, Scheid did ask Hengel to tune his Patek which Hengel delivered to him to try at the Gibbon Ballroom where, however, Scheid complained that it was too sharp. In the course of the evening, he kept checking it with Roman Kahle playing his trumpet, a truly fine trumpet virtuoso who needed little time to convince Scheid that it was now on a perfect 440 pitch. Likewise, Patrick Zwack with a recently serviced clarinet also confirmed that the concertina was right on A:440 with his tuning fork. A few weeks later at George's Ballroom in New Ulm, Scheid's wife reassured Hengel that "the concertina was just fine." Following another tuning in 1965, that particular concertina has held its pitch under heavy use right up to the present moment.

Almost simultaneously, Hengel began actually building and rebuilding concertinas. Tinkering with them already in 1943, he acquired Whoopee John's 1918 Triple Pearl Queen, which he actually tore apart and rebuilt by adding the blocks and reed plates. He reconstructed the 1929 Pearl Queen Triple that had belonged to Melvin Krzmarzick from a C to a quadruple E Flat, but that was back in the 1940s when Hengel was still on the farm. In the early 1950s, the concertina player, Emil Milbrett, had been drafted for the Korean War and Arnold Stimpert at the Orchid Ballroom in Sleepy Eye told Harold Loeffelmacher that Christy could fill his shoes. Thus Hengel more or less dissolved his own "Christy's Band" which he had started in 1947, and on January 14, 1951 began two years of continuous playing for the Six Fat Dutchmen. Prior to joining this widely renowned band, Hengel had a pickup group playing for house parties and local gatherings. For example, he played for the wedding dance of Earl Fridley and Helen Cook on June 5, 1947 at the Avalon Palace in Sanborn [now the Rope and Spur], earning $7.00 for the evening. For this ad hoc team, Hengel recruited musicians like Bill Nissel on clarinet, his son Harold Nissel on bass, and Swede Hammerschmidt on saxophone. The Nissel brothers were German immigrants, Harold the father of current-day concertinist, Marv Nissel. Known during these youthful years as Christ Hengel [from Christian because he was born on Christmas Day], he named his playing team "Christy's Band" which, after their dissolution, became the routine name for Hengel himself. The suggestion for this alteration came from the owner of Dugie's Bar in Clemments, Minnesota, a man who painted signs for Hengel and suggested that Christ change his public name to Christy.

When Hengel ceased playing regularly with the Six

John Friedl and wife Maria in 1903.

John Friedl was working for Otto Schlicht when issued a Social Security card.

Fat Dutchmen in December, 1952, he decided to launch his concertina construction business in earnest.[10] This meant a trip to Chicago where Hengel's friend, Frank Hagert, then working at the Curtis Candy Company, took Hengel by streetcar to see Henry Schuckert. Schuckert could not help but sent them to the Italian Accordion Factory. Unable to assist, the workers in turn sent Hengel to Jack "Wally" Walles, a Polish fellow. Walles was the final owner of the Otto Schlicht factory, who at the end had a partner called Paul Ewald. When Schlicht died on March 26, 1938, Ewald took over the factory which he operated until it collapsed due to his retirement in 1946. Chief stumbling blocks for the old masters were of equal importance, the one that the Russian Red Army was in control of the factories in Chemnitz, Carlsfeld and Klingenthal, and obstructed the export both of instruments and of parts to the West. Secondly, the chief reed makers and filers, John Kummer and John Friedl, immigrants from Austria, were in their eighties and no longer able to continue the business.

Reeds are the heart of a good concertina. In all, there are 374 in each concertina and Hengel, to make his instrument the finest in the world, needed nothing more than good reeds, their source now cut off behind the Iron Curtain. In the pre-World War II time frame, Friedl and Kummer were filing them by hand from high quality bulk Swedish steel.

John Friedl was born December 26, 1873 in the village of Bernstein [Borostyánkő], state of Burgenland, then the western edge of the Kingdom of Hungary. Indicative of the confusion surrounding the national identity of Burgenlanders is the fact that in the 1930 Federal Census John Friedl is noted as born in "Hungary," but then the word is lined out and "Austria" is overwritten. The switch to Austrian nationality for the province had been effected at the Treaty of Versailles in 1919. Both John Friedl and his wife Maria are noted as "mother-tongued Germans." In the 1930 census under the listing of a profession, Friedl is registered as "Maker of musical instruments." A stone mason by trade, Friedl learned at an early age to play several musical instruments long before he emigrated, and had once repaired a mechanical piano to the pleasure of its village owner. Though married and the father of four daughters, John Friedl and his younger brother, Karl, left for the United States on board the German vessel, *SS Kronprinzessin Cecile* from Bremerhaven with arrival in New York on May 11, 1909. Employed in Chicago as a bricklayer's helper, Friedl in 1911 sent for his wife and youngest daughter, Anna, 3, who arrived from Bremen to New York on board the *Barbarossa* May 17, 1911. The Friedl family [missing three daughters] lived in Chicago

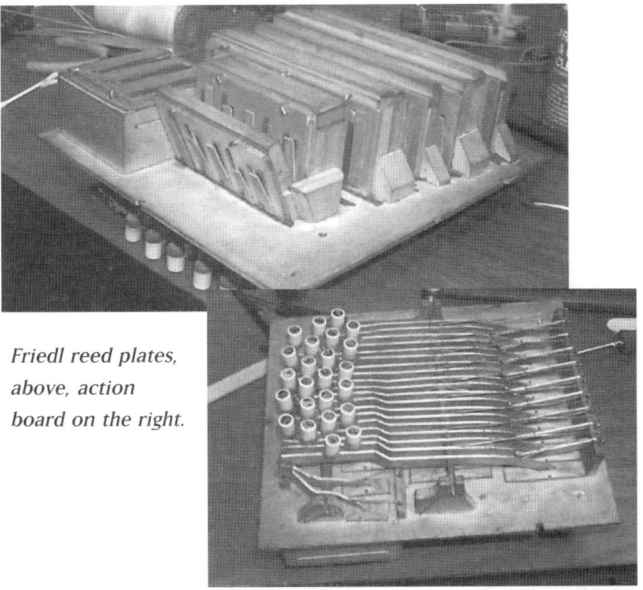

Friedl reed plates, above, action board on the right.

Maria and John Friedl in their home at Christmastime 1937.

John Friedl with fifth daughter, Elsie. John was the father of six girls — four born in Austria and two born in the USA.

Hengel in 1955 at Sleepy Eye works on the 1937 Patek, now owned by Marvin Moravec.

Hengel in 1967 building concertinas in his New Ulm residence at 403 Minnesota Street.

Hengel at his punch press, now sold to Jerry Minar.

at 1633 North Calland Court, today called Kenneth Avenue, south of Armitage and near Grand. Here on May 4, 1913 was born Elsie, the fourth daughter, and on February 17, 1915 the last Friedl daughter, Edith.

Although he intended to return to the Burgenland, the First World War intervened. Subsequent to the armistice in 1918, Friedl sent for the three daughters left behind but only Rose, in 1921, still had the desire to immigrate. The two older ones, having reached young adulthood, chose to remain in Austria with their grandmother. According to the 1917 *Chicago City Directory*, John Friedl was then living at 1633 Kongee Avenue in Chicago with the listed profession of "musician." In January, 1923 John Friedl purchased a two-story tenement house at 1657 North Latrobe Avenue in Chicago, between North Avenue [Highway 64] and Grand Avenue. It was not too great a distance from his cohorts like Otto Schlicht, Rudy Patek and Henry Silberhorn.

But it was here on North Latrobe where John Friedl set up his shop in the basement and produced the majority of his reeds and plates for the Otto Schlicht factory. In 1936, John Friedl was issued his first Social Security card for his employment with Otto Schlicht at 655 May Street in Chicago. May Street at 655 is just south of the Kennedy Expressway between Grand and Chicago Avenues. May intersects near this point with North Ogden Avenue. At the peak of his career, John Friedl built his own concertina [the only one], with Friedl reeds of course, one where the reed blocks themselves are shifted to produce high versus low reed tonality. In the possession of his grandson, it is the only concertina with such reed block shift capability known to exist. Friedl died of a heart attack on July, 24, 1948.[11]

The career pathway of John Kummer is more elusive. Manuscript censuses do not seem to record the right John Kummer (listing four John Kummers in all). However, the *Chicago City Director* for 1917 does mention a Kummer and Siebenaler Store at 1015 Lill Street. Lill is an east-west street located just north of Fullerton [also an east-west thoroughfare], and three blocks east of Ashland Avenue North. John Kummer at this time was living at 1013 Wolfram, a short street running east-west about four blocks north of, and parallel to, Lill Street. The City Directory for 1923 [they were published about every five years] makes no mention of either Kummer or Siebanaler. But in 1928, the *Chicago City Directory* reports John Kummer as the manufacturer of musical instruments, living at 1348 Maplewood and working out of his home at the same address. This address is a north-south street just north of North Avenue and a bit south of diagonally-running Milwaukee Avenue. Thus, Kummer lived in close proximity to the Otto Schlicht factory at 655 May Street and reasonably close to Patek and Silberhorn on Milwaukee Avenue.

Although Paul Ewald took over the Otto Schlicht business in 1938, he retired in 1946. Therefore, Jack Walles bought the remaining Pearl Queen and Patek concertinas along with the old Otto Schlicht factory and its equipment. Meanwhile, it appears, Walles had moved westward to a musical instrument store that operated formerly at 3119 West Cermak Road in Chicago.[12] Although Walles hoped to import accordion parts from Italy, it soon proved impossible because the accordion's two reeds per plate were waxed in place while the concertina required 18 and 20 reeds per plate held with hook screws rather than wax. Therefore, when the Italian factory was unable to make reeds for the concertina, Walles collected the remaining Schlicht parts and stored them in the basement. Henry Schuckert, meanwhile, had been working at the Schlicht factory and now advised Hengel and his companion to travel to the Walles building at 7600 Cottage Grove Street where they met Jack Walles. Attempting at first to buy reeds only, Hengel was told that he could not buy any individual parts because the entire remaining stock of parts was for sale in toto. After serious discussion, Walles and Hengel agreed on a price of $1,500 for the inventory—the reed blocks, keyboards, bellows—whatever was there.

Upon returning to Minnesota, Hengel discussed the matter with his

LaVern Rippley across the street in front of 7600 Cottage Grove in south Chicago.

Walles was a dealer for the Italian Accordian Company. He also bought from Patek and Schlicht. Later, from 7600 South Cottage Grove, he sold the Schlicht equipment to Christy Hengel. Jes and Doris Kragh of Tyler, Minnesota owned a concertina bearing a namplate "Italian Accordion Mfg. Co. Very best — hand made — all types," and the address 7600 So. Cottage Gove, HU 3-4811.

Purchase order from Norbert Wilger, a priest. Sylvester Liebl was his parishoner and influenced the sale.

Christy Hengel posing in his New Ulm, Minnesota shop in March, 1967, two years after leaving Waseca. On display are most of the parts needed to build a concertina. Note that he is still using the brand name Hengel's, which he never abandoned. Minar switched to Hengel without the 's, but has rights to both names.

brother-in-law, Michael Grausam, who worked for Hengel until his death in 2000. When Grausam agreed to fork over $700, Hengel agreed to pay another $800 and they set out for Chicago. It was March, 1953 when an open stock truck owned by trucker Bill Riley of Wanda set as its purpose to fetch the annals of the former Otto Schlicht factory, then owned by Jack Walles and located in his music store at 7600 Cottage Grove on the south end in Chicago. [Today Walles Music continues general sales of music paraphernalia from its address at 6846 West North Avenue in Chicago.] From eight in the morning to four in the afternoon they loaded matériel. Not in a mood to waste time nor money, they then headed back to Minnesota, where Hengel paid Riley $150 for the roundtrip travel and transfer of goods. To be sure, they were no longer at the actual Schlicht factory, which had years earlier closed its manufacture on May Street on the northern periphery of downtown Chicago. Rather, it was owned on an intermediate basis by the Italian Accordion Company, which operated at its own site. Nevertheless, in March 1953, more than a decade after the demise of the masterful Otto Schlicht, Hengel was thrilled to have "his arms around" all the original parts, equipment and tools—the drill press, table saw, kick press—all handmade by the masterful, adroit Otto Schlicht and his support personnel in the vicinity of his May Street operation. In an old brooder house located on the Hengel farm near Wanda, Christy began what would become his half century of concertina production.

It took two years for Hengel to construct his first concertina, accomplished only after his move to Sleepy Eye. The same year in 1955, Nicky Vierling from Iowa, became the first owner of a Hengel concertina. Used to the old Triple he had and the Patek concertina sound he associated with Whoopee John, Vierling complained about the new Hengel for the six months he owned it until Christy decided to buy it back for the original price of $575. Meanwhile, at the pinnacle of its popularity, the Babe Wagner Band was in search of a concertina player when its outstanding concertina player, Elmer Scheid, bowed out after cutting most of the recordings made by the band with Columbia records. In about 1955, the band leaders connected with the young artist, Don Klossner, who, for the following 15 years, played this instrument [Hengel Number 1] with the Babe Wagner Band. After this long stand, Klossner acquired a preference for the Italian-made Stradivarius brand of concertina.[13] Seeking a more flexible output, he provided it with an accordion-type of switching mechanism. When he achieved this with the Stradivarius, Klossner sold Hengel Number One, which ended up in the hands of Butch Wolf, the son of Tony Wolf, near St. Cloud. It was subsequently sold for $1,450 to Ed-Vern Black of Fairfax who owns the instrument currently. Of late, Black refused $10,000 when Hengel tried to buy it back from him. However, at a television show from Mankato in 1996, Black did allow Hengel to play the instrument for the production and the dance that followed—still a beautifully performing instrument.

After Hengel moved to Sleepy Eye, he produced concertinas for Jack Shambour of New Prague, Johnny Helget of New Ulm, Martin Mathwig from Gaylord, and Dennis Scherper from Genola, in Morrison County, Minnesota, who got number four but later sold it to

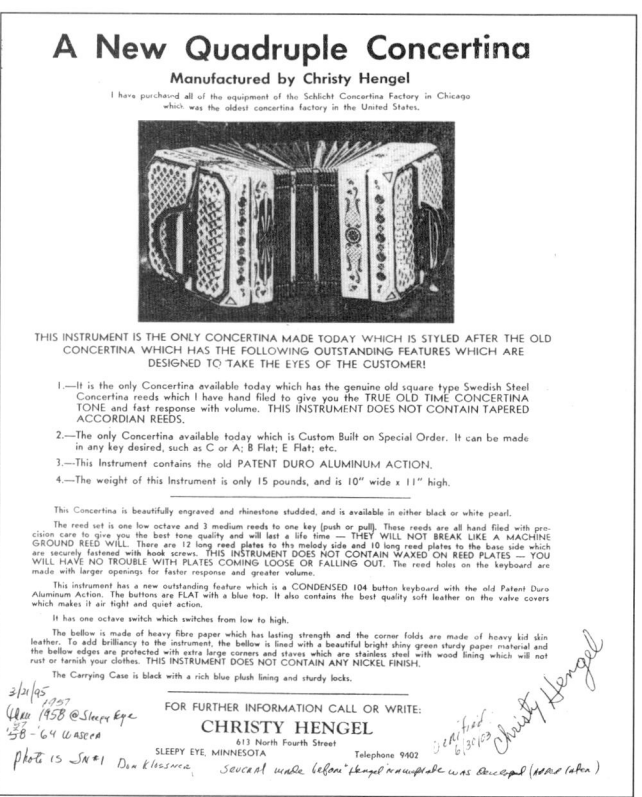

A flyer used by Christy Hengel to market his instruments.

Keith Zwack for $6,500. The fifth one produced went to Larry Dorschner—concluding the series actually manufactured in Sleepy Eye. Hengel then moved to Waseca, although for the time being, he continued production using sequential serial numbers from his original Sleepy Eye venue. The series from 5 through 86, namely a total of 81 boxes, were created during Hengel's residence in Waseca. Slowly gaining market share, Hengel in 1958 joined ranks with Meidel Music Store at 304 North Minnesota to offer a display of the Hengel concertina at the annual Polka Festival. Although the first Polka Day festival held in New Ulm came in 1953 when the city paved the street and sought an appropriate initiation,[14] the succeeding event became so popular that after 19 years, in 1972, it had to be moved from main street [Minnesota Street] to the fairgrounds for better crowd control. However, it was not until the 1958 Polka Day that old time music enthusiasts had the chance to see and order the concertina manufactured by Christy Hengel. Almost overnight some 200 orders arrived and the master could not fill them.[15]

Thus the year 1958 in retrospect was a genuine turning point [a *Wende* in the original German sense of the word] for the instantaneous audience for old time music brought together professional players who experienced the Hengel product. They tried the Hengel concertina and could not believe how well it handled and how beautifully it sounded. In addition to the sharp, distinct but balanced tonal sounds, the instrument was lighter. It weighed around 14 pounds in contrast to the earlier Schlicht instruments that were one or two pounds heavier. And the bellows were smooth and easy to flex, thus skyrocketing the Hengel concertina to the head of competitors in the marketplace. During the Polka Day of 1958, many professionals came into the New Ulm shop, checked out the Hengel concertinas, tried playing them, and gloried in both the ease of manipulation and the high quality of the reed tones.

Much of Hengel's sudden success was due to the reeds. Since after 1945 reeds were no longer available from Germany, Hengel crafted his own. In the earlier years he needed to create them from scratch. Reed making for Hengel began back on the farm in Wanda. It took weeks to punch and trim them by hand, file them to the correct tonal specification and sound, tune them to the exact pitch and then mount them on the blocks. Reedmaking individually was tedious work. Often through the years, Hengel needed to rely on his own skills to produce reeds from purchased steel ribbons. Hengel began to build his reeds on reed forms he created out of oil-hardened steel, crafting it by patterning it according to the exemplars he had extracted from a well-playing concertina. He had to file them down to the exact reed surface, then taper the edges slightly as needed. But then they had to be heat-treated for the required hardness. Once his own self-crafted form was available, though, he could assemble the blank reeds in his specially devised template and mount the whole batch in a vice. Now he could file an individual reed to its perfect tonal shape in a half minute. It was and remained possible to file the reed free-handedly but the outcome was imprecise and crude.

The most admired, highly talented reed maker up to this time had been John Kummer in Chicago. From Kummer, Hengel was originally able to procure reeds. But Kummer filed all his reeds free-hand, for example, in a 1945 Pearl Queen, which Hengel by this time had acquired from Melvin Krzmarzick of Essig, Minnesota. During a visit to Chicago at the Kummer and Friedl work site, Hengel had brought along his reed forms. The master reedmaker, Kummer, was dumbfounded to observe Hengel, the young and inventive journeyman, speed-file his reeds, completing a reed blank in about 20 seconds. Kummer could scarcely believe his eyes. He took one of his own hand-filed individual reeds and matched it against the Hengel reed, rendering a judgment that the Hengel reed, though "speed-filed," was indeed perfectly tuned. The elderly Kummer, then already 83 years old, shook his head in amazement at

Melvin Krzmarzick, the father of Gerald, playing a Hengel C, now owned by Gerald. Melvin plays here with Arlie Rolloff.

the perfect pitch. Hengel was greatly relieved when he was able to procure reed materials from Negrini in Italy beginning in 1969. He still had to rework them a bit to achieve the desired tonal quality, which makes the instrument today's superior product.

Other great advances and "strengths" for the Hengel concertina, in addition to its superb natural ear turning, was the lever action which give it fast reed response. By choosing strong but light bass wood for the outer structure, Hengel was able to reduce the weight of the concertina down to about 13 pounds compared to others which generally exceed 14 pounds. Furthermore, there was the adjustment to the spread of keys. Measured on the right-hand playing side of the concertina from the center row top button to the center of the #18 button on the bottom yields a spread of 5 1/2 inches. Created by Hengel in 1955, this breadth of the hand became the standard preferred by most players. Both German-made and Schlicht-built key spreads were 5 3/4 inches. Star builders however, condensed the hand button spread to 5 1/4 inches. Hengel and Felix Spaeth then decided to try 5 1/2 inches, although Hengel #1 is still 5 3/4 inches. But the 5 1/2 inch spread soon became popular and thus standard for all concertinas, including those made in Italy. An additional advance crafted by Hengel for his concertinas is the supply of air. By making the holes for the air intake and expulsion large, he achieved a reed vibration that was richer, fuller, and more keenly tuned in sound quality. Hengel soon discovered that concertina players appreciated how much easier this new instrument was to play. Among the comments from performers on stage, the "Hengel concertina saved a lot of wear and tear on the arms."

Among the best judges are those who play the Hengel concertina. From a survey of Hengel concertina owners we completed in 2002, a few comments about the quality of the Hengel instrument are worth recording. In answer to a question whether the concertina players surveyed believed the listeners were able to discern whether the concertinist was playing a Hengel or another brand of concertina: virtually all of the 175 respondents maintained that other concertina players are always aware that the Hengel is the preeminent concertina available today. Most agree that the general public is at best somewhat aware of the Hengel as the finest concertina built. But as responding individuals noted — nursing home people wear hearing aids and do not care. Today's preeminent concertina player, Karl Hartwich, says: "Anyone who knows anything about a concertina, knows if he is hearing a Hengel." Here a kind of pattern emerged. The closer the respondent to the New Ulm area where Christy Hengel works, the more likely the judgment that the audience knows whether the concertina is a Hengel or some other brand. Respondents from farther east in Wisconsin believe that the general public is not discriminating enough to distinguish among concertinas. On the other hand, Ernie Stumpf of Belle Plaine, Minnesota states that "Audiences in Wisconsin are very much aware of the Hengel concertina."

Sometimes the respondent laid the difference on the ability of the concertina player — if a skilled player, then the listeners were more likely to recognize that the concertina was a Hengel. A few bandleaders like Gordon Prochaska assert that listeners can detect a Hengel "without a shadow of a doubt." Others are of the opinion that to recognize the Hengel, you have to be quite familiar with many old time music tunes. On occasion the report was less conventional: "I have several concertinas and I call my Hengel the boss. When I take out the boss and play it ahead of an audience, it commands them all to perk up and listen." Intriguing comments include: "Lots of guys want to play a Hengel but they do not want to shell out the money, so they just play their Star or other lesser concertina." The

Joe Malecheski, 1956, in his Chicago home, built bellows for Star, some 3,000 in all. He also supplied Patek and Hengel.

Born in 1933, Felix Spaeth worked on his farm south of Morgan, MN making the wooden parts for Hengel. Photographed in 1954, he died in 1989.

Wendinger brothers also exhibit a touch of wit in asserting, "Audiences always know, which is why we have six Hengel concertinas on stage (three for each brother)." From Fritz Szymkowiak of Stevens Point comes the comment: "The people sure are conscious of it, and all are jealous because I happen to have a Hengel concertina."

Brian Brueggen states: "If you play a Hengel the right way, it rings and resounds like no other concertina and therefore people definitely do know what instrument you are playing." But then there is the comment of veteran Roman Rezac who says simply, "I don't know, but a Hengel sure makes its player look more important." A few like Alvin Chlan of New Prague voices the view that the Hengel is one of a kind, one that holds its value better than money in the bank." Ed-Vern Black affirms that "most people figure it out because the Hengel is better sounding than other brands, with better reeds inside, and a good key action." Johnny Helget is of the opinion that the listener knows right away because the Hengel sound is so great that people ask how it can sound so different from the rest." John Check of Oskosh, Wisconsin offers the view that audiences often ask about the Hengel instrument, "it catches their ear," and has the advantage of offering the most authentic concertina tonal quality. "It is lighter than all the others and its action is superb." A player like Hugo Steven Reinhart of Rochester believes audiences know because the "Hengel is light weight, has great tone, flat buttons, great sound, top notch response and is maintenance free."

Butch E. Hermann of Belle Plaine, Minnesota, tells of his trips to Ohio and Pennsylvania a few times each year to attend polka festivals. There, he asserts, the first question from frequenters is "Did you bring the Hengel?" Others say they came to the dance or the festival only to hear the Hengel. At mutual playing sessions, "everybody wants to play my Hengel box. It's now been played by all the top Polish box players." On his circuit with Prochaska's Little Fishermen Band, Ambrose Kodet believes audiences always comment on the fact that he has his Hengel instruments on stage. "They have an ease of playing, great sound, superb tuning, high resale value and are a copy of the proven instruments that came out of the Otto Schlicht factory in Chicago." And then there is the comment of Jerome Liebsch of Plymouth, but originating from the Little Falls, Minnesota area. Starting with an Arno Arnold double reed he bought in 1951 from Pat Watters Distributing in Minneapolis, he traded the Arnold for a $200 allowance on a Hengel B flat in 1972. "The Hengel has a full sound both on the bass as well as the melody sides. There's a ring to the reeds. It's hard to describe because you gotta own one to know one. I have a Star quad that resembles a Hengel but the full sound just is not there. It seems there is no used Hengel concertina for sale anywhere. The cost is an investment."

Today, some 45 years later, Hengel recalls original sales of an instrument bringing $650 compared to current prices ten times that, $6,500 to $8,000, even $10,000. But he still has not met the total market demand, having crafted some 365 to date, all of which are still playing. In addition, he has reworked and repaired several hundred—the Pearl Queen, Patek, Star, Glass and others. No Hengel concertina has ever been returned for rebuilding, just tune-up and sometimes general cleaning. Thanks to his 1953 foresight in acquiring the Otto Schlicht stock in Chicago, Hengel with his successor, Jerry Minar, today has enough parts to continue the concertina trade, one might say, indefinitely. His bellow maker, Joe Malecheski, supplied hundreds of bellows, to which Hengel has added some made by Adam Lewandowski, both of whom had worked for Rudy Patek and others in Chicago so that today Hengel has a supply of many bellows for future construction of the concertina.

Concertina reeds are a different matter. When inventories from Kummer waned, Hengel found a supplier from northern Italy, but these reeds proved to be of different quality. Housed in the small town of Pavia-Stradella near Milan, the Dallape Accordion Company, equipped with some 300 workers, once supplied a large market. By 1972, however, it was down to just eight workers. When Hengel visited the factory later in 1972, there was just one fellow left making reeds intended mostly for the Dallape accordions. When this reed maker died in 1975, the firm folded and has since disappeared. From this company Hengel acquired the reeds, some 40 sets every three months identified by the brand "Negrini & Borgonovi," which induced some of Hengel's competitors [Brown and Minar] to charge that Hengel was being dishonest when he claimed in radio shows during 1984 that every single piece of his instruments, especially the reeds, were handmade of Swedish steel by him or constituted from remainder materials acquired through Walles from Schlicht. Eventually the matter was resolved by Hengel admitting that his concertinas contained "Hengel shaped reeds," without reference to their national source or specific manufacturing elements.

Aided by his then-wife, Valeria "Josie" Runnerstrom [born August 15, 1926] of Waseca, Hengel was able to produce a concertina in about 250-300 hours. Assisting him with frames were Felix Spaeth of Morgan, who also farmed, as well as Gordon and Bernard Hanson of Owatonna, who made reed blocks, wood frames and did all the plastic laminating. After their demise, the best assistant proved to be Hengel's brother-in-law, Michael Grausam, who started working for Hengel in 1977 until his recent death. Other individuals critical to the production of the Hengel concertina were Otto Heinze of St. Joseph, Michigan who made the air levers, bellow corners, which came from Patek and Anton Wolfe, and engraving from Michael Alex in Chicago. Others involved with engraving and painting included Wayne Borgstahl of Owatonna, Richard Terlikowski from La Crosse, Bernard Henson from Owatonna, Jerry and Beverly Minar of New Prague, along with Ambrose and Lois Kodet of Mankato. Shaping the leather straps were Ralph Vogelpohl of New Ulm and Ivan Sorenson of Darfur, Minnesota. Often Hengel had to make his own lever holders, fiber holders, brass tubing, neck strap holders and clamps.

Playing the concertina requires an understanding of the keyboard map. On the left-hand bass side there are 24 buttons, 28 for the right-hand side. Pulling the concertina in and out doubles the count to 104 keys. However, there are 374 reeds in a Hengel concertina, 150 for the bass and 224 for the right-hand melody. Since Hengel concertinas are quadruple, that means four reeds playing at one time for the right hand, but on the left hand the number is really only triple, except for numbers 1, 5, and 10, which activate four reeds. Pearl Queen and Patek instruments also had only triple bass keys. On the right side are four reeds, including three mediums and a low tone reed. Accordions have similar but tapered reeds, somewhat longer than on a concertina and narrower, which results in faster vibration. Square, rectangular reeds typically are shorter, giving the concertina a broader sound and tone. In the case of the Hengel instrument, the measurements of the box are always eleven inches deep and ten inches high with 28 buttons for the melody on the right and 24 on the left for the bass.

Today the concertina is not only alive but doing well in the hands of the new Hengel owner, Jerry Minar, of JBM Sound, Inc. in New Prague. But Hengel's success is due in part to John Kummer and John Friedl, the reed makers from Germany / Austria, whose creations were and continue to be, the model from which Hengel worked. Summarizing on the route the concertina took to Minnesota, we must briefly review the sequence of

Michael Alex lived at 2003 Fullerton Avenue in Chicago.

Michael Alex, at his Chicago home, engraved the parts for Schlicht, Patek and Pearl Queen concertinas. Here he holds the Hengel #1 for which he did the engraving.

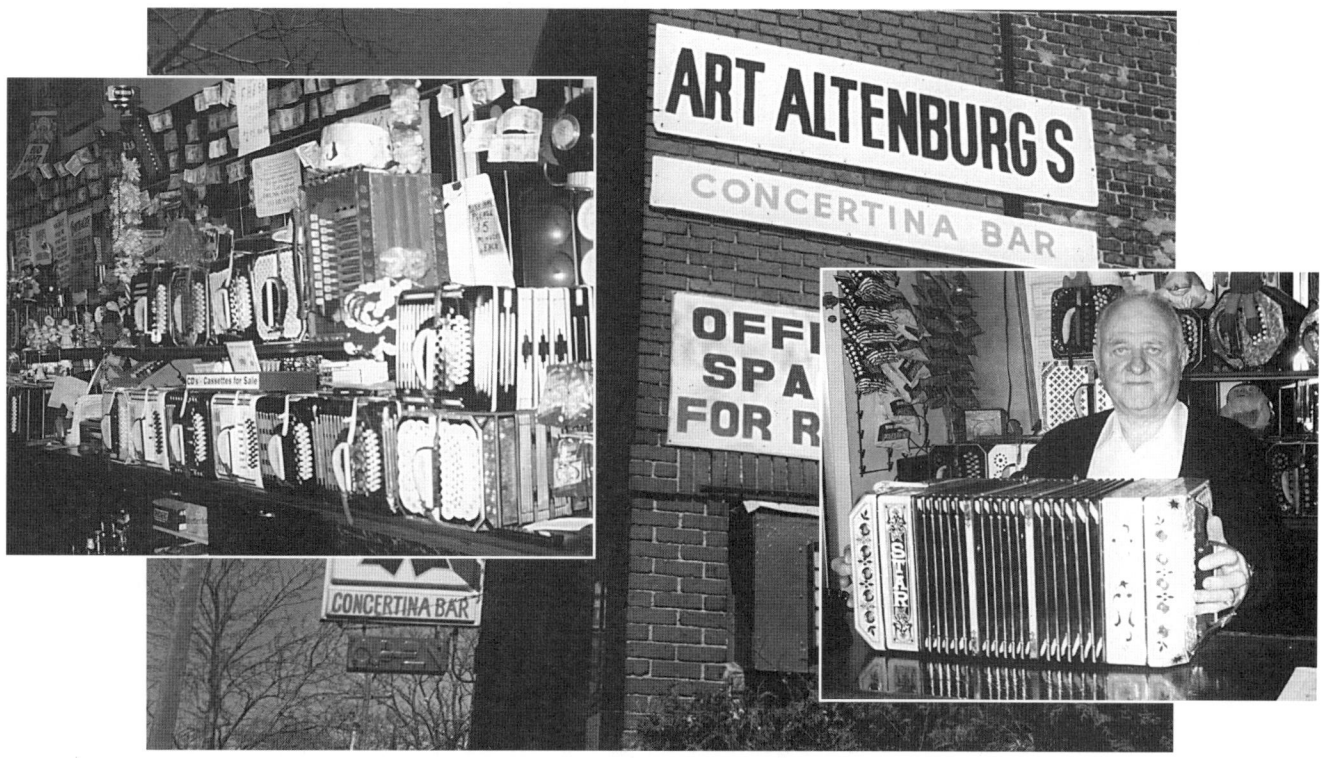

Art Altenburg's Concertina Bar at 1920 South 37th Street, Milwaukee. He is playing a Star concertina at his bar. Photos by Rippley, March, 2002.

concertina events in Chicago. During the heyday of the Chicago concertina, the instruments were either imported directly from the Chemnitz area factories or were bought as parts, which were assembled at the Schlicht factory in south Chicago. Prominent among them was the Brothers Dix firm, which began reed production at Gera in 1866.[16] Great promoters of these instruments built by the Otto Schlicht factory during their prime were Rudy Patek with his "Patek" model and Vitak-Elsnic with their "Pearl Queen" original instruments that date in the United States from about 1910. Getting his start working at the Schlicht factory, Patek in 1926 was asked to go on the road demonstrating the instrument and selling. Soon he began putting his own name on some but apparently kept merchandising just as well the identical "Pearl Queen." By contrast, Henry Silberhorn initially bought all his concertinas at the Arnold and Lange factories in Germany, but upon receipt made minor modifications and changed all their names to "Clarion." When Silberhorn had some concertinas manufactured by the International Accordion Company in Chicago between 1926-1930, he named earlier models the Silberhorn, and in 1938 the Black Beauty, followed by others less well known. Rare owner-players of the Silberhorn concertina live in Chippewa Falls and Ashland, Wisconsin. When International Accordion went out of business, Walter Mosjiewicz continued building essentially the same concertina but called it the "Star," as described in an earlier chapter.

Perhaps the finest collection of the "Star" concertina can be found at the Art Altenburg Concertina Bar at 1920 South 37th Street on Milwaukee's south side. Among his substantial assembly are quite a few 100-year-old Lange concertinas, all playable. But it's the Star brand that predominates, most lined up on the shelves behind the bartender for the enjoyment of patrons. On weekends at the bar, most concertina dance orchestras of the Midwest appear to enthusiastic crowds of fans from far and wide. In Altenburg's agglomeration are some self-crafted instruments including a large oversized concertina completed in 2002. Here, on a tiny stage near the entrance, elderly artisans squeeze out happy time waltzes and polkas while silver-haired men with their golden-aged women circle the tight, elongated dance floor.[17] Also on view are a few odd assortments such as the high, rectangular "accordion style" concertina built by the immigrant Russian artist, Andrew Karpek, of the Karpek Accordion Manufacturing Company (1915) in Milwaukee and called simply a "Karpek."

While Karpek lived and worked in Milwaukee, Altenburg himself derived from the central Wisconsin region around Mosinee between Stevens Point and Wausau, where he once sold Chevrolet cars. From this ethnically Polish and German region subsequently derive other concertina enthusiasts like Pat Watters and teacher-tuner-bandleader-promoter Dan Gruetzmacher, a lifelong devotee of the "Star" from the Merrill-Wausau region, one who, with his wife Susan, has been a "Star" dealer since 1990 through 2001. However, it should be noted that today Gruetzmacher's primary instrument of choice is a New Prague Hengel concertina built by Jerry Minar and delivered in March 2003. [As noted above, the Star emanated from the demise of the International Accordion Company in Chicago about 1930 but was always strictly crafted in the Chemnitz tradition as implemented in America by the Otto Schlicht factory. This factory produced concertinas for Patek, Vitak-Elsnic, Silberhorn, the Kosatkas House of Music and the Kesting Music Store in St. Paul under the names Patek, Vitak, Pearl Queen, Royal and Peerless.] From the International Accordion Company came numerous derivative concertina brand names such as the Schuckert crafted by Henry Schuckert, the Sitek, possibly the Uliska, and the Silverhorn. Following 1930 and the purchase of the company by Mojsiewicz, however, the name of all the concertinas that were built was almost universally rendered simply as "Star."

Back at the primary manufacturing center headed by Otto Schlicht, who arrived from Germany in the early 1900s, production began in about 1910. During the 1920s it accelerated and flowered into the 1930s with individuals like Henry Schuckert, who made the bellows and functioned as the master tuner. Michael Alex did most of the engraving, not only for Schlicht but also for the Star concertinas and other producers in the city.

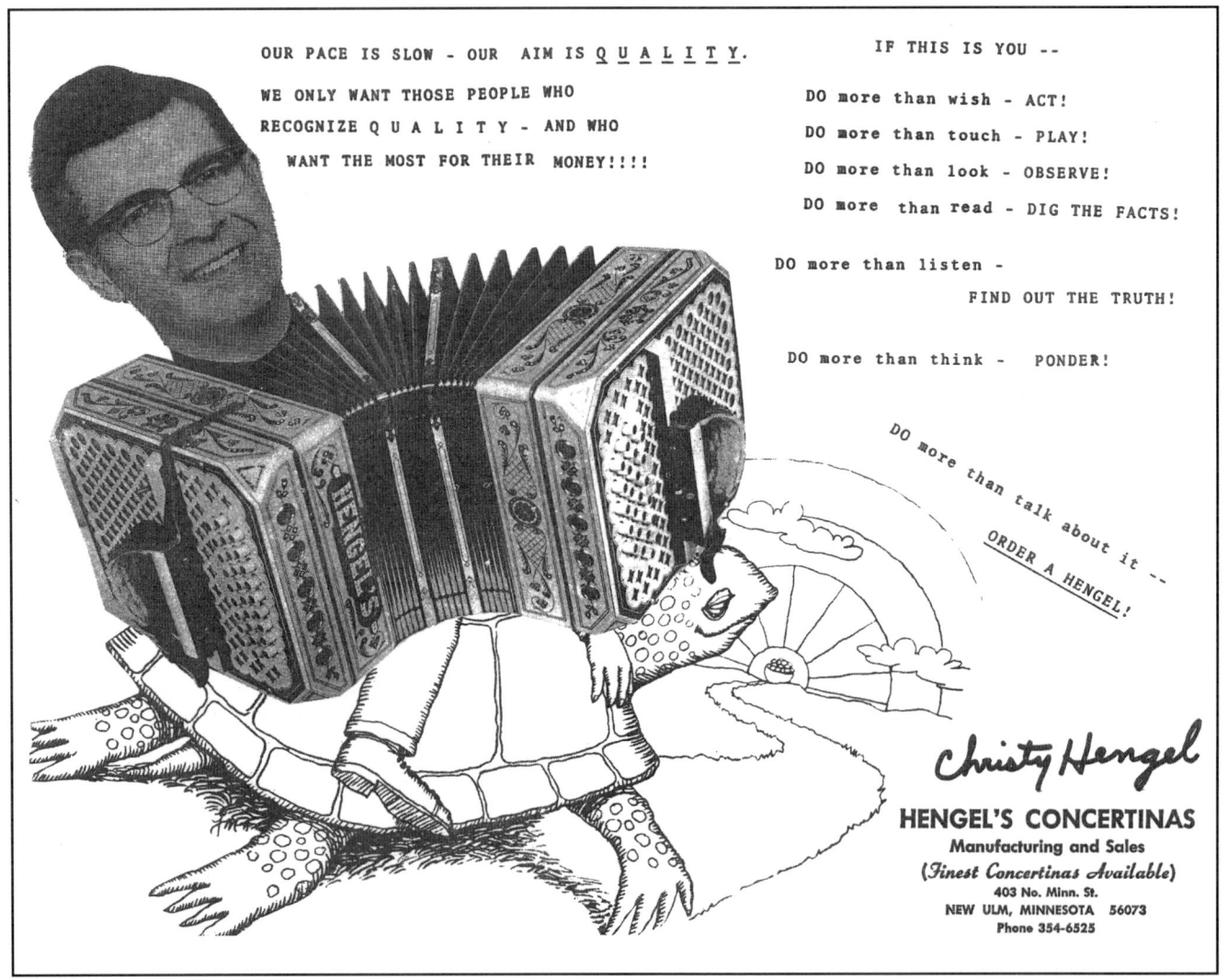

Crafting the reeds from Swedish or German clock spring steel were John Kummer [a one-time tool and die maker], who stamped the reed plates for the Pearl Queen and Patek models, all manufactured by Schlicht. Friedl specialized in polishing the reeds with an emery board, producing a soft finish while Kummer reeds retain visible file marks. Also, the Friedl rivets are rounded while the Kummer rivets are narrow and rectangular. In general, the Pearl Queen instruments had reeds manufactured in Germany at the Chemnitz [Lange] and Carlsfeld [Arnold] companies, or possibly jobbed through Chemnitz and Carlsfeld from Gera and other crafting sites. Otherwise they were hand-filed by Kummer while the Patek concertinas from the same Schlicht factory had many reeds made by Friedl, seemingly the same, although a specially trained ear can tell the difference. Reportedly, in many instances, John Friedl hand-finished his reed plates, rendering them a darker gray but polished look, obtaining reed blanks from John Kummer. All the while, Henry Schuckert, according to experts, was supplying the bellows for many instruments that emerged from the Schlicht factory.

Intermixed among the Schlicht-produced concertinas is the more expensive Excelsior model with reeds furnished directly from Germany, which the Schlicht factory built to "have an accordion sound," according to the 1932 Patek Catalog. Confusing matters for the unsophisticated customer at the Schlicht factory, Henry Schuckert was purchasing hand-filed reed blanks from Kummer and installing these Kummer reeds into his Star concertina. This instrument he named the "Schuckert Supreme," of which only a limited number were sold. From 1926 onward, Joseph Elsnic and his brother, Emil Elsnic, marketed the Pearl Queen from the Schlicht factory, at which time also Rudy Patek was naming these fine concertinas after himself. During his early days spent learning the concertina, Rudy Patek worked at the Otto Schlicht factory, and thus, when he moved into sales on his own in 1926, it was natural to merchandise the Schlicht products. The last serial number stamped on a Patek concertina was #6158 [owned now by Jerry Minar of New Prague], while the serial number on the Elmer Scheid [New Ulm] Patek concertina was #5849. Scheid's instrument is dated September 18, 1937.[18] Thus, in essence, the Patek, the Pearl Queen and even the Star of the 1930s era all comprise a concertina of strikingly similar design and construction, having in some cases even reeds made by the same experts. In the final analysis, virtually all of the concertinas of the 1920s and 1930s were crafted by the artists whose parts the builders assembled into masterful concertinas at the Schlicht factory in Chicago.

When the Otto Schlicht factory passed to Paul Ewald, upon his death in 1938, it retained its sophistication for a time in part because Ewald had worked and learned his artistry on the Schlicht factory floor. Continuing until 1946, the main reason for the rapid demise of the Chicago concertina business was because the Russian Army closed down the German factories. In particular, the large Arnold factory in Carlsfeld was closed when the Russians converted it to a VEB [Volkseigener Betrieb — Peoples' Owned Company, i. e. state-owned]. It was then interwoven with the Klingenthal accordion factories where it began manufacturing the renowned "Weltmeister" brand of accordion, which was in high demand all across the Soviet Union, a nation where the accordion, and definitely not

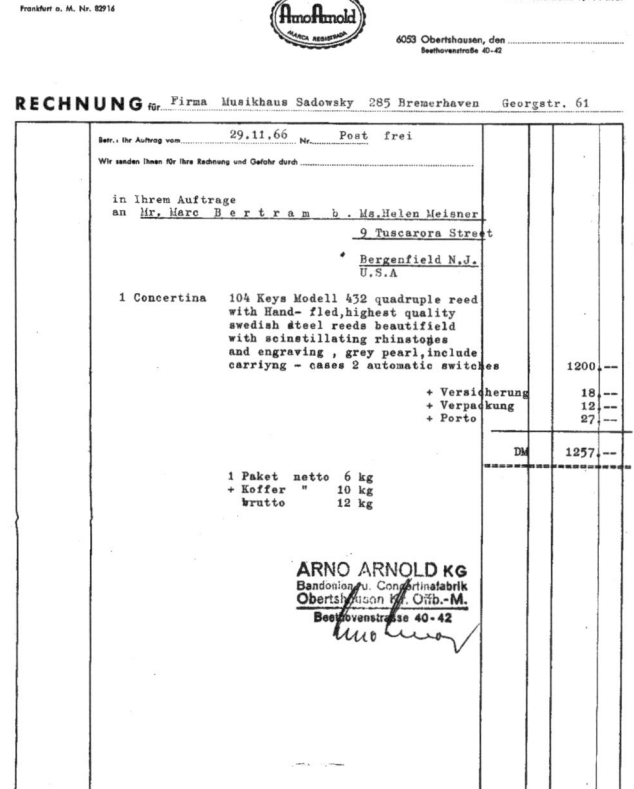

An Arno Arnold Company billing following its move from Carlsfeld to Obertshausen near Frankfurt, West Germany. The concertina billed above is now owned by Alvin Wondra of Montgomery, Minnesota.

the concertina, was in vogue.[19]

Obviously destined for the market in the vast Soviet Union, the Weltmeister accordion was not formally introduced to the United States until approximately the year 2000. However, there is the Senator Paul Wellstone connection. During his final weeks of the campaign for reelection to the Senate in Minnesota, his Beechcraft airplane crashed on Friday October 25, 2002 at the Eveleth-Virginia airport approach, resulting in the senator's death. At a makeshift outdoor memorial site in St. Paul the following day, sitting on the sidewalk in front of the floral sprays, Dan Chouinard played the "Weltmeister" accordion. Wellstone's Jewish parents having immigrated from the Soviet Union, one can at least symbolically link the instrument to his ancestral homeland.[20]

Finally, during the 1960s, there was Pat Watters at 2219 East 42nd Street in Minneapolis. Initially Watters imported Arno Arnold concertinas from the reconstructed Arnold factory near Frankfurt in West Germany, but then imported them from Italy bearing the name "Stradivarius." This instrument was ordered to specifications designed in the Midwest and placed on order at the accordion builder's site of operations in Italy. With a background of sixteen years in music education and merchandising for Wurlitzer and other companies, Pat Watters in 1942 established his own retail store called Watters Music Center in downtown Minneapolis.[21] Struggling for goods in a nation at war, Watters managed to accumulate various pieces, including 15 used concertinas from a shop in Chicago. He relied at first on his experience in selling piano keyboard accordions. But soon Watters developed an enrollment plan for music stores and schools across a large territory, concentrating now on instruments which could easily be played alone, such as the accordion. During this time frame the concertina seemed to fit into his purpose since it could easily provide melody and accompaniment. Following

The former Arnold companies in Germany combined in 1948 to produce the Weltmeister accordion for the Soviet market. Senator Paul Wellstone died in 2002. Here at his headquarters in St. Paul, a mourner plays a Weltmeister. Beginning about the year 2000, Bill Brown in New Ulm began importing the Weltmeister from Klingenthal in Germany. Inset photo: A Weltmeister accordion called officially the Weltmeister Cantora De Luxe B, a high quality instrument built in the 1980s by the VEB Klingenthaler Harmonikawerke.

World War II, as noted above, the supply of reeds and parts were scarce until Arno Arnold of the original Lange-Arnold concertina manufacturing families escaped Communist East Germany and began building a few concertinas once again, now in West Germany. Thus, Pat Watters immediately furnished Arno Arnold with designs for 17 models of concertinas ranging from rather simple and cheap student copies to progressively amateur, semi- and fully professional models which bore fruit, both financially and in a popular vein, when the concertina clubs of old revived. As demand increased, John Bolster's Independent Accordion Service in Minneapolis began servicing the instruments while assisting similar centers over a wide area.

Important to the growth of concertina enthusiasm were such performing artists in east central Wisconsin, especially Dick Rodgers, who logged decades of consecutive television performances carried by more than a dozen local stations. Equally influential was John Check, a professor of educational psychology at the University of Wisconsin-Oshkosh, whose achievements gained him recognition in the Concertina Hall of Fame in 1981, playing his Hengel concertina.[22] Throughout the 1980s, others lending the concertina its regained position in the sun were such recording artists and radio performers such as Tony Wolf, Li'l Wally, Li'l Ritchie and many others. During the 1970s, Pat Watters maintained mailing labels for over 5,000 concertina players in the nation and tried, to a degree, to know perhaps a third or half of them through travels, displays and parties, the first of which he initiated in 1948 as he meandered from Pennsylvania to California to mastermind some 100 parties in all. These he staged by printing and mailing notices, then loaded 20 - 30 instruments in a station wagon for travel to the display center, often spending three or four nights in hotels. On average, each concertina party cost him $100 each, resulting in an overall expenditure of $10,000 for the efforts, which in turn generated commensurate income.

In the far north of Minnesota were other great concertinists who were especially recognizable for their Chicago Polish style. Among the notable were the father-son team, Joseph and William Czerniak of Duluth. Famed for his "Duluth Polka Dots," Joe Czerniak began teaching young Bill to play the concertina soon after his 4th birthday. Already by age 12, Bill was performing locally on his own. During college at St. John's University in Collegeville, Bill played trumpet in concert and marching bands and with some "big bands" of his time. Studying electrical engineering at the University of Minnesota in Minneapolis in 1967, Bill joined the Joe Tomaszewski Polka Band, the "Northeasterners," and in 1971 linked with the Mrozinski Brothers "Aleatoric Ensemble" for dances and recording albums. With wife, Mary Lou, in 1974 Bill formed the "Polka Soul" dance band which continued for nearly two decades until the 1990s when, together, they began the "Bill Czerniak's

This advertisement appeared before 1969, after which Hengel began acquiring reeds from Italy.

Concertina Band," which played throughout the Midwest. In recognition of his talent, Bill was selected by the Minnesota Music Academy as "concertina player of the year" in 1988 and received a similar award from the United Polka Association in 1989. He entered the Polka Hall of Fame in 1992 and the Wisconsin Polka Hall of Fame in 2001. Born on June 20, 1946, his many successes ended abruptly with his death on April 18, 2002.[23]

In reality, of course, the stars like Hengel, Czerniak, Elmer Scheid and dozens more stood on the shoulders of great predecessors. The efforts of Patek, Silberhorn, Vitak-Elsnic, the Glass brothers and others prior to World War II had reaped the fruits of the concertina's heyday when supplies were readily available from the eastern German source. With a musical mechanism that was dead or dying by degrees, Watters did resurrect the instrument, which breathed new life simultaneously into playing the concertina and into the art of "Old Time" dancing in general when he took over *Polka and Old Time News*, turning it into *Music and Dance News*. In the wake of this fast moving vessel of entertainment were the concertina teaching studios that sprang up in Minnesota, among them the Wolf Concertina Studio, the G. S. [George Servatius] Music Service in Melrose, Joe Czerniak's Duluth School of Music, Brown's Store and Distributing Company in New Ulm, Progressive Music Studios, Kesting Music Company in St. Paul, Paul Zelenka and others. Of special note is a man like Ambrose Kodet, who taught some days from 7 A.M. to 10 P.M., giving lessons for purchasers of the Hengel concertina in New Ulm. Likewise robust in the instructional undertaking, if not as gargantuan, was Jerry Minar who taught for the United Music Company of Hutchinson in New Prague. In Wisconsin, similar services were available from Dan Gruetzmacher in Wausau, DeWitz Music Store in Hustisford, Polonia Music in Pulaski, Lincoln House of Music, Mecca Music, Goetsch Music, Graham-Lane Music, Karpek and others in Milwaukee.

For sure, the direct mail advertising of Christy Hengel from his home workshops in Waseca and New Ulm were no small factor in the promotion of his instrument. Devised probably by his wife, Valeria "Josie" Runnerstrom, the advertisements featured many clever eye-catchers coupled with smart word sequences. Picturing a monkey in 1968, the ad begins with "Quit . . . . ing around and order a [picture of a Hengel concertina], the newest in name, oldest in style, and best in quality. This instrument has the true concertina tone!! Contains all hand-filed reeds—therefore, it has no accordion tone!!!" Then again in 1970 he pictured a

Sylvester Liebl in 1950 playing a Lange concertina, which was fitted in Chicago using bellows supplied from Lange in Germany. Later this concertina was overhauled by Christy Hengel.

turtle burdened down with a Hengel concertina with Hengel's own mug sticking out of the bellows and supplied the verbiage: "Our pace is slow — our aim is quality. We only want those people who recognize quality — and who want the most for their money." In 1974 Hengel advertisements harkened back to the 1920s with "Otto Schlicht, the 'Master Builder' of the world's finest concertinas." Hengel boasted his use of "the same dies that produced the masterpiece in the 1930s are still being used in producing the Hengels in the 1970s."[24]

Of equal importance no doubt was the sheet music industry that generated some 4,000 selections from the Henry Silberhorn original library, together with the voluminous offerings of Vitak-Elsnic. These wellsprings were embodied in the Chicago treasure troves of the 1930s but gained prominence in the Midwest from, among other springboards, the improved Silberhorn instruction method available in the Beginner Course offered by the Brown Music Store in New Ulm and by Dan and Sue Gruetzmacher in Wausau. In the late years of the 20th century, new methods of creating concertina music evolved, some at the software hands of computer specialists, and others from the creative, very dexterous and adventurous fingers of players like Karl

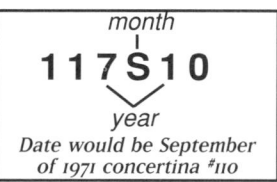

Date would be September of 1971 concertina #110

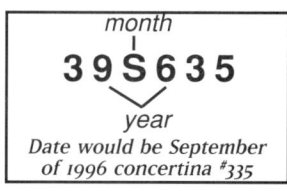

Date would be September of 1996 concertina #335

Sylvester Liebl, originally of Wanda, later of Barre Mills near LaCrosse, Wisconsin.

Hartwich and his Country Dutchmen, Dan Witucki, Gary and Brian Brueggen, Sylvester Liebl, Erwin Suess, Larry Rysavy and others, all playing Hengel concertinas.[25]

One of the greatest masters on the concertina was Sylvester Liebl, born January 18, 1917 in Willow Lake township at Wanda, Minnesota, also the birth hometown of Christy Hengel, both of German Bohemian ancestry. The youngest of 12 children, Liebl's grandfather was also a band leader and music teacher who originated from the Heiligenkreuz region of the Böhmerwald, in today's southwestern Czech Republic. Already at the age of six, Liebl was playing a button accordion, but at 12 switched to concertina, thereafter playing for house parties, barn dances and weddings. With a sister already married in Wisconsin, Syl Liebel in 1934 moved to the La Crosse area where he farmed near Barre Mills, worked in West Salem and played on La Crosse's WKBH radio with his Jolly Germans Band. At the outbreak of World War II, he sought to dampen the German side of things by switching to "Jolly Swiss Boys," never considering, we suppose, that they speak German in Switzerland too. In 1972, Liebl was awarded the "Best Band in the Land" recognition, placement in the Minnesota Music Hall of Fame in 1993, and in 1997 induction into the World Concertina Congress Hall of Fame. For 35 years he was heard on WKTY in La Crosse, then also on WLCX and on WCOW in Sparta, in addition to the countless dances and parties for which he was a life-long mainstay. Pro-players like Karl Hartwich and the Brueggens credit their talent on the concertina to Sylvester Liebl, who died at the age of 86 on May 10, 2003.[26]

Hengel Concertinas used varying unique serial numbering schemes. As a rule, the second and fourth characters represent the last two digits of the year the instrument was manufactured. The third character represents the first letter of the month it was made, and the first, fifth and last characters are the digits of a sequentially increasing number. For example, on the right palm rest is stamped 61-0044 which means the year is 1961 and the sequential number is 44, a concertina that was built while Hengel was still in Waseca. In another example, we have the number 117S10. Here the third and fifth characters represent the last two digits of the year the instrument was manufactured. The fourth character represents the first letter of the month in which it was made, while the first, second and last characters are the digits of a sequentially increasing number of concertinas produced. Thus, for serial number 117S10, the instrument is the 110th made in September, 1971. Still another system can be illustrated from the serial number 39S635. Here the second and fourth characters represent the last two digits of the year the instrument was manufactured. The third character represents the month it was made. The first, fifth and last characters represent the sequentially increasing number of the individual concertinas made. Thus, concertina 39S635 is number 335, which was completed in September, 1996. Observers can also distinguish a Hengel concertina made by himself and one made by his successor, Jerry Minar. Minar spells HENGEL in a vertical pattern from top to bottom [HENGEL], while Christy Hengel labels them using a horizontal pattern from bottom to top [HENGEL'S].

During the first years of production, the name HENGEL'S was not used. Instead, the owner's first name was attached. Approximately in 1958 Christy Hengel recalled his concertinas and installed HENGEL'S name plates. Today both HENGEL as well as HENGEL'S are registered trademarks of JBM Sound, Inc. of New Prague. See the certificate in Chapter 4 about Minar.

One of the crowning achievements in Hengel's life came in 1989 when he was awarded a citation by the National Endowment for the Arts as one of 13 National Heritage Fellows or folk artists. Accompanying the citation was a check for $5,000, as well as a trip to Washington D. C., where Charles Kuralt presided as master of ceremonies for the event.[27] Lending recognition to the event was *National Geographic Magazine*, which sent photographer David Alan Hardy and Rebecca Abrams to the Gibbon Festival in 1990 to focus on Hengel as a National Heritage Fellow. The effort resulted in an article in the January, 1991 issue,[28] an achievement for which Hengel received wide recognition. Then Senator Dave Durenberger received Hengel in Washington, introducing him to some 14 other senators, for whom Hengel played the concertina. In his interview with Charles Kuralt, Hengel played the "New Ulm Polka," making sure that Kuralt understood that all the major New Ulm bands had played it. Harold Loeffelmacher enlarged the name to read, "Minnesota Polka," Elmer Scheid renamed it "Hoolerie #1," Sylvester Liebl stuck with "New Ulm Polka," which prompted today's contemporaries like Karl Hartwich and Brian Brueggen to do the same.

Minnesota Governor Rudy Perpich sent Hengel a certificate commending him "in recognition of your outstanding contribution to the lives of music lovers everywhere, through your creation of America's Number 1 quality concertinas, and to acknowledge that your con-

Christy Hengel played for Charles Kuralt at the awards ceremony in Washington, D.C. taken September 26, 1989. This concertina was built for Michael Grausam, who still owns it.

certinas provide not only delightful polka music but help preserve the cultural heritage of Minnesota."[29] From the White House came a letter from President George Bush stating, "One of America's greatest treasures is our rich and varied cultural heritage. We are all indebted to artists such as you, who have contributed so much to the strength and vitality of the traditional arts

The Concertina in Minnesota. The Hengel Story

in this country." Not to be totally overshadowed by the acclamations, the Minnesota Music Hall of Fame located in New Ulm gave Hengel a special plaque.

Bands and/or individuals with Hengel concertinas (from an early brochure):

    Elmer Scheid - Elmer Scheid and His Hoollerie Band
    Ernie Coopman - The Jolly Brewers Band
    Donnie Klossner - The Babe Wagner Band
    Larry Dorschner - Rainbow Valley Dutchmen
    Lowell Schubert - The Ivan Kahle Band
    Gil Steil - Gil Steil's Concertina Band
    Milo Edel - Milo Edel's Concertina Band
    Wilbert Blohm - The Blohm Orchestra
    Harold Schwer - The Duane Berley Band
    Edwin Kvitek - Edwin Kvitek's Jolly Bohemians
    Dennis Scheper - Dennis' Concertina Band
    Ray Konkol - The Jolly Do-Boys
    Ted Otremba - The Jolly Vagabonds
    Dorine Hinnenkamp - Dorine's Concertina Band
    Sylvester Liebl - The Jolly Swiss Boys
    Murv Adler - Wesley Prescher's Jolly Bohemians
    Ray Trenda - Ronnie & Ray's Concertina Band
    Peter and Paul Wendinger -Peter and Paul Wendinger Band
    Karl Hartwich - The Country Dutchmen
    Marv Nissel
    Leon Olsen
    Larry Olsen
    Leon Helget
    Johnny Helget
    Cletus Goblirsch
    Fritz Szymbowiak
    Tom Kneiss
    Brian Brueggen, The Mississippi Valley Dutchmen
    Kevin Liss, New Jolly Swiss Boys
    Erv Suess, The Hoolerie Dutchmen
    Roman Rezac
    Larry Rysavy
    Lester Schuft
    Luverne Wanous
    Ernie Stumpf
    Ambrose Kodet
    Jerry Minar
    Hugo (Steve) Reinhardt
    Gene Eiden
    Gerald Krzmarzick
    Duane Adler

Photographs from the 1960s depicting the purchasers of Hengel concertinas, taken generally at the home of Christy Hengel. Although Hengel moved eastward from Sleepy Eye to Waseca in March, 1957, he moved back west to New Ulm in 1965 where he immediately had a house built for him by Larry Dorschner, one of his customers, shown here.

Johnny Helget of New Ulm displaying Hengel #3. Helget was not only an expert player, but also a player who could do acrobatic stunts without missing a note.

Larry Dorschner lived in New Ulm and served as contractor for the Hengel home in New Ulm. He purchased Hengel #9, later worked for Bill Brown in New Ulm, but moved subsequently to Menasha, Wisconsin.

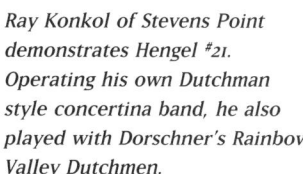

Ernie Coopman of Mankato playing Hengel #11, about 1958.

Ray Konkol of Stevens Point demonstrates Hengel #21. Operating his own Dutchman style concertina band, he also played with Dorschner's Rainbow Valley Dutchmen.

Elmer Scheid, New Ulm, plays Hengel #30. Scheid was the proud owner of a 1937 Patek, ranked among the best in the industry, but thrived also with the Hengel made by his youthful contemporary, Christy Hengel.

The History of the Chemnitzer Concertina

Sylvester Liebl, a trusted beginner on Lange and other concertinas, bought Hengel #31, which he played for the Jolly Germans, later called the Jolly Swiss Boys, from his home at Barre Mills near La Crosse, Wisconsin. Liebl grew up on a farm near the original Hengel farm homestead near Wanda, Minnesota.

Marion Barta of Veseli, Minnesota purchased her C concertina from Hengel in December, 1961. This was No. 46, which was sold in 1995 to Jerry Minar.

Richard Stang of Paynesville, Minnesota plays Hengel #33.

Donnie Klossner, New Ulm, bought Hengel No. 17 in July 1961. Klossner had already been the owner of Hengel No. 1, which had been built for Nicky Vierling of Iowa; however, he did not like it compared to his higher-pitched Pearl Queen, and thus Hengel re-sold it to Klossner.

Leonard Krulikoski was a music retailer under the title United Music Company from Hutchinson, Minnesota, offering various makes of concertinas and also operating a network of teachers for concertina learners.

Born in 1941, Marvin Bulau bought Hengel #42 in 1961 for $700 to replace his heavy "new" Patek and played for Wally Pikal from 1964-1981. His first Pikal band job was at the Blue Note Ballroom in Winsted. German to the core, he works at the Arlington paper and still plays for local events.

Roman Kalina of Lonsdale, Minnesota acquired his No. 37 Hengel concertina in mid 1961; it was subsequently sold to Billy Bartusek.

Lowell Schubert of Oxford Avenue in Delano, Minnesota got Hengel No. 32 in April, 1961. From New Germany, Minnesota, Schubert played for Ivan Kahle from 1960-1966.

Footnotes:

1 LaVern J. Rippley with Robert J. Paulson, *German-Bohemians. The Quiet Immigrants* (Northfield: St. Olaf College Press, 1995), pp. 223 ff.
2 See Chapter One, "German-Bohemians: Their Origins" ibid., pp. 9 ff.
3 Here and below, see the typed manuscript of an interview with Christy Hengel in 1999 by Gerald Krzmarzick of 2612 Fourth Avenue NW in Rochester, Minnesota.
4 See both here and below the photographic evidence in the small book about Whoopee John by LaVern J. Rippley, *The Whoopee John Wilfahrt Dance Band: His Bohemian-German Roots* (Northfield: St. Olaf College Press, 1992), back cover picture and photographs throughout the text.
5 American Folklife Center, *Ethnic Recordings in America. A Neglected Heritage* (Washington, D.C.: Library of Congress, 1982), p. 25.
6 Explained in ibid., p. 12. See also the explanation of folkloric transfer especially as it pertains to the concertina in general in Philip V. Bohlman, *The Study of Folk Music in the Modern World* (Bloomington: Indiana University Press, 1988), p. 116. Others like Werner Danckert, *Das Volkslied im Abendland* (Bern: Francke, 1970) claim there is a substratum or infrastructure by which all folk music is generationally passed, called the *Mutterschicht* (Mother level) for achieving social harmony in the transmission.
7 *U. S. News & World Report* (August 13, 2001), 40-41.
8 Interview conducted by Gerald Krzmarzick in 1999.
9 Even such famous figures in the American labor movement as Walter Reuther strictly adhered to this Germanic tradition. See LaVern Rippley, "Imperial German Socialism in the Life and Work of UAW President Walter Philip Reuther," *The Report 42: A Journal of German-American History* (1993), 43-58.
10 A fine story of Hengel's development as a concertina builder appears in *Entertainment Bits* (December, 1980-January, 1981), pp. 12-13. Editor Doris Pease wrote the story.
11 Letter from John Schnittker, grandson of John Friedl, whose mother was Rose Friedl, 1116 South Douglas Avenue, Arlington Heights, Illinois. Conversation with John Schnittker in New Prague, August 1, 2003.
12 It appears that this store, now known as Walles Music, has since moved to 6846 W. North Avenue, Elmwood Park, Illinois.
13 Don Klossner subsequently played concertina for the Jolly Brewers headed by Ernie Coopman and later by Marvin "Cactus" Stoehr of Elgin, Minnesota. Klossner retains in his possession the musical library of the Babe Wagner Band.
14 See Rippley, *German-Bohemians*, p. 243.
15 Hengel Concertinas in use at dance halls during this time frame are listed in Christy Hengel's promotional newsletters, which are noted here:
For the finest entertainment available, watch the dance bills of your local ballrooms and attend the dances of the following bands and listen to the finest of concertina players playing their Hengel's Concertinas:
Elmer Scheid and His Hoolerie Band, New Ulm, Minnesota—Elmer Scheid has a black B-flat.
The Jolly Brewers, Mankato, Minnesota—Ernie Coopman has a C.
The Babe Wagner Band, New Ulm, Minnesota —Donnie Klossner has a C and a B-flat.
Rainbow Valley Dutchmen, Menasha, Wisconsin—Larry Dorschner has a C and an E-flat
The Ivan Kahle Band, Norwood, Minnesota—Lowell Schubert has a C and an E-Flat.
Gil Steil's Concertina Band, Richmond, Minnesota —Gil Steil has a C and an E-flat.
Milo Edel's Concertina Band, Northfield, Minnesota — Milo Edel has a C and a B-flat.
The Blohm Orchestra, Minneapolis, Minnesota —Wilbert Blohm has a B-flat.
The Duane Berley Band, Waverly, Iowa—Harold Schwer has a C.
Edwin Kvitek's Jolly Bohemians, Lowery, Minnesota—Edwin Kvitek has an E-flat.
Dennis' Concertina Band, Pierz, Minnesota—Dennis Scheper has a C.
The Jolly Do-Boys, Stevens Point, Wisconsin—Ray Konkel has a C.
The Jolly Vagabonds, Little Falls, MN —Ted Otremba has a C.
Dorine's Concertina Band, Melrose, Minnesota—Dorine Hinnenkamp has an E-flat.
The Jolly Swiss Boys, La Crosse, Wisconsin —Sylvester Liebl has a B-flat.
Wesley Prescher's Jolly Bohemians, Elgin, Minnesota—Murv Adler has a C.
Ronnie and Ray's Concertina Band, Owatonna, Minnesota — Ray Trenda has a B-flat.
16 In Germany there were various reed-making factories, perhaps the best known being that owned by the Dix Brothers in Gera. Reproductions of their advertisements appear in the book by Maria Dunkel, *Bandonion und Konzertina* (1996), op cit. pp. 106-7. Other names in the production of concertina reeds are the firm of Rothe & Ruf in Gera, Richard Meinel in Zwota near Klingenthal, Reinhold Glier in Klingenthal, Oswald Meichsner in Brunndöbra, the Sonntag Brothers in Altenburg and Johannes Koch in Trossingen. Cf. Paul Biedermann, *Die Ziehharmonika-Industrie in Deutschland. Eine Studie über die Lebensbedingungen einer Industrie* (Leipzig, 1930).
17 *See* "Milwaukee Untapped," *Food and Wine* (April, 2002), 88.
18 See the end of Chapter 2 listing of all serial numbers for concertinas built by Otto Schlicht and his associates.
19 Interviews with Dieter Seidel in Carlsfeld, Germany, January 18, 2002.
20 *St. Paul Pioneer Press* (October 27, 2002), front page.
21 Here and below taken from a mimeographed sheet of paper written by Mrs. Pat Watters in 1972 at the request of the Michigan Concertina Association for a banquet honoring Pat Watters for his lifelong efforts on behalf of the instrument.
22 Among other sources, see the article "Check makes Hall of Fame" in the *Sunday Post-Crescent*, Appleton-Neenah-Menasha (June 28, 1981).
23 Obituary produced in the newsletter, *Concertina Connection*, ed. Jeannie Enabnit (August, 2002).
24 Hengel brochures boasted many features of his product. Examples follow, quoted exactly without any editorial repairs: For the Newest in Name, Oldest in Style, and Best in Quality: It is the Hengel's Concertinas — favorite of leading concertina artists and Old time dance orchestras.

Mr. Gil Steil in Richmond, Minnesota handles the Hengel in St. Cloud, Little Falls, and Richmond, Minnesota. Inside his brochure, Hengel claims: New quadruple Concertina manufactured by Christy Hengel. I have purchased all of the equipment of the Otto Schlicht Concertina Factory in Chicago which was the oldest concertina factory in the United States. The instrument is the only concertina made today which is styled after the old concertina which has the following outstanding features which are designed to take the eyes of the customer:

1- It is the only concertina available today which has the genuine old square type Swedish Steel Concertina reeds which I have hand filed to give you the true old time concertina tone and fast response with volume. This instrument does not contain tapered accordion reeds.

2- The only concertina available today which is custom built on special order. It can be made in any key desired, such as C or A; B-flat; E-flat etc.

3- This instrument contains the old patent Duro Aluminum action patented by Otto Schlicht.

4- The weight of this instrument is only 15 pounds, and is 11 inches wide and 10 inches high.

This concertina is beautifully engraved, is rhinestone studded, and is available in either black or white pearl. The reed set is one low octave and 3 medium reeds to one key (push or pull). These reeds are all hand filed with precision care to give you the best tone quality and will last a lifetime. They will not break like a machine ground reed will. There are 12 long reed plates to the melody side and 10 long reed plates to the base side which are securely fastened with hook screws. This instrument does not contain waxed on reed plates—you will have no trouble with plates coming loose or falling out.

This instrument has a new outstanding feature which is a condensed 104 button keyboard with the old patent Duro Aluminum action. The buttons are FLAT with a blue top. It also contains the best quality soft leather on the valve covers which makes it air tight and quiet action. It has one octave switch which switches from low to high.

The bellow is made of heavy fiber paper which has lasting strength and the corner folds are made of heavy kid skin leather. To add brilliance to the instrument, the bellow is lined with a beautiful bright shiny green sturdy paper material and the bellow edges are protected with extra large corners and staves which are stainless steel with wood lining which will not rust or tarnish your clothes. This instrument does not contain any nickel finish. The carrying case is black with a rich blue plush lining and sturdy locks.

The masterpiece of the Concertinas — the old type Pateks and Pearl Queens — Custom built on special order. The same dies used to produce the masterpiece in the 1930s are still being used in producing the Hengels in the 1970s.

In his picture of the old Pateks, Hengel shows a "De Luxe" name on the box. Hengel's Concertinas Manufacturing and Sales (Finest Concertinas Available) 403 North Minnesota St. New Ulm, Minnesota 56073 Tel: 354-6525. What are the Hengel's Concertinas? It's a concertina being started back in the 1920s with Mr. Otto Schlicht who was the Master Builder of the World's finest concertinas.

As noted in Chapter One of this book, Hengel repeats: Early in the 1930s advertisements for the Patek concertina bear a photograph of Otto Schlicht and of R. M. Patek which calls Schlicht the American founder and pioneer of the concertina industry, the Master Builder of the World's Finest Concertinas. Checking the fine print we discover that all who have tried to copy Schlicht-built concertinas have been unsuccessful because "there is far more to a concertina than the materials that go into it. It's that mysterious, indefinite ingredient known as CHARACTER." It is the never-ending "attention to the tiniest details, secrets of tones and tone shading, a love for this instrument by OTTO SCHLICHT and his staff of craftsmen. . . all these make up a Patek concertina and give it that something that may be imitated but never reproduced." The advertisement goes on to state that "today each Patek instrument is built under Schlicht's personal direction. Every craftsman engaged in the building of a PATEK concertina has served many years of apprenticeship under Otto Schlicht and no doubt explains why a PATEK concertina is the proud possession of its owner, and wonderful thrill to those who listen to it." Continuing, the claim ends "THERE IS NO SUBSTITUTE for a PATEK Concertina because there is no one else in America who has devoted himself so completely, so wholeheartedly, toward the perfection of this instrument as has Otto Schlicht, who directs the building of every Patek Concertina."

Hengel shows pictures of both Schlicht and Patek. Mr. R. M. Patek, our President, an Inspiration to Beginners and a Friend to Hundreds of Concertina Artists. Hengel then reports: I began doing experimental work on the concertinas in 1943 and in 1953 I purchased all of the equipment and dies from the Otto Schlicht Concertina Factory in Chicago and moved this equipment to Minnesota. It was in 1955 that the first concertina with the Hengel name was put on the market. Even today, the same thing is true — there is far more to a concertina than the materials and parts that go into it. Attempts are being made to duplicate and copy the Hengel concertina, but without the very special dies and this very special love for the instrument and that very mysterious ingredient known as character (the patience for the never ending attention to every tiny little detail, the secrets of tones and tone shading), it will never be reproduced. It may be "artificially imitated." Every Hengel concertina receives my own personal workmanship and is guaranteed to give you supreme satisfaction and many many years of pleasure.

25 See in general the five-volume series, *American Musical Traditions*, especially Vol. 4 "European American Music," ed. by Jeff Todd Titon and Bob Carlin (New York: Gale Group / Shirmer Reference, 2002), pp. 49 ff., with articles by LaVern Rippley, Richard March, Philip Nusbaum, James P. Leary, and others.

26 *La Crosse Tribune*, Sunday May 11, 2003.

27 *Entertainment Bits* (August-September, 1989), front page. Instrumental in nominating and presenting the case for Hengel were Philip Nusbaum of the Minnesota Arts Board and LaVern Rippley of St. Olaf College. Numerous articles in the New Ulm *Review-Journal* e. g. March 5, 1967 and frequently thereafter, as well as the *Free Press* of Mankato, e. g. October 1, 1981, feature various aspects of the Hengel story.

28 Reported by Bren McDowel of the *Olivia Times Journal* and reprinted in *EB* (August-September, 1990), p. 8.

29 Quoted in various papers, including *Entertainment Bits* (December-January, 1990), p. 7.

4

The Concertina Arrives in New Prague: The Jerry Minar Story

A tried and true maxim for the transmission of folklore holds that women, especially mothers and grandmothers, are the primary bearers and conveyors of the art and substance. Nor could this be more apt than in the case of Jerry Minar, born Jaroslav James Minars [*minosh*] on March 22, 1944 in the since-replaced hospital in New Prague, Minnesota. [During his grade school years, at the time when the boy switched from speaking Czech to English, the name was Americanized to "Jerry" Minar.] For indeed it was his mother, Lorraine (Tupy) Minar, who first encouraged the seven-year-old Jerry to take piano accordion lessons, and started him out on a 120 bass accordion. Because she died when Jerry was only 16, she never enjoyed her son as a concertina player, but only as a budding master of the accordion.

A young pupil at St. Wenceslaus Catholic grade school in New Prague, Minnesota, Minar studied first with Sister Imata who saw to it that he gradually phased upward to the 120-bass Titano, a student accordion commonly used for instruction in the early 1950s. The owner of Terlinde Music Store in Minneapolis, Edward Terlinde, from whom the eight-year-old Minar had purchased the Titano, was astonished that Jerry could play by ear the then popular song of the day, "How Much is that Doggie in the Window." Five years later the adolescent Minar advanced to a more professional accordion, this time a 120 bass Hohner. Not to be outdistanced by his wife, the Senior Jaroslav (Jerry) F. Minar, his father, became equally supportive of young Jerry by purchasing the first accordions and later also Minar's first and second concertinas. However, at least in part, the instruments were intended as payment for the youth's contribution to farm work.[1] Some 25 years later, farm income allowed Jerry Minar to build his music business while providing for his growing family. Arriving from Novosedly south of the capital city of Prague in Bohemia during its Austro-Hungarian days as crown colony, the Minars' ancestors reached their Minnesota destination in 1860. Soon they purchased a homestead in Section 13 of Lanesburg Township four miles southeast of New Prague—four miles west of Veseli. In 1872 they relocated slightly, thus owning land in both Sections 11 and 13, land which continues in the family to the present.[2]

When the nun, Sister Imata, doffed her habit following the Second Vatican Council in the 1960s, she became Sister Helen Laura. Wanting to entertain friends

Jerry (Jaroslav) Minar playing the piano accordion around 1953 at the age of perhaps eight or nine. It was his first 120 bass bellow instrument, an Italian creation, built about 1950. This model was commonly used by young learners and, in general, for instruction on how to play the accordion.

A 1962 ad from the New Prague Times offering concertina lessons by Jerry Minar and the United Music Teachers of Hutchinson, Minnesota.

in December, 1976, she asked Minar if she could borrow a 12-bass accordion to play for her guests. Honored and heartfelt by the request, Minar bequeathed to her his original 12-base accordion as a Christmas present— in gratitude for having started him on a trail of bellow instruments.

During his youthful 1950s Minar won various talent contests, some in the local 4-H program, and some in larger venues such as the Minnesota State Fair. By 1959, during his junior year in high school, Minar started giving lessons to younger learners. Soon United Music Company in Hutchinson needed help to offer lessons in the New Prague area and Minar stood at the ready. Teaching in the New Prague City Hall, he was dispatched also to the neighboring towns of St. Peter, Le Center, Le Sueur and Kasota, all down river from Mankato. Under this arrangement, Minar tutored around 35-40 students each week, using a group lesson approach, having 6-8 individuals in each. United Music sold their parents packages that included eight lessons and an instruction book. When the lessons were completed, the youthful protegés could purchase an accordion and continue or they could simply drop out, comforted that they had tried.

The Minar farmstead southeast of New Prague, a bit west of Veseli, as it stands today. Here the first of the immigrant Minar family members settled on section 11 following arrival in 1860 from the region south of Prague. The site pictured above was acquired in 1872 and lies in section 13. Young Jerry's mechanical aptitude started to bud as he was constantly disassembling farm motors, various equipment including an old abandoned threshing machine to figure out what makes them tick. Jerry Minar's music career began in this 1895 farmhouse. His first concertina shop was in an upstairs bedroom. Minar's first concertina lessons were given in this house.

The Concertina Arrives in New Prague: The Jerry Minar Story

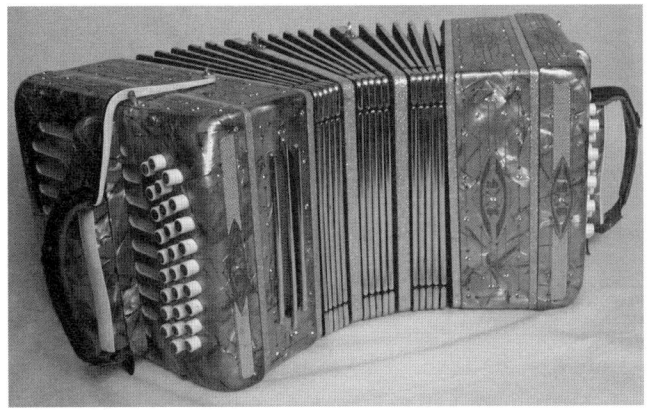

This gray double concertina was built by the Arno Arnold family originally of Carlsfeld near Chemnitz. This third generation builder escaped East Germany following World War II and settled near Frankfurt, West Germany, where he built a large number of concertinas. This concertina bears the registration number D6571 and was completed on December 13, 1960. Acquired in 1962, it was Jerry Minar's first concertina.

The typical nameplate on an Arno Arnold Concertina frequently bears the subheading, "Marca Registrada" signaling that this is an instrument patented in Italy, and using Hohner accordian reeds.

Workers, presumably including Arno Arnold himself, in the family factory at Obertshausen (Kreis Offenbach) near Frankfurt.

In the fall of 1962, the Hutchinson-based United Music Company initiated a plan to offer concertina music lessons under the direction of Leonard Krulikoski, then using the title "Director of United Music Teachers" for the teaching aspect of their operation.[3] A dealer for the Star concertina, Krulikoski functioned from a shop at 946 Osgood Avenue S.W. in Hutchinson, Minnesota. Some of the promotion used to enhance the relevance and popularity of the concertina involved the impetus the concertina was receiving in the hands of skilled and popular old time dance bands. Among them were such well known orchestras as Whoopee John Wilfahrt, the Six Fat Dutchmen with Christy Hengel, the Babe Wagner Band with Don Klossner, the Elmer Scheid Band with Elmer himself fingering the concertina, Norm Wilke and the Little Fishermen, Ernie Coopmann—who played first for the Little Fishermen but later performed with his own band called Ernie Coopmann and the Jolly Brewers, the Jolly Swiss Boys with Syl Liebl, Lester Schuft's Country Dutchmen with Marv Nissel, John Check and the Wisconsin Dutchmen, and others. There were also other great concertinists to be admired, the likes of Johnny Gag, Jerry Schuft, Cliff Mathiowetz, the Wendinger brothers, Emil Milbrath, Lowell Schubert, Marvin Moravec, Roman Rezac, Dorine the Polka Princess, Larry Dorschner, Ray Konkol, Jerry Schmidt, Johnny Helget, Mildred Kamenski, Ray Arent, George Hrica and many more.

Fascinated by the skill and competence these concertina artists exhibited, Minar found his paragons, at which time his father supplied him with a full course and a double-reed gray Arno Arnold "C" concertina, still in Minar's possession. With Leonard Krulikoski supplying

Jerry Minar at the age of 18. The concertina on the left is a "new style" Patek built with waxed reeds in 1962. This is one of the few instruments Patek built on his own after Otto Schlicht ceased production. It has no sound holes and has a plastic air valve.

tips, Minar diligently pursued Course One, consisting of 50 pieces and 12 scales, followed by Course Two, having 20 numbers. The goal of the first course required the student to learn about one number per week and complete the program in a year's time. Among the pieces were such standards as the Barbara Polka, Little Fisherman's Waltz, Isabella Waltz and others still heard today, performable in five key signatures, so that after one year, theoretically, the student knew enough to start his own band. Diligently practicing during the winter of 1962, the young Minar merited the United Music Company's confidence when it began sending him students after barely one month of learning on his own. However, he practiced five hours each day during the off-peak farming season.

That winter of 1962 at the age of 18, Minar traded the Arno Arnold concertina for a white quad-reed Patek "C" concertina. Leonard Krulikoski had recommended a "C" from Hengel, then at Waseca, but noted that the wait would be very long. Although he wanted to place his order, his teacher suggested he take the Patek because, after all, Minar's idols were all playing Patek instruments—Elmer Scheid, Jerry Schuft, Johnny Gag, Marvin Moravec—and, too, Krulikoski had a new Patek for sale on the shelf. Later Minar would learn from Christy Hengel why this new Patek sounded rather dull and misrepresentative—it was one with waxed reeds on individual plates rather than long plates—one of the heavy and less sophisticated instruments Rudy Patek made on his own after moving to the Weyauwega. These instruments resulted when Patek was no longer able to procure his concertinas from the Schlicht factory in Chicago. To hear this from Hengel was disappointing for Minar—but at least he now knew the difference between "Schlicht-produced" Patek concertinas and the later Patek creations. Because Jerry Schuft and Marvin Moravec were good friends, with original Pateks made by Schlicht,

Jay Minar playing the triple reed Pearl Queen owned originally by George Minar, the semi-retired New Prague photographer. It was built by the Otto Schlicht team in Chicago in 1926 with the serial number 3878. Note that years ago concertina players used lap aprons to protect against snagging their trousers. "Geo. S. Minar" is engraved into a bellow frame decoration indicating he was most likely the original owner.

Edward Terlinde specialized in amplifiers and a variety of instruments as well as accordions and concertinas. In addition, he offered instruction and sheet music.

Minar had the opportunity to compare and study the differences in the two generations of instruments and their sound.

Having bought and sold accordions during the autumn of 1962, Minar became acquainted with Edward Terlinde at his music store on Seventh Street in St. Paul. Here, from his basic training as a tool and die maker, Terlinde was retailing accordions on the main floor of his establishment. In his basement he produced microphones for the accordion and on the second floor operated his own print shop for brochures and promotional material. Minar asked Terlinde to tune his Patek to match the one owned by Jerry Schuft. A charge of $60 later, Minar came to understand that Terlinde gave him his first lesson in reed tuning: file the tip to sharpen the pitch, file the lower half to lower the pitch and rid it of excess waves. Although Ed Terlinde had died already in 1981, in April, 2005 Jerry Minar was pleased to acquire Terlinde's personal hand drill from Lloyd Peterson, a fourteen-year employee of the Terlinde Music Store.

Minar also came to realize that the quality of these Patek-tapered, waxed reeds were below the optimum. Reeds found in the early Patek instruments had all come from the hands of the Chicago Reed makers, John Kummer, John Friedl and others, including German-produced "Dix" reeds. Following the end of the Second World War, however, these Dix reeds were no longer available.

This experience brought Minar back to New Prague where he plumbed his family roots for solutions. During 1963 he visited often with his great uncle, George Minar, a semi-retired photographer in New Prague, who had played the concertina all his life. The proud owner of a triple-reed Pearl Queen made in the Schlicht factory, which Jerry Minar subsequently acquired, George Minar showed the young Jerry that a concertina could be tuned by adding small drops of paint that added weight to the reeds. This experimental technique whereby the pitch was lowered without removal of metal from the reed, evolved in due time to an application of melted solder on the reed. Minar also learned that the technique of tuning involved filing on the tip of the reed to make it lighter which would cause it to vibrate faster, thus causing the pitch to rise. Filing on the lower part of the reed makes the tip correspondingly heavier in proportion to the lower flexing part of the reed. Vibrating more slowly, it produces a lower frequency. Reeds vibrate 880 times per second, 440 times, 220 times etc., as the scale is covered. Thus, filing the reeds is a delicate operation because the reeds easily break or deteriorate from even a little bit too much rasping.

While Terlinde did improve Minar's new-style, Patek-built concertina, the older Patek models built by Otto Schlicht were considerably superior. Here the issue is the long-plate riveted, square-designed reed which began to be abandoned in the 1940s in favor of tapered waxed reeds. The latter have merit, e. g. in the musette concertina but they sound more like an accordion, which also has waxed-in reed plates. Minar also learned that there are some high quality grades of waxed reeds. Problematic though that was, Minar discovered as well that waxed reeds are featured in many excellent concertinas. But it so happened that the waxed reed Patek-built concertina had a less than optimal set of reeds. When playing the earlier Patek models owned by Marvin Moravec and Jerry Schuft, Minar came to realize that the long-plate mounting of rectangular reeds is superior in this instance to the tapered individual plates that were wax-adhered to the reed blocks. However, there are cases where the exact opposite is true, leading us to the conclusion that the many variables prove only that reed making is an inexact science. In this instance, the long plate reeds were better at rendering a rich, clear and melancholy sound. Experimenting now in the spare bedroom of the Minar farm house, young Jerry removed some reeds from a Hohner button accordion and installed them in his 1960s

Dance poster showing the Village Concertina Band with Richard Bartusek playing the tuba, Jerry Minar, Patek concertina, and Bohumil Sticha, drums.

Patek to produce a better pitch and a brighter tone. He also discovered that the technique used by George Minar to weight the reed with paint could be duplicated with solder, which was soft and responsive to the file.

Detoured from his pursuit of the concertina, Minar joined the Army Reserve in 1964 to complete his six months of active duty. To overcome the boredom of military marching, he hummed tunes he could play on the concertina. In the evenings he sometimes called home to have his sister, Anita, press out a few notes from various configurations of the concertina to perk up his spirits.

Back from military service in 1965, Minar's opportunity for professional playing dawned. Driving the tractor pulling a digger in preparation for corn planting on his father's farm one spring day, a car stopped on the roadside. Approaching the tractor, a man named Bohumil Sticha asked whether he could play the concertina. Very un-farmer-like, Minar left the tractor poised ahead of the tiller and accompanied the inquirer to the farmhouse where he auditioned for Sticha on the concertina. Because Sticha's brother Leonard was quitting the band to start his own coterie, the Village Concertina Band was left without an artist for its most critical instrument, the concertina. On his Patek, Minar played the "Musicians Come and Play" polka followed by the "Where are the Days of Youth" waltz and was hired to play the four-hour Saturday night stand at the Twilight Club on Highway 55 west of Buffalo, Minnesota. It was a three-man performance, Sticha playing the drums, Richard Bartusek the tuba and Minar the concertina. Although Leonard showed up as a backup concertina player in case Minar would falter, the precaution was needless. It was Minar's virgin accomplishment.

Since bandleader Sticha was a good friend of another New Prague concertina player, Joseph Novotny, Minar got the chance to purchase an Arno Arnold triple-reed E-Flat for $150, though it needed repair. Having played only a C concertina to this point, Minar was intrigued with the E-Flat, reworked it, tuned it and liked the sound coming from the individual plates. The instrument seemed to amount to the same reed structure as found in the Hohner button accordion—probably from the displaced Arnold factory that reopened near Frankfurt and produced these boxes during the 1950s. Held in by hook screws and leathered, the reeds were easily removed like the long-plate reed holders that detach in one piece. From these early concertinas

213 First Street S.E. Minar's concertina shop is in the one-car garage at right.

Minar was self-instructing for future endeavors producing his own concertinas.

Driven now to improve the basics of the instrument, Minar contacted his friends Marvin Moravec and Louis Kukacka of Montgomery. Moravec was the man with the beautiful Patek Deluxe concertina with Friedl reeds that Minar adored. Because Moravec had purchased this concertina from Christy Hengel in 1957, and ever since was thoroughly captivated by the instrument, there was no chance Moravec would sell it and thus Minar could never hope to own this coveted Patek Deluxe. However, Kukacka was also the owner of a black "Star" concertina with long-plate, hand-filed reeds, which Minar was able to purchase. To his great dismay, the concertina had a major malfunction due to incorrect re-tuning and reed repair of the instrument. Luckily, Minar then met Stan Uhlir, who reported that the Stan Jarosz Jewelry store on Lowry Avenue in Minneapolis had a "Star" triple-reed as well as a Silberhorn Snowbird triple-reed for sale. Although Minar purchased these two concertinas, he had trouble in his upstairs workshop at the farm re-combining them with the ill-repaired "Star" he had acquired earlier. With tedious effort, however, he did succeed. Louis Kukacka then acknowledged that he previously owned the Silberhorn Snowbird and did not like it because of its stiff bellows. Monday morning wash day prompted him to hang it on the clothes line with a brick on the lower end to stretch it— but to no avail. Thirty years later, Minar found this very Snowbird model for sale in the Twin Cities. To this Silberhorn triple-reed, Minar added some solder on the tips to produce an octave lower sound and after a time, removed the solder to return it to its original tonal quality. This instrument was sold in the early 1970s and is presently again in Minar's possession. It was Minar's first major reed undertaking.

In 1967 the house at 213 First Street Southeast in New Prague, built by Minar's grandfather in 1948, came up for sale. Jerry Minar purchased this home with its commodious 14 X 24-foot shop, remodeling it later into his music recording studio. This permitted him to move his production to the one-car attached garage, which today continues as one of his workshops. It is particularly important that a reed tuner be unequivocally separated from non-tuning human earshot. When tuning, the artist is constantly repeating the same sound, hoping to discover minute differences that can become irritating to the uninterested. Hence, from 1973 onward, the garage-workshop has proved most supportive for Minar's endeavors especially for tuning concertinas. Symbolically, the garage bespeaks another Minar avocation—old cars. To reach his concertina teaching destinations, he drove a 1956 Chevrolet V-8, double carburetor. Later he acquired a 350 horsepower 1957 Chevrolet of like capability. To Minar there was a close association between the mechanical technicalities and the performance, be it of the automobile engine or of the concertina. Both gulped huge draughts of air and each delivered in direct proportion either power or sound, as the case may be. One can have two identical V-8 engine cars, yet the power and performance of the one easily excels the other. So, too, one can have two concertinas, the one powerful and responsive, the other dull, weak and hard to play — and both may have been completed the same day by the same craftsman. Air utilization is a key factor. The high performance of the tool with reference to the air intake became Minar's deep fascination. As each old hobby car has its own personality, so too each concertina, especially because it is an individual artistic component, has its own temper and disposition which affect its output.

Back in the late 1960s, performing for the Ivan Kahle Band, Roger Kubes was playing a quadruple Patek concertina with a piccolo set of reeds. [Parenthetically it should be noted that the Ivan Kahle Band was invited and played for the first inauguration of President Clinton, going to Washington in 1993.] Jerry liked this Patek concertina and found a similar concertina offered for $350 at Terlinde Music Store in St. Paul. On a quadruple-reed concertina, this means there are 56 low-

[Jerry Minar played the concertina for the Ivan Kahle Band in the early 1970s, and the majority of Kahle's band jobs until 2002.] Here the band appears at the National Capitol where the band played at the invitation of President-elect Clinton for the January 1993 inaugural. In the band are: (L-R) Jerry Minar, who played a Wolfe concertina, accordina and piano accordion; Myron Wolf, saxophone and clarinet; Ivan Kahle, trumpet and drums; Jerry Kahle, clarinet and saxophone; and Jay Pattison, tuba.

Jay Minar, Jerry's son, works nearly full time crafting parts for the Jerry Minar production of the Hengel concertina. Jenny Minar assists with the assembly of reed blocks. Jay is using a small drill press acquired from Bill Brown when Brown Distributing of New Ulm ceased operations in 2002. In the background stands a large floor model drill press acquired from John Bernhardt when Chicago's Star Concertina went out of business in 2000.

Stan Uhlir, originally of Montgomery, then Minneapolis. Here he appears in a 1970 pose with an Echo concertina which he championed in the basement of his shop called Echo Concertina Sales, 4413 31st Avenue South, Minneapolis, Minnesota.

pitched reeds which can be switched by a thumb movement. On this particular instrument, the low-pitched system worked fine, but the upper was weak and pale sounding. Experimenting with his acquisition, Minar found that on the inside, this concertina had reeds machine-ground in Germany. Luckily, he was able to install superior hand-filed replacements from his black Star concertina which gave this particular Patek concertina better performance. When Minar played for the Ivan Kahle band in the 1970s, he traded this instrument to Bill Brown at his store in New Ulm, Minnesota.[4]

Minar's career developed on the personal side when he married Beverly Brunner on May 3, 1969, thereafter fathering five children: Tammy, Vicky, Christy, Jay and Jenny, all of whom are more or less active in music.[5] In that sense, they benefit not just from their father but from Beverly, who plays accordion, piano and renders the vocal parts on several of the Minar recordings. Most dynamic among them, however, has been his son, Jay, who not only began playing the concertina at a young age, but continues performing with two different bands. However, Tammy works as a 'merchandise coordinator for music' at the corporate headquarters of Target

developing strategy to market music. Soon Beverly developed an avocation for decorating the concertinas and, as we shall see, later grew into the business relationship with Christy Hengel and his manufacture of concertinas in the Otto Schlicht tradition. Since both Beverly and Jerry had always liked pianos and since Jerry had already restored their World War I "player," which they brought into their house from the farm, Jerry also took courses to learn "ear tuning" for the piano at the MacPhail School of Music in Minneapolis, Minnesota, a skill he would presently adapt and develop for the concertina. This talent takes him above and beyond what the electronic tuning devices can deliver with their mechanical-electronic readouts. Few tuners today can actually define the term "equal temperament" and without realizing it, they use it every time they tune an instrument. It should be pointed out that prior to about 1930, tuners often made deliberate deviations from today's equal temperament tuning.

Upon joining the Ivan Kahle Band in 1970, Minar began performing at about half the bookings Kahle enjoyed. But a year later he assumed all the assign-

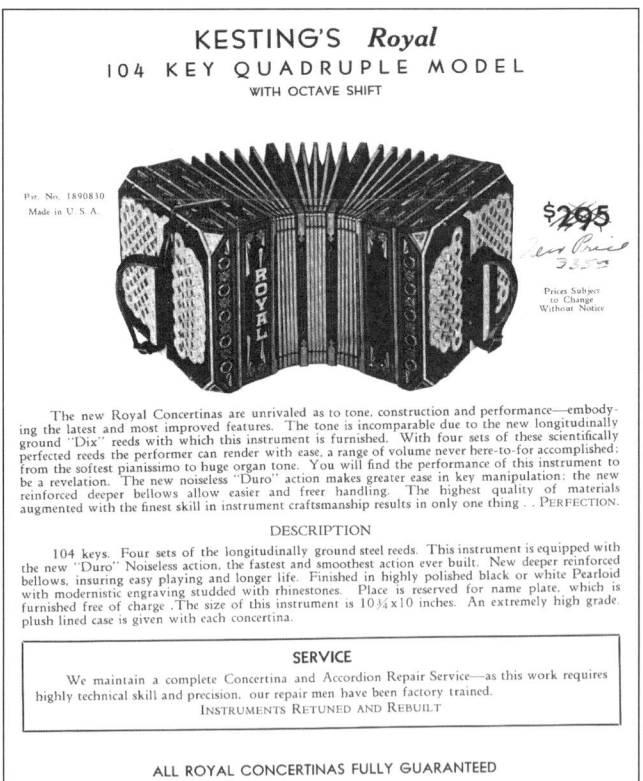

A Royal concertina sold by Kesting Music House under the proprietorship of N. K. Langsten at 32-34 East Sixth Street, St. Paul, Minnesota. Brochure from the late 1930s.

The Concertina Arrives in New Prague: The Jerry Minar Story

Don Barash playing a Royal, the seventh one built by Slim Maser around 1970 in his workshop at 1015 Sperl Street, West St. Paul, Minnesota.

John Mikla [Miklakiewicz] of Baldwin, Wisconsin, playing a New Prague-produced Hengel concertina. Below it on the left is a Royal built by Slim Maser, an instrument procured in 1987 by Mikla. Maser had acquired it from Star Manufacturing but recrafted it in his basement workshop on Sperl Street. On the right is a 1935 Royal built by Otto Schlicht and sold to Mikla by Kesting Music Store on August 2, 1962 for $195. Kesting was located at 34 East 6th Street in St. Paul. The salesman was Paul Zelenka, who grew up a half mile from the Minar farm near New Prague.

A Royal concertina "duro action," which was patented by Otto Schlicht in Chicago, here marketed by the Kesting Music store in St. Paul during the 1930s.

Receipts for John Mikla issued by Kesting Music Store.

Jerry Minar leads the Czech Area Concertina Club performing in the Rotunda of the Minnesota State Capitol in St. Paul, May 11, 2002.

ments full time using an old long-plate Star quad, a Pearl Queen and a Wisconsin-built waxed-reed Patek. These instruments had been built respectively by the International Accordion Company, the Otto Schlicht Factory in Chicago, and Rudy Patek in Wisconsin.

Playing in the band brought Minar into contact with many other concertina players, while it established him as a credible performer two and more nights each week. Among the artists whose acquaintance Minar established was Stan Uhlir, who was building the Echo concertina. Once when tuning concertinas for Uhlir, Minar came upon a white one he liked and bought it in 1971 for $700, the instrument he used for the early recordings by the Ivan Kahle Band. Delving now into the ever-expanding concertina world, Minar in late 1971 bought a Stradivarius E-Flat concertina with low octave musette from Brown's Music Store in New Ulm. To raise the necessary cash, he traded in his Star triple and the Pearl Queen quadruple. In a way, this step was contradictory because Minar had been avoiding the accordion sound. After all, he was already a fine accordion player, but as his taste for the differing sounds evolved, he became intrigued with the sound of the concertina. Thus he bought an Italian-built Stradivarius with waxed, tapered reeds—exactly what he had been fighting up to this point. However, this instrument did provide the low pitch and musette tuning, characteristic of button accordions, a sound that was gaining popularity.

The first concertina of this type resulted when Ray Dorschner persuaded Christy Hengel to build him an E-Flat "Hengel" concertina with four low octave reeds and the musette sound. Most agreed that this alternative to the "C" concertina was refreshing. With a "C" concertina, it is difficult to render flats. But with these alternatives, the concertina gained flexibility in relation to supplementary instrumentation. According to the Silberhorn newsletter, the E-Flat concertina was already making the scene in the 1930s but the "C" held strong sway, particularly in Minnesota. About 1973 Minar met Slim Maser in West St. Paul, a dealer, tuner and occasional builder of the Royal concertina. However, the name "Royal" had been used already in the 1930s for Royal concertinas sold by Kesting Music Store in St. Paul. In the 1930s, they were Otto Schlicht-built concertinas with the trade name of "Royal." As far as can be determined, there is no connection between this new Royal and the old Royal from Schlicht which was sold by the Kesting Music Store. Eventually, however, by using Swedish steel, Italian manufacturers were able to nearly duplicate the German-made originals. From this high quality steel, producers were able to fashion rectangular, non-tapered reeds which were mounted on long, one-piece aluminum plates.

The 1970s is the era when Italian reeds overtook the American concertina industry. Furnished by Negrini & Borgonovi at Via Pisacone 12 in Pavia-Stradella, Italy, these reeds were acquired by Christy Hengel and, eventually, in limited supply by Bill Brown in New Ulm. Probably through Brown, Slim Maser in St. Paul also acquired these Italian reeds and installed them in the few Royal concertinas he built. Although Minar at the time sought to acquire Negrini reeds from Hengel, the competitive spirit interfered and thus Minar satisfied himself with the Royal product constructed by Maser.[6] Now Minar could play his Royal C, his Stradivarius E-Flat, and an Echo concertina from Stan Uhlir that he retuned to B-Flat, giving Minar greater flexibility when performing with the Ivan Kahle Band. In many respects, the best mechanical action among the lot was the Royal, which generated the tone that Hengel concertinas made famous.

From 1967 to 1975, Jaroslav (Jerry) Minar worked days as a civilian employee of the army, maintaining the paperwork required of New Prague's Army Reserve unit.

Lavain Andrew "Slim" Maser (1912-1995) learned to play the concertina as a boy. He married Arena B. Zachow in 1934 and led his own band until World War II. An insurance adjuster at Great Central, he gradually shifted to repairing, tuning and then constructing concertinas until the late 1980s. His "Royal" was built in his home basement on Sperl Street in St. Paul.

But when conscription ended in 1973 and President Gerald Ford abolished the draft, the local reserve units plunged into a tail spin. In a short time, the United States volunteer, paid professional army eliminated the need for reservists as well as the civilian employees, which would have necessitated that Minar relocate. Deciding against a move, he rented a farm with his father, devoting his summers to cash cropping, his winters to music. In addition to giving lessons in his basement facilities, Minar became a retail salesman of Stradivarius concertinas purchased wholesale through the Bill Brown Music Store in New Ulm. During this time frame Minar also placed advertisements in organs like *Entertainment Bits* for "Concertinas, new and used rentals, lessons, music, amps tuning, repairing, trading, new and used button and piano accordions." On occasion he also sponsored a concertina party, e. g., Sunday November 27, 1977 at the New Prague Park Ballroom, free admission.[7] Full vertical advertisements for JBM Sound appeared in the 1980s, offering two, four and eight track recording plus album packages and lists of satisfied customers.[8]

Of course his efforts as a tuner, repairman, and dance player of the concertina continued. Wanting to upgrade what he considered an instrument with room for improvement, Minar began tinkering with his 1971-acquired Stradivarius until he achieved what he thought was an "American-made" concertina sound. In due time, experimenting during performances with the Ivan Kahle dance orchestra, Minar gradually altered his C-Stradivarius long-plate concertina to his own preference. He then colluded with Brown to build a "Stradivarius Deluxe," abandoning the waxed reed concept in favor of long-plate reeds with the result that this concertina rivaled American concertinas coming to market with trade names like Star, Hengel, Echo and others.

Teaching as many as 40 students three nights each week and Saturdays, Minar next became interested in recording for radio advertising and preservation. Using his newly acquired four-track machine, he was able to separate the output of the drum, piano, tuba and concertina, for example, then blend his students' renditions to formulate a simulated dance band. Soon this crafty method of "multi-track recording" motivated his students because they were able to listen to three tracks while adding their own art to generate "whole-band" performances. Having his own 15-minute radio program to advertise concertinas for sale, Minar also interjected generous renditions of his student performers, which greatly inspired parents and relatives of the youthful learners.

Intrigued now with his cybernetic capabilities, Minar expanded to recording dance bands to whom he had sold a concertina and also playing them on his radio program. In turn, this generated recording interests from widely-scattered professionals. One day, Mankato-based Ernie Coopman with the Jolly Brewers, playing both a C and a B-Flat Hengel concertina, expressed an interest in a Minar-modified Stradivarius. Enthusiastic with the hearty sound and the robust rendition of this instrument, Coopman arranged a three-piece band called the "Stagemen" who in March, 1979 released their "Good Luck Album," the first public release for Minar and the first recording for Coopman in 15 years. At this time the eight-track tape was popular, the long play discs were standard products, 45 rpms were still in Juke boxes, and the small cassette was just emerging. In order to meet the deadline for the spring Polka Fest in the Gibbon Ballroom, Jerry and Beverly drove to Dallas, Texas to retrieve their mass-produced creation of LPs, eight-tracks, cassettes and 45s. Achieving a hit at the Gibbon festival, the Minar studio was born![9] Concertina bands liked the familiarity of a "concertina man" studio. Working from his home, Minar could offer a competitive price and thus the fledgling recording studio burst on the scene. From the initial four tracks, he jumped to eight, which sufficed for many years, then, in the late 1980s, upgraded to 16-track production.

Because bands were becoming more sophisticated and increasingly discriminating, Minar now needed to

Jerry and Bev Minar in the basement studio of the Minar home in New Prague. This was the beginning of JBM Recording Studio in 1979. The picture depicts the first recording by JBM, a production by the Ernie Coopman Band. In the photo Bev holds four recording mediums: 33 & 45 RPM, 8-track and tape cassette.

expand by acquiring another 16 tracks plus digital technology, which could be locked together for 30 usable tracks if needed. This meant he did not have to combine instrumentation, for example, a trumpet and a vocal, on one sound track.[10] With innovations stabilizing in 1994, Minar formed his own corporation, JBM Sound, Inc. Assisted by engineer Glenn Wondra, a concertina player in his own right, JBM Sound from 1979 to the present has produced about 400 separate recordings. Crucial to the operation is Minar's son, Jay, who assists in the studio but also plays the piano as a guest performer for some bands, most of which are four- and five-piece units because the ten-piece orchestras cannot be easily accommodated in JBM's physical facility. Furthermore, rather than expanding his studio specialization, Minar plans to concentrate on the manufacture of concertinas.

An interlude opportunity of the mid-1980s occurred when Minar teamed with the accordion player and cameraman Roger Paser with whom he produced videos as compared to just recording tape cassettes. A sound system was needed for such an endeavor which JBM could provide, enhancing and amplifying greatly the volume acceptance of the video camera on its own. Seemingly the world was abandoning simple sound in favor of videos with studio sound, a trend the twosome correctly perceived in its infancy. However, after producing some 20 well received video productions the reality of cost and potential sales soon brought this endeavor to its conclusion. Whereas dance bands could carry small cassette tapes [and later CDs] with them for on-site sales, retailing maybe 1,000 copies of each recording, the reality was that the video would cost at least twice the price, with the result that neither the dance band nor the sound studio could hope to recover production costs. Video work evolved with much 'on location' filming and considerable video editing to create "action-packed" videos. It was however, an interesting and enjoyable venture for both entrepreneurs.

Another of Minar's introductions into the concertina fabricating arena came in 1975 when he met Anton Wolfe of Stevens Point, Wisconsin. Wolfe had arrived to display his concertinas at the Corner Bar in New Prague. At the time, however, Minar's only interest was to acquire reeds for replacement in concertinas Minar was

A TRIBUTE TO R.M. PATEK

Mr. R.M. Patek was a leader in the concertina field. A Patek Concertina is still the concertina others are compared and measured by.

Mr. Patek believed a better concertina could be made in America and has proven it. His constant aim was to make it better.

Hundreds of Patek Concertina owners treasure their instruments. Patek Concertinas command a top resale value wherever concertinas are sold.

I have met many persons that remember Rudy for something he has done for them. He has helped many in the concertina field as well as players without asking or expecting reward.

To me he has been helpful in many ways. He has given me advice and encouragement.

Mr. and Mrs. Patek are retired now and I am sure that their many friends join me in wishing them a long and happy retirement.

WELL DONE MR. R.M. PATEK.

ANSWER TO A QUESTION

Many friends and acquaintances have asked, "Why did you go into making concertinas?" Jokingly I say, "I was a dumb fool". But this is not the reason. I like good music. The concertina makes beautiful music. I remember as a youngster the concertina orchestras of Joe Fisher and "Whoopee" John Wilfahrt. It was at this time that I got what I call the "Concertina Disease". The concertina to me is what the harp was to David.

World War II brought a disruption in concertina manufacturing and a post war rebuilding. With the center shifting from Germany to Italy.

This was, in my opinion unfortunate, for it brought about the piano accordionisation of the concertina. This is not to knock the piano accordion. Each has its merits and supporters. It is wrong to make one in the image of the other, a poor substitute.

These concertinas are very much lacking in the true concertina tone. To bring back this true concertina tone was the reason I entered the field.

In 1967 I purchased part of Patek's concertina equipment and stocks, and have added more of my own. Most notable, reed making equipment. I have made all of my own dies, punches and broaches to make reed plates, and dies and cutters to make reeds. Plus many other items.

A few of the things I make and do; Reeds, reed plates, tuning, reed blocks, action boards, action support rails, valves, frames, celluloiding, engraving, bellows (fold my own), hand rails, hand straps and much more. Plus doing the complete assembly of the concertina.

WOLFE concertinas are truly hand crafted. Every new concertina has my own personal warranty.

ANTON WOLFE
2157 Jefferson Street
Stevens Point, Wis. 54481

Jerry J. Minar
Concertina Sales & Service
213 First Street S.E.
New Prague, Minn. 56071
Telephone: 612-758-4797

On the back of his brochures, Anton Wolfe tells of his relationship with Rudy Patek, one of the greatest Chicago concertina promoters and salesmen of the Chicago era. In turn, Wolfe claims to build strongly on the Rudy Patek tradition.

repairing. Punched reed blanks or reed tongues made of Swedish steel on an aluminum plate were scarce—the only other source in the United States being Christy Hengel in New Ulm. Wolfe gladly accommodated Minar, which led to his being the exclusive dealer for Wolfe concertinas. The new relationship was a positive experience because, up to this juncture, Wolfe had been creating his instrument on the basis of materials he acquired from Rudy Patek in 1967—the concertina Minar was attempting to modify when he became a tuner and repairman during the same years. These were the products Patek had engineered on his own long after he could no longer order his concertinas built by the Otto Schlicht factory in Chicago, using pre-World War II reeds from Chemnitz, Germany. Because the Schlicht remainder supplies had been acquired by Christy Hengel in 1953, Patek had struck out on his own from his new home base in Weyauwega near Stevens Point, Wisconsin.

Having grown up on a farm at Moquah near Ashland, Wisconsin, where he first played concertinas for local parties, Wolfe was experiencing the same dearth of reeds Patek had encountered— which prompted him to create his own, using the square-reed, long-plate design instead of the tapered, waxed reeds. He sold the farm and moved to Stevens Point, where he acquired a former grocery store to house his enterprise. With newly inspired initiative, Wolfe then used his own dies, punches and broaches to make reed plates and

The Anton Wolfe concertina shop in Stevens Point was moved to this converted neighborhood grocery store at 2325 Ellis Street.

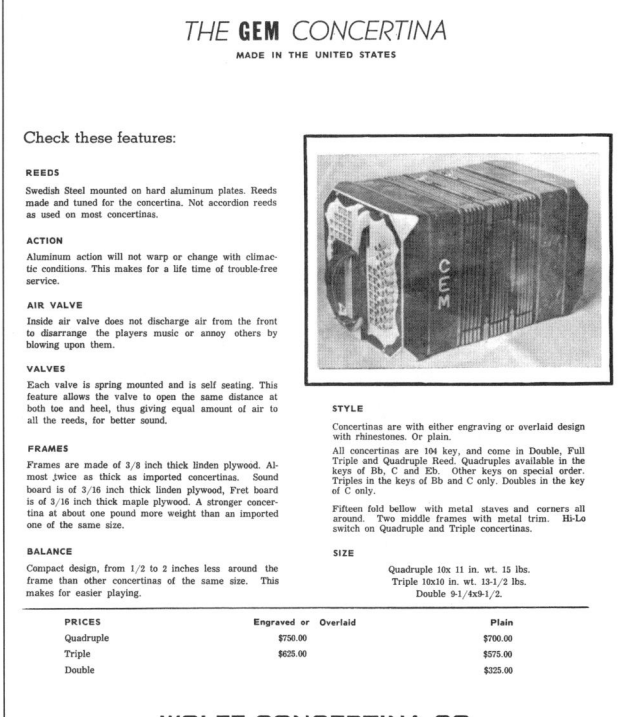

Anton Wolfe published brochures in which he described his "Gem" concertina, this one coming from his Moquah, Wisconsin residence before his move to Stevens Point. In 1967 Wolfe acquired Rudy Patek's stock; the "Gem" in the photo closely resembles the "new style" Patek concertinas.

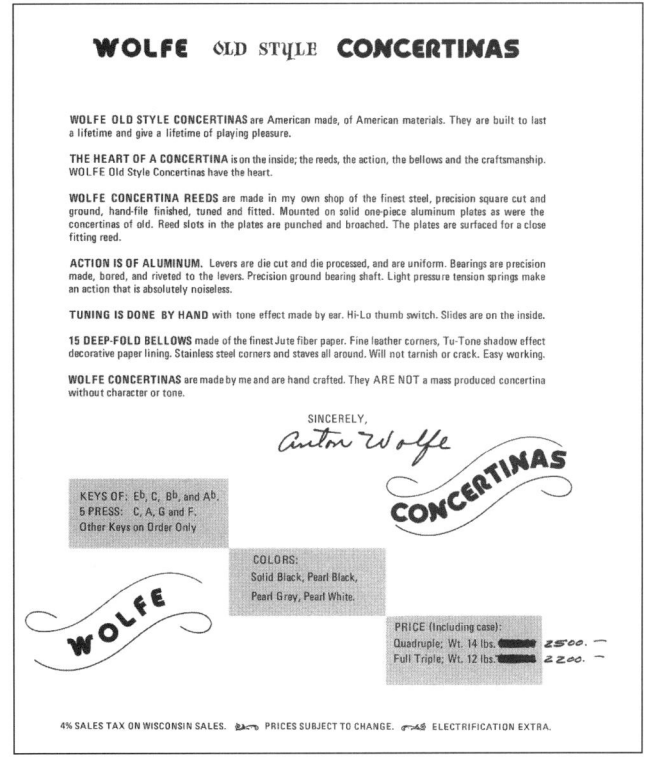

Wolfe advertised his concertinas as being "Old Style" but entirely American-made and of American materials.

Jerry Minar poses with Anton Wolfe near the entry to Wolfe's garage. Although he began work at 2157 Jefferson Street in Stevens Point, Wisconsin, he later moved to the grocery store on Ellis Street.

reeds, so to speak, fabricating his own inventory. Building on the base of the Patek earlier models that exhibited the skill, inventory and reputation of Otto Schlicht and his team, Wolfe honed his own artistic talent to create reeds.[11] Using Swedish blue, also called musical steel, Wolfe struggled to set his reeds on aluminum plates. But always it was Minar who knew how to refine the reed configuration to the exact tolerances for near perfect sound. Wolfe concertinas, as well as the early ones by the same craftsman, but bearing the name Gem and the last ones called Anton Wolfe, owe their artistic sound to the tuning expertise of Minar.

At first, Wolfe did his own engraving but his particular craftsmanship was insufficient for sophisticated works of art. Strictly a do-it-yourself person, Wolfe insisted on creating everything from the bellows to the buttons, from the straps to the corners in his own shop. Eventually, however, he let himself be persuaded to have Richard Turlikowski, the highway patrolman in La Crosse, Wisconsin, do his engraving, a move which significantly enhanced sales. Over the years 1985-90, the Wolfe concertina sold well, though many were less desired in the marketplace than the Hengel products. In an attempt to distinguish the Wolfe concertina, Minar called the instruments the "Anton Wolfe" concertina. His objective was to eliminate confusion with the St. Cloud-based Wolf family, who were also pursuing the concertina business.

During the concertina-making years of Anton Wolfe from 1967-1994, approximately 90 concertinas came to fruition. Of these, the great majority were quadruple reed models, although a few were double and triple reed creations. In essence exact copies of the waxed reed Patek versions built by Patek between 1957-1966, the early Wolfe concertinas emerged essentially from the shop and inventory he acquired from Patek in 1967. By approximately 1970, Anton Wolfe came to the realization he could deliver a better product if he switched to the model with long plate reeds, the time-tested design used by Uhlig, Lange, Schlicht and Hengel. One B-Flat Wolfe concertina bearing the serial number 439 features a complete set of reeds hand filed by Jerry Minar. Manufactured in 1985, this instrument was equipped with six extra keys (three additional buttons), and thus is an unusual 110 key variation. This adaptation allows a more complete high register note because it supplies a note which is an octave above the number four push button. Wolfe and Minar also brainstormed about the bass side in order to create bass notes that are chromatically missing on ordinary concertinas, whereas other notes are duplicated, e. g. numbers 9 and 11 bass, which have the same tone whether the bellows are pushed or pulled.

Throughout the years building concertinas, Jerry Minar and Anton Wolfe also created the "accordina" in the tradition of the German bandonica from a century earlier. It is a concertina played like a button box accordion, which was also produced by the Bill Brown Music Store in New Ulm. In a few instances, Brown modified the Stradivarius and called it the "buttontina." Minar and Wolfe created a half dozen of these cross-

An "Accordina" has the keyboard as a button box accordion. On the bass side it has one half the buttons, 13 in all compared to 24 on the concertina. The accordina opens three valves per button on the bass side. The treble side plays like a three row button accordion. The air lever is on the bass (left hand) side. It is designed for the button box player to get a concertina sound. This is #3 of 5 accordinas built by Wolfe-Minar (#5 was built but never finished or sold).

The Concertina Arrives in New Prague: The Jerry Minar Story

Jerry Minar crafting Hengel concertinas in his shop at New Prague in the first years of the 21st century.

Bill Hlavac crafting the wooden framework on which he mounts the bellows for the new Hengel concertina, here seen in his cabinet shop south of Montgomery, Minnesota, March 21, 2003.

Above, Christy Hengel and Jerry Minar pause at the Hengel shop in the manufacture of bellow staves. Behind them in view is the drill press. Below, Christy Hengel and Jerry's son, Jay Minar, stand in front of the drill press and kick press (foot-pedal cutting press), both acquired from the Otto Schlicht factory that operated on May Street in Chicago, now in possession of Jerry Minar. February, 2005.

bred instruments, a squeeze box something like a button Hohner accordion but with a concertina sound and appearance.

By 1994, however, Wolfe grew tired of life in Wisconsin and moved to Arkansas, where a short time thereafter, he died. Minar in the meantime grew interested in working with Hengel and, as a first step, decorated Hengel concertinas with the equipment purchased from Richard Turlikowski. But before making this gesture, Minar contacted Ambrose Kodet, an experienced engraver and concertina teacher for Christy Hengel during the 1970s. Together with Kodet, Minar and the team motored to Onalaska, Wisconsin, where the deal was consummated. Turlikowski had a broad background engraving for various trademarks— Star, Wolfe, Echo (begun by Uhlir but now built by Robert Novak), Hengel, Eagle (a Star off-shoot built by Richard Raclawski), Galaxy (built by Alois L. Wydra) and lesser brands—truly a well established artist.

At this juncture, Minar was still in competition with Hengel, but acquiring the engraving business drove the two into each other's embrace. Meanwhile, Minar had come to know and admire the Hengel box because he tuned them for many fine musicians — Karl Hartwich, Brian Brueggen, Dale Dahmen, Dale Pexa, Syl Liebl and others. Likewise, in his recording studio, Minar had "engineered" the output of more Hengel concertinas than any other recording virtuoso. Indeed, over 90% of all Hengel-produced instruments in the hands of band leaders, at one time or another, had sounded off in the Minar studios. Admiration had been running on separate pathways until Hengel responded positively to the excellent restoration of some old magnesium engravings so that the Hengel-preferred "pineapple" style of Mike Alex could now be reproduced by the new Minar-Kodet team.

William "Bill" Hlavac's craftsmanship is critical because of his talent to create out of wood. Able to shape and whittle the finest from the strongest and the lightest wood products, Hlavac not only gives birth to the end units he sculpts from wood, but can construct, at a customer's request, simple unadorned wooden end boxes that have classic artistic appeal, e. g. the rosewood frame concertina used by the master player, Karl Hartwich of Trempealeau, Wisconsin and a rosewood/zebrawood frame concertina for young and talented Jon Dietz of Montgomery, Minnesota. But to finish the Hengel-Minar sequence, in February, 1995, Minar broached to Hengel the idea of building the Hengel concertina for, and in succession to, the long tradition Hengel had established. Although it required some 24 road trips back and forth to New Ulm, an agreement was finally struck in September, 1997, that the Minar endeavor would henceforth include production of the Hengel concertina—thus linking this particular concertina brand directly to the Otto Schlicht shop in Chicago, and by extension, all the way back to the Uhlig-Lange and Arnold manufacturing efforts in Chemnitz or Carlsfeld, Germany.

Since the recording studio of JBM Sound had, for over 20 years, been capturing the Hengel concertina sound on tape and compact disk, the Hengel instrument was for Minar not just a familiar device learned from tuning but also from full-band performance. William (Bill) Hlavac of Montgomery, Minnesota, a professional custom cabinetmaker by trade, began building the

Jerry Minar and Brian Jilek [a Czech surname pronounced "Yeelek"], a typical family name in the New Prague - Montgomery area. However, Jilek's ancestry is from the Silver Lake, Minnesota region, where Czech family names are nearly as common as in Montgomery, Lonsdale and New Prague. Today Brian lives with his family in Waconia but operates his tool and die machine shop crafting plastic injection tooling at St. Bonifacius, Minnesota. Minar and Jilek are pictured in front of a CNC (computer numeric control) machine, which is used to engrave the design onto the surfaces of Hengel concertinas.

Bill Hlavac, Jay Minar and Jerry Minar at work in the Hlavac carpentry shop at Montgomery, Minnesota, building the Hengel concertina.

Ambrose Kodet and Jerry Minar play a concertina duet — at the June 26, 2003 meeting of the North Star Concertina Club meeting in the Cottage Grove Legion Hall.

wooden concertina frames and soon also fashioning the celluloid coverings for the new Hengel concertinas. Crafting all of the wooden parts, Hlavac also assists with final assembly of the instrument.

Typical of medieval apprentices and journeymen learning from a master, Minar and accomplices listened, took notes, did some riveting of reeds, set maybe 10 or so, went home, studied their pencil-written notes, placed the balance of the 52 buttons and action plates, then returned to have the work checked, tested, and, in some cases, altered and improved, until a traditional Uhlig, Lange, Schlicht, Hengel product resulted. Often there were references to John Kummer and John Friedl, the reed masters for Otto Schlicht, about fitting the action boards, shaping the reeds, grinding them, mounting the reed blocks with screw hooks and fitting reed plates to the reed blocks. Visiting once again with Hengel, Minar requested an older structural concertina frame, which Hengel selected from his 1964 stock. This frame had been crafted in the so-called pineapple style engraving done by Michael Alex in Chicago before Alex discontinued construction. From this effort there resulted the first Minar-created B-Flat "Hengel" concertina finished on September 14, 1995. During this time frame from February 8, 1995 to September 14, 1995, Minar, with his son Jay and accompanied by Ambrose Kodet, made 24 trips to New Ulm for learning sessions with Christy Hengel.

The second one was a C concertina completed in December, 1995, for Larry Novotny of Montgomery. Third in line was the D-Flat musette for Ambrose Kodet, crafted in full by February, 1996. The fourth was another musette, a white E-Flat for Myrtle Williams, finished in January, 1997. As numbers 5, 6, and 7 reached completion, they were coming out of the shop in New Prague and less and less in need of Hengel supervision, although 28 more trips were required still for the learning process to reach its new "master's" stage of achievement.

Minar was on his way. Next followed an arrangement with Sig Manufacturing, a Montezuma, Iowa firm that cuts plywood with laser precision. Creating the right-side action board for a concertina requires 56 small holes for 28 buttons [each having a double opening] in a board 10 by 11 inches. Cutting these with precision from a mortising bit on a drill press is cumbersome. When the capability of the Montezuma process came to the attention of Minar, the Hengel-Minar duo commissioned Ambrose Kodet, a retired Mankato State University computer science professor, to supply a computer-driven laser cutter program which resulted in a goodly number of boards cut in Montezuma, Iowa.

Thus, from the studio in the basement of 213 First Street Southeast in New Prague, we find the continuation of the Otto Schlicht-Hengel concertina factory as it evolved from Chemnitz to Chicago, New Ulm and currently New Prague, Minnesota. Available also for manufacture are the shop facilities in the attached Minar garage used mostly for tuning and parts, which is amplified also by a back yard shop. Further expanding the operation is a next-door property at 209 First Street, with its basement facilities plus a four-car, garage-like tertiary site at 211 First Street. As space demands are growing, Minar has recently acquired an additional adjacent property at 207 First Street Southeast, which has a nicely arranged modern basement for collateral storage and work. In every respect, this arrangement reflects and even duplicates the arrangement used by the original Schlicht producers who clustered around Milwaukee Avenue in near north side Chicago. Supporting these Minar spaces is the cabinet shop of William Hlavac in Montgomery. Truly, south central Minnesota is the twenty-first century home of the Chemnitzer concertina.

A glance at the history of concertina construction reveals a phenomenon of life that reflects almost all of human interfacing—the rocky road of working partnerships and business relations. Way back in Germany, Uhlig and Heinrich Band cooperated, then split apart. The Arnold family took over from Zimmermann but not entirely without friction. During the early 1920s in Chicago, Otto Georgi teamed with Louis Vitak. Then they brought Joseph Elsnic into the business, shortly after which Otto Georgi left south side Chicago to open his own retail store on Milwaukee Avenue and on North California Avenue, within a dozen blocks of the Patek and Silberhorn enterprises in the Milwaukee Avenue area. During this period of time when the Vitak Elsnic team was vigorously marketing the successful Pearl Queen concertina, Otto Georgi on the north side introduced a similar concertina, but called it the Pearl King to compete with the "Queen."

In the 1940s, anecdotes abound concerning reed worker John Friedl. In one instance, reported by his grandson, John Schnittker, John Friedl was paid a visit by Rudy Patek, the concertina dealer. While Schnittker was too young to know the entire set of circumstances, the story goes that on a previous visit, Rudy Patek had been in a hurry departing the Friedl residence with his 1939 Ford and ran over Friedl's pet cat. This time around, the two argued until Friedl dismissed Patek with the words, "Rudy, you are nothing but a darn crook."

Similarly in the 1960s, Larry Dorschner was constructing the new home and concertina "factory" for Christy Hengel. What brought tempers to a boil is unclear, but the fallout was blatant. Early on, Dorschner was already a fine concertinist and gifted musician, which probably led to his getting the contract to build the Hengel house. Dorschner also purchased two of the earlier Hengel concertinas. When the disagreement arose, Dorschner not only ceased his relationship with the master builder, but sold both his Hengels and went to work for Hengel's competitor, the Brown Music Store.

In the 1980s, concertina dealer and occasional builder Alois L. Wydra of Wisconsin Rapids, broke off his relationship with Star Concertina Manufacturing [International Accordion Company of Chicago] and with a few partners founded the Galaxy Concertina Manufacturing Company for which he ran advertising, "Why settle for a Star when you can have the Galaxy?" Not long after Minar took over the production of the Hengel concertina in the latter half of the 1990s, Ambrose Kodet worked in close association with him. But late in the year 2003, their working relationship soured and Kodet asked to be released from the partnership. The templates Kodet had created were not relinquished and Minar was thereby forced to find a tool and die expert, Brian Jilek, who could operate a computerized milling machine to design and produce the outer scroll work. In the process the idea of templates was eliminated. In its place a sketch is scanned on the

Advertisement for the Alois Wydra Galaxy concertina in Polka Showcase *(1992), a catalog of the Wisconsin Orchestra Leaders Association.*

basis of which a machine can be programmed to operate individually. This technology opens the opportunity for more choices and more customized, "one of a kind" engraving. With the help of wife Beverly Minar, the Minar team plans to implement and offer these new alternatives. However, Kodet and Minar remain active on the local, southern Minnesota concertina scene. Here it should be noted that in 1989 the Minnesota Music Academy presented Jerry Minar with the award for Polka concertina and button box performance.

Just as in Chemnitz, Carlsfeld, and Chicago, the Czech Area Concertina Club is a device to create enjoyment for the players, a market for the instrument, and a social basis for a community of concertina enthusiasts. In the tradition so ably tracked from the Old Country by Rudy Patek, the Bohemian American Concertina Association of Chicago, the Clarion Concertina Club of Tinley Park, Illinois and others, Minar recognized the need for a local concertina club. The initiative for such a group arose in 1995 when James Morris of New Prague wanted Jerry and his son, Jay Minar, to invite high school students to form a concertina marching band. Since the polka has a basic march beat, this music played on concertinas might entice young people to enter the concertina world.

The New Prague City Council was interested in the idea. Soon the candidates for the marching band were in the Town's Edge Restaurant practicing in anticipation of performing for the 1996 Memorial Day program at New Prague. However, that first appearance was met with drizzle and soon the negatives proved insurmountable. To play in the rain with jute board bellows was not the same as carrying brass instruments that shed water. And there was too little power. What if they procured a truck with a roof? But then it would not be a

Jerry and son Jay Minar play a duet on their Hengel concertinas at the Czech Area Concertina Club meeting in the Park Ballroom on July 8, 2003.

Jerry and Bev Minar both "playing" their Hengel concertina in Hengel's shop in New Ulm. This instrument is the Minar-produced Hengel #1, which was completed in September 1995. It took 24 trips from New Prague to New Ulm in Hengel's shop to build this concertina. This New Prague Hengel has engraving believed to be the last completed by Mike Alex in Chicago before his death in 1964. The frame was in Christy Hengel's possession for 31 years before being sold to Jerry Minar for the production of this instrument, New Prague Hengel, No. One.

Anton Wolfe, Fritz Szymkowiak and Al Wydra. Taken in New Ulm in 1976.

marching band. To walk in march step for a mile or two was fine for the young players, but since two thirds of the participants were over 50, the truck would only lend a grandpa image. Elders wanted nothing more to do with pounding the ground.

Instead, they met regularly in Minar's Town's Edge Restaurant. Soon Charlie More put out a newsletter. As president of the State Bank, James Morris funded and subsidized mailing the newsletters, which continued in support of the loosely organized club from 1997 – 2000. Soon thereafter under the leadership of Dave Czaja the club acquired formal status including regular by-laws and non-profit status. But because the restaurant closed at 8 P. M. and the club desired a later evening, they moved to City Hall, with about 35 members. When that proved unsatisfactory, the Union Hill tavern offered them meeting space, but this soon turned negative from the lack of space, the crowds, and the general competition from customers who were non-musically inclined. In order to obtain regular meeting times on the second Tuesday of every month, the next available option was the club room of the Park Ballroom in New Prague. Enjoying ample space, the desired privacy, a comfortable site for some training, a guest speaker, and plenty of open-hearted welcome gestures, the club has grown to about 200 members. Its popularity is increasing and, thanks to the efforts of Minar and others, it hosted the World Concertina Congress Hall of Fame in September 2005.

Also worthy of note in the chronicle of how the concertina has gained acceptance in the public eye is the newly devised exhibit about the history of the concertina, created in early 2004 by Jerry Minar at his Town's Edge Restaurant in New Prague. Here serious as well as

The Czech Area Concertina Club of New Prague taken in 2003
Row 1, from left to right: Mike Shaw, Marion Spetz, Carla Wolf, Jim Bartusek, Timothy Chlan, Jay Minar, Karl Heldberg, Karl Valberg, Pat Fahey, Paul Franzen, Patrick Boulay.
Row 2, from left to right: Roman Kalina, Jerry Krzmarzick, Jerry Minar, Roger Geshwill, Herbert Krenz, Verne Schlueter, Dale Pexa, Myrtle Williams, Ed Brezina, Roman Rezac, Deb Wolter, James Kramer, George Maha, George Marek.
Row 3, from left to right: Ralph Schesniak, Jo Moore, Richard Sauer, Ray Valek, Bernadine Sauer, Raymond Rannow, Eugene Pexa, Rich Holicky, Lyle Holicky, Charles More, Alvin Chlan, Don Lencowski, Dennis Wolter, Al Shimota, Dave Sibinski, Dave Czaja, Clayton Millbrett.
Row 4 and 5 combined, from left to right: Richard Spetz, Georgiana Johnson, Kevin Ruprecht, Gerald Machacek, Pat Kuntz, Bernard Machacek, Glen Tuma, Jim Woukawitz, Butch Herrmann, Charles Mathiowetz, Ron Pashina, Merlyn Jeche, Cactus Stoehr, Bill Hlavac, Leo Lentz, Rose Turek, Myrna Filipczak, John Filipczak, Glen Wondra, David Zellman, Gary Coopman, Lloyd Wysocki, Russ Dietz, George Benusa.
Row 6, from left to right: Tom Goetzinger, Sam Goetzinger, LaVern Rippley, Robert Zoubek, Charles Johnson, Alfred Kuntz, Jerome Fischer, Byron Pearson, Sidney Fredrickson, Matt Anderson, John Blakstvedt, Virgil Logelin, Ken Steltzner, Donnie Klossner, Maynard Ohm.

The Concertina Arrives in New Prague: The Jerry Minar Story

A De Luxe Wolfe built by Minar and Wolfe in 1985. Note the names of the two craftsmen mounted perpendicular to the larger DELUXE plate, serial #439. On a Wolfe concertina, the first digit indicates the size of the concertina. Hence, 4 means a quadruple reed set. The 2nd and 3rd digits tell us it is the 39th quadruple produced.

casual students of the concertina can view the instruments connecting their lineage back to Chemnitz Germany. The display follows their development from Germany to Chicago early in the 20th century. Leisurely, one can read the wall-mounted history and the captions for each instrument. Lined up in chronological order, the pieces easily lay out a visual trail that leads to a comprehensive understanding of a truly inviting, if inadequately understood, musical appliance.

In a manner of speaking, the 1834 Uhlig-Lange Chemnitzer concertina was fabricated not just in Chemnitz but also in Carlsfeld, Johann-Georgenstadt, Klingenthal and other sites literally adjacent to the border with Bohemia, today's Czech Republic. These smaller towns lie easily within 100 miles from the capital city of Prague. One hundred years later, the chief twentieth century center of Chemnitzer concertina production was on the near north side of Chicago where Otto Schlicht, John Friedl and John Kummer, among others, produced for Otto Georgi, Rudy Patek, Henry Silberhorn, Vitak-Elsnic and others. There were two centers for "making" and "forsaking [retailing]" the concertina in Chicago, 700-900 Milwaukee Avenue in the north and 4600-4900 Ashland Avenue in the south. Mainline related fabricators like those for Star and lesser known concertinas were not far removed. Today, the heartland production of the concertina is again within 100 miles of the namesake New *PRAGUE*, this time Minnesota, with primary production having shifted from New Ulm to New Prague. Even less numerous crafters like Robert Novak and his Echo in the Twin Cities and other suppliers at St.

CERTIFICATE OF REGISTRATION
PRINCIPAL REGISTER

The Mark shown in this certificate has been registered in the United States Patent and Trademark Office to the named registrant.

The records of the United States Patent and Trademark Office show that an application for registration of the Mark shown in this Certificate was filed in the Office; that the application was examined and determined to be in compliance with the requirements of the law and with the regulations prescribed by the Director of the United States Patent and Trademark Office; and that the Applicant is entitled to registration of the Mark under the Trademark Act of 1946, as Amended.

A copy of the Mark and pertinent data from the application are part of this certificate.

This registration shall remain in force for TEN (10) years, unless terminated earlier as provided by law, and subject to compliance with the provisions of Section 8 of the Trademark Act of 1946, as Amended.

Director of the United States Patent and Trademark Office

Int. Cl.: 15
Prior U.S. Cls.: 2, 21 and 36

Reg. No. 2,692,879
United States Patent and Trademark Office   Registered Mar. 4, 2003

TRADEMARK
PRINCIPAL REGISTER

HENGEL'S

JBM SOUND, INC. (MINNESOTA CORPORATION)
213 1ST ST SE
NEW PRAGUE, MN 56071

FOR: CONCERTINAS AND ACCORDIANS, IN CLASS 15 (U.S. CLS. 2, 21 AND 36).

FIRST USE 1-1-1957; IN COMMERCE 1-1-1958.

SEC. 2(F).

SER. NO. 76-396,181, FILED 4-5-2002.

ASMAT KHAN, EXAMINING ATTORNEY

Certificate of trademark for the Hengel concertina. Note that the designation Hengel's registration means that the concertina was produced by Christy Hengel in New Ulm. If the nameplate has the name Hengel, it means that the concertina was produced by Jerry Minar at New Prague, Minnesota. However there are exceptions inasmuch as Minar is also at liberty to use "Hengel's."

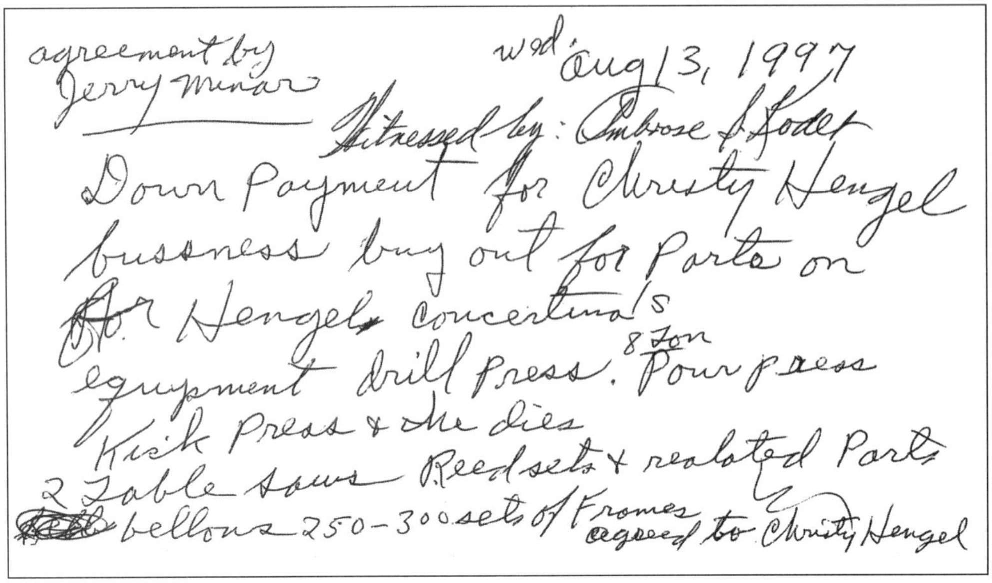

> agreement by Jerry Minar
>
> wed Aug 13, 1997
>
> Witnessed by: Ambrose J. Jodet
>
> Down Payment for Christy Hengel bussness buy out for Parts on Hengel concertina's equipment drill press. 8 Ton Pour press Kick Press & the dies 2 Table saws Reedsets + realated Parts bellows 250-300 sets of Fromes agreed to Christy Hengel

---

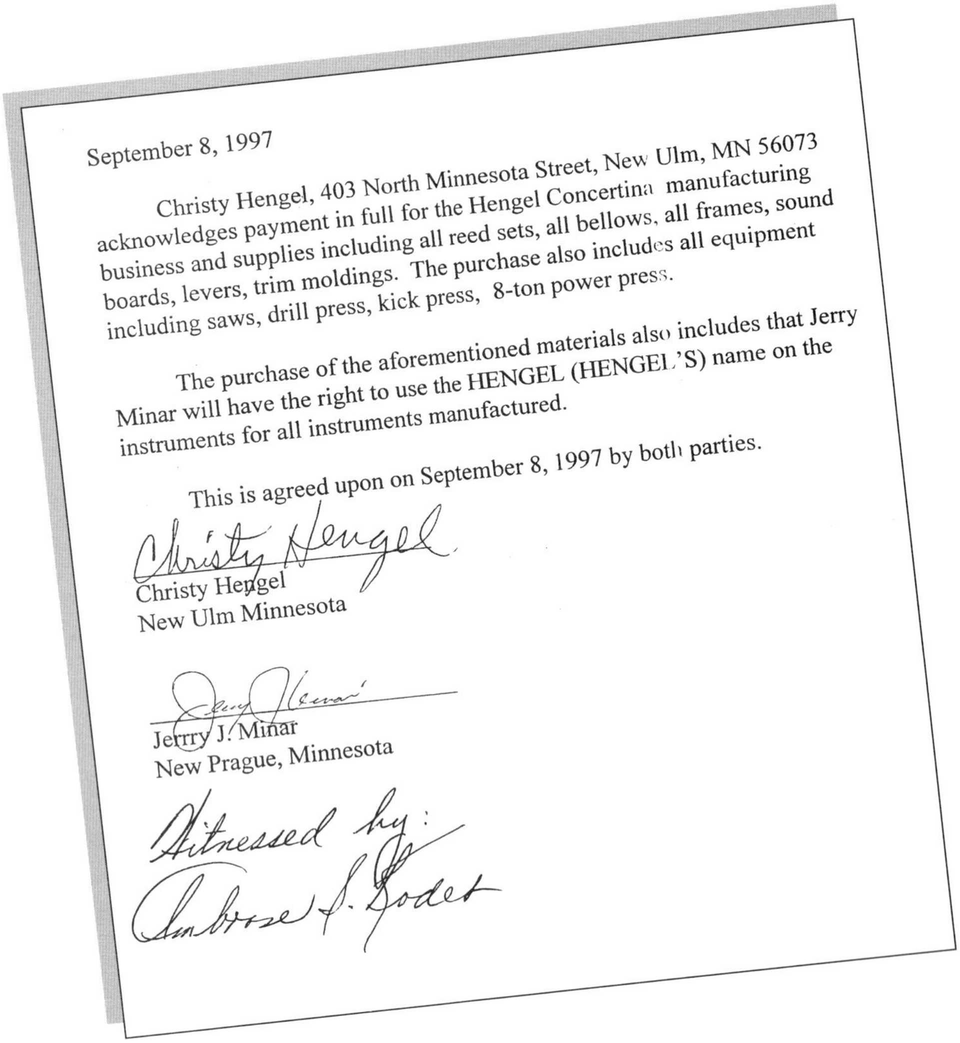

September 8, 1997

Christy Hengel, 403 North Minnesota Street, New Ulm, MN 56073 acknowledges payment in full for the Hengel Concertina manufacturing business and supplies including all reed sets, all bellows, all frames, sound boards, levers, trim moldings. The purchase also includes all equipment including saws, drill press, kick press, 8-ton power press.

The purchase of the aforementioned materials also includes that Jerry Minar will have the right to use the HENGEL (HENGEL'S) name on the instruments for all instruments manufactured.

This is agreed upon on September 8, 1997 by both parties.

Christy Hengel
Christy Hengel
New Ulm Minnesota

Jerry J. Minar
Jerry J. Minar
New Prague, Minnesota

Witnessed by:
Ambrose J. Jodet

Often in the concertina business, agreements were reached in a casual, rather than in a strictly formal, style. Illustrating the informality are the documents at left, which were at first handwritten scratched over, repaired — then slightly more rigidly formulated as seen in the document below. On p. 89 it is clear that the bills of sale were likewise handwritten and carefree. Again, when the remainder of the Henry Silberhorn musical items were transferred to Pat Watters, it was accomplished simply by a handwritten postscript to a letter, as shown on p. 156.

> Christy Name Plate June 23rd 2,000
> made about 1949 use on my 1937
> Ruedy Patek used on 6 fat Dutchman
> 1951-1952 Band
> for Jerry Minar as a souvenier
> signed by
> Christy Hengel

The nameplate from a Christy Hengel concertina, given as a souvenir to Jerry Minar on June 23, 2000.

Taken in 1986, this photo of the Dale Pexa Band of Elko, Minnesota shows the technical team and players at JBM Sound, Inc. in New Prague. First row (L-R) Jerry Minar, studio owner and recording engineer. Dale Pexa, concertina player. Second row (L-R) Roger Passer, video engineer, Christy Peters, guitar and vocals, and Bridget Wagner, drums and vocals. Third row (L-R) Glenn Wondra, editing and sound engineer, Larry Novotny, recording assistant, Fran Pexa, keyboard, saxophone, trombone, and Darcy Skluzacek, keyboard and saxophone. Nineteen years later, as this book is being written, Dale Pexa, Glenn Wondra, and Larry Novotny are involved in Helgel concertina production with Jerry Minar and JBM Sound, Inc.

In September, 1996, Jerry Minar was inducted into the "Concertina Hall of Fame." Above, then New Prague Mayor, Jerry Flicek flew to Benton Harbor, Michigan to be a part of the ceremonies.

Cloud are close at hand. Thus, the contention holds that the nineteenth century of concertina creation encompassed Prague in Bohemia, the twentieth saw a genuine boom in Chicago closely adjacent to Bohemian and Polish neighborhoods, while the twenty-first, in a manner of speaking, is back within the close radius of Prague, albeit, Minnesota.

Below is a partial list of the nostalgic equipment for concertina production acquired over the years from various builders, and now in the possession of Jerry Minar for his Hengel concertina construction.

Otto Schlicht's dies and tooling
Christy Hengel's reed making forms and power press
John Friedl's hand vise for reed making
John Kummer's reed filing jig
Rudy Patek's action spring equipment
Anton Wolfe's belt sander and tooling for action valves
Stan Uhlir's milling machine for buttons
Larry Dorschner's belt sander and reed block forms
Bill Brown's drill press
Star [John Bernhardt] four-ton power press and
   workbench where "Stars" were assembled
Don Roback's tuning table, buffer and polisher
Lavain "Slim" Maser's bellow machine and reed waxing
   device
John Bolster's number stamping set
Ed Terlinde's hand drill
Mike Grausam's (Hengel's brother-in-law) bellow
   exercising machine

Although 12 of the 15 are now deceased, at times their spirits seem to be present in various ways.

Footnotes

1 Minar dictated his life story on tape. The narrative here is a distillation of his personal report which was then verified, where possible, as to spellings, etc.
2 A brief biography of Jerry Minar appears also in *Entertainment Bits* (August-September, 1984), p. 4 with photograph.
3 Leonard and Erv Krulikoski had a dance band in the 1940s. For a time they promoted the accordion, then switched to the concertina and other instruments when its business opportunities seemed brighter. In later times, Leonard Krulikowski bought and operated the King Motel in Hutchinson and for a time also printed platbooks for purchase by county residents. Krulikoski's primary line of concertinas was the Star, although trade-ins resulted in his being a dealer for many other brands as well. He died early in the 21st century.
4 See photographs of the Ivan Kahle Band and articles about its performances in *Entertainment Bits* (October-November, 1979), p. 25. The article also details some of the activities of Jerry Minar during this period of his life.
5 The family is photographed at the Gibbon Festival in 1978. *Entertainment Bits* (October, 1978), p. 27.
6 Some 25 years later, however, Hengel shared his many secrets and helped Minar become an established "Hengel" concertina builder, as will be detailed later in this chapter.
7 *Entertainment Bits* (September, 1977), p. 9.
8 EB (August-September, 1980), p. 31.
9 His new studio is featured at length in *Entertainment Bits* (December-January, 1980), p. 32.
10 See his expansive advertisements and photograph in his New Prague shop, ibid., (February-March, 1980), p. 13.
11 See his photograph with handcrafted parts of his concertina ibid., (April-May, 1983), p. 15.

5
Promotion and Midwest Distribution of the Chemnitzer Concertina

Although in previous chapters we have seen the likes of Silberhorn, Patek, Wilfahrt, Brown, Georgi, Watters, Hengel and others promoting the Chemnitzer concertina, in this chapter the various newsletters, promotional posters and individual devices employed to popularize the instrument take center stage. Neither of the big-band performers during the 1930s-1960s nor the large dance hall operators could have made it to the top of the concertina world without an assist from radio, newspaper bookings, poster promotion, and mass audience appeal. They also depended on mailings, dance periodicals and the communication networks they created, especially in the rural, small towns of the upper Midwest. Sometimes the newsletter brought results. To be sure, advertising was important, but such devices as the concertina club composed of fans and amateur players also helped popularize the concertina. At other times, such mechanisms as the World Concertina Congress Hall of Fame generated the honorary award needed to impel mastery of this difficult, but rewarding, musical device. Honors motivate—both as pertains to the performing artist and to the public listener.

Of key importance to the concertina's early growth in the Midwest was the "Concertina Players Magazine," which first appeared in November, 1927 from the desk of Henry and Carl Silberhorn, publishers and editors, at 516 Milwaukee Avenue in Chicago. In it the chief spokesman for the concertina, Henry Silberhorn, called the concertina the "world's most complete instrument." Constructing his supportive argument, Silberhorn grants that the violin is the world's nearest perfect instrument, but it has to be accompanied by a piano. True, the

According to the 1904 Chicago Directory, Silberhorn operated at 1130 Lincoln Avenue, presumably a typographical error since he clearly exhibits 1120 in the photo. According to the 1909 Directory, he was operating at 1916 Halsted. Both are important Chicago streets today. Photo from Trina Silberhorn Dalton, Riverside, California.

piano itself, as well as the organ, are rather complete for solo performances, but these two instruments cannot be carried from place to place and are forbiddingly expensive. Wind and string instruments are ineffective without accompaniment. Thus, there could be no comparison to the concertina, not even to the accordion [which surely could also stand and play alone without accompaniment]. Silberhorn, as dealer and sole promoter of the "Clarion" concertina, was bent on raising the bid for the importance of concertinas in general. Surely there is a link between the fact that Silberhorn's first Clarion was built in 1927, the same year he initiated the newsletter and the same year he published a special edition of his instruction book.

In this first issue of his "Concertina Players Magazine," editor Silberhorn laid out a comprehensive platform, which was to unite concertina players into one big family. He wanted to make the concertina more popular, to improve its instructional methodology and to help "each player become an expert." Pictured handsomely on page two, Henry Silberhorn argues that the concertina is an organ on your lap, close to your eyes and ears, convenient to your hands, comfortable to handle—an easy means to home entertainment and, in his view, "easy to play." It was thought complete also because the musician can render the melody and bass, suitable for unaccompanied performances. "When going on a picnic or perhaps a vacation it can be transported easily and always affords a great deal of pleasure." Silberhorn argues further that unlike the average instrument, the concertina is complete because it has the melody and the bass accompaniment in one device.

Convinced he could attract the up-to-date musician, he chimed: "If you drop your concertina, you drop behind the times."

Silberhorn pleaded that the concertina compelled the player to retain eye contact with the audience. For those who play the accordion, he insisted, the player's eyes drift downward to the keyboard, because the fingers have not memorized the set of buttons and can sequentially strike the keys only with eye coordination. With the concertina, the hands were pointed forward. Fingers manipulate the key stubs from memory—like a typewriter—eyes and face forward, at best in contact with the listeners. In cases of necessity, the eye can be focused on the music stand, yet periodically connect with the audience. Always, Silberhorn boasted his perfect arrangements, "easy to read, easy to play." To be sure, his phrases led easily to the

The Henry Silberhorn journal began in November, 1927, as yet unnamed. Note that he invites his readers to invent a title.

advertisement for his "Sixth Improved Edition" of his own *Instructor for the Concertina*, available from his office for $1.25 on the cover of which was touted, "To learn to Play the Concertina without having Previous Knowledge of Music."[1] In this first issue of his newsletter, Silberhorn already mentions the popular concertina bands of that era, among them the Mitross Family Orchestra of Chicago, the Charles E. Scherzer group of Saginaw, Michigan, and the Whoopee John Wilfahrt Concertina Orchestra of New Ulm, Minnesota—including mention that they broadcast over Radio Station WCCO in Minneapolis.

Also in this first issue, Silberhorn notes that because of the small demand for Bandonion music, he has discontinued publishing music for that instrument—an indication that, already during the 1920s in Chicago, the bandonion, popular in Germany and South America, never quite made it in the American Midwest. In addition, he invites the public and his readers to furnish a title for his new publication, requiring that suggestions reach him before November 23rd and that the winner would receive $10 for his selection. Already in the second issue, the newsletter has a name, *Silberhorn's Booster*, "for the Advancement of the Concertina," a title submitted by Phil W. Beitel of Norway, Michigan. Receiving notice of his success, Beitel responded that he was immensely pleased, that he had been a concertina player for the last 25 years, and that he always preferred the arrangements offered by Silberhorn. Wishing everyone a Merry Christmas and a Happy New Year in the December, 1927 issue, editor Silberhorn mentions the hundreds of suggestions that poured in from all over the nation. Reasons given for the judges' selection of "Booster" were its simplicity, clearness, ease of remembering, and clarity of purpose. Others receiving honorable mention had suggested appellations such as the Concertinist, Concert-Tone, Voice of the Concertina, Concertina Broadcaster, Buttonettes, United Concertinists, Concertination, and a bit farther afield, Squeeze-Box Educator, as well as Melody.

In addition to offering music for many song titles, Silberhorn now advocates his "Symphony of tone and volume" instrument, the Silberhorn Clarion Concertina which, he boasts, can raise money to exceed its purchase price with all the dance jobs that would result. At this stage of his boostership, Silberhorn is glad to reprint the letters of players telling how they learned to play the concertina without the aid of any instruction book. Surprising for the day, Silberhorn tells how he traveled by automobile from Milwaukee to Seattle, down to San Francisco and back to Chicago— everywhere playing the concertina to people along the way. They are ordinary people who had never heard nor seen a concertina—some indication of the region in America where the concertina, then as now, was truly at home— in the Midwest.

Silberhorn was not only a publisher but also an original arranger. Here he writes a Christmas song for the concertina, called "Stille Nacht"/Silent Night.

The famous Reeperbahn, meaning the street where the ropemakers created rigging, had become a street for sailors to meet women of the night. The title of the piece is "At Night on the Reeperbahn Street."

Listed too are musical numbers for the concertina, among them many with German and Bohemian names, e. g. "Tief im Böhmerwald," and "V Lese, Valcik," a tribute to the concertina's place of origin, the German Erzgebirge, a mountain chain adjacent to the border with Czechoslovakia. Additionally, and unsurprisingly, the Clarion concertina was advertised, "A" internationals, costing between $150 and $200 for the Plain or Pearl Flower, beautifully equipped with 104 keys. Give them a concertina for Xmas [sic], Silberhorn advised. With his arrangements we get not only single numbers and notes but bass chords indicated in a separate space at the bottom of the staffs. Frank Schmidt, Silberhorn's master teacher, comments that you need to master the long notes first, then concentrate on the actual music that renders the melody.

In the *Booster* we learn also about problems with importing concertinas. An individual writes: "I sent to Germany for a concertina and they sent me a different keyboard. Can you send me a chart to change the numbers on the music?" To which Silberhorn answers self-promoting: "Yes. We want to warn all players against the practice of buying from a distant country where you are unable to return goods not satisfactory" [sometimes Silberhorn's English syntax betrays his German birth]." "We have a Carlsfelder keyboard now, that was bought from Germany by a local customer. He waited three months after he sent the money and then got an instrument he couldn't play." [We may assume he received a bandonion instead of the regular Chemnitzer concertina.]

Other announcements are reminiscent of long since forgotten endeavors: From L. Zimmermann of Big Prairie, Alberta, Canada, came a letter stating that the question and answer section of the *Booster* was a real success; that the W. C. Oldenburg Concertina Orchestra of Henderson, Minnesota would be playing on Radio Station WCCO in Minneapolis; that Charles E. Scherzer and his concertina orchestra were responsible for the popularity of the concertina in the Saginaw, Michigan area. The Booster also brought details about various old time dance bands, many in Minnesota. For instance, John Dietzel of Hamburg, Minnesota was satisfied with his concertina as well as being content with the co-leader of his band, George Hölz of Cologne, Minnesota, who was busy playing in south central Minnesota.[2] Always in the *Booster* there was a little joke: Having sold someone a concertina on approval,

Readers enthusastically made suggestions for the Silberhorn magazine from which Henry selected "Booster" with a clever subtitle.

Silberhorn dunned the purchaser for payment, to which he received the response: "Pay for dat musick? You said in tree weeks dat concertina pay for heemself."

Sometimes Silberhorn editorialized that the concertina player should always get the most money of any member of the dance band because the instrument was the hardest to play. Moreover, as if to justify his own retail business, that it was the most expensive to purchase. He also boasted new quarters for the Silberhorn Chicago studio, no longer located at 516 but at 519-521 Milwaukee Avenue, obviously just across the street from his original work site and pictured on the last page of the April, 1928 issue. Some of Silberhorn's literature specifies that his shop is at this address on the second floor, of 519-521, near Grand Avenue and Halsted Street.

In response to a question, the master salesman elucidates on the reed and tonal pitch of the concertina — I have a 104-key concertina tuned in natural A. Can it be tuned to International C? Answer: "We don't understand what you mean by natural A. Before the War [WW I, 1914-1918], all concertinas were tuned in high pitch [piccolo]; since the war all concertinas are international or low pitch (440 vibrations). An instrument tuned in low pitch can be played with other instruments. All concertinas are really in the key of C, but for many years they have been called key of A, because the No. 5 press is A. An A concertina can be tuned down from high pitch to low pitch." In the next column Silberhorn promotes his new musical numbers, among them the "Mariechen Waltzer" (Marysia Walc), a new arrangement with names of the chords which accompany this popular waltz.

Promoting their orchestras via mention in the Booster were the Emil Berkhahn Concertina Band from Bonduel, Wisconsin, the Otto C. Rettke S & R Concertina Orchestra of Fairmont, Minnesota, the Alfred Schultz Band of Chief, Michigan, John Stypa of Kansas City, Missouri, the Niclai Wekseth Band playing on WKBH Radio in La Crosse, Wisconsin

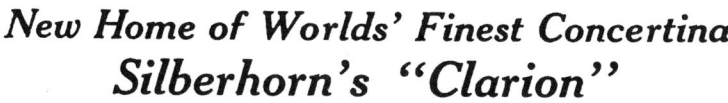

Above is Silberhorn's new building at 519-21 Milwaukee Avenue which he was occuping in April 1928. This appears to be the same structure that stands there today. Right, the building in March 2002.

CATALOGUE OF MUSIC FOR THE CONCERTINA

Arranged and published by

HENRY SILBERHORN

519-21 Milwaukee Ave.
Chicago, Ill.

HOME OF THE FAMOUS
CLARION CONCERTINA

CATALOGUE OF MUSIC FOR THE CONCERTINA

This General Catalogue is complete up to May, 1932, and is classified into all the various kinds of music listed in the Index. There are over five thousand different pieces of every variety to select from. The majority of this music, representing a life-time of accomplishment, has been arranged and published by Henry Silberhorn during the past forty-six years. Music published by other dealers is also listed.

HENRY SILBERHORN
"The Concertina Specialist"

"To the Concertina Player:

"My whole life has been devoted to the Concertina and the Concertina player. I learned to play Concertina in the year of 1886, at a time when there was practically no music or instruction book for the Concertina. Having studied music for some years previous to this time, it was possible for me to arrange Concertina music for myself and other players in a short time. Thereafter, I taught hundreds how to play Concertina and in 1910 published an Instruction Book which proved to be the basis of the practical Concertina method of today and the foundation of its importance as a musical instrument. Thousands of pieces have been arranged and published by me for the Concertina as well as several improved editions of the instruction books.

For many fine arrangements in this catalogue, I am indebted to Mr. Frank F. Schmidt, an able and distinguished Concertina player and arranger. Mr. Schmidt has been my pupil and assistant and is well fitted to make arrangements according to the practical methods I have established.

I believe in the Concertina and its future. Everywhere—everybody likes its tone and it is bound to become a nationally popular musical instrument if the individual player will strive for faultless performance."

Yours for success,
Henry Silberhorn.

Catalog used by Silberhorn, shown approximately in its original size. Note the promotional message Silberhorn writes to the concertina player, printed on the inside cover.

and the Zims Novelty Concertina Orchestra of Pittsburgh. Also in the February, 1928 issue, Silberhorn explains that Theodore G. Rittenbaugh of Pine Grove, Pennsylvania wanted a new concertina that would last as long as the Lange instrument his father had purchased 30 years earlier and handed down to his son. The Rittenbaugh son now wanted an instrument that would last as long as that fine old Lange concertina. The answer? Of course, another Lange—imported by Silberhorn from Germany. Immediately following this little story is the pitch that Lange is the world's finest double-reed concertina, while the Silberhorn Clarion is the finest triple-reed concertina made. For quality, workmanship, tone, volume and price, these instruments could not be equaled anywhere. Thus it is obvious that the import of Lange concertinas continued well into the 20th century when they easily held their own against the American-produced instruments. Of course, those being built at the time in Chicago by Otto Schlicht, the Glass family, the International Accordion Company under Kadlubowski and others mimicked their German forerunners in almost every respect.

On occasion, Silberhorn offers his version of the history of the concertina, for instance in the March and April, 1928 issues of the *Booster*. While most today agree that the credit for the first Chemnitzer goes to C. F. Uhlig in 1834, Silberhorn earmarks the first one to Zimmermann at Carlsfeld in 1821 [an impossible credit because Zimmermann was not born until 1817]. Otherwise, the lineage is about as we know it today and as detailed in our earlier chapters. Not out of touch with the concertina's emigration history, Silberhorn from time to time mentions also the success of the Bandonion as used in the Argentine tango orchestras in the 1920s and 1930s. As we know today, the bandonion is vastly more popular in Argentina than anywhere in the United States or Germany.[3] Even as the concertina historically is at home close to the Czech border in the Erzgebirge range, so too Silberhorn is pleased when he receives orders for concertina sheet music from a Mr. Ruzicka in that then-young, independent nation of Czechoslovakia. Always, Silberhorn is glad to sell the Clarion concertina, noting in every issue of the *Booster* the "name 'Clarion' means bell-like or clear as a bell. A clear and ringing tone carries farther than a dull tone. That is why the Clarion concertina is the ideal orchestra instrument." But he also stocks used, trade-ins of many other brands, notably the Lange, Arnold, Pearl Queen, and others.

Though free to those joining his mailing list, some readers kept sending in a dollar and more to cover the costs of the new *Booster*. And always there were budding concertina orchestras hoping to gain publicity from a mention in this ever-growing *Booster*. We learn of the John C. Scharbach Peppy Three Concertina Orchestra of Reedsville, Wisconsin, the A. E. Boissoneault concertina concerts rendered on WSKC Radio in Bay City, Michigan, as well as the Slocum Lake Trio Concertina Orchestra of the Villa Park Inn on Slocum Lake. Some wrote from farther away—such as John Gottfried with his concertina orchestra of Cayuga, North Dakota, Merton Birmingham of Hortonville, Wisconsin, Francis Schutte of New Brighton, Minnesota and, closer to home, Paul Kuczynski and John Papa of

LaVern Rippley wearing a Silberhorn t-shirt created long after Silberhorn's demise. It was intended to promote Silberhorn remainder merchandise handled by Pat Watters and later Dan and Sue Gruetzmacher. Rippley in 2004 is holding a 1920 Pearl Queen concertina sold by Georgi-Vitak and bearing the serial number 2490.

The History of the Chemnitzer Concertina

Central Wisconsin Club, 1996 [Credit: Ronald Rux & Al Beyer]
Front Row: Ronald Rux, Frank Legner, Mary Novitzke, Barbara Rux, Robert Novitzke, Edward Olshanski, Millard Ringle, Arnold Scheu, Al Kanitz, Ronald Gliniecki, Marlin Novitzke, Joseph Konecny, Paul Kramas.
Back Row: Larry Pyan, Lucy Kvamas, Daniel Kurth, Ervin Lawrence, Arnold Sundell, Willis Loesel, Kurt Hackbart, Bill Volland, Alfred Beyer.

Milwaukee Concertina Club - January 15, 1967 [Credit William A. Hayden]
Front Row: Young man with white shirt, unknown; Danny Lowell; behind him with bald head, unknown; Woman with corsage Concertina Millie Kaminski; to her left, Boots Buroce; unknown; Erv Leamone with dark rimmed glasses. Behind Leamone looking to the right is Chester Myeski; Back Rows: standing is Micky Stys; seated behind Boots Buroce, eyes downcast, is Ray Ulkowski; standing with concertina near microphone is Irvin Kwas; below the microphone with head bowed is Carl Panfil; standing and framed by the door is Hank Jacobs; to his left standing next to the drum set is Max King; the drummer is unknown. The photo was taken in Milwaukee January 15, 1967.

Promotion and Midwest Distribution of the Chemnitzer Concertina

Milwaukee Concertina Circle
This is the cover of a piece of music intended for the Milwaukee players. Note the date of 1902, hence well before the advent of Pearl Queen and Patek instruments, but subsequent to the 1893 introduction of the Lange instrument to the United States. It appears that most players are holding pre-1900 Lange models.

Chicago Concertina Club
To all appearances, this is a 1900s picture of the American Concertina Circle or a Chicago concertina club. Its director, H. C. Wilke, has a Chicago address. The concertinas seem to be Lange models, perhaps built for Majestic or Wunderlich but supplied from the Lange factory in Chemnitz.

Chicago who, however, on that occasion played in Wausau, Wisconsin for Labor Day, 1928. Dropping into the story, according to the January/February 1929 issue, was Joe Starcevic of Hibbing, Minnesota who, according to his letter, had learned well by following the Silberhorn method, in which he also boasted the high quality of the Clarion concertina. Repeatedly there are testimonials and success stories: Frank R. Soukup of Long Beach, California, Eli Zunich of Buhl, Minnesota, Stanley Wasielewski of Chicago, Walter Crown of Detroit, Erwin Drallmeier of Hinsdale, Illinois and Henry Meyer of the Chicago Bandonion Club—in which his two sons play Clarion quadruples rather than the bandonion (March/April, 1929). In the same issue on the back cover is the Henry Bobzien Band of Des Plaines who had taught many beginners as well as performed frequently at dances.

Concertina circles and clubs were also growing. In Chicago the Bohemian-American Concertina Association was chartered June 29, 1929 by members Jerry Stirek, Edward Fik, Anton Swoboda, George Pisarik, Joe Placatka, Joe Brousil and Laddie Prazak. With 100 members by the 1950s, they played at Sokol halls during the winter and at picnics in the summer. In Detroit there was the Musik Verein Frohsinn meeting every week, and in Milwaukee the Concertina Circle composed of John Blanching, Rudy Brugger, Mike Brugger, Thomas Pipp and William Ackerman entertained regularly, all playing concertinas and one on drums. Meanwhile, Silberhorn editorializes about the distances his sheet music travels, reaching players from Maine to California, from Washington state to Florida—every state in the Union—with occasional orders from Canada, Mexico and Europe. For a brief period, the concertina had become a national instrument.

But of equal interest to his reading public were the photographs and identifications of concertina orchestras, e.g. in the September 1929 issue: Frank's Comedians featuring H. E. Rau on coronet, Jacob Geib on drums, Frank Spiczak on concertina, Joe Stepan on clarinet and saxophone, and Rudolf Stepan on piano and guitar. Regularly they were given high profiles on Radio KSTP in St. Paul and WNAX in Yankton, South Dakota. Equally enthusiastic are the likes of Stanley Sereika of Medford, Wisconsin, William Rostalsky of Wausau, Wisconsin, Robert Geisler of Glenshaw, Pennsylvania, Rudolph J. Marek of Chicago and Herman Waller of Webster, South Dakota. Waller claimed to have traveled 461 miles through mud and rain that summer, just to play old time music for local dancers. In Volume III, No. 4, Christmas 1929, we learn about M. Mertzacker of Howard Lake, Minnesota and about the Silver Tone Melodians of Chicago, a Bohemian musical group with concertina led by Frank Suchan. In the Spring 1930 issue we meet John Hernandy and his concertina of Two Rivers, Wisconsin, Otto Rindisbacher of Rice Lake, and Joe Musilet of Cologne, South Dakota, as well as Julius W. Tantow of Merrill, Wisconsin. Then there was Edward Havlicek and his concertina orchestra of La Crosse, Wisconsin, and William Swoboda of Hutchinson, Minnesota, the latter boasting about his mass media contribution playing on Radio Station WDGY in the Twin Cities.

Offering us a glimpse at the Chicago concertina club scene, the *Booster* reports on the newly founded Clarion Concertina Club inaugurated by Ernest Silberhorn in Summer 1930. At the time it had 13 members who met every two weeks for fellowship and music. Also reported in the magazine is the feat they performed by driving a colonnade of 18 autos to a local picnic of 200 people,

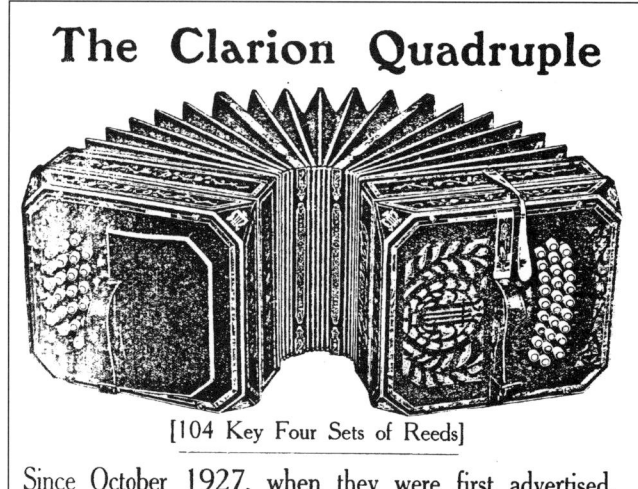

This was the best concertina available in 1927. Usually the Clarion was imported from Germany with the name "Clarion" attached in the Silberhorn shop.

Promotion and Midwest Distribution of the Chemnitzer Concertina

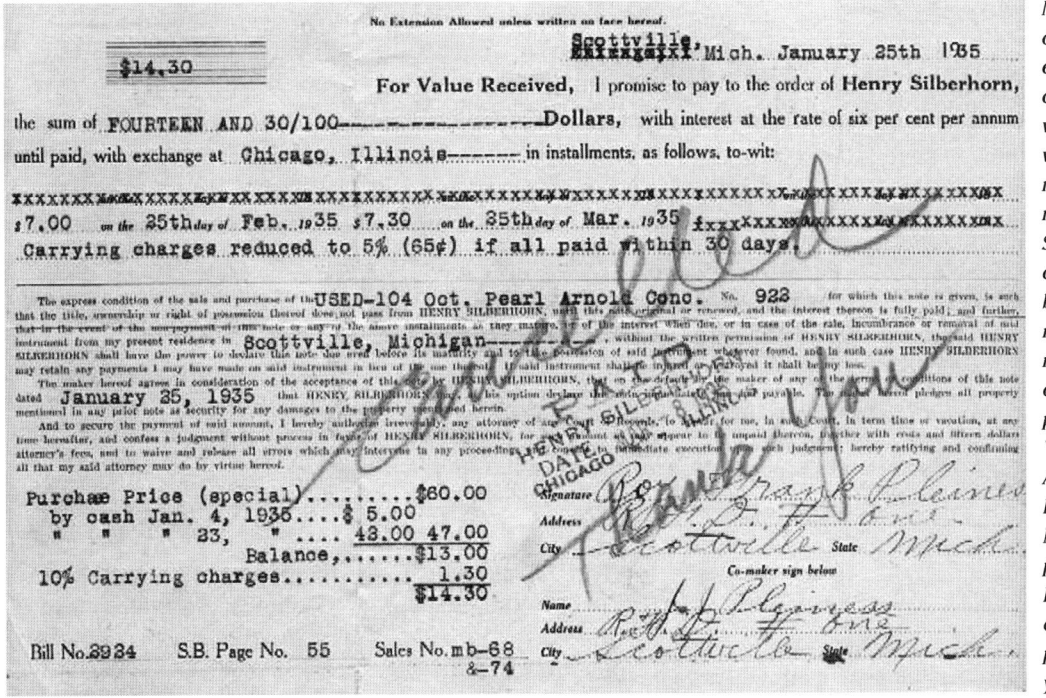

Notice that Henry Silberhorn offered credit to the purchaser of a used Pearl Arnold concertina. It is not clear what kind of instrument this was, since the double designation Pearl and Arnold never appears elsewhere. Starting in about 1930, concertina wood structures began to be covered with nitrate celluloid plastic material available in a variety of colors and attached in marble pattern called pearloid, "Pearl" for short. This Pearl Arnold had a contemporary look. From Scottville, Michigan [near the mid-state port city of Ludington] Roy Frank Pleines made payments on his $60 instrument until paid during the Depression year 1935.

Note the different makes of used concertinas available at the Silberhorn outlet: Arnold, Lange, Majestic, Pearl Queen, among other brand names.

Silberhorn describes the satisfying effects worked on a player by a good concertina.

→ 141

their version of a stunt to boost membership.[4] In tune with the tough economic times of the Great Depression the following spring and summer, the Clarion Club persistently held sway with 22 members. They performed for the benefit of the unemployed, for example in the Masonic Temple at Blue Island, Illinois [on 127th Street in a southern Chicago suburb], to an audience of 1500 dancers. Between sets, as reported in the paper, the revelers refused to leave the floor —cheering and clapping their hands for more and more music.[5] During the same period, Silberhorn was careful to cover his concertina world territory, mentioning Joseph L. Fisher, whom he acclaims as the most successful old time concertina orchestra in the state of Iowa. In the Depression year of 1931, Fisher's orchestra played 355 jobs, mostly in Iowa, but including some in Illinois and Wisconsin. Also in the *Booster*, Herman Engel of Chicago gets credit for having continuously played the same concertina on which he began playing 39 years ago. According to the article, he started taking lessons from Henry Silberhorn when the latter was operating from his site on Dayton Street in Chicago. Dayton is one block west of North Halsted at Diversey, a short distance from his subsequent business site on Milwaukee Avenue.

During the depths of the Depression, Silberhorn began to market a rather unknown brand, the Loyola concertina, which he called well built with the most modern design and finish, "the same as the many well-known concertinas that have been made and sold for years," meaning the Clarion which, to no surprise, continues on center stage in the *Booster*. Still, Silberhorn claimed the Loyola Octave, or double-reed, had the loudest and best tone of any double-reed concertina made, and that it was available in a style that was attractive in appearance but cheap in price. He also offered triple-reed models with quadrupled contra bass Loyolas, which were available in 106-key triples for $165. This was probably an imported German-made concertina because the Chicago builders never produced a discount model during the 1930s. In the identical issues, to no one's surprise, the Clarion is touted for having the most remarkable features: "Easy, quick-speaking reeds of finest steel, tempered to tone and hand filed to the exact key—delights the Clarion owner most of all. All reeds speak together. The full-throated performance of a Clarion will please you. The most outstanding feature of the Clarion is its rich, clear TONE and powerful pure VOLUME. . . . No squeaks and no rasping roughness but a clear and tremendous volume of tone that sounds above other instruments and carries to the farthest corner."

Despite a depressed market in 1932, the Clarion was selling for $285 - $300, reflecting its rating against the Loyola and others. Here it should be remembered from chapter one that the "Clarion" may have been imported directly from Germany. However, they could have come through the showrooms of Otto Georgi, who imported them from F. Lange in Germany before the craftsman and repair specialist, Otto Schlicht, had arrived in the United States. Subsequently, Silberhorn also bought or ordered directly from the Star company which bought certain materials from Schlicht. Georgi also sold reed plates to Kadlubowski. In 1902, as will be recalled, Georgi partnered with Louis Vitak, a retailer of Czech origins, to form the popular firm of "Georgi and Vitak," a retail business which in the mid-1920s ceased when the co-workers fell into disagreement and parted. Thus the Silberhorn "Clarion" is clearly a mainstream instrument that trails forward from Uhlig, Lange, Georgi, Schlicht and others to the concertina's present-day producers, Hengel and Minar.

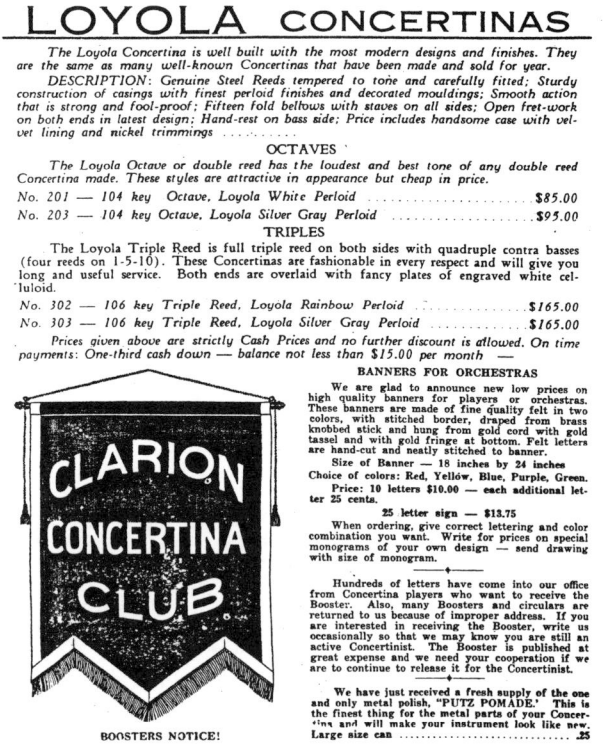

Silberhorn describes his Loyola brand of concertina.

Sample newsletter headings from one of Silberhorn's chief competitors, the Vitak-Elsnic Company from south Chicago.

At the close of 1932 and the election of Franklin Roosevelt as president, Silberhorn in his Christmas issue believes there would now be hope for the future as articulated in an article, "Better Days are Coming." Silberhorn was glad to have concluded "a year that has been a tough battle for most of us, a year that made our heads whirl with such words as 'prosperity is around the corner' — 'a new deal'! But the most magic and electrifying word of all has been B - E - E - R. We probably won't have beer by Christmas but we'll have it soon—so they tell us. And all of you who remember the good old times B. P. [before prohibition] know that there'll be more parties and more dances that will look to the concertina player for music. *Nazdrowie* and *Prosit* will be the pass-words to good cheer! Then we will all turn our faces to the future and go forward with confidence to the better days that are to come. . . . For the occasion, Henry Silberhorn has written a new Beer Waltz Medley."[6] In the same issue of the *Booster*, the master announces that the preeminent concertinist, Henry Schuckert, tuner and arranger, is directing a concertina club on the south side of Chicago, made up of a cluster of amateurs and professionals who meet regularly for pleasure and practice. Here we recall that Henry Schuckert [along with John Kummer and John Friedl] was one of the renowned reed makers described in chapter three, from whom Christy Hengel purchased a repository of materials before becoming heir of the Otto Schlicht factory, whose linkage to Minnesota is a key focus of this book. The Henry Schuckert music store was located at 8222 South Ashland Avenue in Chicago.

With reports of concertina success from across the nation, Silberhorn mentions Alfred Schunk, who had bought a concertina from Silberhorn nine years earlier. He reports on his 13 years running "Schunk Melody Monarchs." Warren Henrichs and Glen Leder assist with red hot barn dances taking place in North Dakota, each musician earning $10 per

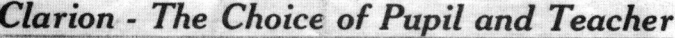

A sample page from the Booster.

Henry Schuckert, a builder of Star concertinas, sometimes placed his own name of "Schuckert" on the instruments. Here he holds a typical 1950s Star.

night. In like manner, William A. Niemeyer of Palatine, Illinois is quoted for writing: "What would all the players do if the house of Henry Silberhorn would not be in existence? I bought several instruments from you for myself and other people and everybody was satisfied. One concertina I bought in 1910, 22 years ago, and it is in good condition today and I did not put it in the corner either. I use it today yet and it has seen a good many nights for dancing purposes." Always, of course, such words in the *Booster* keep up the boosting, especially of the Silberhorn agency, one of the rock solid enterprises that made the concertina an important instrument in American folk music. Occasionally Silberhorn complains about costs of his publications. To cover his 60-page catalog, he needs to sell 4,000 sheets of music. To publish each issue with a run of 2,500 *Booster* newsletters, he needs to sell 2,500 sheets of music.

In the same framework as Silberhorn were the catalogs which Rudolph M. Patek supplied from his Patek Music Company at 835 Milwaukee Avenue in Chicago. Though located almost next door to Silberhorn, these printed products were different inasmuch as obviously they were designed more than the Silberhorn organ to sell the Patek products. Also, Patek's publications were less oriented to the matter of teaching and instructing and hardly at all to the business of creating new music. In his own right, however, Patek was a leading musician with a powerful personal interest in concertina players. As noted in chapter two, Patek built a few concertinas, primarily after his move to Wisconsin in the 1960s, though earlier he had assembled and altered some concertinas. In his boom time as a concertina

A typical inside first page of a Rudy Patek catalog. Note that he promotes his own Patek instruments which, however, were actually crafted by Schlicht on May Street around the corner from the Patek store.

Wenzel Fischer (1895–1966) of rural New Ulm, Minnesota. Fischer was a self-taught concertina player. His love for the instrument opened up an appreciation for the concertina and its music. Wenzel prepared others to follow by giving music lessons. He sold mostly "Star" concertinas after World War II until his death, although here he is playing a Lange.

promoter, Patek relied on suppliers in Germany and on Otto Schlicht in Chicago. Repeatedly, Patek acknowledged Schlicht as the American founder and pioneer of the concertina industry who was commissioned to create the products Patek would promote and sell.

As noted on page 53, Patek was comfortable offering his "liberal" guarantee: "Patek concertinas are so carefully made from such fine materials that we can gladly offer an unusually liberal guarantee—If any Patek Concertina experiences trouble because of defective workmanship or material we will repair it absolutely free of charge if sent to us postage prepaid. In addition to this, all pearl work is fully guaranteed for five years, all woodwork is fully guaranteed for two years and all reeds for one year. This liberal guarantee is given to you in writing."[7] While not concentrating on learning to play the concertina, Patek nevertheless shows samples of how the notes and the number systems can be mutually supportive for the beginner, allowing him to allege that "although the most beautiful of all musical instruments, the concertina is the easiest to master. No previous knowledge of music is necessary. Concertina music is written so you can understand it. Each key is indicated in such a clear way that you can tell at a glance which one to press. And it only takes a few lessons to gain a complete knowledge of the entire keyboard." For the layman, there might be a degree of hyperbole in the Patek assertions about easy and speedy skill acquisition.

Equally hyperbole-enhanced is some of the boosterism Patek exhibits about his Patek line of concertinas. And in these instances, he implies that he is personally and intimately involved in production, but as shown previously in other texts Patek entirely disclaims his own direct craftsmanship in concertina construction. One of these Patek Deluxe concertinas, a 1937 vintage, was acquired by Wenzel Fischer of New Ulm in 1948 for $400. It is currently owned by his son, Jerome Fischer, of New Ulm. Under the headline for his new Patek Deluxe, in large letters Patek extols: "Custom Built on Special Order for Musicians Who Want the World's Finest Concertinas."

So fine, so beautiful, so distinctive that only a limited number will be made. And each of these will be master engineered on special order only. We've put everything we know, the most complete knowledge about Concertina making in the world into the producing of this model. And so perfect must these instruments be that it requires eight to ten weeks to make just one. In tone quality, in the accurate and delightful producing of lovely music, this Concertina is beyond compare. From the gentlest musical whisper to the full, rich power of organ volume each note is delightfully true. Ordinary beauty pales into insignificance when compared to the loveliness of the Deluxe. Its pure white mother-of pearl, gleaming in a shimmer of irridescence covers like a lake of glistening snow above the black and gold overlay studded with jewel-like stones. Specially deep bellows of the strongest, lightest fiber material known, are covered with attractive art leather, and further adorned with beautiful emerald material. Extra length reeds are hand filed from the finest musical steel, and are tested and retested for tone, and fitted into duraluminum plates. The reed channels are carefully cut out by hand assuring accuracy in the finest detail.[8]

Even though Patek never assumed the teaching role that Silberhorn touted, he did maintain his own school for instruction in playing the concertina. Private instruction was available from capable teachers; thus, catalog readers were invited to contact the company for details. Parallel to its selling objective was the repair and tuning of concertinas, which included not only the concertina but also the bandonion, piano and chromatic accordion. Also available were sample music contract forms to protect the musicians as well as ballroom operators in case of any dispute. Concertina music—if out

A full scale support music store, Patek taught his concertina purchasers how to manage their own business affairs by selling them contract forms for performance expectations.

A page from the Patek book telling clients how to play the concertina.

Note that after Patek moved farther to the northwest, but still on Milwaukee Avenue, he continued marketing his school along with his specialty concertinas. These are post-World War II products made in Italy, not those from the Schlicht factory.

and published, Patek had it—was sold in special chorus arrangements or for the concertina in manuscript form. Patek also provided concertina emblems for coat lapels, nickel plated to make the musician "stand out like a million dollars." His instruction book promotions, however, were, perhaps intentionally, oblivious to the Silberhorn versions, claiming that for many years the concertina field was desperately in need of a clear, concise, self-instruction book written in the English language. Although Patek carried the Silberhorn instruction book in his repertoire of such materials, he also marketed another one of his specialty books entitled the *Concertina Self-instructor* in both Polish and English, compiled by the well-known teacher, Maryan S. Rozicki. Thus, Patek was indeed a full service retailer ready to provide products to satisfy a wide range of demands. In many mediums, Patek waxes eloquent about the specially-built concertinas he plans to offer for sale in the future.[9]

Another promoter of enormous consequence resulted from the backbone personalities at the Vitak-Elsnic company. As noted above, concertina importer (sometime assembler or builder), Otto Georgi, in the

```
                    FROM
          Name ........................................
          Town ........................................
          State .......................................


                 VITAK-ELSNIC CO.,
                    EVERYTHING IN MUSIC
                  4815 SO. ASHLAND AVENUE
          51st ST. STA.            CHICAGO, ILL.
```

Louis Vitak and his nephew, Joseph Elsnic, operated a full-service music store on the Chicago south side directly west of the famed Chicago Stockyards.

MODERN QUALITY
  TRADITIONAL STYLING
    IT'S A VITAK-ELSNIC EXCLUSIVE

THE **"PEARL QUEEN"** CONCERTINA

THE MASTERPIECE OF ALL CONCERTINAS

These instruments are made to our strict PEARL QUEEN requirements as they have been made for over 50 years.

FULL PRICE ONLY $850.00

FEATURES

COLOR:
  All white with deluxe scroll engraving and vari-colored rhinestones inlaid. Full size white buttons with green tops on a standard size 104 key keyboard.
REEDS:
  Quadruple blue Swedish steel reeds.
BELLOW:
  Stainless Steel staves and corners all around the colorfully lined bellow which has 15 folds, 2 middle frames and neck strap hooks. Staves and corners are wood lined for more permanent glueing.
ALUMINUM ACTION
WEIGHT: UNDER 16 LBS.
SWITCHES:
  A shift lever on the right hand or melody side provides a varied tonal effect by allowing you to choose between high or low octave.
MICROPHONE PICKUP INSTALLED
FELT LINED CARRYING CASE INCLUDED "FREE"
KEY:
  Available in B♭ & C. Special keys on request.
VITAK-ELSNIC CO. 4815 S. Ashland Ave. Chicago, Illinois 60609

Here Vitak-Elsnic promote their Pearl Queen concertina. However, the fret plates appear to be of Star manufacture. Perhaps the Star Company built a few for Vitak-Elsnic.

IT'S NEW
  IT'S DIFFERENT
    IT'S A VITAK-ELSNIC EXCLUSIVE

THE **"JET QUEEN"** CONCERTINA

PEARL QUEEN QUALITY WITH EUROPEAN ECONOMY

Made to our strict PEARL QUEEN requirements by dedicated Italian craftsmen in answer to your requests for a quality instrument at a reasonable price.

FULL PRICE ONLY $539.95

FEATURES

COLOR:
  All white with deluxe scroll engraving and vari-colored rhinestones inlaid. Full size white buttons on a black standard size 104 key keyboard.
REEDS:
  Quadruple blue Swedish steel reeds.
BELLOW:
  Stainless Steel staves and corners all around the gold lined bellow which has 15 folds, 2 middle frames and neck strap hooks. Staves and corners are wood lined for more permanent glueing.
ALUMINUM ACTION
LIGHT WEIGHT (UNDER 17 LBS)
SWITCHES:
  5 switches on right hand side with musette, bandonion, concertina or master, clarinet and bassoon effects.
MICROPHONE PICKUP INSTALLED
FELT LINED CARRYING CASE INCLUDED "FREE"
KEY:
  Available in B♭ & C. Special keys on request.
VITAK-ELSNIC CO. 4815 S. Ashland Ave. Chicago, Illinois 60609

This post-World War II concertina was built for the American market in Italy and re-titled by Vitak-Elsnic to tie back to the traditional Schlicht product, the Pearl Queen.

The History of the Chemnitzer Concertina

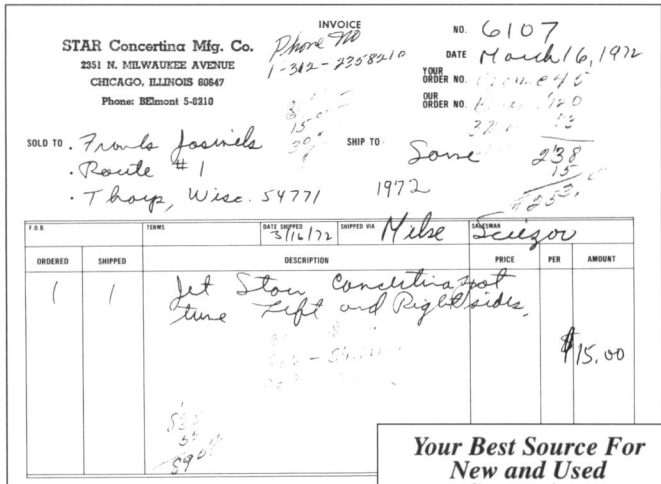

Here the former Italian-American Accordion Company has tuned a Star concertina built by the Kadlubowski father-son team on North Milwaukee Avenue. The customer is from Thorp, Wisconsin, a Polish community on Highway 29, where the Star was especially popular. Brochures featuring the Star Concertina sometimes boasted the "Big Concertina Reed, for those who want the finest in tone, styling, and performance: The New Star "Streamline." They also offer the Star Beauty, the Star Special, and the Star 130 Streamline. There were nearly 3,000 Star concertinas manufactured, between two and three per week between 1940 and 1960 according to the last owner, John Bernhardt, who built 60 with waxed reeds and 60 with long plates.

When Bernhardt retired in 2000, his last serial number was 3,995. He had four people working for him, among them Italian-born tuner, Lucio Lorenzetti at the right pictured tuning a Star, who died February 13, 2003.

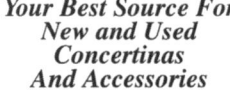

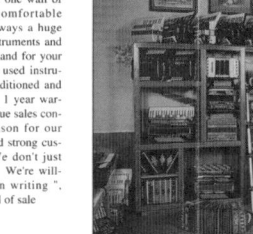

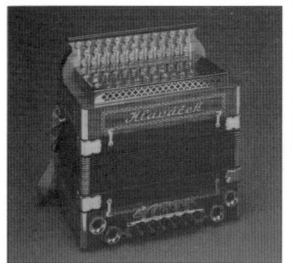

Note that the Star company is now located on 60 Martin Lane in Elk Grove with showrooms on West 35th Street in Cicero, Illinois. On the left, note that Star is much more than a concertina store.

first years of the 1900s had worked with Louis Vitak. But when their relationship fell on hard ground in the early 1920s, Vitak teamed up with his nephew, Joseph P. Elsnic, to create the "Vitak-Elsnic Company" located at 4815 South Ashland Avenue in Chicago. While selling and promoting mostly sheet music in many languages [Polish, German, Lithuanian and Bohemian predominating among the offerings], they also offered items from special collections such as a catalog supply of concertina music written by the able Henry Schuckert. They also fostered concertina music for the piano accordion and sold new and used concertinas that paralleled the Patek models produced in the Schlicht factory, also bearing names like the "Pearl Queen" in the 1920s. In the 1960s the Jet Queen concertina was being built in Italy to have Pearl Queen quality with European economy. Supposedly, it was made to the formerly strict Pearl Queen requirements by dedicated Italian craftsmen and imported to Chicago. Its intended market was in answer to requests for quality instruments at a more reasonable price. Available in both B-Flat and C, the Jet Queen was all white with deluxe scroll engraving and vari-colored rhinestones inlaid, full-sized, white buttons on a black, standard size 104-key keyboard. It had stainless steel staves and corners all around the gold-lined bellow, which contained 15 folds, two middle frames and two neck strap hooks. First and foremost, Vitak-Elsnic merchandised its more traditional standby, the Pearl Queen, "made to strict requirements for over 50 years." By way of price comparison in the late 1960s, the Pearl Queen was available for $850, while the Jet Queen sold for a mere $540.

During the Depression years, Vitak-Elsnic and Patek sought to boost sales by their publications. Vitak-Elsnic from 4815 South Ashland Avenue in Chicago published many specialty catalogs offering their wares, especially sheet music, but also their own small newsletter, called "Concertina News." More than really a newsletter, the four-page items were flyers with items for sale.[10] In the "News" the company offered sheet music for prices ranging from 15 – 75 cents and usually were grouped according to their demand clientele. Thus always included were numbers for Polish musicians, sometimes arranged by Elsnic, for Bohemians, and for Germans. Then there were the many concertinas for sale, often used but "cleaned, repaired and tuned" so they could be guaranteed to be in good playing condition. Generally concertinas came with a free case and ten musical pieces of the buyer's choosing. In the lineup were such makes as the Majestic, the Lange, the Wunderlich and, as might be expected, many bearing the name Pearl Queen. However, there were also such unusual names as the Pearl Flower, the Seifert [from the Seifert Brothers near Chemnitz, Germany] and a few billed simply as "German make." By contrast, in his "Booster," Silberhorn frequently offered the brand names of Lange, Seifert, and

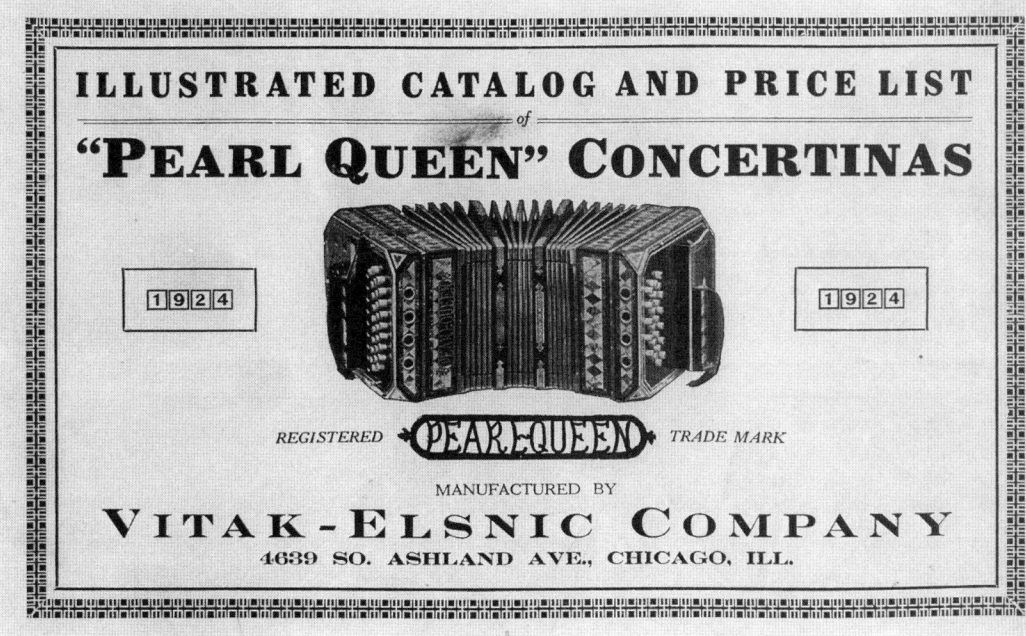

This 1924 catalog with a green cover features many Pearl Queen models with excellent reproduction yielding near-perfect facsimile views of the original intstruments.

Pitschler [a brand barely known in the United States today]. In the Silberhorn listings, furthermore, confusion is deepened by the availability of concertinas bearing names like the Pearl Flower and the Pearl Inlaid, which he subheaded as Arnold instruments. They were Arnold-built with a fancy pearloid covering.

As we have seen in earlier chapters, the Star concertina was the outgrowth of Kadlubowski and Mojsiewicz. It is likely that these builders imported from Germany many parts as well as ready-built concertians. However, the Star manufacturers retailed their instruments from their own corporation and repair shop at 2351 Milwaukee Avenue in Chicago. This location on Milwaukee Avenue was northwest from Patek's store at 835 Milwaukee, the W. H. Sajewski store at 1017 Milwaukee and other lesser-known stores located on side streets in this more southeastern district along Milwaukee Avenue. Later, Star moved to 60 Martin Lane in Elk Grove Village, Illinois.

As noted in a previous chapter and as reiterated in their promotional materials, the Star Company reaches back with its old world pride and craftsmanship to 1926, but now in the 1930s offers not only concertinas and accordions, but also amplifiers and expert repair services. At their musician-owned and operated company, the owners stocked a complete line of concertinas, a unique library of rare concertina sheet music, and a full line of accessories. Boasting their product, Star designers offered a five-year guarantee, any instrument in C, B-Flat, F, E-Flat or the low octave C in various colors, black, white pearl, red pearl, and blue pearl. After the company moved to 2618 West 59th Street in Chicago, sales were promoted for the various Star models in the price range of $1,000- $1,300, with a special Eddie Lash Star Streamline going for $1,190. Whether the very competent salesman and concertina player, Edward "Eddie" Lash [Laszczak, of Polish parentage detailed in chapter two], actually made any concertinas is doubtful though his presence as a player and promoter on the concertina scene was indeed noteworthy. Lash set out frequently from his Chicago base, travelling northward with a station wagon filled with concertinas and returned a day or two later empty except for the extra orders he had collected en route for a variety of products, including Star, Patek and Pearl Queen concertinas.

As articulated expressly in chapter three, the real successor to the Otto Schlicht and Otto Georgi, Patek and Pearl Queen concertina builders, together with their experts in the craft of reed making, John Kummer and John Friedl, was Christy Hengel of New Ulm, Minnesota. Like the many promoters and manufacturers who preceded him, Hengel also worked hard at the necessity of promotion. Through the late 1960s and 70s, taking his cue from Silberhorn and other famous personalities, he too mailed newsletters to his list of interested individuals. In them we conjecture various facts and features that parallel the older masters. In his July 15, 1968 issue, Hengel addressed an invitation to his fans using New Ulm Polka Day as his lure.[11]

On July 29 that year, folks were urged to see his

Hengel advertisements always stressed the difference between Schlicht-produced Pateks and Pearl Queens vs. Star concertinas by the International Accordion Company. Here he touts Schlicht's patent for the Duro Aluminum Action and the square rectangular rivited reeds on long plates vs. wax-mounted reeds. Some players believe that the Star quadruples of the 1920s outperformed the Schlicht-built quads of that era. This forced Schlicht to develop his Duro Action in the early 1930s to compete with Star. After World War II, Star switched to waxed reeds which Hengel considered inferior.

display in the former New Ulm Surplus Store across the street from the American Legion, and not just see but play the Hengel concertinas in the exhibit. "My little square-built salesmen will not pressure you with sales talk—you can play the concertina and be your own judge. THE PROOF OF THE PUDDING IS IN THE EATING. The Hengel concertina is the only truly hand-made concertina available on the market today. All other brand concertinas are available through many, many, many other salesmen and peddlers—and some distributors advertise that 'Salesmen are welcome.' This is proof that the term 'hand-made' is being used by other distributors as a sales gimmick which is used to describe ASSEMBLY OF THE PRODUCTS." [12] For sale on shelves stocked with used instruments were models like the Silberhorn Black Beauty, the Star quad, an old type Star, a Patek quad, several Pearl Queen models, one Clarion, a Glass, as well as some piano accordions. Hengel's concertinas all were listed for sale at prices ranging between $200 and $400 while his accordions retailed at prices that were much cheaper. Of course the Hengel concertina was always described in superlatives, "the newest in name, oldest in style, and best in quality."

Like his predecessors, Hengel also sold sheet music, copies of the best known old time dance numbers, at his home in southern Minnesota. While his competitor at Brown's Music Store was also actively supplying the market on a broad front, and would eventually acquire the enormous collection of musical notes from Vitak-Elsnic in Chicago, Hengel stocked a supply of notes on paper that challenged the Brown heritage from Vitak-Elsnic—even though Hengel himself could not read a note. Always there were used concertinas. In late 1968, Hengel offered three Lange Triples, key of C with about $170 price tags, instruments that had to be over 30 years old. When the year 1969 reached its summer high point, Hengel announced that he was discontinuing the display party. However, he would have his own "factory" open on Polka Day, located at 403 North Minnesota Street. Even though everyone was invited, he warned, people might have to take turns entering his shop. This pattern carried forward to Polka Day 1970 when he set up a small platform outside his house to showcase his concertina and related wares. This time, though, he offered a concert scheduled for the Sunday afternoon before Polka Day, July 26, which amounted to a recital by Hengel concertina students and their teacher, computer science Professor, Dr. Ambrose Kodet of Mankato State University.

During the summer highlights of 1970, Hengel used his shelves to feature for sale several Stars, a few Pateks and some Pearl Queen instruments, and even an old Arno Arnold concertina from the 1950s. In 1971 Hengel's emphasis on a tone of excellence continues subtly,

In the center of the picture is Randy R. Dorschner of Appleton, Wisconsin. On the left is Keith Zwack, and on the right is Eldred Doell. They are holding and bragging about owning Hengel concertinas, 4, 5, and 6 built sequentially by Hengel. The #5 instrument was owned by Larry Dorschner from 1958 to 1965 when Hengel bought it back but sold it again to Randy Dorschner in 1998. Randy also covets Hengel #9 an E-Flat concertina with Musette tuning.

"Hengel concertinas are limited—we only want those customers who recognize quality and who want the most for their money. Quantity brands are available—if you don't want much for your money—want to spend your money right now—[then] don't look at a Hengel. OUR PACE IS SLOW, OUR OUTPUT LIMITED, OUR AIR IS QUALITY—THE RESULT IS A HENGEL CONCERTINA." Depicting this motto in his advertising is a concertina with Hengel's head popping out of the bellows, riding on the back of a turtle. For sale in 1971, in addition to the Patek, Pearl Queen, Star, Schuckert Star, Stradivarius, and Lange triples, were such off-brands as the Majestic triple, Liberty triple, a few with the name Stradi. The Stradi is not the same as a Stradivarius sold by Watters. Rather, it was a beginner's single, double or triple reed instrument that had the unique feature of button numbers implanted into the button tips.

By 1972, Polka Day had moved out to the Brown County Fairgrounds for better containment by the municipal authorities of the crowds that assembled, some of the more youthful, for the opportunity to buy and consume beer. With regrets that he would miss many visitors at the little shop downtown in his home, Hengel decided to stay home and wait with open doors. Even if the real polka festivities and heir to Polka Day was moving to the Gibbon Ballroom 18 miles north of New Ulm, the public would still be welcome to his place of manufacture. In his newsletters of that period, Hengel affectionately represents his concertina as the genuine descendant of the great Otto Schlicht "Master Builder" from the 1920s and 30s—which, indeed, it was. To better underpin his claim, Hengel reprints a page from the Patek catalog [quoted in chapter two of this book] where Otto Schlicht is honored as the American founder and pioneer of the concertina industry. Hengel also stresses the fact that no imitators have been able to copy Schlicht, reiterating exactly what Patek had claimed to market his Patek-named instruments throughout the 1930s. The Patek concertinas are of the highest quality because they were built by Otto Schlicht and his crew. Concluding this accolade to Schlicht and Patek, Hengel writes: "I began doing experimental work on the concertinas in 1943 and in 1953 I purchased all the equipment and dies from the Otto Schlicht Concertina Factory in Chicago and moved this equipment to Minnesota. It was in 1955 that the first concertina by Hengel was put on the market. The first Hengel concertinas had a generic nameplate the next few, the first names of their owners. Only in 1958 did he put Hengel's on the box and then recalled a few already sold to implant his trademark name. Hengel did not attend the newly constituted Polka Day at the Brown County Fairgrounds, known in 1972 and subsequently as Heritage Fest. New Ulm's Polka Day was no more.

But Phoenix-like, Polka Day needed only to switch venues to revive. From Friday, July 27, through Monday, July 29, 1973, Cliff and Katie Hermel subsumed Polka Day with a new title when they staged Musikantenfest at the

Aerial view of the parking lot at the Gibbon Ballroom on the east edge of Gibbon, Minnesota, probably in 1973. At the right, Katie and Cliff Hermel, who were inducted into the World Concertina Congress Hall of Fame in 1993.

Gibbon Ballroom. It was no longer in New Ulm, but the skilled promoter, Christy Hengel, immediately recognized this new opportunity to showcase his Hengel concertina. It was a question of seizing the moment because the Hengel concertina would be vibrantly in action at the ballroom where the majority of the orchestras were equipped with none other than Hengel concertinas. A Hengel, after all, was the mainstay instrument played by the artists fronting such bands as the Wendingers, Johnny Helget, Elmer Scheid, Syl Liebl, Ray Dorschner, Rodney Ristow, Jerry Schuft for Earl Schmidt, for the Lester Schuft Band, Ivan Kahle, the Six Fat Dutchmen and many others.

As a means to advocate his Hengel concertinas in the year 1975, Hengel wrote in a mutually supportive vein, boosting the Gibbon Fest where again orchestras would be using a Hengel instrument to best exemplify their individual musical arts and styles. In addition to presenters of the previous year, Erwin Suess, Harvey Becker with the Riverside Dutchmen, the Jolly Swiss Girls from Cochrane, Wisconsin, Norm Wilke with the Little Fishermen and others were scheduled to play. In the mid-summer 1975 July issue, Hengel returns to his reliable comment that the Hengel concertina is indeed unique. In Hengel's opinion, it was a time when the concertina market was being flooded with three-dimensional quickies—"quickly made, for a quick buck and a quick loss of money!" Again for sale at Hengel's store are used boxes like Pearl Queen, Stradivarius, Star, Lange, Arno Arnold, as well as additional models.[13]

Though the Hengel newsletters were obviously self-serving and of limited duration, *Polka and Old Time News* was similar, and was likewise short-lived. Issued by C. B. Brown under the ownership of Lindstrom-Brown Publications in Minneapolis, the monthly promoted the concertina tirelessly.[14] This Brown was a brother to Bill Brown, Sr., whose concertina enterprise was on South Broadway in New Ulm. Not surprisingly, there were the

Polka & Old Time News Magazine lasted but a few years.

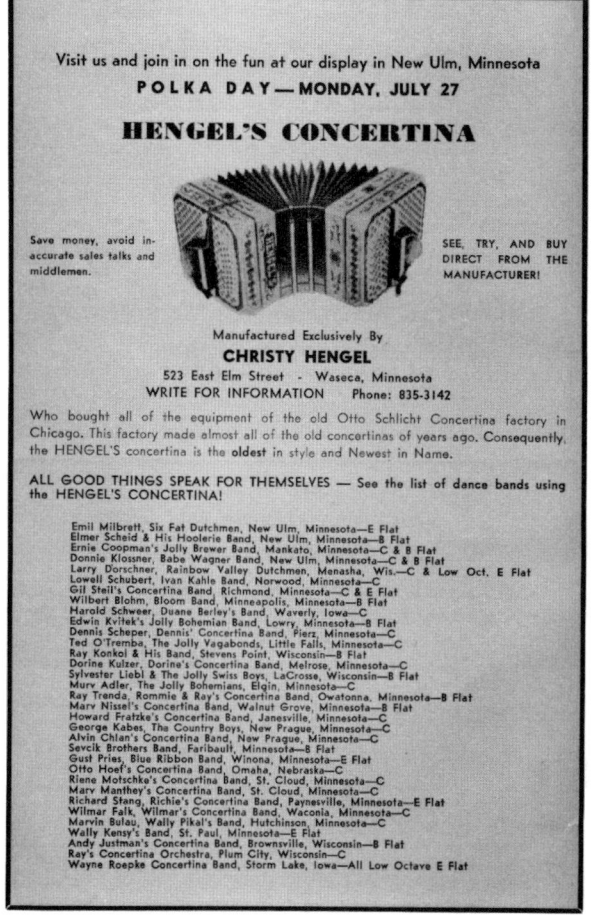

The back cover of the July, 1964 issue of Polka & Old Time News, *carries Hengel's advertisement.*

usual advertisements from Brown's Music Store for sheet music, lessons and concertinas. Informative are the listings of old time dances, e.g. at the Prom Ballroom on the Midway in St. Paul featuring an old time band every single Thursday night with a half hour broadcast of each band's program on radio. Bands scheduled for November, 1963, were Elmer Scheid, Whoopee John, the Earl Schmidt Band featuring Jerry Schuft, and The Six Fat Dutchmen, all concertina bands. In the first issue in 1963, several concertina orchestras supply their dance dates—Elmer Scheid, Ernie Coopman, Norm Wilke, Dick Rodgers and others. Likewise, the radio stations offering concertina performances are given: KXEL from Waterloo, KOEL from Oelwein, Iowa, WPLY of Plymouth, Wisconsin, KTOE of Mankato, KDHL of Faribault, KASM of Albany and KRBI of New Prague and St. Peter, all in Minnesota. Christy Hengel advertises his concertinas "being played by all of the leading old time dance bands in Minnesota, Wisconsin, Iowa, Illinois, Nebraska and South Dakota."

In the second issue, Vern C. Bank of Kaybank Recording Studio City Recordings of Minneapolis, having just assumed ownership of Pleasant Peasant and Golden Wing recording organizations, explains his acquisition of various catalogs and thus boasts of the many LP albums he has for sale from his Studio City division. Pleasant Peasant was formerly owned by C. B. Brown, the editor-publisher of the innovative *Polka and Old Time News*. Drawing special attention in this issue is Elmer Scheid, who initiated his own band in 1951 following great performances previous to that with Babe Wagner and The Six Fat Dutchmen. In January we learn a bit about the Ray Dorschner Rainbow Valley Dutchmen, for whom Larry Dorschner was the concertinist as well as [parenthetically] the general contractor for the Christy Hengel house at 403 Minnesota Street in New Ulm. From Pulaski, Dick Rodgers with his concertina gets a review for his dance schedule and his DECCA recordings in the March 1964 issue. In the same issue Christy Hengel advertises his replica of the Schlicht-built concertina, stressing that he is the builder in the United States whose concertinas do not contain imported reeds—Hengel being the only United States producer who makes his own reeds. Hengel further propounds with his own words, "the Hengel's is the most durable concertina on the market—it has the beauty of expert workmanship and the rich concertina tone."[15]

Useful knowledge in the April 1964 issue is the listing of companies that record old time music.[16] Of the bands now listing their schedules in the *News*, only The Six Fat Dutchmen play every single night of the month. Leonard Krulikoski at the United Music Company in Hutchinson runs a full-page advertisement for the Star concertina, demonstrating that Hengel indeed had multiple competitors in his backyard. In the May 1964 issue are pictures of Ernie Coopman playing his concertina in his band and of Harold Loeffelmacher shown in connection with his brief biography. Here, for the first time, Stan Uhlir at 4413 31st Avenue South in Minneapolis, advertises his Echo double reed Concertina, "designed and engineered in the USA, handcrafted in Italy by Moribidoni, the famous accordion builder." Concertina bands listed as having high frequency appearances per month (15 or more nights per month) include the Earl Schmidt and Jerry Schuft Orchestra of Cologne, Minnesota, Tony Wolf and the Deutschmeisters of St. Joseph, Elmer Scheid of New Ulm and Dick Rodgers of Pulaski, Wisconsin.

Ray Konkol receives the photographic nod in the June 1964 issue with folded arms over his two concertinas, one a Hengel. Born at Stockton near Stevens Point in 1931, Konkol started playing the concertina at age 12, did his time in the navy, and upon his return started his own band in Stevens Point in 1960. Also in this issue is an article about the Kewaunee Federation of Musicians Local 604 at Algoma, Wisconsin, representing in their

LaVern Rippley poses at the gravestone of the famous TV concertinist, Dick Rodgers, in the cemetery of Pulaski, Wisconsin, July 24, 2004. In the background is the gravestone of his parents, showing Rodziczak, the original spelling of the Rodgers name.

words, "the largest concentration of Bohemian nationalities in the country. The most frequently scheduled band in June is Dick Rodgers (Richard Rodziczak) from Pulaski. The July 1964 issue explains New Ulm's Polka Day, begun in 1954 and continuing until 1970. Too, the Echo II Concertina is advertised as "the only compact concertina with the tone quality and volume of a quadruple. New in beauty, tops in performance." Also in this issue, Krulikoski in Hutchinson takes out a full page advertisement for the Star King Concertina, the one produced for Lenard Krulikoski of Hutchinson to compete with Hengel. Christy Hengel followed suit with his back cover advertisement inviting people to visit his display in New Ulm on Polka Day, Monday, July 7, 1964.

Announced in the August 1964 issue is the stock acquisition by Pat Watters of the Henry Silberhorn library of concertina music, consisting at the time of 3,000 unlisted and as yet only nominally marketed concertina arrangements. Frequently-playing bands highlighted in this issue include Earl Schmidt/Jerry Schuft and Tony Wolf with the Deutschmeisters. In September 1964, Christy Hengel receives the biographical notation. The October 1964 issue offers a letter from Al J. Kunz, the 78 rpm record collector who was featuring on local radio stations the many folkloric numbers recorded by early concertina bands. Norm Wilke, as leader of the Little Fishermen from Le Sueur, got his mention for organizing the band in 1952. Like all other issues, the December 1964 issue of *Music and Dance News* brings a number/note arrangement, "Christmas, We Remember," for the concertina by LeRoy (Silvers) DeWanz. In January 1965 the Ray Dorschner Rainbow Valley Dutchmen concertina band gets a special highlight. Of additional interest is a letter writer who inquires how to convert regular music to concertina music, while another, Walter M. Mroczek of Sunland, California remarks that the Los Angeles Concertina Club still exists. Into the bargain, the editor offers a chart supplied by Pat Watters telling readers how to transpose any concertina to a different key without having to switch to a differently tuned concertina. This was the concertina slide rule allegedly invented in the 1950s by Hank Jacobs at Karpek in Milwaukee, but in actuality having previous origins. Much earlier, e. g. Henry Silberhorn from his address at 5942 North Talman Avenue in Chicago had marketed a vertical version of the slide rule.

Interesting, too, in the January 1965 issue is an announcement by Pat Watters about new Lange concertinas. Of course they were not Lange concertinas at all, but Arno Arnold instruments featuring the so-called Sonatone balanced action with square-cut, hand-made reeds completed from Swedish steel on individual short reed plates. Arno Arnold had escaped from the Carlsfeld region of East Germany at about age 60 in 1952 and began an imitation instrument made famous by the former Ernst Louis and the Alfred and Paul Arnold concertina factory in Carlsfeld, which had been closed by the Russians at the end of World War II. From his site at 40-42 Beethovenstrasse in 63179 Obertshausen (Kreis Offenbach am Main) a bit southeast of Frankfurt, he built a relatively significant number of concertinas for export to North America. In turn, from his Minneapolis site, Watters was selling these 1960s-built concertinas with "the usual Arnold Lifetime Guarantee." In his literature Watters boasts that the Arno Arnold concertinas now uphold a heritage stretching back over 100 years. They had anodized reed plates, 5-piece laminated wood reed blocks, airtight leather gaskets, super air capacity with lifetime bellows and the patented "BALANCED ACTION," which made for lightning-fast easy fingering.

In February 1965, the *Polka and Old Time News* changed its format to an 8.5" X 11" size and single color renditions, black and white, seemingly to save money. Though it claimed nearly 10,000 subscribers, the magazine soon mysteriously ceased publication and vanished

Pat Watters receiving the World Concertina Congress Hall of Fame award in 1976.

from the scene. During this era, though, Watters Distributing operated expansively at 2219 East 42nd Street in Minneapolis and called itself the World's Largest Concertina Handler. Pat Watters was indeed among the greatest concertina promoters in the world during his heyday in the 1960s.

Despite the fact that the Brown journals, like the Hengel newsletters, were obviously self-serving, other publications were simultaneously promoting the products offered by its writer. Among the best examples are those issued by Pat Watters on behalf of his distributing company, which continued from about 1964 through the 1970s and into the early 1980s. Billed officially as *Music and Dance News, International Old time 'oom pah,' Popular,* the Watters publication, unlike the Brown journal, enjoyed coast to coast distribution. Amid the wares available from Watters were countless sheets of music and, above all, that Watters creation—the Stradivarius concertina.

Of special interest in the Watters newsletters, however, are the varying biographies of concertina dance bands. Tony and Betty Wolf's St. Cloud Deutschmeisters appear frequently with text and in differing photographic poses. Of course it did not hurt that they were Stradivarius dealers. Headlined in the April, May, June 1967 issue is Harold Loeffelmacher with The Six Fat Dutchmen, of whom there were seldom 6, none fat and usually 11 on stage. Recording for Dot and RCA Victor recording studios at the time, the Loeffelmacher band was sub-headed as the "nationally known radio and TV stars coast to coast and Canada, featured on the Lawrence Welk and Dave Garroway shows." During this time frame in the 1960s, The Six Fat Dutchmen were playing 325 nights, and rolling up 100,000 miles annually on their bus playing in the upper Midwest with occasional swings into Canada and Texas. Capping 13 straight years at the Nebraska State Fair was the occasional trip to Los Angeles—not to mention the Dave Garroway Show [predecessor of *The Today Show*] one time when it broadcast from St. Paul.

True to his mission and in a way serving his own cause, Watters, next to the article about Loeffelmacher, featured Emil Milbret, the concertinist for The Six Fat Dutchmen during a 16-year period. Concluding with his own boost of the instrument, Watters asserts "all people who are in any way interested in the concertina should give Harold Loeffelmacher a big hand for keeping the concertina in the eyes of the public and in the hands of good players all of these many years. This has been of great value to the concertina image." It should be noted however, that Loeffelmacher always used Schilcht-built concertinas, rarely Watters-marketed products. Willing to append his personal advice, Watters urges the importance of concertina displays and parties to maintain and create interest in playing the concertina. Taking credit for his own efforts, Watters pens the lines "There is a general opinion throughout the country that the editor

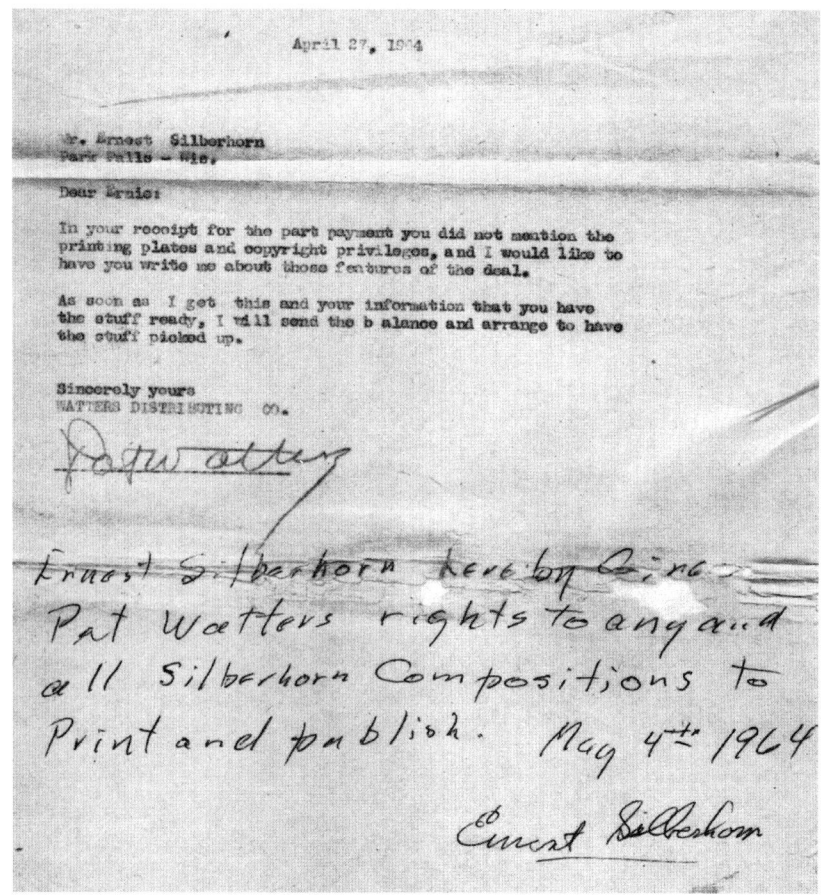

With this letter in 1964, Pat Watters acquired the entire remainder materials from Henry Silberhorn, bequested by his son, Ernest. The collection includes many original manuscripts by the likes of Henry Schuckert and others.

of M & D and the owner of Watters Distributing Company deserves a big part of the credit for bringing about a tremendous upsurge in concertina interest and number of players that is evident all around, by having hundreds of displays and concertina parties, starting 17 years ago [i. e. 1950], and extending throughout Minnesota, Wisconsin, Illinois, Indiana, Nebraska, Pennsylvania, Michigan, the Dakotas, and others." [17]

Watters from his store in Minneapolis continuously offers concertina music from the ample storehouse of the Silberhorn library as well as used instruments, all in "excellent" condition, cleaned and tuned, guaranteed. Among them are the historical triple models from Alfred Arnold, the Carlsfeld factory in the Erzgebirge, the newer Arno Arnold, numerous versions of the Star from Kadlubowski, the Pearl Queen from Schlicht for Vitak-Elsnic, always the Stradivarius, and frequently the lesser version called the "Stradi." Whether pure fact or embellishment, Watters clearly takes credit for the quality the Stradivarius definitely embodies. In a report about the concertinas offered by him, Watters expands:

> All of the features [of the Stradivarius violin] are built into the Stradivarius concertinas. Three years ago, Pat Watters, owner of Watters Distributing Company, went to Italy and Germany, as well as the European countries, taking with him models of all the finest concertinas that had ever been made with orders to the oldest and largest of manufacturers of steel reed bellows instruments to produce the finest concertina of all times. Instructions included the use of the finest of Swedish Blue Steel reeds obtainable, the finest of reed valve leather, the finest of seasoned, resonant woods and free-acting, trouble-free bellows. An artist's delight—Stradivarius. But more so, a bonus, the Watters development of action which has been used on the fine German concertinas imported by this firm, known as 'balanced action.' Watters together with John Bolster of the Independent Accordion-Concertina Service of Minneapolis invented this action through the mathematical equation of PLM, which is Pivot, plus Leverage, plus Motion. . . . No other Italian made concertinas have the high quality handmade reeds, top grade American Jute for bellows, seasoned selected woods, acoustically measured reed chambers, and mathematically designed, balanced, key action. [18]

Sue and Dan Gruetzmacher pose in front of the Silberhorn collection they acquired from Pat Watters at a price of $4,000, now stored in the attic of their home near Wausau, Wisconsin. Photo by LaVern Rippley, December 6, 2003.

Watters also distributed 33 rpm recordings of polka bands, including then-famous disks featuring the concertina by itself. For example, the All Star Concertina Vol. 1 offers concertina numbers by Elmer Scheid, Ray Konkol, Bill Brown, Don Morris, Babe Wagner, Ray Dorschner, Ernie Coopman and others. On the jacket for the recording called "Concertina Holiday" are numbers by Ernie Coopman, the Deutschmeisters [Tony and Betty Wolf], Bob Mastel, Don Morris, Earl Schmidt the trombone player, Elmer Scheid and Roman Rezac among them. Included on the same page are pictures and a brief blurb about Concertina Eddie [Edward Rickert] and Concertina Millie [Mildred Kaminski of Milwaukee] with her album "Concertina Moods," billed as two albums of 100% concertina music, but containing harmonics that fool the listener to believe there were other instruments in the mix. From the outside area come concertina stories via reporters Nick Kramer of Milwaukee, Sue Gruetzmacher [wife of Dan], plus a host of others. Often, Texas is a favorite, revealing that, until the age of 24, Watters grew up—as he puts it—picking a hundred bales of cotton by hand, wearing out 40 nine-foot sacks and 10 pairs of knee pads.[19] Thus, during this late 1960s period, Watters sometimes features old time bands from Texas, such as Bill Mraz of Houston and Gil Baca with their troupes from Fayetteville, Texas. Generally, these were not concertina bands as we know them, but clearly they do exhibit the Czech musical heritage that always flavored the southern Minnesota "Dutchman" concertina style in the 1930s, a trend which continues decisively to the present.

During the late 1960s as concertina playing needed some life support, Watters in his newsletters boosted the tradition of the concertina club. Thus, he featured the Tony Wolf Concertina Band of St. Joseph, Minnesota, which in 1955 performed concerts using some 45 members playing concertinas. Not unexpectedly via such write-ups, Watters was able to boost his own business by contributing to the success of these clubs.

Glowing in the light of the Wolf concertina achievement because he could sell concertinas to the club members, Watters also graciously promotes the Tony Wolf Distributing Company of St. Joseph, as well as the George Servatius (G. S. Music Store) retail business of Melrose, both of whom thrived by selling Watters imports into the German region surrounding St. Cloud. In 1955 and later, Watters built on his 1930s reputation for operating 21 retail stores in which the Wurlitzer accordion was his mainstay. Now it was the concertina's chance to turn him a handsome profit.

In the same post-World War II era, Watters became a climacteric importer and distributor of the Arno Arnold concertina, for which he organized schools and

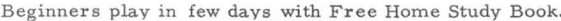
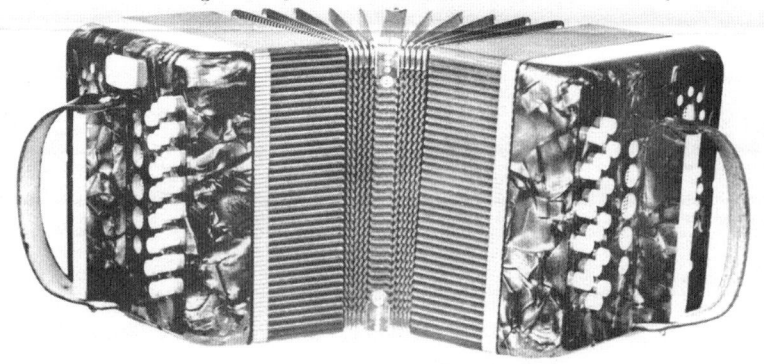

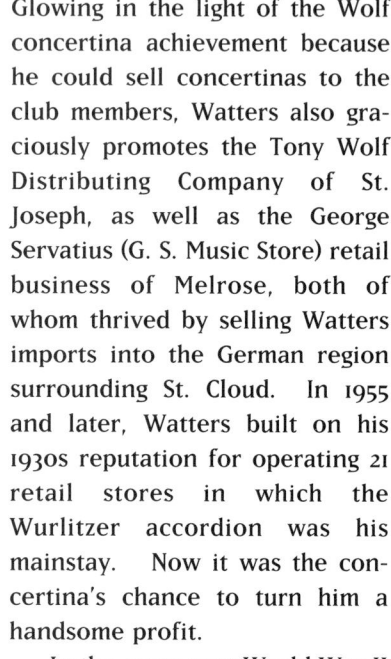

Both George Servatius (left) of Melrose and Tony Wolf (right) of St. Joseph, Minnesota promoted the Arno Arnold concertina. For beginners, Bastari in Italy built the Stradi pictured at the left to look a bit like the Arno Arnold. Arno Arnold, born March 28, 1893 in Carlsfeld, founded his own concertina manufacturing company in 1949 at Obertshausen near Frankfurt am Main. He died there on November 20, 1970.

clubs along the lines of his previous accordion advancement activities. Featured alongside the Wolf Concertina Band in his *Music and Dance News* in 1968 is a reprinted photograph of a 1939 gathering of Wurlitzer accordion players. Some 350 in all, the group was sponsored by Watters in a performance for the Federated Teachers Service Corporation at its third annual gathering given this time at Roosevelt High School in Minneapolis.[20] On the back side of this special issue about Wolf are also photographs of the July 1967 Fifth National Concertina Festival held at the Granite City Ballroom in St. Cloud. Intended was an outcome in which the concertina might achieve mass appeal identical to that of the accordion. Without a doubt, it never did, but with its Bohemian and eastern German roots it has nevertheless proven to be durable in the upper Midwest.

After achieving remarkable success that approached a breath of national exposure in the latter 1960s, Watters seemed at the pinnacle of his career. Suddenly, for reasons not entirely clear, he decided in 1968 to sell his concertina inventory, which featured largely the Stradivarius and his Arnold instruments, to Bill Brown of New Ulm. Headed by William W. Brown, the Brown Music Company already enjoyed a powerful tradition in the promotion of old time music, as well as the concertina and other instruments to play it. At this juncture, Brown seized the opportunity to build upward from the Watters network for Arnold, Stradivarius and used concertinas. However, Watters kept in his bailiwick the sheet music business, proudly boasting his ownership of the 4,000 items acquired from the famed Silberhorn library to which he had added some 3,000 from other publishers so that he could claim his inventory of titles topped 7,000. Brown became well equipped with sheet music after acquiring the Vitak-Elsnic material in 1986. In addition, Brown Manufacturing in the early 1970s was producing the "Brown Concertina" and retailing other musical merchandise as well. In his own right, he was already a strong promoter of the concertina and its paraphernalia.

In the course of his active career it is believed that Bill Brown built between 50 and 60 of his own brand name concertinas. He also sold guitars, keyboard sound systems and a wide array of musical accoutrements. From his store at 2208 South Broadway opposite the Holiday Inn in New Ulm, Brown also owned copyrights

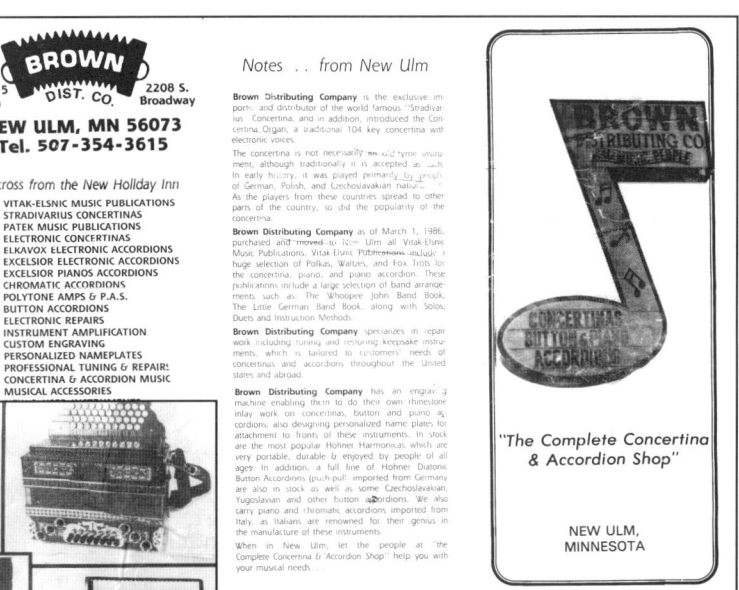

Advertisements for the Bill Brown distributing and musical retail business in New Ulm, Minnesota. Note his rightful boast to have acquired the Vitak-Elsnic musical remainder in 1986.

to the music of Whoopee John and arrangements like the Snow Waltz and the Red Raven Polka. Assisted by his son, Jim, Bill Brown also made the Buttontina, an instrument that allowed button accordion players to sound as though they were playing a concertina. The Brown establishment, billing itself during the 1980s as "The Complete Concertina & Accordion Shop," was especially proud in claiming to be the "exclusive importer and distributor of the world famous 'Stradivarius Concertina,' even though the Browns were exclusive only in the latter years of its import into the United States.

At the root of Watters' decision to disengage from the Stradivarius concertina, apparently, was his planned move to Mosinee. Already servicing concertinas in this central Wisconsin location was Dan Gruetzmacher [husband of *Music and Dance News* reporter, Sue Gruetzmacher], who offered repair and tuning at 1019 South Fifth Avenue in Wausau [now at T3136 Calico Lane, Wausau, Wisconsin 54403]. Long acquainted with Watters, having stayed at his house when studying the repair business and learning the concertina from John Bolster in Minneapolis, Dan Gruetzmacher was a natural for teaming with Watters. Inspired by his father, Dan Gruetzmacher took lessons from Fred Schaefer of Merrill, Wisconsin. At the age of nine in 1941 he played his first job with the family band for a wedding. Playing off and on in the meanwhile, Gruetzmacher was drafted into the army in 1955 and for 18 months performed his military "duty" by entertaining in Alaska. In 1967 he joined the Jolly Gentlemen, which changed names in 1974 to the Dan Gruetzmacher Orchestra.[21] Inducted into the World Concertina Congress Hall of Fame in 1979, Gruetzmacher is among the versatile players who exhibit mastery in playing the concertina. He can perform in any key with bass fill-ins that most players cannot achieve. In like manner, he can slip from Slovenian to Polish, German and Tyrolean styles with the utmost ease. After many appearances and recordings as the Gruetzmacher Orchestra, the band evolved into the "New" Gruetzmacher Band until Dan retired from Kraft Foods altogether and from the band business as such. Gruetzmacher did, however, continue to aid Brown in an advisory capacity while he assisted with Stradivarius concertina distribution in Wisconsin and Michigan. Also, Dan taught the concertina for decades, tunes the instrument for others, and is especially proficient in playing the bass side of the instrument.[22]

Dan Gruetzmacher at his home on Calico Lane near Wausau, Wisconsin demonstrates his Stradivarius concertina for LaVern Rippley on December 6, 2003. Gruetzmacher also owns a B-Flat Hengel concertina built in New Prague.

Dan Gruetzmacher at his home near Wausau, Wisconsin plays a Hohner concertina bearing the serial number 11334F, one of the few Hohner concertinas known in America. At Trossingen in Baden-Württemberg [far from Chemnitz and Carlsfeld] Hohner specializes in button box and piano key accordions. Photos by LaVern Rippley, December 6, 2003.

Included in the *News and Dance* announcement of the Brown Stradivarius acquisition is a brief biographical entry about the Browns in New Ulm. Founded by the senior Bill Brown in New Ulm and reaching back to the early 20th century, Brown's Music Store continued for generations, partly due to the versatility of his father. Both Bills were able musicians. They played various instruments and managed their own old time bands, which they fronted for decades on the dance circuit, at the New Ulm Polka Day and for other engagements. Being of retirement age and inclination, Watters "is happy that the trade relations he has so carefully and solicitously nurtured is in the hands of such an energetic service-dedicated organizational master as Bill Brown."[23] From this point forward, Bill Brown serviced sales in the western part of the upper Midwest states while Watters, with Gruetzmacher, handled Wisconsin and the eastern segment of the concertina market area. Together, they had the "Stradivarius" built in Italy with the so-called PLM [Pivot, Leverage, Motion] action—equipped with keys mounted to the rods with individual bearings.

Having been called by publicists "the Daddy of Wurlitzer accordion," Watters [pictured for the article] also reveals how he came to the concertina. An accordion man to begin with, he found it comparable and superior to the accordion as a solo and ensemble instrument, but one that had never enjoyed extensive promotion while the accordion's boosting, in the opinion of Watters, had already reached its maturity. In spite of the public's preference for the accordion, Watters contended, there were considerably more sheet music arrangements available for the concertina than for any other instrument except the piano and the violin. Motivated, and, in some respects absolutely driven, Watters traveled thousands of miles through upper Midwestern states visiting players and entertainers to gather a list of over 4,000 players. Of these, he claimed to be personally acquainted with over 2,000. To develop and cultivate his contacts with foreign suppliers, Watters also learned to read the German, French and Italian languages, a remarkable accomplishment on behalf of the concertina he loved so dearly.

From his new address on Route 3, Box 239, Mosinee,

The Masthead of Music and Dance News *for February/March 2004 headlines the 40th anniversary of the Wendingers Brothers Concertina Band.*

Wisconsin 54455, Watters continued his support for the concertina with the reprint of a photograph of the Milwaukee Concertina Circle Club of Milwaukee, composed of 21 concertina players accompanied by horns and a large drum on which was printed the date of the band's origin, 1889. Quite likely this was not actually the founding date of the concertina club. A concertina player born in Graz, Austria who had not arrived in the United States until 1910, Carl Griessbacher of West Allis, Wisconsin supplied Watters the picture. Griessbacher also alleged that around 1900 there were a half dozen Milwaukee concertina clubs, undoubtedly with German Lange boxes imported by Georgi and Vitak in the Chicago retail business. Also pictured are concertina club players from Pittsburgh. A letter from Duane Pichelman Enterprises of 420–16th Street S.W., Waverly Iowa, explains the success Watters enjoyed for sponsoring Concertina Day in Waverly. They were planning a fall "Iowa Concertina Festival."[24]

Settled now in his retirement home, technically at Knowlton on Lake Dubay [of which structure there is a picture on the front page of the first 1969 issue], Watters could relax a bit while still fostering the concertina and its playing fans. Featured in the first issue published at his new address in the fall of 1968 is John Check sporting his Hengel concertina. With his Wisconsin Dutchmen, Check had just been named Polka King of the state.[25] Check was good publicity for Watters because as chairman of the Department of Psychology at the University of Wisconsin-Oshkosh, he brought style from academia though his fame during this era as a concertinist came instead from his dance hall performances and his regular appearances on WLUK TV in Green Bay. Until his retirement from the university in 1987, Check showered the concertina with his ability as player, distinguished himself for his compositions, dance appearances, media events and for his role as a professor at the university.

In the same issue Bill Brown advertises his Stradivarius sales and service from New Ulm, while Dan Gruetzmacher runs advertisements for tuning and repairing at his Wausau residence. Also advertising for the first time are the Ray Stolzenberg Enterprises (and the Northern Playboys), who seek dance jobs. Stolzenberg also offers to buy used instruments and trade them at his 704 Tenth Avenue NW office in Austin, Minnesota 55912. Highlighted also with an agreeable photograph in this fall issue is Eddie Lash, the "King of

Concertina players appear on the Bandwagon Show, Mankato Television KEYC in 1986.
Row 1: Lori Nissel Ebel, Reuben Fenske (bending at the waist), Carmen Lochner, Cletus Goblirsch, Rudy Witthus, Christy Hengel, George Marek, Eddie Mathiowetz, Norbert Gag, Norman Hall.
Row 2: Ernie Coopman (standing below), Joel Stumpf, Alvin Chlan, Butch Hermann, Jay Minar, Jerry Minar, Marv Nissel.
Row 3: Larry Novotny, Ambrose Lewandowski, Russell Dietz, Peter Wendinger.

the Concertina," from Chicago, who had recently visited the Gruetzmacher booth at the Wisconsin Valley Fair in Wausau. Lash [Edward A. Laszczak] of Chicago was inducted into the World Concertina Congress Hall of Fame for his superb salesmanship of the concertina as well as for his ability to play it.[26] In the same issue, Servatius from Melrose reports on the national concertina festival at St. Cloud, with the winter version planned for January 26, 1969 and the next annual concertina festival to be held on July 20, 1970, again at St. Cloud.

After Watters departed Minnesota territory, his newsletter focus expanded to the more national scene, mentioning players: Vernon Drozd in Texas, Buddy Ketter in Los Angeles, George Hrica of Oak Park near Chicago, Bill Czerniak and his Nesgoda Naturals of Duluth along with the Duluth concertina club, an old photograph depicting 18 middle-aged men in the Western Pennsylvania Concertina Club, presumably Pittsburgh, Eddie Kurziel of Rothbury, Michigan and Ray Dorschner for whom Ray Konkol of Stevens Point was the concertinist. Center-folded in the Watters issue of July, August and September 1969 is a cursory history of the bandonion with photographs of Heinrich Band (1821-1860), and of Carl F. Uhlig of Chemnitz, credited as inventor of the concertina, as well as an historical piece about the Star Concertina Company of Chicago.

As detailed in a previous chapter, the Watters item mentions that the Star concertina factory began in 1926 under Walter Kadlubowski, Sr. and Walter Mojsiewicz at 2351 Milwaukee Avenue in Chicago and continued until its sale in 1963 to Walter Kadlubowski, Jr., though founders and tuner Mojsiewicz and Kajetan Perkowski still continued working for the new owners. Star concertinas at the time were being distributed by the Brown Music Store in New Ulm. Chief among the offerings of Bill Brown, however, was the Stradivarius which he acquired from Italy and merchandized [with Watters,

Bandwagon program KEYC, Mankato Minnesota. New Prague High School Polka Band.
First Row: Megan Ryan, Beth Otto, Amanda Gerold, Jacob Youngberg. Second Row: Curt Wick, Trevor Murchison, Justin Malecha, Samuel Jirik, Amanda Stocker, Susannah Rosival, Nathan Thompson, Michael Hennes, Jacob Gysland. Tuba - Christopher O'Dell, Piano - Melissa Wolf, Drums - James Callahan, Concertina - Timothy Chlan, Megan Pint, Dustin Bardon. Teacher is Sandra Gallagher. May 28, 2004.

Gruetzmacher and others] until his shop closed in 2002. As noted above, Brown also bolstered his appeal by holding most of the Vitak-Elsnic sheet music. However, the Gruetzmachers at Wausau also continue their sales of these products, in particular the sheet music once assembled by Silberhorn in Chicago.

Watters' third issue of 1969 features promotionally-inspired front page coverage of Tony and Betty Wolf's 37 concertina students. Now the Watters argument is that these students would function as multipliers in the concertina marketplace. As each grew in competence, he or she would start combos and orchestras or become teachers. In turn, Watters argues they have already brought in pyramidal clienteles for the concertina by recruiting hundreds of new players who would or did buy the instrument. Standing in the picture are both Betty and Tony Wolf, with Pat Watters at the extreme right, sons Ambrose and Arnie with daughter Lola, also in the photograph—taken presumably at St. Joseph, Minnesota.[27]

Ranging by this time more or less nationwide, Watters' reporters offer briefs from the primary concertina centers of the nation: George Hrica from Chicago and Charlotte King from Pittsburgh. King tells the story of Bill Moltz, who serves as president of the Pittsburgh Concertina Club. In Wausau, Sue Gruetzmacher reports about Joyce Koutecky appearing with Lou Prohut in Omaha and singing in both Czech and English. We learn about G. Luch Ladewski from the Indiana steel mills, Eddie Lash in Chicago and Walter Kadlubowski Jr., who at the time is actively heading the Star Concertina Company. Accompanying these reports are advertisements for the Stradivarius by Brown in New Ulm ["Excellence is not an accident—nothing has been left to chance"] and by the "eastern" sales center for Stradivarius, Dan Gruetzmacher in Wausau.

During 1970, Watters published for his readers a photograph of the 1929 Des Plaines Concertina Club, which consisted of 14 men bearing the names Linneman, Gunther, Bobzien (teacher), Minx, Kempke and Schuknecht, seated; standing, Zerrien, A. Ahrens, G. Ahrends, Forsyth, Sallee, Lang, Linneman and Gutekunst. Pictured, too, is the Continental Concertina Club of West Bend, Mequon and Grafton, Wisconsin, near Milwaukee. Last names of the members pictured are Klaman, Landowski, Kiefer, Eickstedt, Rennicke, Sickstedt, Ohm, Stanczyk, Emig, Herthem and Brunner. Also showcased is Irving DeWitz, a loyal tribute to this promoter of the Stradivarius on behalf of Watters. DeWitz had distinguished himself over a 40-year time frame for his concertina sales, especially the 1960s Watters' import from Italy. On the *Music and Dance News* front cover this time is the now familiar photograph of Irving DeWitz with his eight-year-old daughter, Lucille, taken about 1930, when the concertinas were available only from Germany or from the builders in Chicago. This father-daughter team represents their Hustisford, Wisconsin DeWitz Music Store, where he taught 500 of his players, championed his own and local concertina clubs and orchestra groups, and, with his son, Robert, diligently

This Wunderlich concertina bears the Uhlig trademark, slanted corners with the harp logo. Thus it can be assumed that the instrument was built for the retail outlet of Wunderlich by either the Arnold enterprise in Carlsfeld or the Uhlig-Lange factory in Chemnitz. This one is a double reed owned by Ambrose Kodet of Mankato, Minnesota.

Above is an early model of the Majestic built by the Lange company in Chemnitz, a 76-key instrument acquired by Kodet from Christy Hengel of New Ulm in 2004. It has the peculiarity of an air release hole in the back, called by some players the "shirt sucker." The front is plain.

John [Czech] Check, retired professor at UW-Oshkosh, Wisconsin began his first dance band in 1939 at Stevens Point. When teaching at Flint College in Michigan, he started the "Michigan Dutchmen" in 1959. After returning to Wisconsin in 1966 he started "The Wisconsin Dutchmen."

Hartford, Wisconsin Radio Station WTKM at the Chandelier Ballroom where John Check emceed the afternoon program. Taken March 19, 2005.

marketed the Stradivarius concertina. It is this photograph that appears on the "Ach Ya" recording jacket for the history of German Music in Wisconsin.[28]

A brief feature of the 1970 dance magazine by Watters relates about Harold Zimmerman of Union, Michigan. It brings the family down two generations with a photograph of Charles, Jack, Harold and Charles Sr., who played along using an ancient "Wunderlich"[29] concertina. This instrument purportedly was purchased generations earlier from Henry Silberhorn, and is described as being still in good condition. According to the story, the Zimmerman family can boast owning two Star, one Glass, two Arno Arnold, one Patek and four Pearl Queen concertinas—in a manner of speaking, displaying at their home a mini-museum history of the concertina and its circuitous pathways within the United States. Though rare, the Wunderlich concertina actually comes from the C. A. Wunderlich Company of Siebenbrunn in Saxony [on the western periphery of Markneukirchen, Siebenbrunn being a suburb, which is no longer autonomous on today's maps]. It can be argued that the Wunderlich is among the best concertinas to be imported from Germany, superior to Lange. The best guess is that the Wunderlich was actually built for the Wunderlich sales people by the Ernst Louis and later the Alfred Arnold Company in Carlsfeld until about 1930. It employs the standard Max Scheffler keyboard equipped with double reeds, and, like various other concertina products, was sold under the retailer's name. C. A. Wunderlich himself was probably not a concertina builder but a musical distributor who sold concertinas and other instruments he acquired from generic producers.

Repeatedly during these early 1970s, John Check [Jan Czech, born near Rosholt, Wisconsin] is featured, partly because of his excellence as a concertina player, but in part because he offers testimonials to the Stradivarius used often during this era for his WLUK TV appearances in Green Bay, Wisconsin. A photograph of his band during its prime in 1970 appears in the popular collection of old time band photographs. At the time he is accompanied on his concertina by Dave Marvin, Don Hale, Ray Wifler, Willie Zeamer, LeRoy Wolter, Tim Morrissey, Dick Altreuter and Neil Wilson.[30] Holding his Ph.D. from the UW-Madison campus, Check became a professor of educational psychology at the University of Wisconsin-Oshkosh in 1966, which post he continued until his retirement in 1987. Throughout his career, he diligently cultivated the concertina, playing for dances, radio and television in the Midwest. His "Wisconsin Dutchmen" produced over 15 recorded albums, some of which feature the 100 polkas and waltzes he authored. In recognition of his "promotion" of the concertina, he was inducted into the World Concertina Congress Hall of Fame on October 3, 1981 at New Ulm, Minnesota, playing for that event a Hengel instrument.[31] Check continues actively playing annually at the Allenton, Wisconsin, concertina festival, at the Hartford, Wisconsin, radio concertina festival in March and throughout the year.

Late in 1970 in the Watters publication, Sue Gruetzmacher reports on the Michigan concertina clubs, including the ones at Caspian, Muskegon, and Union, of which Harold Zimmerman—mentioned above—was both a member and a dealer for the Stradivarius. In the succeeding years the Michigan Concertina Association grew by considerable proportions. A club unto himself, in a way, was Eddie Rickert of Milwaukee, who, with his wife Ellie, was known across the Midwest as "Concertina Eddie." In March 1971, Dan Gruetzmacher and wife, Sue, founded the Midwest Concertina Club at Wausau. In the 1980s this organization evolved into the Central Wisconsin Concertina Club, then for a time branched off into the Goodtimers Concertina Association, which is now defunct. Simultaneously in Wisconsin, salesmen were active, selling especially the Star concertina and making a few on their own, among them Albert Wydra in Wisconsin Rapids [e. g. the Galaxy]. Wydra died December 31, 2003 at Riverview Hospital and was buried from St. Casimir Church in Stevens Point on January 3, 2004.

A genuine mainstay of concertina clubs was the Union, Michigan troupe headed by Jack Zimmerman. On March 19, 1972, the club, called Midwest Concertina Fans, held an annual bash with a host of guest performers, including Paul Futa from Indiana, Danny Boratyn of Toledo and Charles Vagrosky of Elyria, Ohio, Joe Stulga of Chicago, Ed Star of Gary, Tony Stimac of Lackport, Ilinois, Edward Kettmann and son from Lockport, and George Hrica, plus many others from Illinois.[32] During this period, Zimmerman of Union, Michigan "renames" his hometown village Zimmyville and bills his orchestra simply as Zimmy's, an illustration of "named" promotion at its best. Other concertina clubs in the Union, Michigan vicinity included the St. Joe Concertina Club of Michigan City. In Milwaukee, Wisconsin there was the Milwaukee Concertina Circle and, it appears, the Alpine Village Concertina Club.

Not far from Wisconsin or Michigan were the active concertina clubs of Chicago, all promoting the instrument both by subtle and more aggressive methods.[33] During the first half of the 20th century, the Chicago clubs were everywhere. Among the most prominent were the Bohemian-American Concertina Club [sometimes called Association, later of Berwyn, Illinois], which is cited frequently in the obituaries of the individuals whose death notices appear in the *Chicago Tribune* newspaper index. Others in Chicago were the Star Concertina Club, the Alpine Village Concertina Club, the Clarion Concertina Club, those championed by Rudy

This photograph of Irving DeWitz and his daughter, Lucille, of Hustiford, Wisconsin dates to approximately 1928 and has been used frequently to illustrate the role of teachers and promotion of the concertina.

This gray Patek concertina is #5466, therefore, a 1934 production model. In the picture on the next page we find the history of this concertina as written on the bottom of the reed plates. Note that it was tuned by Christ [sic.] Hengel in 1953, then of Sanborn, Minnesota. It was tuned in 2004 by the JBM team and converted to triple medium reeds on Hengel plates.

Patek, the Good Times Concertina Club, the St. Joe Concertina Club [in southwest Michigan] and countless others. Advertised from time to time in *Entertainment Bits* is the "47th Street Concertina Club," which featured George Stevens, the dancing violinist.[34] More than just a club, it was a band available for bookings. In a few distant states, like Pennsylvania and especially the City of Buffalo, New York, there were clubs, e. g. the Buffalo Concertina Club, from time to time one or two in California and in Nevada the Reno Concertina Club.[35] All clubs provided entertainment and companionship for the players, but all were primarily and unabashedly promoting the concertina. Sometimes a concertina club was informal. For many years groups of concertinists played on radio and television, notably on the Mankato KEYC Saturday night "Bandwagon" show. The performances continue today sometimes by local, more mature players, but occasionally by youth groups.

Frequently the story of an individual concertina is hidden on its inside. On the other hand, the repair and builder personnel are thereby not just recording their contributions but promoting their services. Thus, for example, a gray colored Patek concertina built in 1934 by Otto Schlicht bears the serial number 5466. It started its life in the key of C, a quadruple with piccolo reeds on the treble side. At some point it was reworked into a B-Flat instrument, accomplished by melted solder on the tips of the reeds. In January, 1953, this concertina was owned by 'Christ' Hengel of Sanborn, Minnesota, before he began merchandising himself by the name of Christy. Reportedly, this occurred only after a printer making dance band bills for Hengel spelled it with the 'y' thus giving it a more melodious name which Hengel liked and perpetuated. In 1953 when Hengel bought the Otto Schlicht equipment and remaining stock, the concertina was tuned by Christy Hengel and later in 2004 by Jerry and Jay Minar. In the meantime, the concertina was owned and played by Ernie Reck of Arcadia, Wisconsin, Mel Branstad in Minnesota, later by Byron Pearson in Red Wing, Minnesota, by Harlan Bussmen in Nebraska, and subsequently by Elmer Nienkark in Waterloo, Iowa. Finally in 2004 it ended up with Jerry Minar in New Prague where it was refurbished by Jerry and Jay Minar with Bill Hlavac at JBM Sound exchanging the piccolo reeds for three medium and one low reed combination.

Returning our attention to Pat Watters, we note

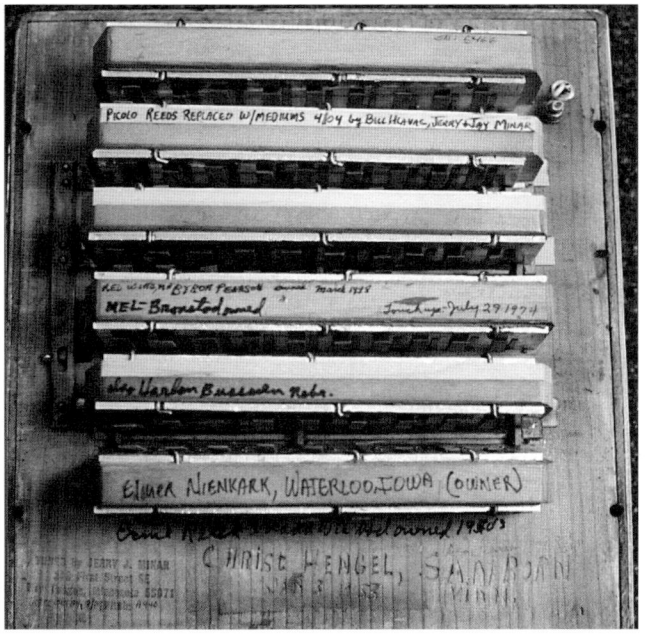

Timothy Chlan plays the concertina with fellow New Prague high school students on KEYC Television in Mankato, May 28, 2004.

that in 1974 he promoted the Gibbon Ballroom's July weekend as the "Big 1974 Concertina Jamboree." To the surprise of no one, he intended thereby to advance his own products. In his publication, he made mention of a 63-page booklet for learning the rather simple, hexagonal, English concertina and boosted Bernard and Barney King as the world's only professional twin concertinists [of course, on Stradivarius instruments]. He also called attention to the Kings' new Good Times Concertina Club, as well as the Bohemian American Concertina Association's members of Chicago, Henry Dauer, Frank Losos and Steve Palla, who were playing regularly for the Olympic Savings and Loan Association in the Chicago area.[36] Over the years *Music and Dance News* became more universal, reporting on harmonicas, accordions, stars like Welk and Eddie Blazonczyk, Dick Pillar, the former president of the national polka organization, and giving considerable effort also to promote the Polka Music Hall of Fame. The organ also acquired a new format, expanding from the 8" x 11" layout to a small newspaper look with the same number of pages. In the January, February and March issue of 1978, Watters pictured attendees at the 1977 World Concertina Congress Hall of Fame Awards program—among the recipients, Dennis and Adeline Wilfahrt for their father, Whoopee John, President Jack Zimmerman, Tony and Betty Wolf, plus others.

In early 1979, the World Concertina Congress tour, sponsored by Pat Watters and Jack Zimmerman, drew headlines with photographs of members meeting Austrians at Seefeld, a few miles north of Innsbruck. They had no inkling where the real cities of the con-

Bohemian American Concertina Association taken in 1949. *Officers for that year were George Stovicek, President; Mike Prevender, Vice-President; Laddie Prazak, Secretary; Anton Hovorka, Treasurer; Frank Sirovy, Sergeant-at-Arms; Edward Antczak, Trustee; Charles Snyder, Trustee. Seated from L–R [interweaving both rows]: Edward Dusek, Joseph A. Fencl, George Hrica, unknown, Rudolph Marek, Frank J. Groom, Victor Johnson, (center behind the drums) Frank Rychtik, Mike Prevender, Charles Triner, Fred Schaffek, Laddie Prazak.*
Standing L–R (interweaving both rows): George Stovicek standing low down without a concertina, James Herda, Richard Knize, Joseph Knize (concertina widely drawn to the right, Joseph Guzo (with violin), Edward Antczak, John Hofbaueer (without a concertina) Frank Christensen, Charles Burian (without a concertina) Martin Senica, Vince Brezinsky (hands clasped), Charles Snyder, Jack Simon (with saxophone) Chester Biernek, James Syndel (with saxophone), Laddie Kravcik, Edward Curin (upper rear without concertina) James Pittra, Anton Hovorka.
Note that the concertina has always been associated with both Bohemian and German immigrants and only secondarily with the Polish element in the United States.

certina were located. Also highlighted was the St. Joseph Concertina Club of Michigan City, Indiana, which had been newly organized in 1976. Fans during this period wrote to suggest that the Watters publication, *Music and Dance News*, though an inanimate object, should be elected to membership in the Polka Music Hall of Fame. For example, letter writer Charles M. Carlson of Minneapolis pens: "During the last 14 years you have enhanced polka music interest by publishing on what you aver is a 'break-even' cost basis. . . .[yours is] a music paper which entails not only the cost of publishing but expensive travelling to festivals and conferences, [and the] taking and reproducing of innumerable pictures. . . ."[37] Nobody acted on this advice but it does suggest the appreciation readers expressed for the Watters effort. Advertised now in most issues were the Czech Records offered by the Nebraska Record Company at Schuyler, featuring, among others, Al Grebnick, Ernie Kucera, Moostash Joe, Eddie Janek, the Omaha Brass Band, Math Sladky, the Bouncing Czechs and others.

What is noteworthy in the paper's many lists of players and bands is the continuous affinity of the Bohemian with the eastern Germans, replicating in persons living in the United States the geographic and cultural source of the concertina and its music. Also notable is the mention Watters makes of the annual World Concertina Congress with its April 1st deadline for nomination of new candidates. Lists of nominees needed to reach Secretary Jack Zimmerman in South Bend, Indiana, well in advance of the official meeting at the county Concertina Club in Union, Michigan.[38] The purpose of the Congress was as much to promote the instrument as to honor its players. During the early 1980s as well, Watters promoted European travel to Germany and Austria, a technique to showcase the instrument. Offerings were made in the name of the World Concertina Congress and managed by Jack Zimmerman, Treasurer of the organization living in Mishawaka, Indiana. Photographs show Chet Lasik and his Concertina Jamboree Celebration at Cafe Europe in Chicago, a record jacket with numbers like the Orphan's Lament Waltz, Ukrainian Girl Polka, German Woods Oberek, Happy Lover Waltz, plus others, none of which fit well into the Minnesota concertina tradition. Pictured too is Robert "Whoopee Bob" Nowitzki playing a Stradivarius in the Tomahawk, Merrill and Wausau areas in an effort to promote the coming Concertina and Bandonion jamboree scheduled for Middleton, Wisconsin.

The St. Joe's Concertina Club of St. Josep [Benton Harbor], Michigan, taken about 1975.
Front Row (L–R): Carol Liedtke, Clarence Tylisz, Louis Stupeck, Frank Liedtke, Christine Senerek. Middle Row: Casey Bruzdzinski, David Bruzdzinski, Joe Dusza, Phil Dusza, Ted Yagelski, Al Chalewa, Barney Katzmarek, Eddie Senkowski, Mike Morrisroe. Back Row: Ken Yagelski, Rick Yagelski, Stan Yagelski, Mitch Kmiecik, Dick Kamont, Mickey Srovec.
Tylisz operated bands from Michigan City, Indiana; the Brzdzinski father-son team are from Calumet City, Illinois. Ted Yagelski operated bands from Michigan City during the 1950s. Ken Yagelski is playing a Patek while most others are playing Star concertinas. Kamont from Michigan City is known for his Polka Party radio shows.

Tiring a bit and admittedly somewhat more driven by his used concertina and sheet music business than by editing the *Music and Dance News*, Pat Watters in 1981 began to combine two quarters into one.[39] He now lists all the members by that date in the

World Concertina Congress, alphabetically with state of residence: Roger Andersen, MI; Lyle Anthony, MI; Ray Anderson, WI; Virgil Baker, MI; Henry Beyer, MI; Rodney Beyer, MI; Rodney Bolterstein, MI; R. B. Bruckner, MI; Robert Babcock, MI; Robert Boneske, WI; Ronald Buczko, IL; Edward Benson, WI; Vilas Bartlet, WI; Leo Bartlet, WI; Richard Bjoraas, IN; Al Czerniak, WI; Joseph Czerniak, MN; George Carter, MI; Chester Chandler, WI; Edmund Dutkiewicz, WI; Henry a Dulak, WI; Bernard Dobrowolski, WI; Billy Ewert, WI; Pat Faux, WI; Paul Fudurick, WI; John Foytek, WI; Raymond Gumberg, MI; Dan Gruetzmacher, WI; Eugene Fraffunder, WI; Maureen Harju, MI; Kenneth Hawkins, MI; Eileen Hawkins, MI; Dale Henrickson, MI; Clarence Hack, WI; Taina Hawkins, MI; Dale Henrickson, MI; Clarence Hack, WI; Cliff Hermel, MN; George Hrica, FL; John Hennes, MI; Joseph F. Harast Jr., Il; Stanley Jansen, MI; Wilbur Jensen, MI; Walter Li'l Wally Jagiello, FL; Stanley Kazlauskas, MI; Mitchel Kulswiak Jr., MI; William Kucaitis, MI; Frank Kucera, CA; Michael Kukura, MI; Alfred Nanitz, WI; Victor Kuchera, WI; Ed Kettman Jr., IL; Earl Kops, MI; Burney King, WI; Barney King, WI; Walter Kuncaitis, IL; Joseph Kulisz, MI; Joesph Kujanick, IN; Ted Kiewicz, IN; Frank Kubik, WV; Michael Katich MI; Steve Kalder, WI; John Koppa, WI; Dave Kramas, WI; Bonnie Kurth, WI; Heinie Kriewald, WI; Don Kleinschmidt, WI; Joseph Lenzo, MI; Stephen Litwin, NY; James Legner, WI; Louis Legner, WI; Frank Legner, WI; Gordon Lemke, MN; Elmer Livanec, MI; John Marek, MI; John McKillop Jr., MI; James Miskosky, MI; Michael Milosh, MI; Jerry Minar, MN; Orland Mean, MI; Archie Maxim, MI; Jerry Macey, IL; Russell Maki, ID; Robert Mathiowetz, WI; Joseph Malchowski, WI; Bill Moltz, PA; Robert Nowitzki, WI; Gordon Normand, WI; Marion Nowogurski, MI; Roger Novak, WI; Stanley Nowicki, WI; Edward Olshanski, WI; Casimer J. Piusis, MI; Stanley Palusewski, MI; Nancy Paluszewski, MI; Paul J. Peshel, IL; Edward Regina, MI; Millard Ringle, WI; Bernard Rekowski, WI; LaVern Soberalski, MI; Jerry Stedronsky, MI; Paul Sweeney, MI; Edward P. Schultz, MI; Ray Stolzenberg, MN; Michey Svorek, MI; Frank Stanczewski, NY; Arthur Schmuldt, MI; Robert Storch, MI; Arnold Sundell, WI; Robert Schwartz, WI; Joseph Starck, MN; George Servatius, MN; Albeert Tabaczka, MI; Peter Tarczon, MI; Albert Villadlsen, MI; Carl Voigt, WI; Charles Vagrosky, OH; John White, MI; Barbara Wisniski, MI; Pat Watters, WI; Harry Weber, IN; John Whalley, WI; Anton Wolfe, WI; Adam Wanta, WI; Neil Wayne, England; Bill Wilkerson, MI; Harry Wroblewski, IL; Donald Walser, MN; Tony Wolf, MN; Jessy Zalis, MI; Edward Zalis, MI; Richard Zatarga, MI; Raymond Zelasko, IL; Chuck Zimmerman, WI; Jack Zimmerman, IN; Harold Zimmerman, IN. Clearly, in the early 1980s, the membership is a Michigan and Wisconsin organization despite its title of "world" and even these two states can be reduced to east central Wisconsin, south-western Michigan and northern Indiana; Iowans and Minnesotans are negligible.

This membership list is appended with a secondary grouping of names to whom are added those more recently joining the World Concertina Congress. The names included familiar pioneers of the concertina as an instrument: John Bernhardt, IL; George Burkhard, PA; Harry Dolata, WI; Gloria Dzekute, WI; Joseph Fronek, IN;

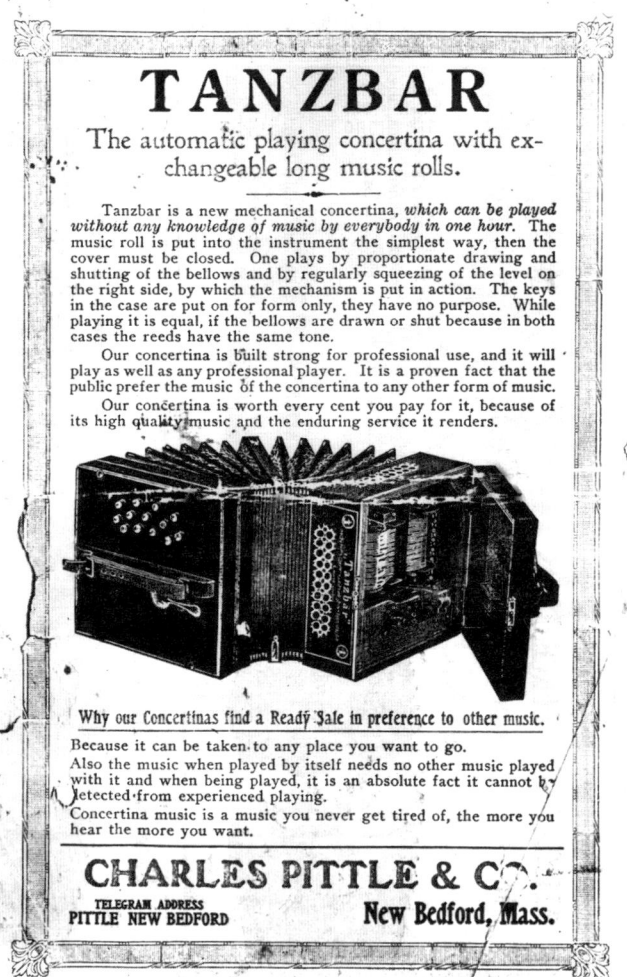

This German built tanzbär [dancing bear] has its original nameplate with the umlaut over the ä. When promoted in America by East Coast retailers, the umlaut was dropped. See also page 24.

Leon Floweors, IL; Frank Goetsch, WI; Peter Glazik, Il; Charles Hellwig, IL; John Hennes, IL; Suzie Henkle, MI; Frank Jasinek, WI; Giles Kahr, WI; Wm Red Ketter, CA; Joseph L. Kiebles, IL; Paul Kramas Sr., WI; Mildred Kaminski, WI; Chester Konieczki, IL; Bruce Libby, WI; E. P. Loranz, MT; Henry Munich, WI; Andrew Misure, NY; Lorraine Meyers, WI; Varney Nitka WI; Alelx Novogroski, IL; John Nowak, OH; Ralph Noll, WI; John J. Oberstar, MN; Casimir J. Pienizek, IL; Max Peters, WI; Helmut Peters, IL; Louis Proudfit, IN; Anton Procevicz, OK; Albert Piselac, PA: Peter Perveiler, WI; Les Petersen, IL; Stanley Peterson, WI; Sydney Peterson, WI; Stan Prankuys, IN; Eddie Rickert, FL; Walter Roback, MN; Don Roback, MN;Andrew Roll, MO; Adolph Strauss, PA; Art Schmuldt, MI; Ernest Silberhorn, IL; Edward Skrzekut, IL; Chester Srutkowski, IL; Leo-Irene Wittsche, MI. The then-inducted Hall of Famers among them were Watters, George Hrica, Rudy Patek and Stanley Nowicki.

At the 1981 Minnesota State Polka Festival at the Bel Rae Ballroom in Mounds View, the date of Sunday, June 21, was publicized as concertina day. Bands appearing included Bill Czerniak, Renata & Girls, as well as the Wendinger brothers. At the International Polka Association Festival the same year at the Red Carpet Inn in Milwaukee were many bands from there and Chicago, some with concertinas. All the while Watters continued to offer for sale the Stradivarius and now the Stradella Italian-made new concertinas plus many second-hand Pearl Queen, Glass, Patek, Star and Arnold concertinas. Always center stage during this era was John Check with his Stradivarius concertina, although he traded it for a Hengel, and, especially in later years, more often than not, played this new Hengel. Also reported by Martha Czerniak in 1981 are the successes the Czerniaks had in the Duluth, Minnesota area promoting the concertina—ever since Joe first acquired one from Watters in 1965.

After a long and powerfully active career on behalf of the concertina, Pat Watters died in 1982. According to his brief obituary, Bennett "Pat" Watters died on Sunday, July 18, 1982 at St. Joseph's Hospital in Marshfield. At the time, he had been living at 1572 Iris Lane, Mosinee. Born on September 21, 1902 in Texas, the son of Ralph and Alice Patrick Watters, he married Marie Fondow in Antigo, Wisconsin, on May 16, 1936. From then until 1968 he lived in Minneapolis, where he pursued his career operating a music store. After moving to Knowlton, Wisconsin, he continued to sell musical instruments and also to publish *Music and Dance News*.

His survivors included not only his wife but also a son, Daniel, and two daughters, Charee and Judith, who were living in the Twin Cities. Most of the Watters remaining retail merchandise and related operations had been transferred, effective October 1, 1980, to Gruetzmacher Concertina Sales at Route 3, Box 334A, [now T 3136 Calico Lane] Wausau, Wisconsin.[40] Sue Gruetzmacher continues actively marketing the Silberhorn sheet music acquired from Watters.

Dance bands spawned from Watters' efforts with the Czerniak endeavors include Renata and Girls, the Dick Jaski Beaconaires, Dennis Zuk, Jim and Jeff Dobosenski, Ted Dobosenski, Polka Sweethearts, Harmony Stars, the David Greczyak Old Timers, and Leroy Lahti of Wisconsin, plus the Greg Czerniak Music Inc. enterprise. The Czerniak sons of Joe, Bill and Greg made the record album "Twin Concertinas" according to Father Joe's arrangement.[41] In the late fall of 1981, the publication reports the death of concertina master, Tony Wolf, in St. Joseph, though Betty carries on. Anton J. Wolf was born March 4, 1916 in New Prague and died on June 24, 1980 in St. Cloud, Minnesota. His funeral was on June 26, 1980 at St. Joseph's Parish in St. Joseph. Admitted also to the Concertina Hall of Fame that year were Ray Stolzenberg of Austin, Minnesota, as well as Casey Siewierski and Lou Prohut of Chicago. This time around, the World Concertina Congress meeting in New Ulm offered sessions headed by Jerry Schuft, an on-stage show by Frank Stann, and award recipients Joe Czerniak of Duluth and John Check of Oshkosh. The masterful Check is once again credited not only with fronting his Wisconsin Dutchmen for decades, but for composing over a hundred pieces of music for the concertina.[42]

More recently, three original music manuscripts of John Check were requested and then donated to the archives of the Music Museum at the University of South Dakota. Many other compositions, some 50 in all, were donated by Check to the Wisconsin Music Archives in the Mills Music Library in Madison. Accompanying the deposit were albums, compact discs, plus other items so that today the University of Wisconsin Music Archives has 84 of his original tunes and recordings of these scores for researchers and historians of popular music.[43]

Earlier in this chapter the promotional efforts of Bill Brown have been detailed. In all respects the Brown family [Bill and Helen Brown of Brown Distributing in New Ulm] were great promoters of the concertina in

Minnesota. Not only did they market the Stradivarius for Watters, they also built their own concertinas with parts from abroad and some created domestically. Of particular note was their acquisition of the Vitak-Elsnic Company's supply of music for accordion, concertina and other instruments that functioned for more than 50 years in Chicago. Marketing the Pearl Queen concertina built by Otto Schlicht and his team, Vitak-Elsnic bought the Colonial Music Company in the 1930s to give their distributorship nationwide capability. When business waned in the 1960s, their sales declined steadily, concluding with their transaction of inventories to Bill Brown in 1986. The Browns reproduced and sold from the original Vitak-Elsnic catalogs. Assisting the elder Brown in repair were Vince Sandhurst, Donald Klossner and David Ayer, who worked on electronics. Brown's three eldest sons traveled, making sales for the distributorship. On and off for a good 20 years Brown played trumpet, tuba and concertina with The Six Fat Dutchmen, Babe Wagner, Fezz Fritsche, Clem Rhode and with his own Brown family concertina orchestra. For his many efforts and talents, Bill Brown in 1986 was inducted into the World Concertina Congress Hall of Fame. However, in March 2002, the Brown firm ceased operations.[44]

In a different category but a 1986 inductee into the World Concertina Congress nevertheless, was George Servatius of Melrose. Continuing in business from his Melrose, Minnesota home, Servatius began his career over 50 years ago on the ballroom circuit. From his neighbor and friend Tony Moening, playing a concertina on the back porch, Servatius learned the concertina. A few years later when Moening got married, he traded in his "costly" concertina for a "cost-saving" washing machine. Be that as it may, Servatius inherited the area's concertina clientele orbit from Moening, though 20 years later they joined each other to found the Melrose Clown Band, which proved such a success that it remained in demand for 30 years thereafter. Together with Moening and more so with Tony Wolf's Deutschmeisters, Servatius played for and assisted with various concertina festivals and in 1973 initiated "George's Big Annual Concertina Party." Known today as the GBA, Servatius annually assists with the April concertina party

Richard "Farmer Rich" Brown plays entirely by ear. Although born in Chippewa Falls, Wisconsin in 1957, he has lived since 1964 in Cleveland, Wisconsin, where he has worked as a chicken farmer and a carpenter. Heading the Polka Meisters Band, he is especially proud of, and skilled with, his Star shell in which he has installed reeds crafted by John Friedl and extracted from an old Patek Deluxe. His B-Flat instrument rings especially clear when rendering Dutchman-style numbers. Taken March 20, 2005 at Chandelier Hall in Hartford, Wisconsin.

Born in 1952 in New Prague, Minnesota, Gary Pikal learned to play an Arnold triple concertina in 1964, aided by lessons from Jerry Minar. In 1970, accompanied by his father, he ordered a Hengel key of "C" concertina from Christy Hengel, but did not get delivery until 1976. In the meantime, he bought a Star quad from Stan Uhlir in Montgomery. The year 1970 was the start of a playing career when he entertained at the local FFA banquet, which resulted in "Gary's Concertina Band." Soon after, the band added players and renamed the group to "The Sound Arrivals," which operated until 1977. After a short pause, a reconstituted group was formed and called "The Revival Band." The Revival Band operated from 1978 through 2001 and was performing 50 to 75 dance jobs per year, throughout the state of Minnesota. Using the acquired Hengel C and an E-Flat Stradivarius concertina Pikal acquired from Minar, the band played a mix of polka music and "rock and roll." Currently Pikal has regrouped and is performing as the "St. Wenceslaus Polka Worship Group," doing church music.

held at the Melrose VFW Club. In the 1950s, Servatius on the concertina was supported by musicians Jack Pfau of Freeport, Erv Mayer of Meire Grove, Dick Hiemenz of St. Cloud, Louis Schley of Sauk Centre and Louis Kunkel of Melrose. Assisted by his wife, Nellie, Servatius continues his concertina repair, musical score sales and his enormous interest and ability with the concertina.45 His promotional efforts have resulted in considerable success for the concertina in central Minnesota.

Perhaps nothing today is more effective in promoting the concertina than the Internet. Type in the word on any search engine and the sites scroll up profusely. Names particularly worthy of mention for their concertina websites include Loren Schaeffler, Chris Timson, Paul Schwartz, Dan Melander, Karen and Wim Wakker, Dan Gruetzmacher, Harry Geuns, Terry Knight, and Steve Litwin. Ken, Rick, Stanley and Ted Yagelski are especially noteworthy for their photographs and World Concertina Congress listings. Two worthwhile websites in Germany are http://www.uni-bamberg.de/ppp/ethno-musikologie/Konzertina/K-Men%FC.htm and http://www.chemnitz-concertina.de/de/index.htm, which tell and show the status of concertina history and examples through the instrument's history.

Useful especially are three sites
1) http://www.concertinamusic.com/sbox/timeline.html
2) http://www.concertinamusic.com/sbox/links.html
3) http://www.concertinamusic.com/sbox/wcchof.html

Without a shadow of doubt, it is the website with its capabilities for music and sales that will keep the concertina at the forefront of investigators. However, it is unlikely that this method of promotion will ever be able to surpass the instrument being played. Sales will still need to allow the customer to finger the product, to manipulate its buttons and bellows before the tones in turn will sell themselves. Buyers and enthusiasts cannot be created by viewing a picture of the instrument alone. The hall, the display, and the skill of the performer enjoying good acoustics will remain the best promotion of the concertina. e-Bay auctions can display; they can but are not yet accurate in demonstrating the tactile and tonal quality of the musical goods.

Footnotes

1 Of course, there were other documents and booklets for instruction on how to play the concertina. An example is the "National Self Teacher for Concertina, 76, 94, or 102 Keys (Square Shape)," which sold for the price of 25 cents plus 2 cents for postage, by the Chart Music Publishing House in Chicago in 1919, an 18-page document which included some simple melodies like 'My Country Tis of Thee,' 'Home Sweet Home' and the 'Spanish Waltz.' Many more are listed in the chapter explaining how to play the concertina.

2 Also, members of this band, in addition to Dietzel playing his Clarion concertina triple, include Art Muchler on clarinet, Dooley Hoeltz on saxophone, William Schoen on drums and George Streu on coronet, as described in the newspaper and reprinted by Silberhorn: "John Dietzel and his old time concertina orchestra of Hamburg, Minnesota stopped here a short while en route to Minneapolis where they broadcast over WCCO radio station that afternoon at 2:30. The old time program lasted until 4:00 o'clock and the reporter, together with many of the local citizens, greatly enjoyed listening to the fine program of this band of old time musicians. They rendered several numbers of old time favorites which certainly were appreciated. They are excellent musicians when it comes to playing old time music."

3 Here and below, Silberhorn's *Booster* (June/July 1928), p. 6.

4 *Booster*, (Summer 1930), p. 10.

5 *Booster*, Vol. 14 (Spring 1932).

6 *Booster* (Christmas 1932), front page.

7 *Patek Concertinas* (a catalogue of products from about 1932.) In 1937, effective July 1, Patek sends the catalog with an insert showing "new price list of Patek concertinas" leading to the conclusion that the original catalog dates from a few years earlier, possibly still from 1932.

8 Catalog, p. 12.

9 The 1935-37 Patek Catalog, p. 21.

10 See *Concertina News* published by Vitak-Elsnic Co., Chicago Illinois, Volume 5, No. 5 (Fall 1931).

11 At this juncture the factory is at Hengel's home at 403 North Minnesota Street in New Ulm, although the letterhead is still Waseca where he had resided preceding his move to New Ulm.

12 The Hengel newsletters are available at the home of Ambrose Kodet in North Mankato and through the preservation and collection of concertina history by Jerry Minar in New Prague, Minnesota.

13 The year 1976 seems to be the end of the Hengel newsletters.

14 *Polka and Old Time News* began publication in 1963 and concluded already in 1965. In the course of its brief life It offered interesting and familiar material along with informative advertisements.

15 On the back cover of *Polka and Old Time News* Hengel bought an ad in which he lists the artists who then are playing his instrument in their bands: Emil Milbrett, Elmer Scheid, Ernie Coopman, Donnie Klossner, Larry Dorschner, Lowell Schubert, Gil Steil, Milo Edel, Wilbert Blohm, Harold Schwer, Edwin Kvitek, Dennis Scheper, Ted Otremba, Ray Konkol, Dorine Kulzer, Sylvester Liebl, Murv Adler, Ray Trenda, Marv Nissel, Howard Fratzke, George Kabes, Alvin Chlan, Sevcik Brothers, Gust Pries, Otto Hoef, Reine Motschke, Marv Manthey, and Marvin Bulau.

16 Artists' Life of Orange, CA, Columbia of NY, Cuca of Sauk City, WI, Decca of NY, Dot of Hollywood, CA, December of Stevens Point, WI, Gold Star of Appleton, WI, Jay Jay of Chicago, IL, Lodestar of

Minneapolis, MN, Northland of Wausau, WI, Pleasant Peasant of Minneapolis, MN, Pageant of Juneau, WI, Polkaland of Sheboygan, WI, RCA Victor of NY, and Soma of Minneapolis, MN.

17 *Music and Dance News; International-Old time 'oom pah' Popular*, (April, May, June 1967). See also a brief history of the concertina by Pat Watters in *Polka & Old Time News* (May, 1964), 11, reportedly condensed from an article in *Music Trades Magazine*.

18 Ibid., p. 3.

19 Front page, *Music and Dance News* (January, February, March 1968).

20 Ibid., p. 2.

21 Sara Bredesen, "Back to One. Concertina Celebrity Retires from Professional Life, Plays for Fun," *The Country Today* [Eau Claire, Wisconsin], Section C, *Country Market*, front page.

22 http://www.gruetzmacherconcertina.com/. On December 7, 2003 I attended his "final" dance for the public held at Hatley, east of Wausau, which no one believes will be absolutely his last such endeavor.

23 Ibid. Music and Dance News (January, February, March, 1968), p. 2.

24 *Music and Dance News* (April, May, June 1968).

25 Ibid., October, November, December 1968

26 http://www.concertinamusic.com/sbox/images/ eddielash1964.jpg

27 *Music and Dance News* (July, August, September 1969).

28 *Music and Dance News* (April, May, June 1970). DeWitz also sold farm machinery and pumps. Most of all, though, he was in love with the concertina. Cf. James P. Leary, "The German Concertina in the Upper Midwest" in Philip V. Bohlman and Otto Holzapfel, *Land without Nightingales* (Madison: Max Kade Institute, 2002), pp. 202-203. The picture appears on p. 204. See also the recording "Ach Ya—Traditional German-American Music from Wisconsin" (Madison: Wisconsin Folklife Center of the Max Kade Institute, 1986), two discs.

29 Letter from John Bernhardt, last builder of the Star Concertina, July 19, 2002. The owner of two Wunderlichs, Bernhardt in his letter reports that the Wunderlich concertinas were probably built by Ernst Louis Arnold and later by Alfred and Paul Arnold in nearby Carlsfeld—as reported to him by Chris Wagner, "Das Akkordeon oder die Erfindung der popularen Musik." See also Hans-Peter Graf, "Concertina und Bandoneonkultur: Organisierte Arbeiterfreizeit in Deutschland zwischen 1870 und dem Ende der Weimarer Republik," in Sabine Schutte, ed., *Geschichte der Musik in Deutschland* (Hamburg: Rowohlt, 1987), pp. 212-236.

30 *Bands. Old Timers Picture Album* No. 2, originally collected and printed by Der Cammack, a bass horn player in Mankato, Minnesota, available from Dennis Brown, Lakefield, Minnesota 56150.

31 *Sunday Post-Crescent*, Appleton-Neenah-Menasha, Wisconsin, June 28, 1981.

32 *Music and Dance News* (April, May, June 1972).

33 One of the early Chicago clubs of 1895 is pictured in the book *Land Without Nightingales*, op cit., p. 199.

34 *Entertainment Bits* (February 1979), p. 32.

35 Reported by Edwin Suterko of Reno and others.

36 *Music and Dance News* (April, May, June 1974).

37 *Music and Dance News* (January, February, March 1979), p. 4.

38 *Music and Dance News* (October, November, December 1980).

39 *Music and Dance News* (January, February, March, April, May, June 1981).

40 *Mosinee Times* (July 22, 1982), p. 4. See also the *Mosinee Times* (August 5, 1976) for a special article by editor Ann Brill about the lives of Pat and Marie Watters of Knowlton, Wisconsin.

41 *Music and Dance News* (January, February, March, April, May, June 1981).

42 Ibid. (October, November, December 1981).

43 *Music and Dance News* (June, July, 2002), p 9.

44 Entertainment Bits (October and November 1986), pp. 4-5, with pictures.

45 Brochures and newspaper clippings gathered during an interview with Servatius at his Melrose home June 26, 2003.

6
How the Concertina is Played

During the course of the Chemnitzer concertina's history, most fabricators offered techniques about how the instrument would and should be manipulated. All proponents of the concertina since its creation in 1834 insist the concertina may look formidable but is really beginner-friendly. Some view the prospect of producing music from this mysterious square button box as being so simple the player would never need to know how to read notes. To this day, many concertina musicians still do not read notes and when they do, they often transpose them into a digital system. Along with notes on clefs, erstwhile instructors have devised a workable system of numbers. If the number has a carrot, ^ , then the bellows are pushed. Un-capped, they are pulled apart. Early on the scene manuals to help novices learn the concertina seem to originate on both the German and the English sides of the instrument's history.

From those documents which use the word "German," it is safe to conclude that they target the Uhlig models first and foremost.[1] From the perspective of 2005, we might point out that expanded keyboards never really caught on in the United States. In South America the bandonion retains popularity with many more keys than the American Chemnitzer concertina. Instruments with 102 keys in the 1920s grew to 104 keys, which remains the standard arrangement to this day. The 130 key pattern configured by Albert G. Nechanicky, "Nicky", using 124 and then 130 keys in the 1980s, was another attempt which never ignited performers' fancies. Concertina players in the upper Midwest said: "Too big, too heavy, too expensive, just don't need

The Alfred Arnold Company sold its concertinas with a special cylinder to retain the screwdriver tool for easy access to the inside — notably mounted on the left near the hand strap in the photograph. The harp depicted on the corners is reminiscent of the Uhlig-Lange logo.

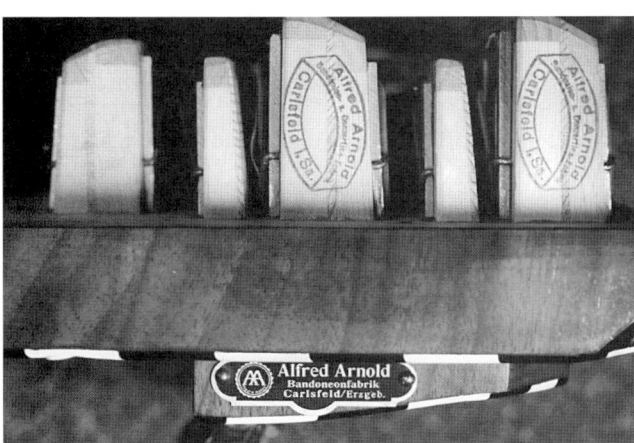

Note that the Alfred Arnold Bandonion and Concertina fabricators prominently stamped their name and address on the inner reed blocks of the concertina. This one's serial number is 109022, dated March 28, 1939, and owned by Jerry Minar.

→ 175

more keys." That the Chemnitzer concertina enjoyed international status by the mid 19th century is indicated by its inclusion in books like Hector Berlioz' *Instrumentationslehre*. Born in 1803, Berlioz lived his entire life in France and died in Paris in 1869.[2] Also, the instrument was showing up at industrial fairs all over Europe. In 1851 Carl Zimmermann of Carlsfeld exhibited his wares in London. In 1855 at the exposition in Paris, Heinrich Band came from Krefeld. When Europeans came to Chemnitz for a musical instrument showing, Christian Friedrich Reichel came from nearby Waldheim, Carl Friedrich Uhlig arrived from his store on Rosenplatz to display instruments, as did Ernst Louis Arnold from Carlsfeld.[3]

In the Jerry Minar collection of memorabilia are flyers from 1850 displaying "Praktischer Selbstlehrer für Concertina mit 58 und 74 Tönen" (a practical self-teaching method to play the concertina) by Carl Zimmermann of Carlsfeld in Saxony. This self-instruction manual is of considerable interest to the learner because it is the first known manual issued in both German and English, on identical facing pages, including dual hand and button tables for finger positions.[4] There can be little doubt that Henry Silberhorn and other American publishers had access to this booklet. Mentioned also in mid-19th century lists of teaching materials for the concertina are manuals such as the one written by the Krefeld music teacher, Heinrich Band, inventor of the Bandonion. His *Accordionshchule für 40- und 44 tönige Accordions, oder die Kunst, bei einigen Notenkent-*

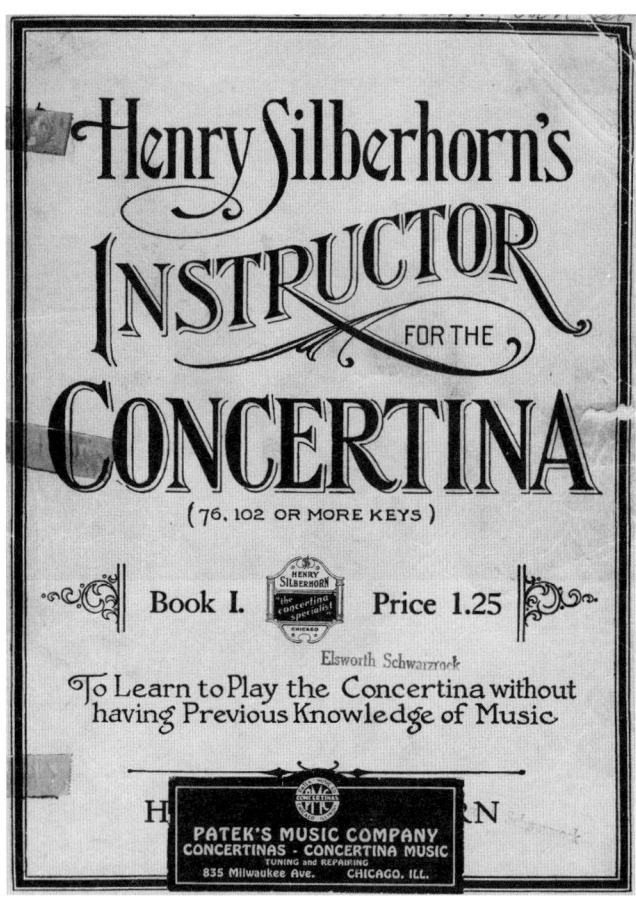

The Silberhorn instructional manual went through many editions. The one pictured above is called the Sixth Improved Edition of Book I and bears the date of 1927, "international copyright secured." In evidence is the overlaid label at the bottom, showing that it was sold by the Patek Music Company at 835 Milwaukee Avenue in Chicago. It was sold to Elsworth Schwarzrock of Bird Island, Minnesota.

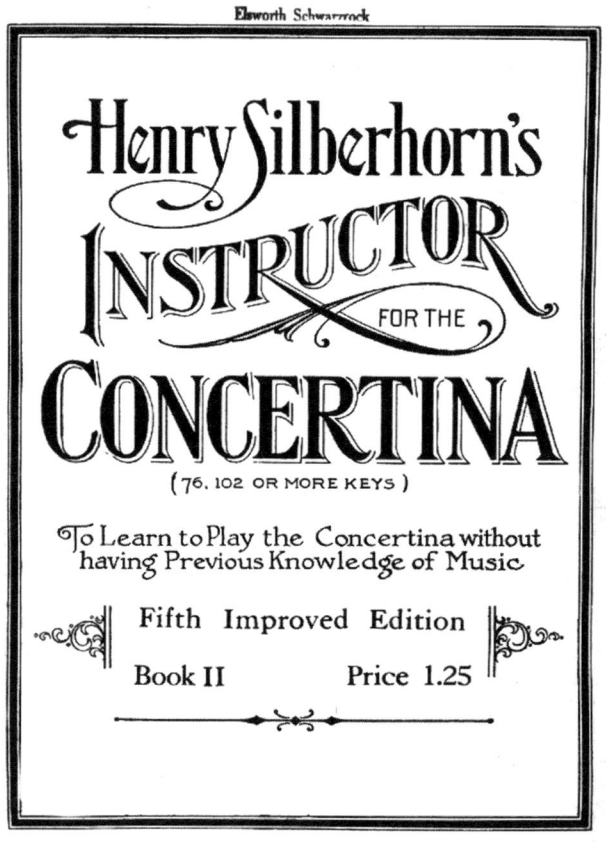

Silberhorn's Book II builds on the first book, the one shown here being the Fifth Improved Edition bearing a date of 1921, "international copyright secured." The Silberhorn books were probably first printed in 1910. Silberhorn moved his operation from Milwaukee Avenue to 5942 North Talman Avenue. The earliest letterhead from this address is August 22, 1943. As late as March 4, 1954 he is still at the Talman Avenue address. This copy is from his last retail site.

nissen in kurzer Zeit selbst ohne Lehrer die schwierigsten Musikstücke spielen zu lernen [Accordion school for 40 and 44 key accordions—or the art of learning to play the most difficult numbers with little or no knowledge of notes and without a teacher] is a good example.5 There is likewise little doubt that Band had access to the instruction books of Zimmermann in Carlsfeld and vice versa. Others in Germany were prolific in the printing and distribution of publications how the instrument is played. Largest and best known was the Oskar Seifert publishing house in Eppendorf which issued the Seifert'schen Notenausgaben [Seifert's Concertina notes, which were, of course, just numbers on clefs] for concertina and bandonion.6

Among the earliest American teachers to publish a methodology how the concertina is played today, however, is the preeminent Chicago teacher, Henry Silberhorn. On the cover of his Catalogue of *Music for the Concertina*, Silberhorn addresses the concertina player.

My whole life has been devoted to the Concertina and the Concertina player. I learned to play Concertina in the year of 1886, at a time when there was practically no music or instruction book for the Concertina. Having studied music for some years previous to this time, it was possible for me to arrange Concertina music for myself and other players in a short time. Thereafter, I taught hundreds how to play Concertina and in 1910 published an Instruction Book which proved to be the basis of the practical Concertina method of today and the foundation of its importance as a musical instrument. Thousands of pieces have been arranged and published by me for the Concertina as well as several improved editions of the instruction books. For many fine arrangements in this catalogue, I am indebted to Mr. Frank F. Schmidt, an able and distinguished Concertina player and arranger. Mr. Schmidt has been my pupil and assistant and is well fitted to make arrangements according to the practical methods I have established. I

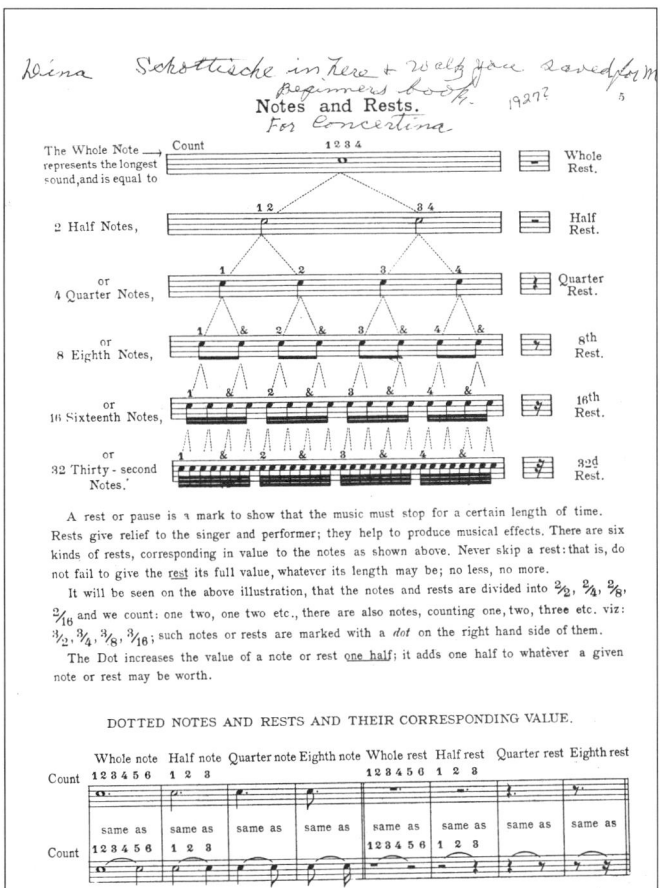

The rudiments of music theory from Silberhorn's book.

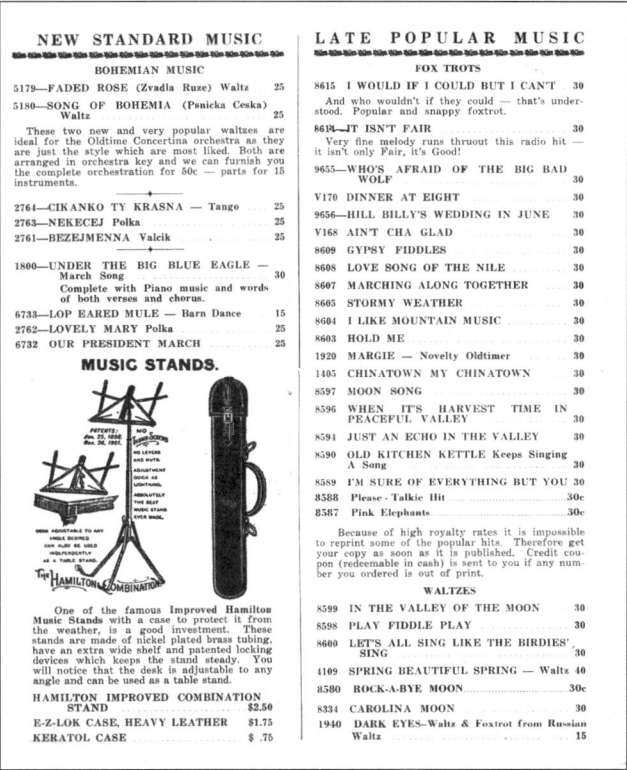

Note that Vitak-Elsnic, both of Czech heritage, pushed Bohemian music in their sales catalogs.

believe in the Concertina and its future. Everywhere— everybody likes its tone and it is bound to become a nationally popular musical instrument if the individual player will strive for faultless performance.7

Perhaps one of the first to suggest the simplified approach by which the novice need not read a single note, but only digits, Silberhorn in his 1927 edition of the 60-page booklet, secured an international copyright. However, the method of instruction seems to rest heavily on the German publications that preceded him. On the cover of Silberhorn's instructional manual, the author proudly stamped his own coat of arms and the words: "Henry Silberhorn, the concertina Specialist, Chicago."8 The very first publication of a Silberhorn booklet occurred as early as 1910. Once it appeared, it became overnight the supportive tool which, during the next decades, became the best recognized method of instruction for thousands of players. On the title page near the bottom, the following words appear: "To learn to play the concertina without having previous knowledge of music," words which Silberhorn reiterates in his preface, elucidating that the book is expressly for the benefit of beginners who have had the desire to play a concertina and cannot afford to learn under a teacher. But Silberhorn continuously urges that his manual also offers many great advantages in helping someone well posted in music, especially a good violin player, to switch to the concertina.

Before launching his technique in the inner core of his book, Silberhorn provides at the very outset, under the cover, the keyboard for concertina, right hand or treble clef, and left hand or bass clef, as copyrighted by him in 1911. These he glosses with both notes and the alphabet scale, sharps and flats included, which correspond to a number on each button, some being fractions, zeros and the like. By pages six and seven, Silberhorn deals with the function served by a musical staff, time, and accent. He explains the values of each measure, whole notes, half notes, eighth notes, etc. Soon his self-teaching method proceeds into eigth and triple notes. Then he explains the sharp and flat mechanisms with their annotation and moves on to expression and articulation. Quickly he has explained crescendo, pause, trill and the use of embellishment, sometimes called the cadenza, and the ad libitum found in music, always with notes in a staff example. Pages 10 and 11 gradually ease us into the use of grace notes, repeat signs, abbreviations, and characters with certain indicators, their Italian terminology, all more or less well translated into English. [See figures A and B below].

Under the assumption that all this verbiage is digested immediately by the beginner, Silberhorn is ready to lead the student into hand and finger positions. Obviously Silberhorn's long explanations make concerti-

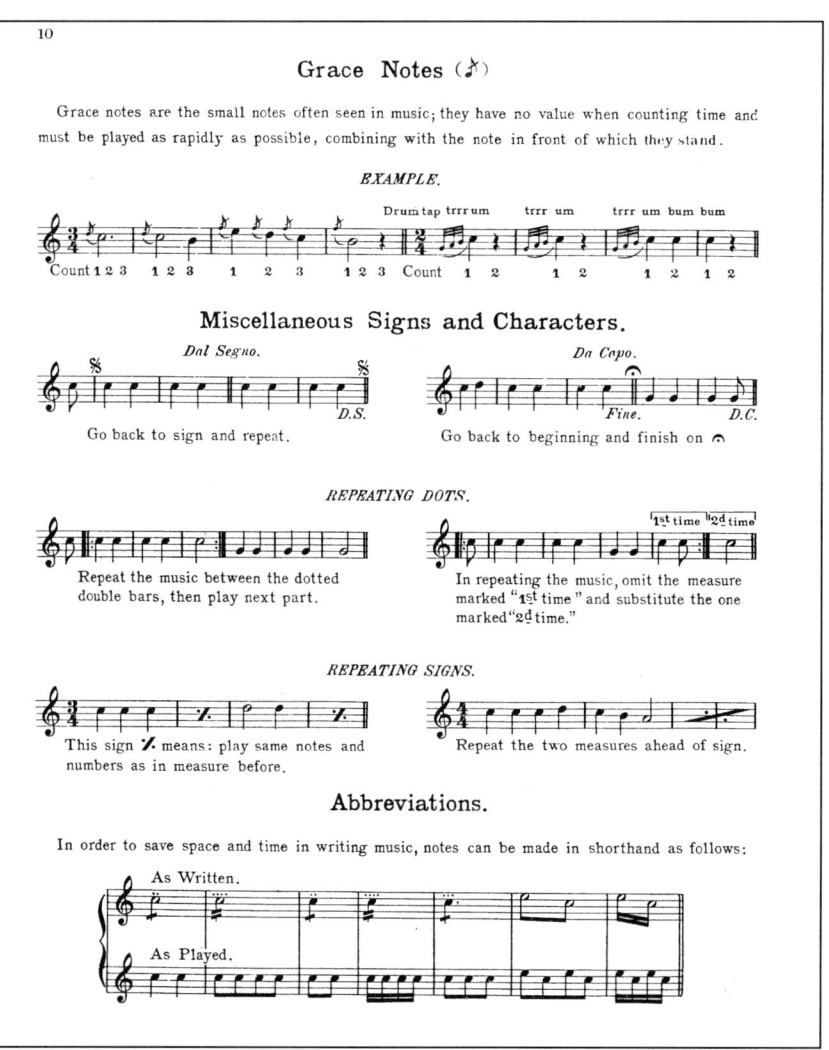

Figure A. Above, Silberhorn offers instruction to the beginner for reading basic musical scales and the time value of certain notes. At the bottom is his scale with abbreviated noting.

na playing seem formidable. For this reason the Wolf method called "a simple approach with instruction & easy pieces," was created in 1957. Some contemporary concertina players affirm that the Silberhorn book is really a good refresher course, one that becomes useful only after the player has manipulated the instrument for a good ten or twenty years. Today few players take the time to finger B-Flat or A-Flat on a C concertina as was expected in 1927 and earlier. Having concertinas equipped in various keys, the performer can simply change instruments rather than changing keys on the same one. Sketches serve the purpose and each of the four fingers on each hand is assigned a Roman numeral, the left hand being an inversion of the right, both index fingers having number one. Now the enterprising starter is ready for some exercises for each hand. Counts and beats are required for each fingering exercise. Pretty soon Silberhorn has his amateur practicing a waltz, then some eighth notes for a Schottische and, finally, a more rapid polka with legions of eighth notes. To be sure there are lots of scales for the left hand, for the right hand, with the advice of Bach when playing scales—"each ought to resemble a string of pearls in which all the pearls are of the same size, and each touches the next without adhering to it." Halfway through the book, the rookie can play "Home Sweet Home," the "Kitten Waltzes," the "Mabel Waltz," and others. More hand exercises and the student is ready for syncopated melodies, amusement exercises, daily scale practice for the right hand, and more until the book note concludes on page 60.

Not that Silberhorn was original in his method. As noted above, German-language books in the 1890s showed beginners how to play the concertina with almost identical layouts for the hands and a number system that equates with what Silberhorn offered. That should come as no surprise for, after all, Silberhorn was an immigrant from Germany.[9] Likewise, in her book on the bandonion and concertina, Maria Dunkel incorporates the same hand charts ascribing the key layout and the numbering system to Carl Uhlig, naming it the "Uhligsche Kernzone," but offering another slight variant called the "Zimmermannsche Kernzone" after Carlsfeld's Carl Zimmermann. As discussed in an earlier chapter, Zimmermann immigrated to Philadelphia from his previous association with the Arnold factory in Carlsfeld. In both the German and the American traditions are the 104-key system called the "Schefflersche" from Max Scheffler, who fabricated concertinas in Chemnitz beginning about 1890 in collaboration with Max Neubert and Richard Lindner. Dunkel's book offers similar systems to explain the bandonion keyboard and learning system, one which is intentionally left out of consideration here.

Because the buttons on the concertina were arranged, not in any

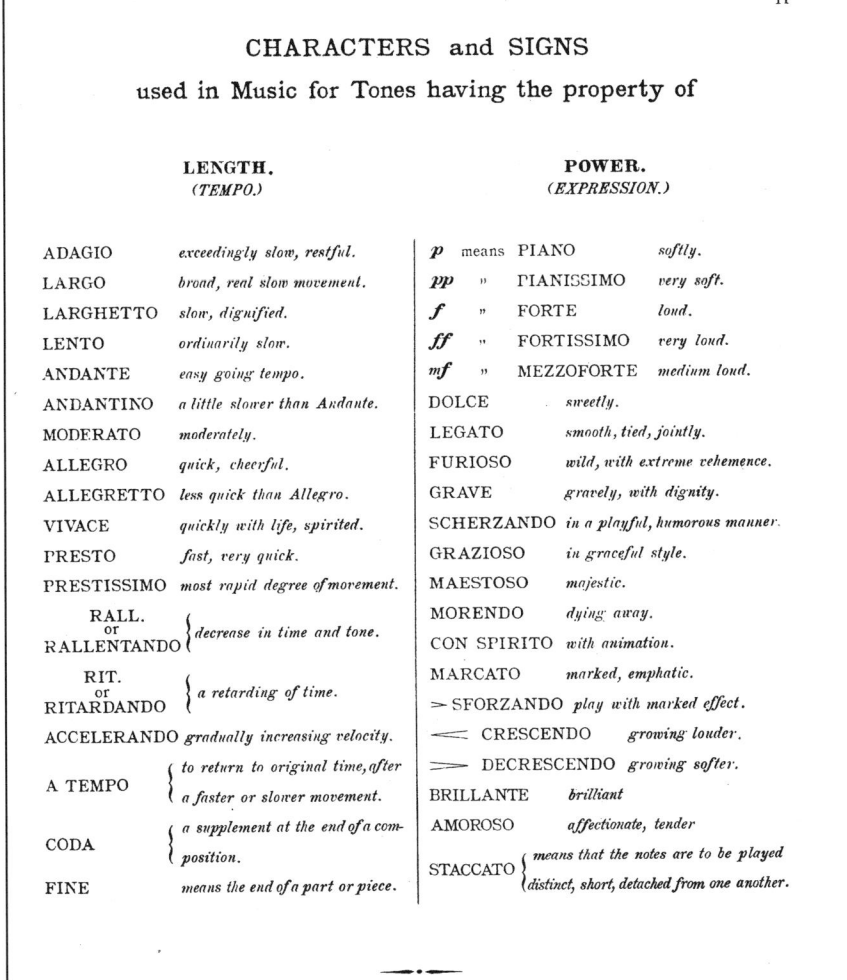

Figure B. Here Silberhorn outlines the instructional verbiage of music, primarily words derived from the Italian but valid for all musical notation.

logical sequence to the musical scale but, like the American typewriter, with reference to frequency of usage, self-teaching of the concertina seemed easy, especially to the already competent artist. Thus, Richard Scheller published his *Symphonetta-Schule für den Selbstunterricht. Nebst Beilage der Allgemeinen Musiklehre von C. A. Herm. Wolff, Kapellmeister und Lehrer der Musik* and issued it from the publishing house operated by Ernst L. Arnold at the Arnold factory in Carlsfeld.[10]

The business of self-teaching the concertina, known in Germany as 'self instruction,' replicates over time throughout the United States. In addition to the Silberhorn mainstay book for teaching the concertina, there were such booklets as, for example, the *National Self Teacher for Concertina* [76, 94 102 keys, square style] by Joseph Fischer, published by the Chart Music Publishing House in Chicago in 1919. Also available from this publisher were "self teachers" for violin, mandolin, ukulele, banjo, guitar and just about any other instrument the customer might want to learn to play. As with Silberhorn's method, the instructions are straightforward, building from simple notes on each hand to scales for 76- and 102-key concertinas, advancing to the use of sharps, flats and certain minor key scales and chords. Soon Fischer has his neophytes playing a simple waltz, "Old Folks at Home," "My Country 'tis of Thee," the "Bohemian Waltz" and others. Even in these books for instruction, the apparent proximity and affinity for the Bohemian aspect of the concertina's history is in evidence. A few teaching schools in Chicago included offerings with or without live teachers from the many music stores as well as in other publications including the "Concertina Self-Instructor" by Maryan S. Rozicki.

On occasion Henry Silberhorn offered in supplementary pamphlets his "Page on the concertina method, Hints, Helps and Advice" for the learning concertina player. In one of those undated pamphlets which promote his Black Beauty concertinas and various sheet music, Silberhorn writes:

Over twenty years ago . . . the House of Silberhorn came out with a 122-key concertina which was gratefully acclaimed by most of the better players of that day. Later Louis Solar originated a 124-key [concertina] which also enjoyed its vogue. The final improvement by the House of Silberhorn was the 128 key which has been conceded the most practical key board for the concertina. The 128 keyboard was built around the original 102 so that the player did not have to relearn an entire keyboard but could easily learn the use of the extra keys. This was a definite improvement and a real advance in the technique of concertina performance. The right hand or melody side of

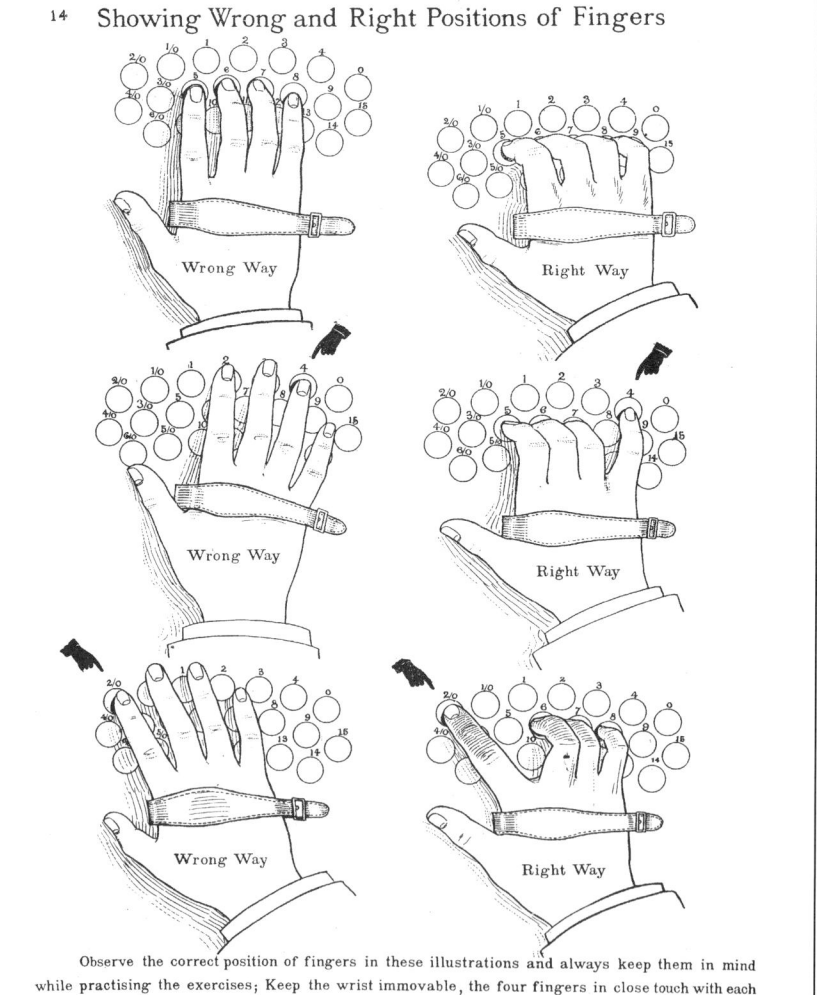

Fingering instruction chart.

the 128 key has a fourth row of keys on the top of the regular keyboard for additional notes down the scale to low violin G. You can thus play melodies both high and low octave without the need of a shift key or low octave set of reeds. Each of these new keys, both press and draw, is the same note and they are placed in position close to their octaves or harmonics. On the left or bass side there are four more buttons (low bass) — two below No. 1 and 5 and two above "Cross" and 2/0 — making the bass side complete to play all sub-basses and chords in music both press and draw.[11]

Other instructors and their printed texts of explanation are sometimes detected from the newsletters of the concertina stores in Chicago. The Vitak-Elsnic music establishment, "Successor to Georgi & Vitak," at 4815 South Ashland, in 1931 recommend Silberhorn's *Instructor* first and foremost as the best instructional manual available. But Vitak-Elsnic also pushed the *National Self-Teacher*, "prepared for those who do not wish to study with a teacher," and one by Rosyckiego, in which the "explanations are in Polish and English and contains many good teaching pieces."[12] In addition, Vitak-Elsnic routinely included a few pages of "How to Play the Concertina" in their 3" X 11" blue catalogs bearing the title *Concertina Music, Instruction Books and Supplies*. To be sure, the "Pearl Queen" champions of Chicago also wanted to sell sheet music and thus listed the "easiest" pieces best suited for beginners under the title "Grade 1," then moving higher to "Grade 2," "Grade 3," and so on. In Grade 1 were such numbers as "Ach du lieber Augustin," "Du, du liegst mir im Herzen," the "Isabella Waltz," the "Lauterbach Waltz," and also some numbers that seem to us not that easy to play, the "Katrina Polka," the "Lindenau Polka," and the "Little Fisherman Waltz." Those listed in Grade 2 seem familiar enough to us, among them the "Barbara Polka," the "California Polka," the "Martha Polka," and Whoopee John's theme song, the "Mariechen Waltzer."

In Chicago, too, were the likes of George Hrica, who in later life had retired to live in Plantation, Florida. An artist, inventor, instructor, and developer of endless new techniques, Hrica offered his Hrica Clinic to give beginners, amateurs and professionals instructions in techniques of introductions, fill-ins, breaks and endings that differentiate a performance from drab to spirited. According to concertina promoter, Pat Watters, Hrica was the most traveled concertina missionary and teacher of the concertina. He demonstrated the instrument's capabilities for musical fields ranging from jazz, rock, folk, international, to classical and traditional. He also engineered and built the "organtina" which embodied selec-

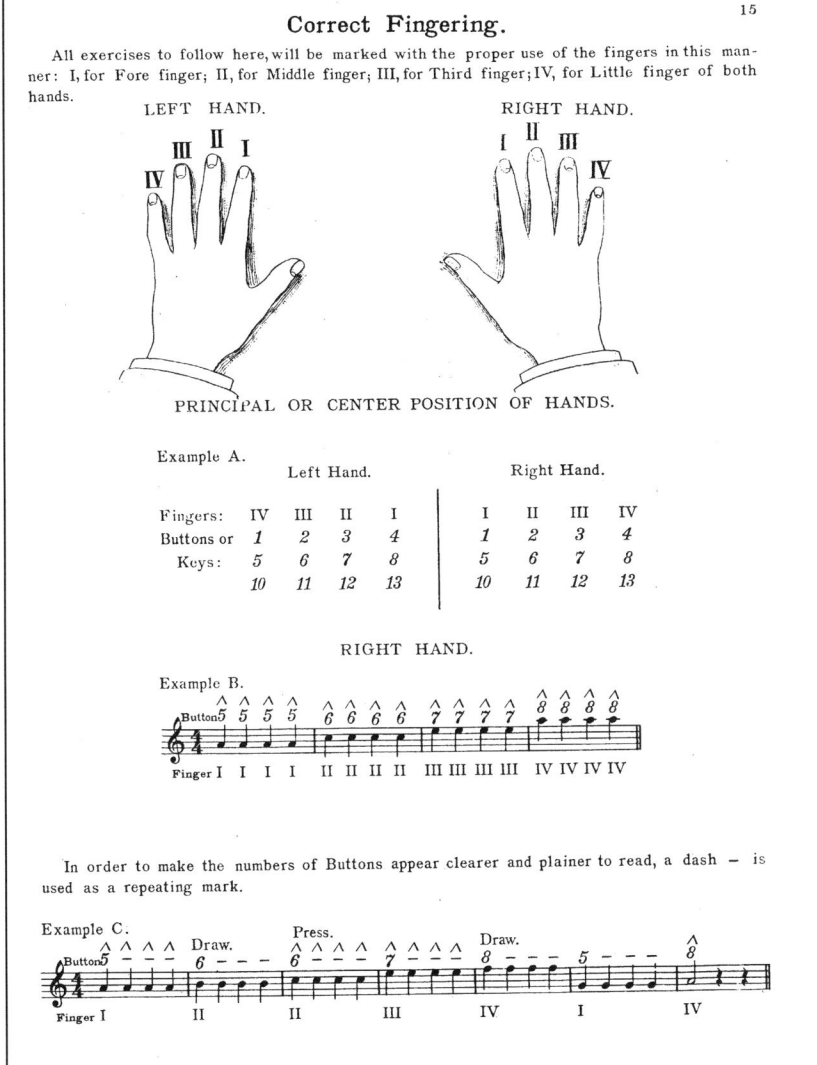

Fingering chart for teachers of the concertina.

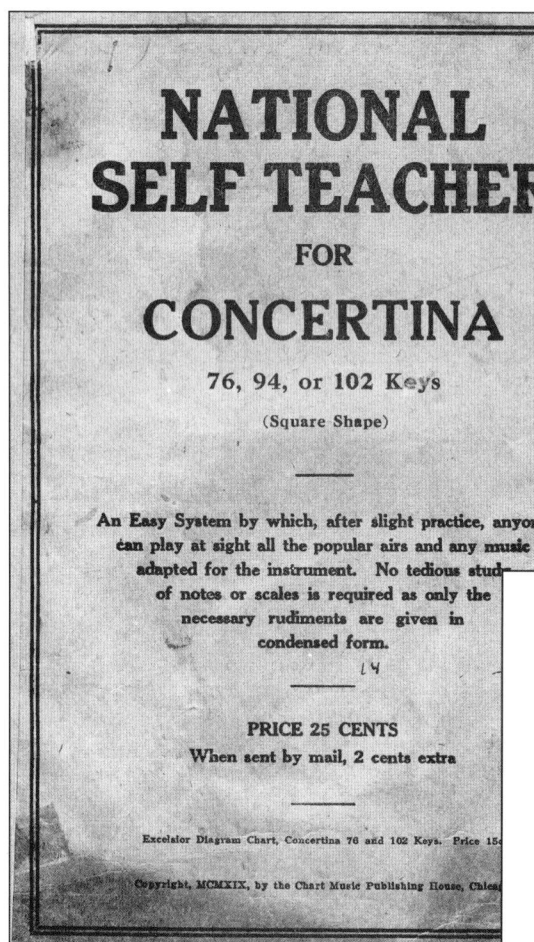

The National Self Teacher, one of many manuals devised by players to teach the concertina.

German Style Concertina. In other printings the title varies to *Wolf's Concertina Course: A Simple Approach with Instruction & Easy Pieces.*[13] Although written and prepared by Betty Wolf of the Tony Wolf Deutschmeister Band in St. Joseph, Minnesota,[14] the book was published in 1957 by the M. M. Cole Publishing Company at 251 East Grand Avenue in Chicago. In her preface Betty Wolf promises that her years of experience are brought to bear in this self-instructive book. She asserts that it supplies all the necessary material so that the beginner can learn to play the concertina without any previous knowledge of music, clefs, notes or scales. Not to be ignored is the *Brown Concertina Method* from the Bill Brown music store in New Ulm. Also there is the Frank J. Converse *Deluxe Concertina Book.*

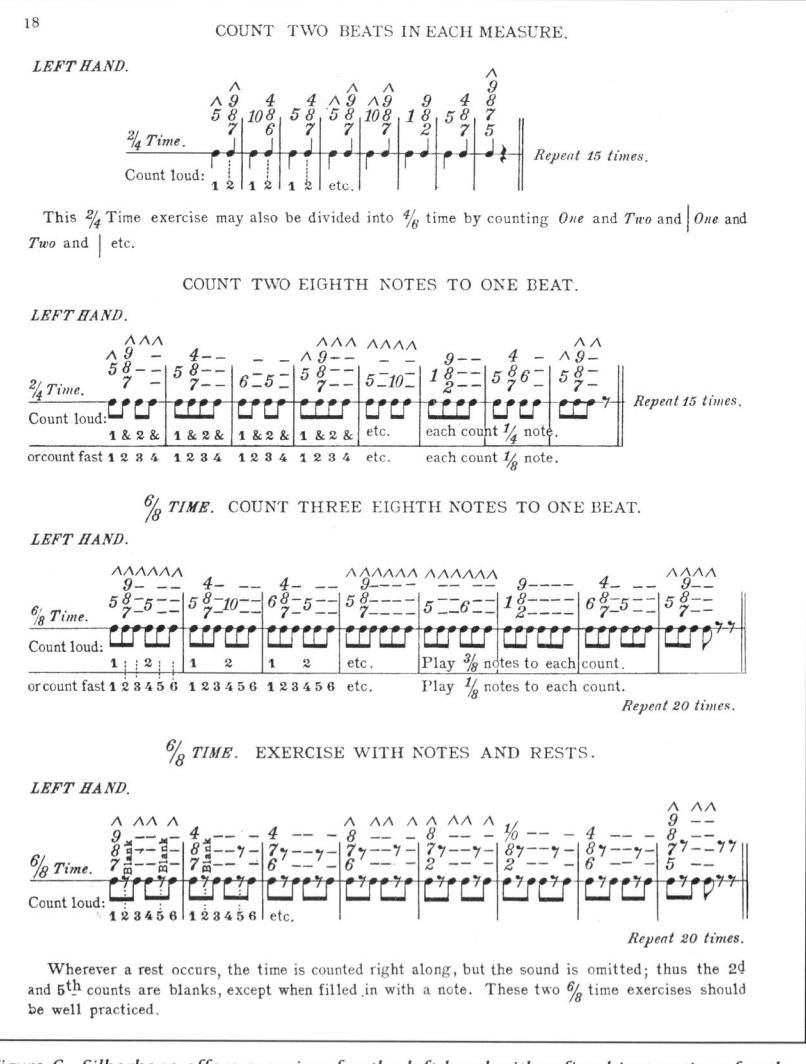

Figure C. Silberhorn offers exercises for the left hand with refined instructions for the proper time and beat.

tively organ and concertina voices. Hirca's creations were prototypes for the electronic systems known as MIDI [Musical Instrument Digital Interface], commonly in use today. In addition, there was Albert B. Nechanicky of Spokane, Washington who prepared *Nicky's Instructor* for the 130 key concertina he built. Included in his book are many simple movements that enhance the music. His manual contains 20 full tunes and many charts of scales, chords, fingering and keyboard charts.

Not just Chicago, but also Minnesota and other states witnessed forthcoming authors of books for the self-taught player, e. g. *Wolf's Concertina: Arranged especially for the Beginner of Any Age;*

How the Concertina is Played

The first 25 pages consist of easy and simplified instructions concerning the fundamentals that are necessary for learning, followed by simplified pieces to further instruct and encourage the beginner. As with any music teacher, Betty Wolf admonished that regular daily practice is still the real mother of success. Not surprisingly, Wolf uses simple but familiar pieces like "Twinkle, Twinkle Little Star," "Old Mac Donald," "Jingle Bells," and "Little Brown Jug," but soon graduates to melodies like the "Barbara Polka," a number which exemplifies the strong German-Bohemian heritage, its lyrics available in either tongue, Czech or German. Further encouraging the powerful identification of the German players with those of Czech origin was the presence occasionally of Wolf at the

Above is the cover of the instructional volume written by Tony and Betty Wolf of St. Joseph, Minnesota and issued in 1957 by the M. M. Cole Publishing Company at 251 East Grand Avenue in Chicago. It has 64 pages which, like Silberhorn, offers an introduction to music in the early pages, then progresses to the concertina, the correct position of the fingers to play the 52 buttons that render 104 key notes. After the first 25 pages, the book provides notes of familiar tunes to help the learner feel satisfaction: Twinkle, Twinkle; Yankee Doodle; Jingle Bells; even the Barbara Polka.

Figure D. Above, Silberhorn supplies exercises for both hands, paying attention to time and punctuation of the left hand accompaniment.

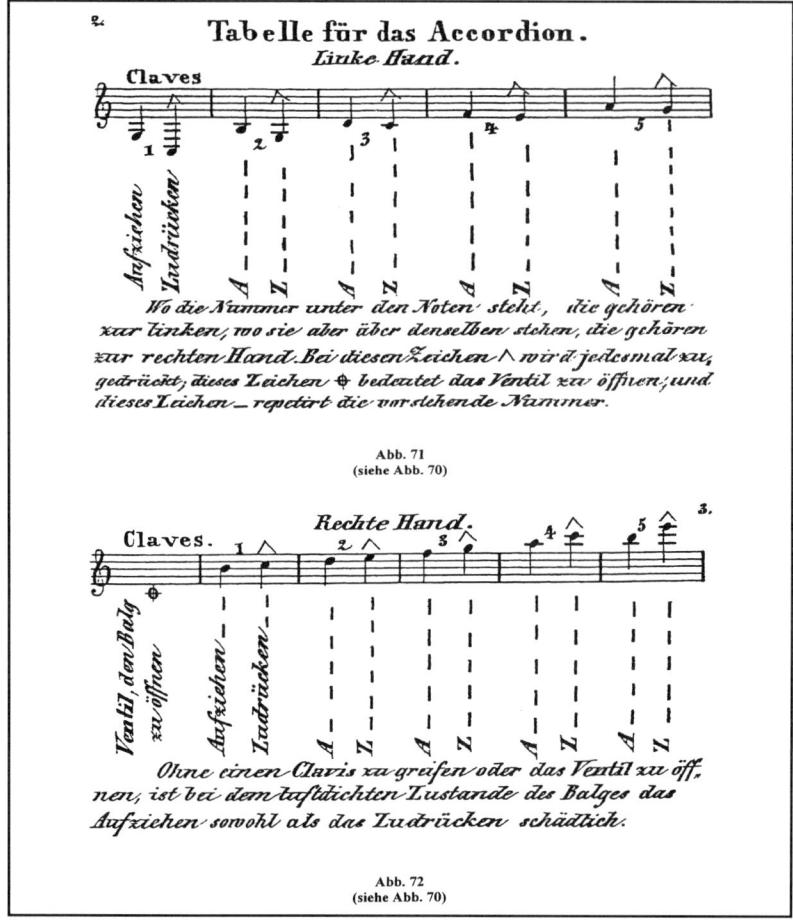

Karl Oriwohl in his volume Das Bandonion (Berlin. 2004), p. 333 offers instruction for the "Accordion," though he really means the concertina or bandonion. This illustration is offered to demonstrate how closely the German instructional manuals were copied by those prepared from such sources for the American concertinist. Note that the carrot marking ^ is used on both clefs.

Neighborhood Inn Store opposite Town Edge Restaurant in New Prague. The link between the German traditions of St. Joseph in Stearns County and the Czech proclivities of New Prague, Montgomery and Lonsdale was, and remains, whole.

Fairly well known in Minnesota were the instructional efforts of Minnesota concertina promoter, Leonard Krulikoski, then using the title "Director of United Music Teachers" at Hutchinson. Others were Ambrose Kodet, Jerry Minar, Joe and Bill Cerniak, Bill Brown, Tony and Betty Wolf as well as George Servatius of Melrose. Early on the Wisconsin scene were the watchmaker, Ernst Hauke, and Irving DeWitz of Hustiford, Wisconsin. In Illinois, Stanley Nowicki, Henry Bobzien, George Hrica, Rudy Patek, Frank Schmidt, Henry Schuckert, Joseph Stacy, Wally Stark and Edward Starzynski stand out. In central Wisconsin, the most prominent teacher was Dan Gruetzmacher of Wausau, and in the Milwaukee area John Bondowski, Thomas Smigielski and Ed Teikowski.[15]

Today, to be sure, there are methods available on the Internet which explain how the concertina is to be played, the best by Loren Schaeffler.[16] Edwin P. Suterko of Reno Nevada, born June 11, 1928 in Chicago, offers for sale simple left and right hand paper charts for the learner. Inducted to the World Concertina Congress Hall of

How the Concertina is Played

Fame at Wausau in 2001, Suterko started on a Lange concertina at the age of nine in 1937. His letter and number system enables the player to syncopate the numbers to notes on paper and thereby to transpose numbers to the chromatic scale. Other sources offer alternatives by video cassettes teaching the English concertina. These methodologies were produced by enthusiasts of the hexagonal model for the English Wheatstone concertina.

Shown here is the melody side of a 104-key concertina, a key of 'C' instrument. The circles represent the buttons. The number above the button is the number that is stamped on the actual concertina. The digit in the center of the button shows the note played during draw and the note played during press. The inverted "V" or carrot ^ above the note on the right side of the button indicates a press note. The notes on the melody side of a 'C' concertina range from C3 on a piano notation to F sharp 6 (with Hi switch) for a total of 31 notes—adequate explanations for the learning beginner, one would think.

Keyboard for concertina right hand, melody side

As is obvious, there are two sides of the concertina. Shown below is the bass side of a 104-key concertina, a key of 'C' instrument. The circles represent the buttons. The number above the button is the number that is stamped on the actual concertina button assembly. The music note on the staff in the center of the button shows the note played during draw and the note played during press. The carrot above the note on the right side of the button indicates a press note. The notes on the bass side of a key of 'C' concertina range from G1 to A5 on the piano keyboard.

Keyboard for concertina left hand, bass side

Chords are achieved by playing three buttons at the same time. A G-Major chord is made by playing the 2-3-4 buttons while pressing. The G-Bass is the 1-press. A D 7th chord is made by playing the 2-3-8 buttons or the 3-8-9 buttons because a full 7th chord consists of four notes (hence 2-3-8-9) while drawing the bellows apart. A player may do inversions of a chord (re: play 1/0 button instead of the 9 button, the F sharp note then being one octave lower). The D Bass button is the 1-draw. An F Major chord is made by playing the 7-3/4-0 buttons while pressing. The F Bass is the 2/0-press. A C Major chord is made by playing the 4-3-2/3 draw. The C Bass is the 0-draw. The most common and easiest key signatures to play on the "C" concertina are G, D and A.

Sample Concertina Music Score in Key of G

In the example supplied here, the numbers above the staff are the buttons to be pressed on the melody (right) side to sound the proper note. If there are more than two numbers, the top number is the melody and the lower the harmony. The numbers with the carrot ^

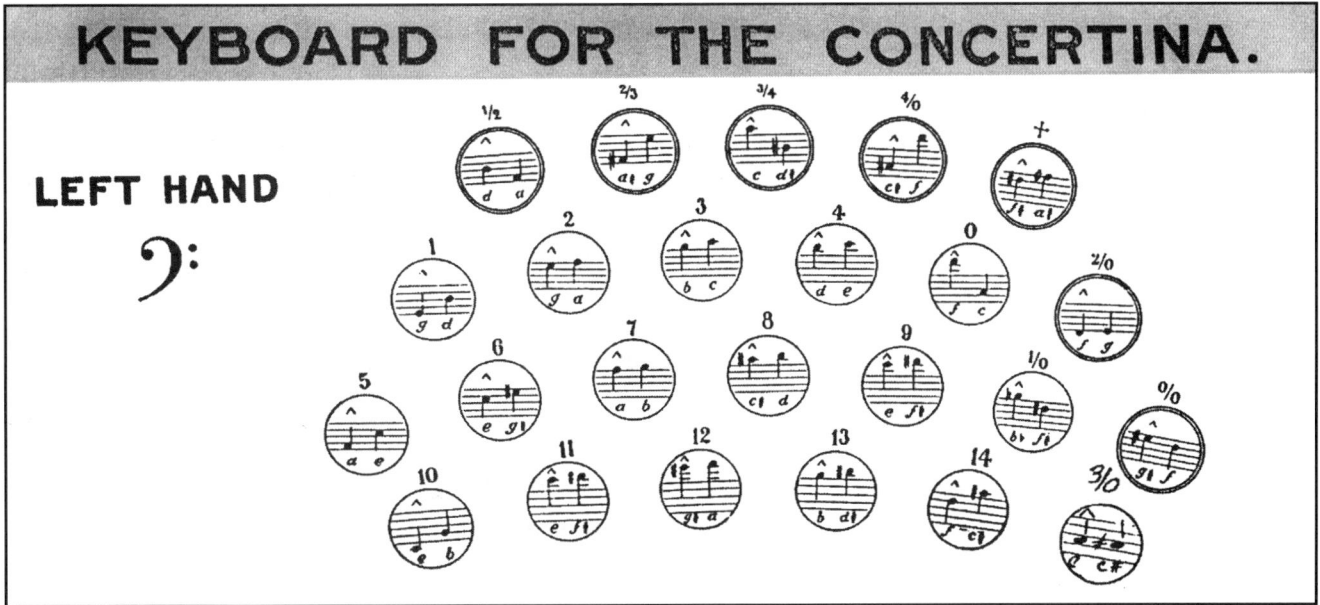

above them tell the player to squeeze the bellows together when playing. Those without the carrot ^ tell the player to draw (or pull) the bellows apart. The bass and chords are played on the bass (left) side of the instrument. Almost all commercial music sheets show the fingering with the numbering system for bass side chords that is similar to the melody side of the concertina. However, in some cases, the score may show only the chord fingering, e.g. G, D7, C, D, etc.

Concertina music is typically written for a key of C concertina. A "C" concertina plays the actual notes represented on the music staff. All other key concertinas are actually transposing the music to other key signatures even though the keys are fingered the same way. In most cases this is an advantage, because, for example, a "B^b" concertina and a Trumpet ("B^b" instrument) then can both read the same concertina musical sheet with an exact match. Both read the key of "G" and produce the key of "F" or both read sheet music in key of "C" and play in "B^b." A typical polka is comprised of 112 measures of notation, although some could be longer. The tempo is about 53 to 58 measures per minute. A waltz is about 144 measures long, its tempo about 52 to 54 measures per minute, the piece lasting about two and one half minutes.

When playing today's Chemnitzer concertina, the note of C is rendered by the #3 button on either side of the concertina while pulling the bellows of the concertina apart. The usual 104 key Chemnitzer has 24 buttons on the bass side and 28 buttons on the melody side of the instrument, each button having two notes: 24 plus 28 = 52 times 2 which gives 104.

The following figure shows the right (melody) keyboard and the respective notes played by push and draw, along with defining the octave key, i. e. the push 2/0 octave is the 16 key.

Right Keyboard Melody

When mention is made of a Double, it means two reeds for the draw and two for the press on the melody side, one medium and one piccolo, or two mediums, or one medium and a low. A Low Triple has three reeds for draw and three for press on the melody side, one low and two medium. A High Triple contains three reeds for the draw and three for the press on the melody side, two medium and one piccolo. Finally, a Quad has four reeds for draw and four for press on the melody side, typically one low and three medium. However, many were made with one low, two meduim and one piccolo reed.

Reed Information

To observe whether the concertina is a 'Double,' 'Triple' or a 'Quad" is to remove the melody side (right hand) keyboard cover. Remove the air valve cable. Most end cap keyboards are fastened with either 3 or 4

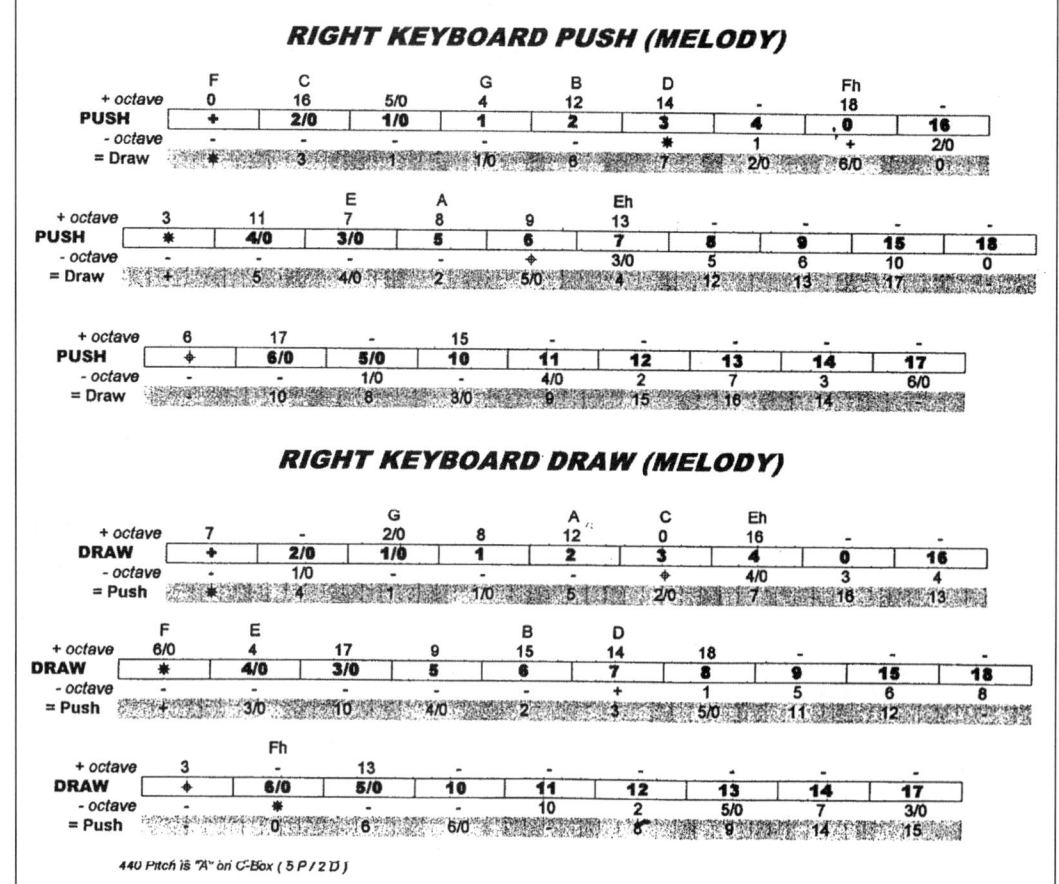

screws. Once the screws, (or pins), have been removed, the keyboard lifts off easily. Air pressure from the bellows may "assist" with keyboard removal. Do not remove the reed plates. Count the number of reeds that are mounted on the outside surface of the reed plates. These are reeds that sound in "Press." (There is an equal number of reeds on the inside surface for the "Draw".) Divide the number of reeds on the outside surface by the number of buttons on the melody side. The result is two for a "Double," three for a "Triple" or four to a "Quad." Not all the reeds have 'leathers' on them. The keyboards made in the pre-plywood days (approximately until the WW II era) are fragile and crack easily. Set the cover loosely on top of the keyboard and line up the buttons with their respective holes with a toothpick or something similar. Install the air valve cable. If the air valve cable has a leather washer, it goes underneath the air lever. Sometimes reaching through an adjacent hole will help to align the buttons.

Types of Reeds used in Chemnitzer Concertinas

Long plate reeds: The original reed designs date back to the origins of the concertina and are still in use today. They were used exclusively in the Pearl Queen and Patek instruments manufactured by Otto Schlicht, Christy Hengel and other manufacturers. The Star concertina, being built originally by an accordion company, may have either long plate or individual waxed reeds.

Photo of an Arno Arnold concertina from a Watters Distributing Co. advertisement. The photo below is an example of individual plates with hook screws, known as pinned reeds.

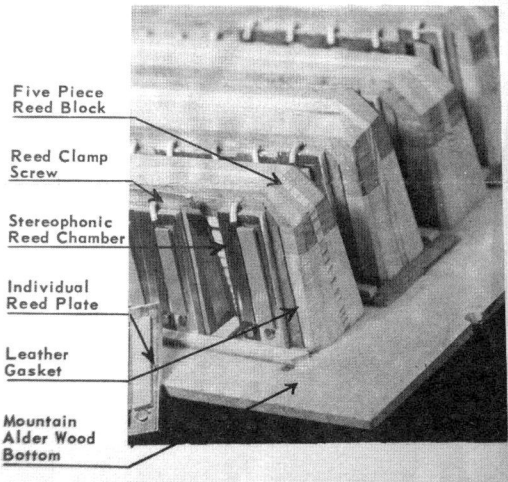

Pinned reeds are individual short plates like those for waxed reeds mounted on reed blocks with leathers, having pins and screw hooks like long reed plates.

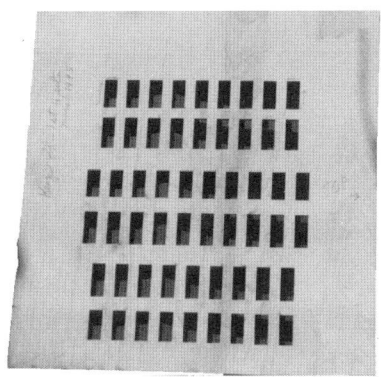

Sound board without reeds mounted and with no action mechanism.

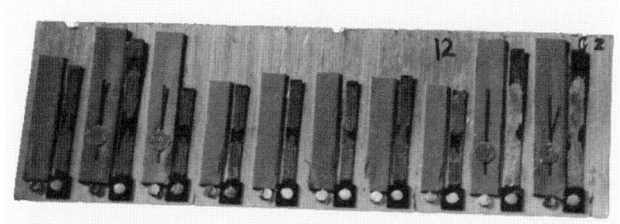

Long Plate Reeds

Sound board with reed blocks without reed plates. Note the three "screw hooks" waiting to lock down the long plates.

The History of the Chemnitzer Concertina

Sound board with reed blocks and reed plates. Here the hooks have been closed against the long plates.

Wax reeds

Wax-type reeds: This reed concept was essentially "borrowed" from the accordion industry. Note that each individual reed set is waxed in place.

The concertina action mechanism

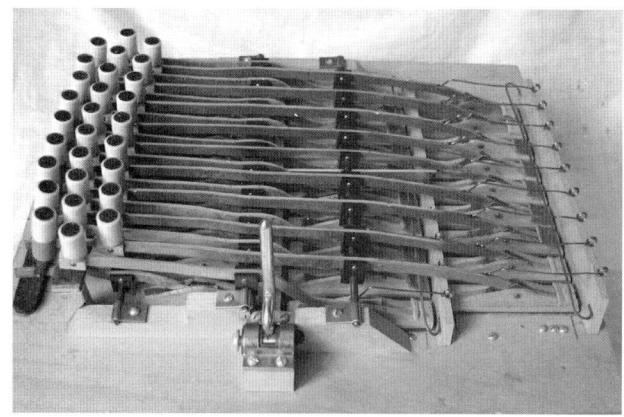

Above is a Hengel Treble or melody aluminum mechanism—right side action.

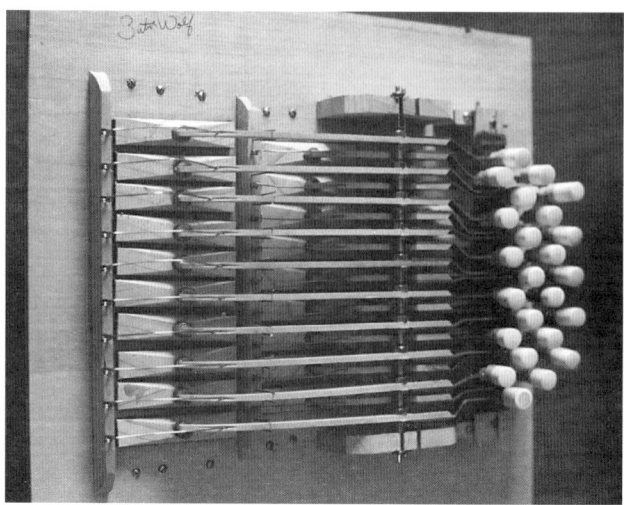

Arno Arnold bass—left side action concertina mechanism. A wood action. Note that Ambrose "Butch" Wolf owned this concertina.

Concertina keys

The most popular concertinas manufactured are in the Key's of: C, B^b, E^b, A^b, D^b (or C-sharp), G, F, and D respectively.

Since the 1950s, many concertinas are tuned musette [in a manner of speaking, systematically off-tuned]. The E^b may have many reed configurations:
3-mediums & 1-low
3-lows & 1-extra low
4-lows with 1-low tuned musette
2 mediums & 2-lows tuned musette
1 medium & 3-lows tuned musette

Melody side switches and their effects.

Single switch: Typically, this device switches out a low reed to allow medium reeds to play, rendering a high sound. A Quad concertina switches from 4 to 3 reeds and a triple switches from 3 to 2 reeds, whereas a double switches from 2 to 1 reed. On a concertina tuned with musette, the switch will switch in/out the musette-tuned reed. Musette tuning occurs when one set of reeds is tuned either sharp or flat to produce a button-accordion waver effect. In a manner of speaking, one set of reeds is "out of tune." Actually, musette tuning is favored by Czech musicians, along with others, of course.

Key of Score — Bass Chords (most commonly used)

Key of Score		Keys:			Keys:			Keys:	
F	F push	2/0	7, 3/4, 0	C7	0	3, 4, +	Bb push	2/3	4, 0, 1/0
C	C draw	0	3, 4, 2/3	G7 push	1	2, 3, 0	F push	2/0	7, 3/4, 0
G	G push	1	2, 3, 4	D7 draw	1	3, 8, 9	C draw	0	3, 4, 2/3
D	D draw	1	2, 8, 9	A7 push	5	2, 7, 8	G push	1	2, 3, 4
A	A push	5	7, 8, 9	E7 draw	5	6, 8, 4	D draw	1	2, 8, 9
E	E push	10	11, 12, 13	B7 draw	10	2, 7, 13	A push	5	7, 8, 9

Bass chords most commonly used

Above is an example of the most frequently used chords.

Multiple switches: On an American-made instrument, the switch does the Hi-Lo as described above. The second switch typically switches a musette-tuned reed in/out.[17] The Star concertina, which was manufactured in Chicago, produced on a 8-switch model which included an additional switch on the bass side. However, the majority of Star instruments had but one switch. The Italian-made instruments, such as the Stradivarius, typically offered 5 switches, their design borrowed from the piano accordion industry. They are typically labeled "Master" (all reeds), "Musette" (3 reeds), "Bandonion" (2 reeds, low and medium), "Clarinet" (1 medium reed), and "Bassoon", (1 low reed). Occasionally repair shops (e. g. JBM Sound, Jerry Minar) make modifications to the "Bandonion" and "Clarinet" switches rendering the instrument able to play 3 reeds and 2 reeds respectively, notably in a musette-tuned instrument, to produce the effects found in the American instruments described above.

Playing the Concertina

Several books teach the beginner how to play the concertina. As mentioned previously, they include Henry Silberhorn's Instructor for the Concertina, Books I and II, the Tony and Betty Wolf book, the one from the former Brown's Music Store in New Ulm and the one produced by United Music Course. Many instructors, along with experienced concertina players, suggest students focus on learning the scales (the melody side keys of 'C', 'G', 'D', 'A', 'E' and the chromatic scale), both push and pull. Teachers also strongly suggest learning the most frequently used chords on the bass side.

Tips for practicing the concertina

1. Note the time signature (number of beats per measure) before you begin to play.
2. If, when you play you have difficulty with the rhythm, count the beats for each measure slowly out loud or silently to yourself.
3. Use correct position and fingering — this increases accuracy and helps prevent fatigue.
4. Work on the musical score in sections. Master each section before proceeding. If you have difficulty coordinating both hands, first play the _right hand alone_, then play the _left hand alone_, then play both hands together.
5. Test yourself by playing the section or phrase _correctly_ three times in a row.
6. Play the entire piece _slowly_, section by section, to identify and correct all errors.
7. Allow time to think about expression, phrasing, tone changes, bellow direction, etc.
8. Listen to yourself— try to match the sound you hear with the sound you want to play. Tape record your playing and hear yourself as others do.
9. Give yourself a break from practicing by playing something just for fun!

Stanley Darrow, _How to Practice_ (Westmont, N. J.: Acme Accordion School).
http://trfn.clpgh.org/free-reed/essays/darrow.html

1. Select a suitable area in your home for practicing and organize this area with your music.
2. Develop a system or plan for practicing. Practice at

the same time and place each day.

3. Memorize your music and begin each practice by playing all the songs you have learned.

4. In addition to the songs you know, practice major and minor scales each day.

5. When learning a new piece of music, proceed slowly. *To learn fast, practice slowly.*

6. Note the key and the time signatures of each piece. Count or tap out the rhythm.

7. Work slowly, relaxed, and gently. Learn one step at a time. Play each part many times.

8. Build a good foundation of your music, and add to it as you learn.

9. Ideally, beginners practice one hour a day. Build up to an hour and a half practice each day.

Maintenance for the Concertina
Cleaning[18]
Pledge or Liquid Gold
Polish wood and celluloid covered instruments
Goo Gone — Removes grime and sticky materials
4/0 Steel Wool — shines stainless steel bellow parts
Metal polish — Tarnite metal polish, Braso, Wenol and Flitz remove tarnish from metal parts on old concertinas. It is always safest to clean the bottom first. Be sure to periodically examine the bellows for loose trim parts. Loose corners (metal on celluloid) should be repaired. It is recommended that no harsh chemicals (i.e. Auto polish, Acetone, etc.) be employed since they could remove stones and result in repainting or resetting the stones. Also the celluloid and engraving could be damaged.

Bellows: remove dust carefully with a soft brush. The colored foil on the bellows is delicate and prone to fading. If the bellows appear to be weak or caving in, they should be reinforced by a qualified repair shop.

Storage: Wipe down after you finish playing, especially if sweat has fallen on the instrument. Sweat eventually will remove the paint. Leave instrument outside the case to air dry. Do not store instruments in a basement unless the humidity is controlled. A Hengel concertina stored in a wood pile for security reasons resulted in moldy bellows, staves, and warped inside parts. Nor should the instrument be stored in a hot attic. Keeping the concertina in the carrying case allows it a gradual transition to changes in humidity. Any repair or cleaning on the inside of the instrument should be left to a qualified repair shop.

Heat and Cold: Avoid extreme heat or cold, e.g. in an automobile trunk. Always allow the instrument to warm up before playing, the best approach being to leave the instrument in the case to reach room temperature. This reduces the risk of condensation. Never leave a concertina with waxed reeds in the summer sun. The wax can melt and the plates will fall off their mounts.

Smoking around instruments: Burn marks from dropped live ashes are impossible or at best difficult to remove. Cigarettes placed between buttons —— explosive nitrate material in fret plates may cause an explosion.

How to play with concertinas in other keys
This chart is simple to use. Two examples follow:

Assume you are playing a "C" concertina from sheet music written in the key of "G". Since your instrument is a B♭ you must find the key to play. Go from left to right in line No. 1, until you come to the "G" at column 11. This is the sheet music key. Next go down to line No. 3, which is the B♭ concertina line and your answer, is "A". Therefore you must play in three sharps to match the

The Chicago standard Press "5"		1	2	3	4	5	6	7	8	9	10	11	12	Line
A	C concertina	A	Bb	B	C	C#	D	Eb	E	F	F#	G	Ab	1
C	Eb concertina	F#	G	Ab	A	Bb	B	C	C#	D	Eb	E	F	2
G	Bb concertina	B	C	C#	D	Eb	E	F	F#	G	Ab	A	Bb	3
F	Ab concertina	C#	D	Eb	E	F	F#	G	Ab	A	Bb	B	C	4
Bb	C# concertina	Ab	A	Bb	B	C	C#	D	Eb	E	F	F#	G	5

The schematic above shows how to play the concertinas in a variety keys.

accompanying instrument. Now let's assume that the person above has a "C#" concertina and yours is an E♭. The sheet music remains the same, namely, it is written in "G". Go from left to right in the 5th line until you come to "G" in column 12. Go up to the 2nd line. Your answer is "F". The "E♭" instrument fingers the key of "F" while the "C#" concertina fingers the key of "G."

How to determine in what key a concertina is crafted

Your Concertina: (American Standard)
C	Concertina 'C' Key	push 2/0	draw 3
B♭	Concertina 'C' Key	push 3	draw 7
E♭	Concertina 'C' Key	push 5	draw 2
A♭	Concertina 'C' Key	push 7	draw 4
D♭	Concertina 'C' Key	push 2	draw 6

(D♭ is the same as C#)

If the concertina key is unknown, press the No. 5 button on the right hand side and compare it with a piano. It should match one of the five keys on the extreme left column on the chart. Note that pulling the right or left number 3 button will tell you the concertina key.

The following chart shows the most commonly used bass chord runs (primarily for concertina with electronics installed). However, they can also be selectively used when switching chords.

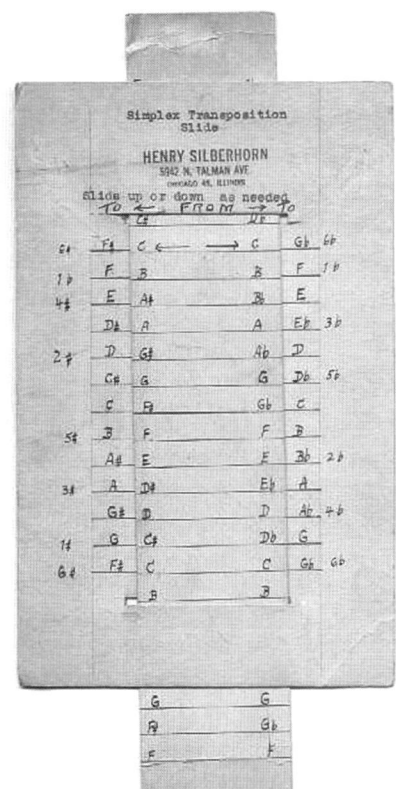

Here is a slide rule devised to help the concertina player shift keys instead of shifting instruments. Many concertinas are built in the Key of C, some in B-Flat, etc. Note that from the early days of concertina playing, experts had devised slide rules to cope with the key shift as needed to blend with varied band instrumentation.

Bass Runs for the Concertina

KEY OF "G"

G to D7	Push	1, +, 10
D7 to G	Draw	1, 5, 1/0
G to C	Push	1, 5, 13
C to G	Draw	0, 10, 1/2

KEY OF "A"

A to E7	Push	5, 0/0, +
E7 to A	Draw	5, 1/0, 14 or 6
A to D	Push	5, 13, 4/0
D to A	Draw	1, 3/0, 10

KEY OF "D"

D to A7	Draw	1, 3/0, 10
A7 to D	Push	5, 13, 4/0
D to G	Draw	1, 5, 1/0
G to D	Push	1, +, 10

KEY OF "C"

C to G7	Draw	0, 10, 1/2
G7 to C	Push	1, 5, 13
C to F	Draw	0, 1, 5
F to C	Push	2/0, 10, 1/2

Note: Press the first note twice for Polkas (takes 2 measures)

Bass Runs

Key coordination is best accomplished by using the slide rule offered by Hank Jacobs and Leo Franicke (deceased) at the Karpek Concertina and Accordion Company in Milwaukee. Distributed free of charge at Polka Days in New Ulm in the late 1960s to garner attention for the Karpek studio, the rule has been downsized by Ambrose Kodet of North Mankato. This handy slide rule makes it easy and flawless to transpose a concertina built in any key so that it plays in harmony with all other instruments or concertinas, no matter the key in which they are played or tuned.[19] However, the slide rule is neither original nor specific to the Karpek Company, for, much earlier, Henry Silberhorn from his address at 5942 North Talman Avenue marketed a vertical version of the slide rule.[20] Another vertical version is attributed to Ed Hermann. In the 1960s a similar chart, but not exactly the same as the slide rules, was offered by Pat Watters from his Distributing Company on East 42nd Street in Minneapolis and the evidence suggests that there were various others.[21]

Occasionally technical assistance was offered through the catalogs and newsletters. For instance, around 1929 Rudy Patek explained his "important addition to concertina playing. . . ." A new range was suggested as follows: "The Patek Concertinas, 104 keys, triple and quadruple reed are now installed with a No. 11 draw on the melody side (right hand) low D sharp, which is greatly needed in various passages and chords." He goes on to explain that if a player finds some old music with No. 11 draw F sharp, he should use the No. 8 draw instead. Patek adds that he has added on the bass side new notes 3/0 press C Bass, and 3/0 draw C sharp. "Experienced concertina players and teachers will be pleased to have this improved scale with which the player will be enabled to play with better harmony and chords."

To be sure, this improvement allows the information that the Patek Music Company maintains its own school of instruction for the concertina. "Private instruction is available from capable teachers who understand the concertina, and who know how to impart their knowledge and ability to play to the pupil. If you are interested in brushing up on the finer points of playing, come in and let us explain. Or, if you're not in town, write for details." Interestingly, almost identical instructions were being printed in the Vitak-Elsnic catalogs at the time, indicating that it was the Otto Schlicht producers who were creating the improvement and the technique and not the individual retailers of the period.

Henry Silberhorn in his pamphlets under the heading "Hints, Helps and Advice" gives pointers. 1) To

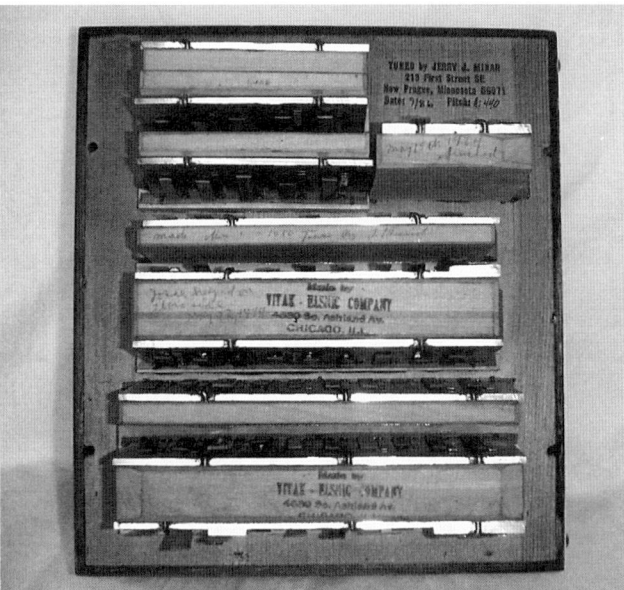

This is the inside view of a Pearl Queen 104 key triple reed concertina with serial number 5122, completed May 1, 1930, #16 in the colored section. When Christy Hengel in New Ulm tuned this instrument, he entered the note that Ma Runnerstrom [his mother-in-law] had assisted him, May 1, 1984. On the treble side he notes that "Ma" Runnerstrom died on Saturday May 5, finally finished Thursday May 31, 1984. On the bass side, Hengel wrote, Josie [his wife] helped May 15, 1984, May 22, 1984 finished. At another spot in the concertina is the note May 1, 1930 tuned by J. Vicevich. Elsewhere are printed the words, Made by Vitak-Elsnic Company 4639 South Ashland Avenue, Chicago, Illinois. And at another place, we find the notation, tuned by Jerry Minar September 1986. Thus, the inside of a concertina sometimes incorporates the life courses of those who handled it.

The inner mounting of reeds in a Pearl Queen concertina. Note how diligently Patek and other dealers stamp their identities on the inside of the concertina reed mountings.

keep your concertina carrying case in good condition and protect it against weather, apply liquid shoe dressing; allow to dry; then apply coating of Simonize or auto wax and rub down. 2) Keep reeds in good condition by dusting them off with soft brush occasionally. Dust absorbs moisture in air which rusts reeds. 3) Bellows wear out in folds where dust is allowed to accumulate and grind away. We have in stock a few fine bellow brushes, made of natural ebony black, one quarter inch by seven inches – stiff pure bristle. Keep bellow folds clean!! 4) Some concertinas with bass-box can be changed to open fret-work at a small cost. Ship your concertina to us, we must see it before an estimate can be given. 5) Bad light where you play? We have just the thing—Acme Music Lite, a practical and convenient music stand lite, which adjusts to any angle and clamps on stand, table or wherever wanted.

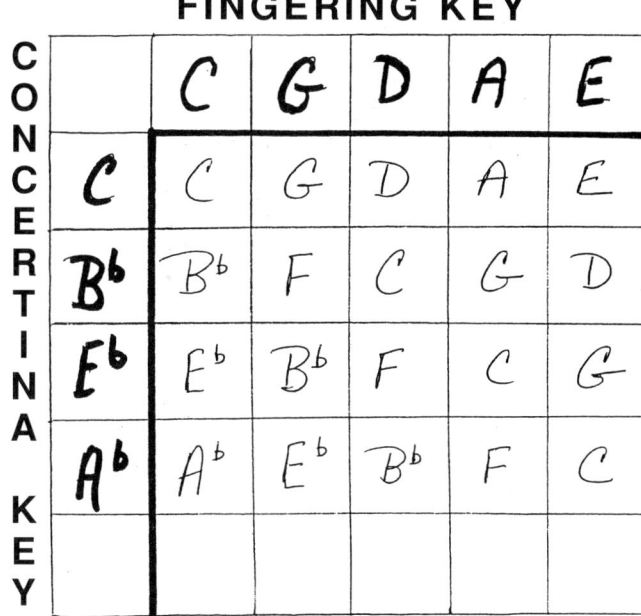

Above is a simplified chart for transposing the concertina built for one key, as noted on the left column, into an alternative key, as noted on the top row. A far more thorough, if more complicated, chart appears on the following page. This one was devised by Jerry Minar.

Before Rudy Patek moved to his store at 835 Milwaukee Avenue he operated at 769 Milwaukee. Possibly this was the site where he partnered in early times with Otto Georgi on the north side of Chicago. Of interest here is the stamp on the inside of a concertina he either built or serviced. He promotes his Columbia Records and music in Slavish [sic, we would expect Slavic], Bohemian, German, Slovenian [now once again its own nation but until 1993 part of Yugoslavia. However, the political combination of the Duchy of Krain [capital was Laibach] into Yugoslavia occurred only after the Versailles Treaty in 1919. He also has music for the Krainers, a relatively small settlement to the south of Austrian Styria and northern Slovenia. Best known today for Krain music is the popular Slavko Avsenik.

Note that before Patek moved to 835 Milwaukee Avenue and promoted exclusively his concertina as built by Otto Schlicht and his co-workers, he boasted his being the "exclusive agent for the celebrated Pearl Queen concertina." Later, the Pearl Queen was marketed by Vitak-Elsnic exclusively. However, as has been mentioned frequently in other chapters, both the Patek and the Pearl Queen are the same instrument built by Otto Schlicht, and their serial numbers interweave with each other.

The History of the Chemnitzer Concertina

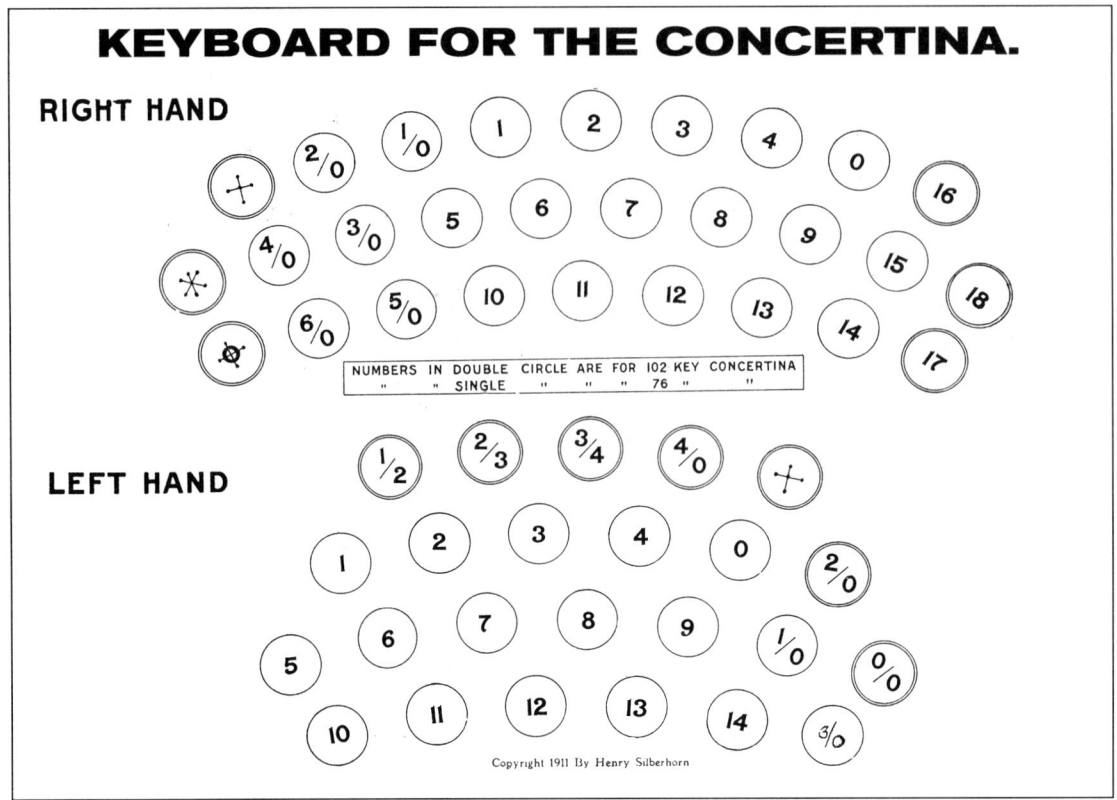

The keyboard for concertina comes from the Henry Silberhorn instruction manual.

The above chart instructs the player how to transpose concertinas built in one key to play in another key when required for harmony with other keyed instruments. Some credit Hank Jacobs of Milwaukee for inventing this slide rule. However, versions of it were widespread in Germany. The first replicas were introduced by Henry Silberhorn in Chicago.

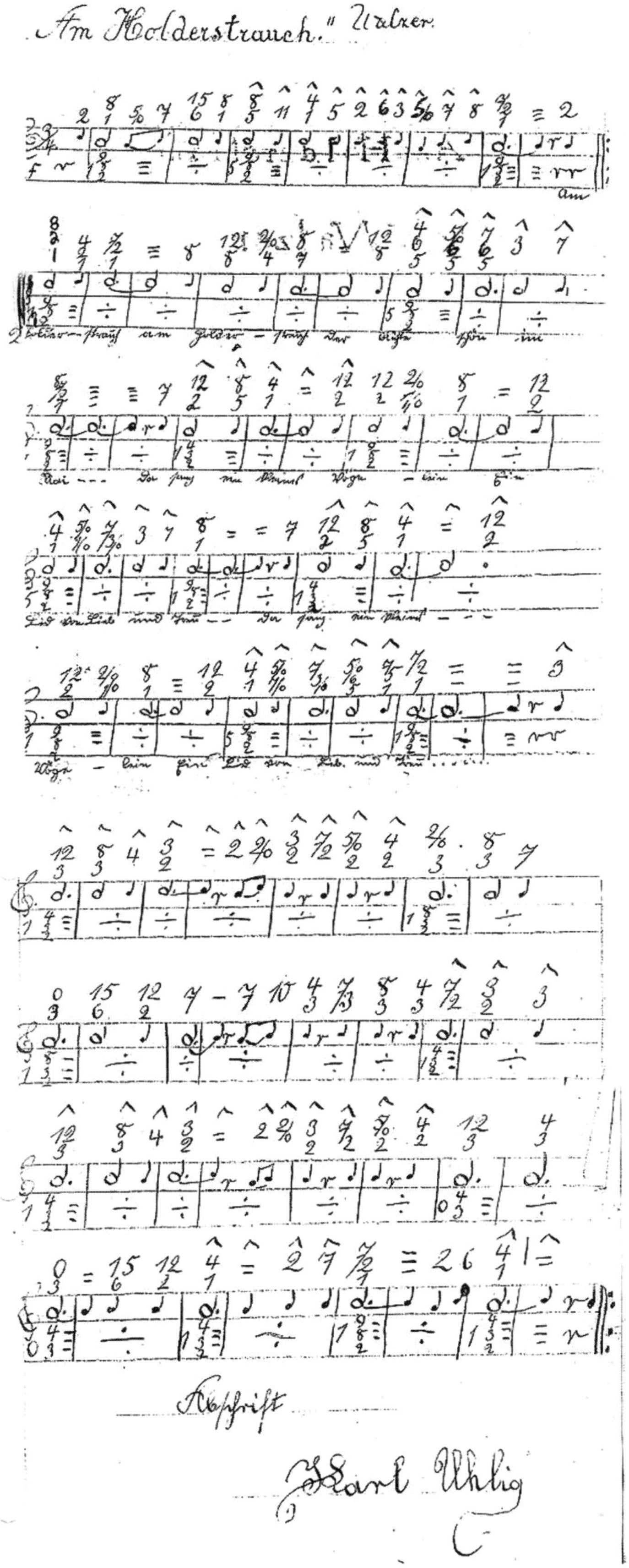

How the Concertina is Played

This document of music was probably annotated and signed by Carl Uhlig, the inventor of the concertina. It appears to be composed for the 76-key German Scheffler system, but can be reworked minimally and played using the American Scheffler system. Devised at this early date with the numbers of notes corresponding to buttons on the concertina, this piece is called the Holderbush Waltz.

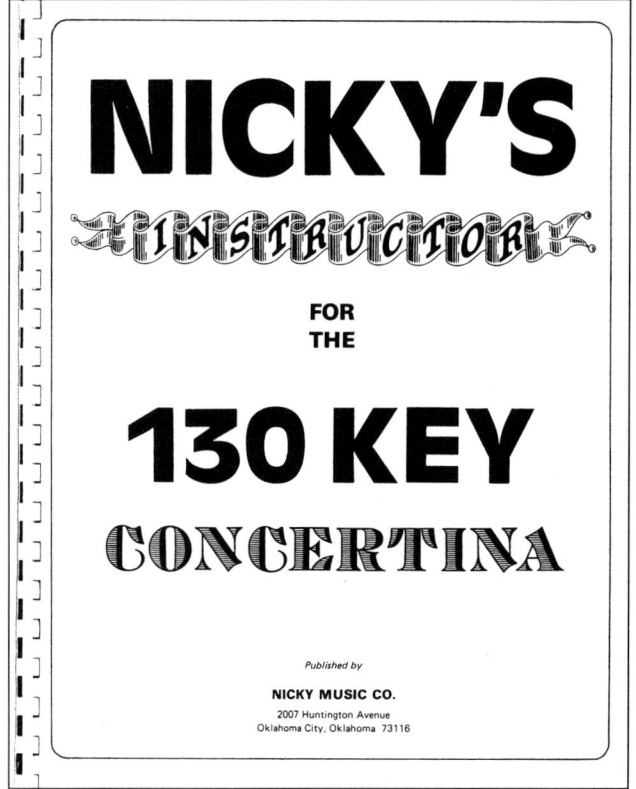

Instruction book compiled by Albert G. Nechanicky.

Footnotes

1 Here in chronological order are early books for instruction on the concertina, mentioned also in Chapter One.

> 1857 *Instructions for the German Concertina*
> (New York: W.A. Pond)
> 1860 *Howe's new school for the German Concertina*
> (Boston: Elias Howe)
> 1869 *Guide for the German Concertina*
> (Winner, Septimus. Boston: Ditson & Co.)
> 1869 *Winner's new primer for the German Concertina* (Winner, Septimus. New York: W.A. Pond & Co.)
> 1879 *Eclectic school for the concertina*
> (Boston: E. Howe, Chicago: Howe & Grant)
> 1919 *National Self Teacher for Concertina 76, 94 or 102 Keys (Square Shape)* (Chicago: Chart Music Publishing House, 1919).

2 Hector Berlioz, *Instrumentationslehre*, ergänzt und revidiert von Richard Strauss, Vol. II (Leipzig: C. F. Peters, 1905), pp. 428 ff. See also Hector Berlioz & Richard Strauss, *Treatise on Instrumentation*, trans. Theodore Front (New York: Edwin F. Kalmus, 1948), pp. 401 ff.

3 Maria Dunkel, *Bandonion und Konzertina* (Munich: Katzbichler, 1987), p. 163-4.

4 The full title page to the book is *Praktischer Selbstlehrer für Concertina mit 58 und 74 Tönen* [eine leichtfassliche Anleitung in höchst kurzer Zeit das Concertina selbst ohne Lehrer geläufig spielen zu lernen, mit besonderer Rücksicht auch auf Solche, denen es bisher am musikalischen Kentnissen fehlte] (Carlsfeld in Sachsen: Carl Zimmermann, Eigenthum des Verfassers, no date).

5 Mentioned in connection with the Hofmeister Catalogs from Leipzig in 1852, in Hans Luck, *Die Balginstrumente—Ihre Historische Entwicklung bis 1945*, Teil 2 Handbuch der Harmonika-Instrumente (Kamen, Germany: Karthause-Schmülling, 1997), p. 52.

6 Beginning in 1844 there was a plethora of instructional books printed in German for learning the concertina. The publishing of such books accelerated in the 1860s and boomed until World War II. A sampling of such books is included below.

C. A. Scherbauer, *Praktische Anleitung zum Erlernen der Concertina* (Munich: Aibel, 1865).
Otto Luther, *Concertina-Schule* (Leipzig: Zimmermann, 1888).
Arnold Haupt, *Schule für Concertina mit 40 Tönen* (Hamburg: Ahrens, 1900).
F. E. Lange, *Schule für die 76 tönige Konzertina* (Leipzig: Stoll, 1902).
P. Angelot, *Neuste praktische Schule für das Konzertina* (Berlin: Köster, 1908).
Mariana Rozycki, *Skola na Koncertine i Bandoniom* (Chicago, 1916).
Fritz Bauer, *Lernt Konzertina spielen* (Leipzig: Ahrens, 1933).
F. Hahnel, *Konzertina-Schule* (Berlin: Burbach, 1937).
Paul Frey, *Neue theoretisch-praktische Schule für Konzertina* (Berlin: Köstler, 1938).

These and many more instruction books for the concertina are listed in Karl Oriwohl, *Das Bandonion* (Berlin: Oriwohl, privately printed, 2004), pp. 219-235.

7 This advice by Silberhorn is from the inside cover of his sales catalogs, as shown in Chapter Five "Promotion and Midwest Distribution of the Chemnitzer Concertina." This particular quote has been reproduced there on the right hand column.

8 There were various editions of Henry Silberhorn's *Instructor for the Concertina* (76, 104 or more keys), the one in my possession being actually the 6th edition which Silberhorn claims was greatly improved with a number of pages added "to meet the requirements of present day music, made 'UP TO DATE' and will serve its purpose better than ever." Prolific in his supply of printed materials, Silberhorn was on the book circuit with multiple enticements, e. g., collections of German folksongs for concertina, among them standard numbers like "Freut euch des Lebens," "Ein Jäger aus Kurpfalz," and "Deutschland über alles." See *Sammlung beliebter deutscher Musikstuecke fuer die Concertina*, herausgegeben von H. Silberhorn, Chicago, 1913.

9 See e. g. Emil Geier, *94 Tönige Concertina Schule* (Leipzig: Verlag Edmund Stoll, 1897). In his introduction to this volume, Geier explains: "The 76 key concetina is still one of the most popular instruments, out of which has been developed the 94-key instrument. The latter have been crafted expertly by the firm of F. Lange, formerly C. F. Uhlig, in Chemnitz. Since this 94-key instrument is in great demand, we offer this teaching method [dated at Chemnitz July 20, 1897]. See also especially Dunkel, pp. 52 ff.

10 Dunkel, p. 89.

11 Pamphlet in the files of the author.

12 "*Concertina News*" (Winter 1931-32), Vol. 5 No. 6.

13 Copies made available to me by George S. Servatius, 32999 County Road 168, Melrose, Minnesota 56352.

14 Residence at 25 Second Avenue Northwest, St. Joseph, Minnesota 56374.

15 See James Leary, "The German Concertina" in Bohlman, op. cit., about teachers p. 203.

16 http://www.newulmtel.net/lorens/

17 Hence, a total of 4 tonal possibilities: 1) low musette, 4 reeds; 2) high musette, 3 reeds (low switched out). 3) low straight tuning, 3 reeds (medium playing musette switched out; 4) high straight, 2 reeds (both low reed and musette medium reed switched in/out.

18 Much of the advice provided here is available on websites. Nearly a century ago, Henry Silberhorn was offering the same advice and parallel products for care of the concertina, though of course different brands. See http://www.concertinamusic.com/sbox/links.html and link to Silberhorn's "Hints, Helps and Advice."

19 Contact Kodet at 474 Forest Lane, North Mankato, MN 56003, Ambrose.Kodet@MNSU.edu.

20 Photo can be viewed on the Ken Yagelski web site.

21 The Watters chart was reproduced in the short-lived Journal, *Polka and Old Time News* (January, 1965), p. 16.

7

Entertainment and the Concertina

When the Chemnitzer concertina was invented in Germany in 1834, it was and has remained strictly an eastern German instrument. It was far more at home in Saxony than elsewhere in that disjoined [until 1871, redivided in 1945] and later reunited [1990] German nation. Never was the concertina a genuinely German instrument. Though the concertina lived in isolation in eastern and Bavarian Germany, the bandonion was for a half century popular in the manufacturing and mining Ruhr district along the Rhine in the north. Certainly the concertina was never the primary bearer of melodies in Bavaria where "um pa pa" music was, and remains, very much at home. The accordion, the zither and voiced song lyrics crooned in dialect assured that. Nor did it make its way to Austria in any but isolated instances. Folkloric to the core, the Austrians relied on their horns, their reed clarinets and accordions to alternate with dialect songs and yodeling.

Founded in Chemnitz, the concertina was fashioned there by Uhlig and Lange as well as subsequently in smaller towns south and east of there—especially at first by the Zimmermann, then the Arnold factory in Carlsfeld and then by the Reichel factory in Waldheim. It later appeared on the market from the Seifert shops in Waldheim and in the multi-musical surroundings of Klingenthal. This small town is situated directly on today's boundary between Saxony and the Czech Republic. Following its beginning in 1834, the concertina quickly moved eastward through Bohemia but "settled" only in selected communities, tarrying a bit later in a more worthy, but also temporary, home in Poland. Currently, no neighborhood in Poland is known to serve as a home for the concertina. Regardless of geographical location, the concertina always belonged to the common man. At the heart of the matter when playing the concertina was folk music for dancing and singing. Some said it was the poor man's organ. Others conceived of it more broadly as a folk instrument. Many found it the best instrument for the single performer, one not in need of the support from added musical instruments. Thus it was an inexpensive source of music because one performer could stand alone and offer "the whole band." Never was the instrument welcome in the concert hall. Its sole purpose was entertainment not of the high brow but of the folk, be it for the players themselves, their listeners or the dancers.

As it applies to the concertina, entertainment means many things. It implies amusement, diversion, relaxation, recreation and enjoyment. It also suggests festivity, merriment, gaiety and jamboree. It could indicate an element of "show business," theater, and merry-making but it would never extend to athletics, sport, gaming, or reveling. Playing a concertina might encompass showmanship only if operated in the way that a few skilled concertinists can play the instrument while engaging in acrobatic maneuvers. No matter how played, the notion of entertainment with the concertina insinuates sociability, gregariousness, affability, and congeniality in groups.

There is something of the party element in concertina playing. We of course associate it with dancing. Seldom is it played for singing in group fellowship. Rather, it connects more than likely to masquerades, costumes, and specialty attire. Played well, it renders pleasure to the ear, but also to the eye as the rhythm of the end plates wax and wane to and from the billowing bellows. Also eye appealing is the abalone, mother-of-pearl which glistens on the two reed-holding shells, often ornamented with designs and name plates. Communicated to the audience is a certain gusto, zest, and relish. But it also supplies intellectual pleasure for those who grasp the complicated nature of its operation. The concertina delights if it does not gratify; it treats and pleases though it does not regale or revel. It glad-

An Arno Arnold concertina produced in 1939 prior to World War II, plain in color and design with slanted corners on which are mounted the Arnold logo. Owned by Marvin Moravec.

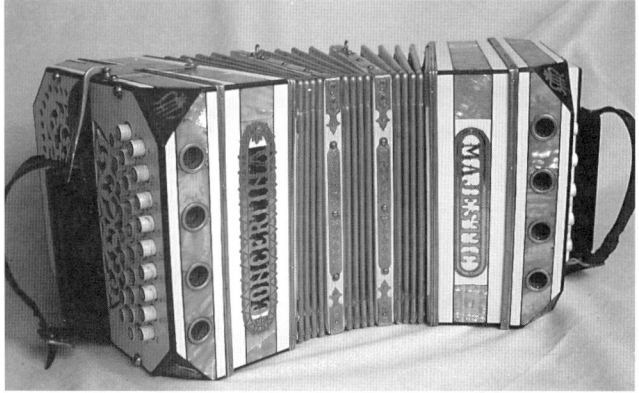

A Majestic concertina produced for the American market, probably by the Lange company in Chemnitz. Notice the Uhlig harps on the corners. Owned by Jerry Minar.

A combination concertina probably assembled in Chicago using parts shipped from Germany. This concertina has the Patek brand name but most of the exterior, including the bellows, is definitely of German manufacture. However, the internal parts, notably the reeds and the buttons, are identifiable as having Chicago manufacturing. Owned by Jerry Minar.

dens and thrills but it does not bewitch or intoxicate. In the end, the concertina offers dancing, especially old time, European favorites like the waltz and the polka.

In this chapter, the focus is on those sites and locations which have provided and still supply the locales for entertainment—primarily dance halls. It also converges on those bands which have kept the concertina as their core instrument in providing musical entertainment for the dance halls. Although dance halls as successors to the house party and the hay barn dances thrived between 1920 and 1980, there are still many more functioning dance halls than can be counted on one's two hands. On weekend afternoons and evenings, the old time dance still offers engagements for dozens of concertina bands. However, these venues are generally small towns situated across Minnesota, Wisconsin, and northern Iowa. While such orchestras as the Whoopee John Wilfahrt, the Six Fat Dutchmen, the Babe Wagner and many other bands once played 360 and more nights of the year, a concertina orchestra today can have 100 engagements and not be performing in frequency above its competitors. Often, though, these performance opportunities take place with multiple bands in alternating two-hour entertainment stretches, almost always, it turns out, in rural townscapes. The change from large city sites can be described as a shift from a single band performing four to five hours for a wedding,

One of the rare examples of a concertina built by the Hohner Company in Trossingen, Baden-Württemberg, called the Echo. The eight beveled corners have the letters "MH," which stands for Matt Hohner. Owned by Jerry Minar. One speculation is that the "Hohner" company (the harmonica and accordion giant in Germany) was testing the market with a few concertinas, which Matt Hohner called the "Echo" (in parallel to the Echo harmonicas being built in his factory). Years later, first Stan Uhlir and subsequently Robert Novak, began building and marketing a concertina with the name "Echo," now strictly a United States product. Note on p. 160 that Dan Gruetzmacher is playing a Hohner.

anniversary, retirement, or just a dance to support an organization like the local firemen to fests where various bands concatenate for a full and even multiple-day event.

Midwest locales for such performances at dances would include Gibbon, New Prague, Waconia, Rochester, Hamel near Minneapolis, Mankato and the St. Cloud area of Minnesota, as well as suburbs of the Twin Cities and on the Iron Range. In Iowa, Durant near Davenport, Cedar Rapids, Spillville, Clear Lake and others are representative. Nebraska can boast Wahoo, Wilber and smaller Czech towns around Omaha and Lincoln. Wisconsin has Pulaski, Kewaskum, Wausau, La Crosse, the Wisconsin Dells, Fountain City and the suburbs of Milwaukee, e. g. Allenton, while Illinois with Chicago is waning. A few sites in Michigan's Southwest come to mind. Which brings us to the secondary theme of this chapter—the concertina is not just a folk instrument for the common man, but also is definitively a "rural" instrument. It just is not at home in the big city, except in very ethnic neighborhoods like northeast Minneapolis. Even in Polish Chicago where the concertina lives, it appears to be becoming more popular among Bohemian communities than in others.

As for North America, with the exception of a few earlier arrivals in New England and in Philadelphia, the Chemnitzer concertina did not seriously make its way to the United Staes until it arrived for the 1893 Columbian Exposition in Chicago. As detailed in Chapter Two, in Chicago it was first imported and sold by Germans and Czechs who soon began building their own, feeling very at home in the Polish neighborhoods where they worked and sold. The concertina also gained a solid foundation in the Polish settlements of Buffalo in New York. It has thrived in southwest Michigan and northern Indiana around South Bend where the German population sustains it. Farther to the north of Chicago, it gained status in Milwaukee and in central Wisconsin [Pulaski, Wausau, Stevens Point and the region] where a mixture of Poles and north German Pomeranians have been its true champions. As we have witnessed in previous chapters, certain individuals, neither German nor Polish, have been among the instrument's most diligent promoters. Pat Watters must have been Irish, Silberhorn was German, Patek was Czech as is Minar in New Prague, Minnesota. Lash, originally Edward A. Laszczak, was Polish to the core of his soul. Hengel is Bohemian-German, Vitak and Elsnic were Bohemian, while Gruetzmacher of central Wisconsin is German. Brown of New Ulm was Yankee American in a German-American town. Also German was Harold "Zimmy" Zimmerman of Union, Michigan [on the Indiana border] as is his son, Jack Zimmerman, of South Bend, Indiana. Without the Zimmermans' initiative and support for the

Wausau, Wisconsin concertina learners with their instructor. *Dan Gruetzmacher. Front Row L-R: David Pazio, Ronald Zastrow, Vern Doering, Roger Wilk, unknown. Back row L-R: Dennis Halkowski, Jeff Falkowski, Henry Kuklinski, David Malinowski, Dan Gruetzmacher. [All appear to be playing Arno Arnold concertinas.]*

World Concertina Congress Hall of Fame and their promotional activities, there would be a far smaller concertina presence in the Midwest today.[1]

Thoroughly at home in southern Minnesota, the concertina has always experienced a close affinity with German and Bohemian musicians. Whether offered in Minnesota's New Ulm, New Prague, Webster, Hutchinson or Montgomery, whether in St. Joseph, New Richland, New Hope or New Brighton, whether at Silver Lake, Gibbon, Rochester, Owatonna or Waseca, the style of playing and the melodies rendered by the concertina developed on their own and independently, but always with either Czech or German characteristics. In southern Minnesota, styles varied considerably. The "Dutchman" renderings held little similarity with the tunes, melodies and beats that developed and prevailed among the Polish settlements in northeast Minneapolis. They are likewise starkly different from the Yugoslav [Slovenian, Croatian, Serbian] features of concertina music on the Minnesota Iron Range and Duluth.

Minnesota names like Tomaszewski, Mrozinski, Czerniak, Bzdok bespeak band leaders of a strictly Slavic stripe. Bruno Rudzinski, who recorded on RCA Victor already in 1928 made Chicago something of a concertina performance capital. Eddie Zima followed with the "Circus" polka and similar numbers on Capitol Records which made him the godfather of Chicago-style Polish concertina music. Successors to these standbys are Lil Wally Jagiello who brought along concertina players with names like Casey Siewierski, Al Piatkowski and Jerry Darlak. Chicago was, and still is, home to the Cicero Concertina Circle, a concertina club that has been meeting in the Chicago area since 1919. It meets on the first Friday evening of each month at Drexel Hall, on the northeast corner of 36th Street and 54th Avenue in Cicero, Illinois. Frequent performers at Drexel Hall include, almost exclusively, players of the Polish heritage, boasting names like Chester Sukacz, Joe Warput and Joe Stulga; other common players in the Chicago area were Ed Jakubowski, Diane Pawelczyk, Florian Pawelczyk, Chester Sukacz, Stas Micek, Rick Bubula and Hank Dziekan.

Milwaukee concertina teacher Stanley Nowicki (1894-1983), stricken with the loss of his sight in adulthood, was not only an expert instructor but also a highly respected concertina performer, artist and arranger. He lived at 1531 West Maplewood Court in Milwaukee. Chicago's [and Florida's] George Hrica is best identified as Bohemian, but remained an all-around superb Chicago-style concertinist hardly surpassed for his ability with the concertina. In many respects, it has always been the talent of the player rather than the exact brand name of the instrument that has made the concertina "proud." Players like Hrica, Bill Czerniak, Eddie Lash, Eddie Blazonczyk with his Versatones, along with Frank J. Stanczewski and Al Tucholski of Buffalo, New York [who played every third Wednesday with their Buffalo Concertina Club] do as much for the concertina

Chicago Concertina Club. Note that most players are holding imported Lange concertinas from around 1900.

A long-time member of Chicago's Bohemian American Concertina Association (BACA), George Hrica was not only an innovative concertina player but also served as a founding member of the World Concertina Congress. He provided leadership during a stint as First Vice President and was subsequently inducted in 1976 as a member of the WCC Hall of Fame. Most recently Hrica made his home in Florida where he died on February 12, 2005.

bandonion in the early 1930s playing the waltz quadrille, she soon switched to the concertina. In 1936, she acquired a Pearl Queen double with which her teacher, Al Giese, started her by giving a few lessons. It being the Great Depression, she could not afford further schooling and became entirely self-taught. Her father, Harvey Lemke, was German, which accounts for Millie's comfort with German and Slovenian tunes. As a Bullard lathe operator at International Harvester in Milwaukee, Millie worked close to Karpek's Store, which she browsed often to acquire newer concertinas. Through it all, the

as the instrument did for them. Frequently the Star brand is loved by Polish players, the Silberhorn, Clarion, Patek and Pearl Queen along with the Hengel are more desired by German-style players.

A few peak performers in the Milwaukee and Chicago areas have preferred the Karpek products and those of the Glass Brothers. Other expert players have included especially Concertina Millie [Kaminski], who can perform in any style. Though Millie started on the

An Arno Arnold "Slim Line" concertina owned and played by Ambrose Butch Wolf, the son of Tony and Betty Wolf of St. Joseph, Minnesota, before his tragic death.

Concertina Millie [Kaminski] from Milwaukee playing her Star concertina at the Gibbon Festival in Minnesota, July 22, 2004.

Robert Novotny of Sleepy Eye displays his array of concertinas, including two Hengel and two Stradivarius models.

Star brand remained her favorite, although she also fingered different makes at places like Eddie Teikowski's Music Store. Directing various bands during her long career, always under the general name of Concertina Millie, Kaminski continues her artistry at gatherings and on the job, despite the loss of her truck driver husband, Edmund Kaminski, who died in 1993.[2]

Another high-quality performer on the concertina in the Milwaukee area was Henry Jacobs of Cudahy, who worked for the Karpek Accordion operation.[3] As mentioned in Chapter Two, George Karpek took over from his Russian-born father, Andrew, who died in 1942 and carried the business forward at 820 South 16th Street until his death in 1988.[4] Playing concertina for southside weddings and parties, "Hank" was a tool and die maker, a common career for concertinists. Although Karpek's concertina building waned over the years, repair boomed and in between he built a few of the so-called accortinas, half concertina, half accordion. Likewise skilled was his associate, Max King [stage name for Ervin Kuczynski], a brother of the more famous Pee Wee King, who almost always stuck with the accordion rather than the concertina. Along with Thomas Smigielski and John Bondowski, later joined by the very distinguished father-son Blazonczyk team, these concertinists were representative of the Polish-style tradition of entertainment with the concertina. Additional peak performing concertinists during the 1970s and 1980s in the Milwaukee region were Len Behn, Ben [Carter] Dobiecki, Albert [Alvin Gastomski] Roberts, Walter Kehl, Irvin Kwas, Eddie Rickert, Ervin Taczala, Harlan Zwiefka plus others. Younger players who have excelled on the concertina in the Milwaukee area include Donald Gralak, Bryan O'Donnell and James Monson.

A Star "Streamline" concertina from the 1950s bearing the Serial Number 1567, which indicates a completion in early 1954. A Star completed in October, 1953 bears the number 1523. Working backwards we note that a Star with the number 1413 was completed on February 13, 1952. Yet another was issued the number 1445 with the completion date stamped inside as June 7, 1952. In other words, 33 concertinas were built in 16.5 weeks. This means that Star manufacturing in Chicago was producing about two concertinas per week. Note that the Streamline was patterned after the look of the 1950s automobiles, which displayed shiny chrome and rounded corners.

A newspaper that assisted the concertina in a direct way to offer entertainment to large crowds of people at dances was the bi-monthly *Entertainment Bits*. It began publishing in the spring of 1973 when issued by the Minnesota Ballroom Operators Association [MBOA] under its president, Lee Hens. Accentuated prominently in the first issue were such enduring stars as Tony Wolf and the Deutschmeisters from St. Joseph, Minnesota. Playing the concertina in traditional southern Minnesota old time music style, Tony was joined by his wife, Betty, and their family. Equally present, however, was the Joe Tomaszewski band, with his concertina offering blends of country and Polish polkas. From start to finish, the dichotomy of southern and northern Minnesota is directly in evidence, even within the first issues of this ballroom operators' organ. Essentially, *Entertainment Bits* existed for the administrators of the large dance halls like Bel-Rae in New Brighton [later Mounds View], the Spectacle Lake in Cambridge, the Gibbon Ballroom, the Island Ballroom in Bird Island, the Algon in Alexandria, the Riverside in Carver, the Taylors Falls Barn Dance Ballroom in Taylors

This is a 19th century Uhlig clearly showing the "U" logo midpoint in the nameplate on the right.

Falls, the Terp in Austin and many others frequently appearing in this paper. Often in this periodical, Polish bands at their polka festivals used an accordion, which in the organ's earlier days seems to have taken priority over the concertina.

Entertainment Bits began publication in the spring of 1973.[5] In his "corner" of the paper, the President of the MBOA in this first volume spells out the goals of the publication. He reports that the Association had been formed many years before in 1927 with concerns for "the continuity and continuation of Polka and Old Time music. . . . The business has changed dramatically [but] the Association today still exists for the same reasons that the organization was formed in 1927. The World's Largest Annual Polka Festival organized by the MBOA in 1970 was first held at the Metropolitan Stadium in Bloomington, Minnesota and was dedicated to the purpose of showing the young and old the fun that can be had with polka and old time music." Lee Hens, President. Thus, the same "battle" to gain the yearnings of a more youthful dancing clientele seems to have trailed from the 1920s through the entire 20th century in tandem with a half-century-long craving to inspire young musicians to play the concertina. Waning since 1950, the concertina as a source of entertainment to large crowds has actually held its own through the turn of the 21st century.

On display frequently in early issues of the paper are such dominating concertina players as Tony Wolf and the Deutschmeisters for which Tony was the champion concertina player [probably an Arno Arnold as best deciphered from photographs], having received by the 1980s ten citations from the MBOA and having played continuously for 19 years on KASM Radio in Albany. Tony Wolf of Richmond and Betty (Arnold) of Eden Valley, Minnesota began their musical careers together at Pearl Lake, Minnesota in 1938. Since 1954 at their home in St. Joseph, they taught concertina, published a book to teach learners, and sent their students to concertina festivals across the states. In the summer of 1973 the band boasted the support of their daughter Lisa, who in 1965 at the National Concertina Convention in St. Cloud, was declared the youngest concertina player in the United States.[6]

Portrayed via advertisements in *Entertainment Bits* during the 1970s are such additional well-known ballrooms as Proch's in Ellsworth, Wisconsin, the Palms Ballroom in Renville, the Diamond Point Rancho between Sauk Centre and Long Prairie, the Algon in Alexandria, the Clarissa Ballroom in Clarissa, the Spectacle Lake in Cambridge [which collapsed during the Blizzard of the Century, January 11, 1975], various additions to the Gibbon Ballroom, the Blue Moon at the Lyon County Fairgrounds in Marshall, the Sauk Centre

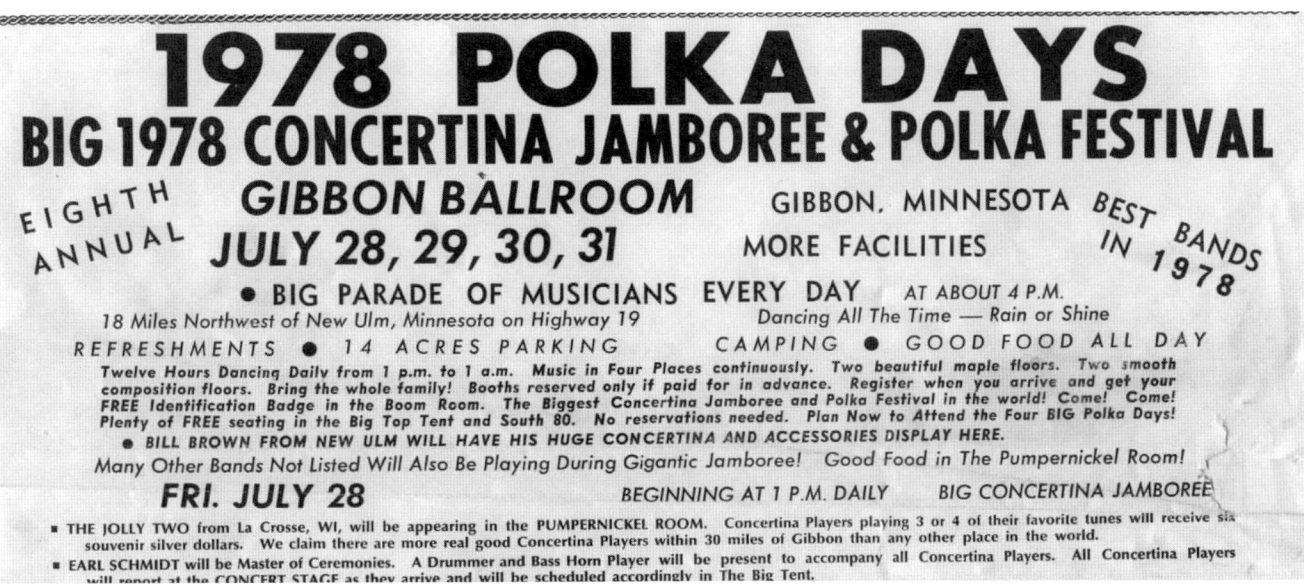

From the early 1970s to the present, the Gibbon, Minnesota festival offered four days and evenings of dancing on its mammoth grounds at the east end of Gibbon. Notice that Bill Brown from New Ulm displayed his concertinas there. Also note the claim that there are more concertina players within 30 miles of Gibbon than anywhere else in the world. Earl Schmidt of Cologne served as master of ceremonies for the concertina jamboree and did so every year including 2004. The Gibbon Ballroom went silent in 2005.

Coliseum, the North Star at Carlton, the Blue Note in Winsted, the Paradise in Waconia, the Pla Mor at Glencoe, the Lakeside in Glenwood [built in 1909, it burned to the ground on June 7, 2003], the Majestic in Cottage Grove, the Marigold on Nicollet Avenue in Minneapolis and the Prom in St. Paul—all operating at "full steam" during the 1970s and 1980s.

Seemingly it was the instigation of Cliff Hermel, the ballroom operator most successful in bringing Polka Days from New Ulm to Gibbon, that gave Gibbon the edge in championing some of the best concertina players in the world. In 1978 for example, the fourteen acres of parked cars and the crowds covered the entire field east of Gibbon. Yearly there was and continued to be a huge concertina jamboree. Hermel unabashedly named Gibbon the "concertina capital" of the world, which in 1993 garnered him a place in the World Concertina Congress Hall of Fame. When he died in 1999, the ballroom complex passed to Richard Seeboth of New Ulm and has been operated by him since then, but is scheduled to close following the 2004 Polka Days bonanza.[7] Born in Milwaukee, Seeboth continues to live in New Ulm where he serves as county commissioner and has rendered 12 years of service as vice president of Heritage Fest.[8]

Steadily items appeared in *Entertainment Bits* from editor Doris Pease, who summarized current and historical events from the ballroom perspective of concertina music. Pease was an appropriate personality. Born in Springfield, Minnesota, she spent her teen years dancing to the music of world class concertinist, Whoopee John Wilfahrt, the Six Fat Dutchmen, Elmer Scheid and many other fine concertina bands. Later she lived for a time in Olivia, then in Faribault and finally in Coon Rapids, from where she wrote many of her columns. Her experience, however, reached back to Willmar radio station KWLM, writing for the *New Ulm Journal*, the *Redwood Gazette*, *Olivia Times Journal* and lesser periodicals. Publication of the *Bits* was at the Osseo, Minnesota Press where she formatted and issued the paper.[9] It then moved to St. Joseph, Minnesota where it was published under the title, *Music and Dance News*, edited by Denis Dalman and published by Janelle Von Pinnon. In mid-2005, the paper passed to the Herald Journal Company, Box 129, Winsted, Minnesota 55393.

In the summer of 1973, Governor Wendell Anderson proclaimed July 8 'Polka Day' in Minnesota, to the delight of ballroom owners and musicians alike. With 31 ballrooms on board, the association was always thrilled to accept new applications—from the Horseshoe Lake Ballroom in Browerville, the M & M Ballroom in Montevideo, the Playland in Watkins, the Pine Camp in Pine City, all in Minnesota. Big halls like the Falls in Little Falls, the Coliseum on Lake Street in Minneapolis, and the Medina a bit west of Hamel, Minnesota were all on board. Showcased intermittently during these early 1970s are concertina bands like the Katzenjamers of North Mankato including Der Cammack on the bass horn, Clete Frederick on drums and famed Johnny Gag with the concertina. Given top billing too are the likes of "Jumping, Tooting Wally Pikal." The owner of a music store in Hutchinson, Pikal performed clown acts playing three coronets at once, with or without backup from his band which included Jerome Kadlec on saxophone, Marinus Fasching clarinet, Bob Busacker piano, Cy Vanyo on drums, Ray Moran on bass and Marvin Bulau on concertina.

Often the paper produced excellent entries about the concertina and its artists. In the fall of 1974, Doris Pease wrote affectionately that Vern Steffel of St. Louis Park would be reviving the Whoopee John Wilfahrt Band. Following its demise with the death of John Wilfahrt's son, Pat, in 1966 [John died already in 1961], the library of 350 polkas and 400 waltzes would pass to Steffel from surviving son, Dennis, in St. Paul.[10] In the same issue she reported the introduction of a new instrument, called by *Entertainment Bits* the "Accordiontina" as introduced by the Riverside Dutchmen from Glencoe and Hutchinson. However, the instrument was devised by Christy Hengel of New Ulm and played by Harvey Becker. It had a rectangular reed design on long plates. A bit later Jerry Minar in New Prague, George

The Accortina above was made in the late 1970s or early 1980s by the George Karpek Company in Milwaukee. Note that it has two bass units for the left hand, an accordion bass attached, and a concertina bass lying flat on the table.

Karpek in Milwaukee and others were creating another variation of this instrument, one that came and went with ephemeral whims common to the entertainment world. Thus, in essence, there were three different instruments tried by various inventors. The Accortina pictured on page 204 was made by Karpek in Milwaukee. The Accordion-tina, which is a piano accordion with Hengel long plate concertina reeds and the Accordina, which was created by Anton Wolfe and Jerry Minar, is pictured on page 120. Brown Distrubuters of New Ulm built a similar instrument called the "Button-Tina."

In the same issue is a story about Bill Brown, the concertina builder and music store proprietor of New Ulm, depicted with his musically talented three sons, Jim, John and Bill Jr., who had just returned with a trophy from the Mid-American Music Association contest held in Kansas City.[11] Also noteworthy is the Erv Reutzel creation of the "Hoolerie Bohemians" Dance Band at Blue Earth, Minnesota where he was employed during the day as a radio sports announcer. Of interest here is his concertina player, Leonard Drattota of Jackson, and the fact that he named the band "Bohemian." It contrasts with the varied use of specifically German names attached by Elmer Scheid and Erwin Suess as the "Hoolerie Dutchmen"—all fine concertina bands, of course, ambivalent about being German [Dutch which stems from Deutsch] or Bohemian. Few seem to have understood that the music and the instrument was German, and that the preeminent concertina players in Minnesota were of Bohemian or more specifically German-Bohemian origin.[12] Some wonder about the word "Hoolerie," a term first used by Bohemian-German Emil "Dumphy" Domeier, who liked to hear the concertina played in the high switch which he called Hoolerie. At first Hoolerie [sic] but spoken as if it were "Hoolerei." Later, clarinets supplied the main thrust of this high pitched style. No one can claim the word or the style is Bohemian, Bavarian, or simply German. What interests us, historically speaking, is that there had always been a geographical, political, and cultural proximity of the German and the Bohemian—the same holding true for the concertina itself and for its origins in and around Chemnitz.

Occasionally the Polish of Minnesota connected with the Polish concertina lovers of Buffalo, New York, e. g. when the Golden Stars, Wanda and Stephanie, came to the Majowka [pronounced *mi-off-ka*] or "May Day" celebrations at the Bel-Rae Ballroom in Moundsview. It was sponsored in 1975 by the Holy Cross Polish Parish at

John Filipczak playing his concertina at the V.F.W. Club in Cottage Grove, March 2004. He is the bandleader of The Classics, of northeast Minneapolis origins, though John now resides in Grantsburg, Wisconsin. John is playing a concertina built by Walter J. Roback of 3555 2½ NE, Minneapolis. Prior to his death, Roback had been a railroad worker who traveled frequently between his home and Chicago where he often met, conversed, played concertinas and exchanged construction ideas with the Star concertina team. Walter Roback's son, Don Roback, was also active with concertina repair out of his home shop. Don Roback passed away in February 2004.

Harvey Becker, of Glencoe, Minnesota, is playing the Hengel-built accordion-tina for the Riverside Dutchmen. This instrument is a piano accordion with which Christy Hengel offered to replicate the unique sound of his concertinas.

1621 University Avenue NE, Minneapolis, Minnesota 55413. The next day concertinists from Buffalo appeared at Carlton near Duluth in the North Star Ballroom. The young performers had appeared previously with Joe Tomaszewski and his Polish Band.[13]

Also on February 9, 1975 Joe Czerniak of Duluth and Bill Czerniak of Shoreview entertained as sponsors of a concertina party at the Polish American Club in St. Paul. At the event they featured their talented students from the Duluth area: Roger Juntenen, Tim Telega, Jeff and Jim Dobesinski. Performing, too, were artists like Rufie Granda, Dave Sowada, Gordy Lehrke, Bob Sobinski, Jerry Pitzen and Joe Kaczmarczyk, with special performances by Ed Chesney from northern Minnesota. The article stipulates that the Czerniaks are the Minnesota distributors for the Star Concertina Company of Chicago. From time to time in *Entertainment Bits*, Bill Czerniak at 747 Gramsie Road in Shoreview, Minnesota advertised his "Star Distributing" agency, offering music, repairs and lessons. The same "Authorized Concertina Sales and Service" was available by Joe Czerniak at 701 Martha Street in Duluth.[14] Among the many recordings of Bill Czerniak was his special album entitled "Mr. Concertina." Prominent in the winter 1975 issue of the paper was the "Cavaliers" band of Cloquet near Duluth, composed primarily of guitars but led by Todd Dobozenski on the concertina. The latter described his music as "Polish sound with lively brass and full-bodied accompaniment as well as the concertina which gives it the Polish sound." Seeking examples of players who featured the Polish sound, it should be noted that the term would remain empty without mention of John Filipczak and the Classics, led by John, an expert concertinist. Calling himself at times the "Polish Pavarotti," John and his team offer many Polish vocals alongside straight melody on concertina at performances and on recordings available from his Grantsburg residence.

In 1976, *Entertainment Bits* penned a special story about Joe Czerniak for his Polka Day, June 27, running from noon to midnight in the North Star Ballroom in Cloquet. Duluth concertina player Joe Czerniak, played Star concertinas since he was eight years old. At 12, he started playing solo for the entertainment of others. The son of Polish immigrants, Joe Czerniak as an adult, often played with his son, Bill, and other relatives. The writer credits Czerniak for his role in teaching hundreds to play the concertina. His first real student was his son Bill, who began at the age of seven. But the Polka Day he organized was his most rewarding for bringing on stage the many students he had instructed, among them the Dobosenski brothers, Jeff and Jim, as well as Tim Telega and Roger Juntunen.[15] Since May, 1974 Bill Czerniak with wife Mary Lou operated the band called Polka Soul, starting at a wedding in Morris, Minnesota but moving ahead to record among others, "Concertina Encore." Polka Soul gave Bill the opportunity to express his unique concertina style. Performing at all of the major polka festivals, Polka Soul soon gained a national following because of its unique, energetic and solid sound. Bill published approximately 50 original polka and waltz tunes, many of which were recorded on the dozen LP's on which he has recorded. From his home base in Shoreview, Bill Czerniak was inducted into the IPA Polka Music Hall of Fame in 1992. William G. 'Bill' Czerniak passed away at the age 55 on April 18, 2002.

M. J. Recording, Inc. Czech Records with Joe G. Spellerberg Jr. as President and Jo Ann Sobczak as Manager contributed its share to the popularization of the concertina. Located in Dodge, Nebraska, it favored old time dance music which, for many Midwest orches-

Life-sized figures carved by Art Feser at Hutchinson for Dotty Wendinger: Paul and Peter Wendinger. February 20, 2004 at Turner Hall in New Ulm.

Karl Hartwich and Pete Wendinger on stage in Turner Hall at New Ulm, February 20, 2004.

George Servatius at his shop in Melrose, Minnesota, playing an Arno Arnold concertina, June 24, 2003.

Hugo (Steven) Reinhart of Rochester, Minnesota, in 1987 playing a Hengel concertina in his home study with another on the shelf, plus a button box.

tras, meant the concertina. However, reports indicate correctly that the concertina was never as prominent or dominant outside the upper Midwest as the presence of Czech and eastern German immigrants would indicate. For instance, the Math Sladky Band from Waverly, Nebraska, begun in 1952, played frequently for such events as the Wilber Nebraska Czech Days, the Pla-Mor Czech Days in Lincoln, and across the states of Nebraska, Iowa and South Dakota. Prominent in his band for some time was Gawaine Dvorak, who was equally able on the accordion, button or keys, and the concertina. During this time it was the only band in Nebraska with the concertina sound.[16] Subsequently the band could be reached at Math Sladky Band, 5340 Zeamer St, Lincoln, Nebraska, 68524. Of late, however, fine concertina players in Nebraska include especially Edward Malina, Jan Lhotak, Lonny Hansen, Kenneth Shuda and Ron Kantor, all of Czech heritage.

Worthy of extra attention in 1975 were the Wendinger brothers, Peter and Paul, who that summer appeared with Marv Herzog in Frankenmuth, Michigan, where 312,000 people heard and danced to their talents. On the circuitous pathway to Michigan, the Wendingers stopped for performances in St. Charles and later at Sioux City, Iowa's Oktoberfest. The two brothers embarked on playing with an appearance at Polka Day 1962 in New Ulm where they purchased concertinas from Christy Hengel. Concertina lessons for them started the same year from Leonard Krulikoski of Hutchinson, Merle Zuehe and Janette Weber, continuing later with John Helget, Linda Schroeder and Ambrose Kodet in New Ulm. Their first formal appearance came at John Deere Days in Gibbon in January, 1964. Early on, each of the brothers took turns playing with Harold Loeffelmacher's Six Fat Dutchmen. Members of the band were Barry Franta, Red Slanders, Leonard Hanson, sometimes switching with Leonard Sellner, Donald Hoffman and Fritz or Welles Zimmerman on the bass horn. Later the Wendingers were joined by trumpet players Clarence Prahl and Robert Rheaume and eventually Gary Gleisner. Recording started with Czech Records in 1971, who did three albums followed by Johnny Durham of Cedar Rapids, Iowa. Later the band did some ten recordings with JBM Sound in New Prague. In 1975 the Wendingers pioneered with their first polka mass held at home in St. George, Minnesota.[17] Busy with farming in their middle years, they have for decades been successful also in their travel business, practically circling the globe with their land and sea offerings, on occasion with the band's accompaniment. On February 20, 2004 they feted their fans with a 40-year celebration at Turner Hall in New Ulm where their slide show supplied the visual, their band the audio entertainment.

Bohemian-German by heritage, the Wendinger style contrasts sharply with the well-known Polish approach to playing the concertina. Infrequently, the two styles blended into an enjoyable mixture. For example, on December 5, 1976, Polish-style Bill Czerniak staged a concertina party at the Riverside Ballroom in Carver where he broadcast live on KSMM of Shakopee and in the hall displayed various brands of concertinas. The following March 6, 1977, an impromptu group of con-

Erwin Suess, World Concertina Congress Hall of Fame Inductee and famous bandleader for many decades, at his home in North Mankato, Minnesota.

Christy Hengel in his shop at New Ulm and Hilary T. Mohr. In June, 2001 Hengel is touch-tuning Hengel concertina #11, which was completed in 1958 for then-bandleader Ernie Coopman of Mankato, who in 1958 had just purchased the Jolly Brewers Orchestra from Bruno Randles.

Carl W. Neuman of Waupun, Wisconsin playing a Hengel concertina. Neuman bought his first concertina from his teacher, Irving DeWitz, at his Music Store in Hustisford, Wisconsin.

John F. Check, retired professor of educational psychology at the University of Wisconsin-Oshkosh, at home on Bismarck Avenue with his Hengel concertina. Retired from his band, Check continues his old time music WTKM radio show in Hartford, Wisconsin.

certina players entertained the MBOA convention at the Medina Ballroom in the Twin Cities in fine Polish style. Wanting to offend neither the Dutchman nor the Polish style fans, they were followed by the German-Bohemian Whoopee John Band with Vern Steffel to supply music for the evening dance. That summer *Entertainment Bits* honored Kathryn and Cliff Albert Hermel as owners of the Gibbon Ballroom, who were credited with sponsoring the "biggest concertina jamboree" in the world. Hermel was born March 18, 1918, in Mankato, to Adolph and Marie (Kroeger) Hermel and graduated from Nicollet High School in 1934. From their hometown of St. Peter, the Hermels, with his father, A. H. Hermel, had owned the Swan Lake Pavilion near Nicollet, which had been torn down. He owned the Gibbon Ballroom since 1961 and greatly expanded it over the years. Although Cliff never played the concertina, he did drum for the Valley Dutchmen of St. Peter and owned various bands. For his sponsorship of the concertina, and in particular for bolstering the Gibbon Polka Fest from 1972 to the time of his death at the age of 81 on October 31, 1999, Hermel was inducted into the World Concertina Congress Hall of Fame in 1993. It was his promotion of the instrument that garnered for him that honor.

Tony and Betty Wolf of St. Joseph were also inducted to the Concertina Congress Hall of Fame on October 28, 1977, for which they received broad coverage in *Entertainment Bits*.[18] Weekly during that time frame, the Wolfs pushed their concertina music on Saturdays from KASM 1150 in Albany. With the help of Pat Watters, they became a concertina distributorship for the Arno Arnold and later the Stradivarius, receiving orders from far and wide. Marketing the Watters line of concertinas in the St. Cloud area, the Wolf family was joined by George Servatius in Melrose to sell the instrument in

Tony Lis of Stanley, Wisconsin poses at the Hengel Shop in New Ulm when he acquired his concertina in June, 1994.

Jerry Schuft plays Karl Hartwich's rosewood Hengel concertina at Gibbon, July 24, 2003.

On the left, Eugene Bertrand holding a Hengel and Bob Novotny with a Stradivarius at Sleepy Eye, Minnesota in 1995.

central Minnesota. A parallel distributor for the south, Bill Brown, did the same from his outlet in New Ulm. Sometimes in parades and at dances, the Wolf band appeared with Watters above a sign, "Wolf's Watters Concertina Distributing Co.," giving us an indication of their close relationship. Expanding their scope, the Wolf family not only sold but also taught the concertina and hired concertina teachers, e. g. in New Prague and Montgomery, Sister Valeria, the school music teacher at Holy Redeemer School in Montgomery, Minnesota, also gave lessons on the concertina. The Wolfs' Deutschmeisters Band got its start in 1958. By 1977 they had produced 13 albums of recordings and, as noted previously, had been awarded many citations from the MBOA. In many respects, the Wolfs carried on and built to fruition a tradition in Stearns County that reaches deep into German history and the immigration of German Catholics to that region.[19] A great loss to the concertina world was the untimely death of Ambrose Butch Wolf, who died January 4, 1990 at the hand of his deranged wife, at the age of 47.[20]

Of considerable importance in boosting the concertina during the late 1970s was the rise of the Renata Romanek Band with their title, "Girls, Girls, Girls," students of Joe Czerniak in northeastern Minnesota. Female concertina players had always been rather sparse in number. Besides Renata from Cloquet, there were Theresa Telega and her concertina from Duluth with Holly Hill on violin and Debbie Tillman on drums.[21] Booking out of their home at 427 Highway 33 in North Cloquet, Minnesota, the Girls, Girls, Girls Band put out many fine musical albums with Renata on her Star concertina.[22] Equally influential from northern Minnesota during the late 1970s was the Iron Range Governor of Minnesota, Rudy Perpich. On various occasions at the Bel Rae Ballroom, special festivities took place in the Governor's honor, including e. g. the Perpich Polka Ball on Sunday, January 22, 1978. Offered were a polka mass with Father Perkovich. The dancing that followed took place to the Jerry Schuft Orchestra representing the Dutchman style and the Mrozinski Brothers, the Polish approach. Through his terms in office, Perpich was generous in proclaiming official Polka Days for Minnesota. Of course Governor Al Quie and subsequent governors likewise never shied away from proclaiming Minnesota Polka Day.[23] While the concertina was never front and center at these events, the music of the instrument was heard clearly. Peter and Thomas Mrozinski, along with Schuft, played the concertina often and vigorously.[24]

From Brownton, Minnesota, Gerald Erich "Jerry" Schuft, born in 1936, the son of Erich and Martha (Tietz) Schuft, had been playing concertina with bands since

Randy Dorschner of Menasha, Wisconsin, hovers over his Hengel concertinas — which he plays for the family old time band, Rainbow Valley Dutchmen.

Bruce Libby of Roberts, Wisconsin, demonstrates his Hengel concertina above his Royal by Slim Maser and a Stradivarius.

1954. His first concertina came from Wenzel Fischer in New Ulm who shipped it by train to Brownton. Practicing and memorizing, Jerry annoyed his father with the squeaking and wheezing, but in a short time achieved consummate skill on the instrument. Initially it was parties and bars, his first paying job at the Hamburg Hall basement for fox hunters' merrymaking. It lasted so late that, when he returned home after sunrise, his mother said "church starts at 9:30." To allay her anxiety, Jerry emptied his pockets of more than $30, most of which she made him dump into the collection basket. A few short years later in 1957 he joined the Ivan Kahle Band in Norwood, performing some four nights a week on average. Complementing his night work was a day job repairing reed and brass instruments for Doug's Music Shop in Glencoe, which involved upkeep on instruments for 47 high schools.[25]

From 1968-1999 Schuft also originated and ran the Rainy Water Conditioning Company, serving the Hutchinson area. From 1960-1970, he first joined and then co-owned the so-named Earl Schmidt Band in Cologne, parading on the circuit of ballrooms including the Prom in St. Paul, the Marigold in Minneapolis, the Serf in Clearwater, Iowa and George's in New Ulm. This led to purchasing the second half of the Schmidt Band in 1970, which lasted for 15 hectic years leading to his retirement in 1985. Schuft then sold all his instruments, equipment and music library except his favorite concertina, a 1932 Patek.[26] No doubt a fine introduction to the musical ability of the Jerry Schuft Band is left to us in his recordings. In 2004 he released Volumes 5 and 6 on CD and cassette. Number 5 features the band at a 1980 appearance in the Gibbon Ballroom with Frank Melmer, Ron Hahn, Earl Schmidt, Hillary Haag, David Retka and Jerry Schuft. However, Volume 6, entitled "Come, Spend an Evening at the Sokol Auditorium in Omaha, Nebraska" may be his best. After 17 nights en route performing continuously in Texas and neighboring states, the band executed a string of numbers for recording artist Ron Nadherny, assisted by Earl Schmidt, who announced this realistic, in-the-dance-hall, peak performance of the Jerry Schuft Band.[27] Jerry Schuft died of a heart attack on June 15, 2004. Posthumously on November 5, 2004 he was inducted into the Minnesota Music Hall of Fame.

Well-known orchestras like the Marv Nissel Band announced their reorganizations in the newspapers. Nissel was born on a farm near Walnut Grove and took up the concertina while his father and grandfather were playing with Christy Hengel's band at Wanda. In 1979 Marv Nissel was featured with a photograph of himself and his three Hengel concertinas for harmonious interaction with his players.[28] A concertina player for the Cliff Hermel Band in the 1950s when it operated from St. Peter, Marv Nissel in 1978 put together a new band with his wife Carol as the vocalist functioning also as chief bookkeeper and scheduling supervisor. In 1987 the Marv Nissel band was voted the number one variety band for the State of Minnesota by the Minnesota Ballroom Operators Association (MBOA). They also won numerous MBOA awards for their outstanding contributions to the ballroom industry for top quality dance music. In 1988 Carol Nissel was selected as one of the top five vocalists from the State of Minnesota by the Minnesota Music Academy in Minneapolis, Minnesota. Playing with his orchestra in the early 1980s were Larry Roepke, Arnold Olsen, Larry Olsen, Carol Nissel and Dale Tolk.[29] Currently the band consists of Marv on concertina, Carol on keyboard bass piano and vocals, daughter Lori on trumpet, fiddle, concertina, drums, and vocals and daughter Jodi on drums, fiddle, soprano and alto saxophones, as well as vocals. Also appearing with the band is Mike Moldan on trumpet and drums. With his feeder pig operation north of St. George, Minnesota, Nissel has been fully occupied by day as well as by night.

The youthful Frank Kinayski Band from Eau Claire, Wisconsin got its Minnesota start at the Mrozinski Brothers' Polka Super Sunday on April 9, 1978 with Mark Pieplow playing the concertina.[30] Young in 1978 was the

Larry Novotny of Montgomery playing his three favorite instruments for the St. Paul Czech festival (CSPS Hall) on Seventh Street, St. Paul Minnesota, September, 2004.

word also for the Zwack Brothers Band with Gary and Keith, both able to handle the concertina at dances booked from their home in Brooklyn Center, Minnesota.[31] Their foursome included Paul, Dave, Jim, Gary and Keith, the primary concertinist. Equal in popularity, if not exactly in age, was the Billy Bartusek Band with its Bohemian style from New Prague. They started in 1963 when Billy acquired his first concertina from his father. Breaking with tradition was his composition of two guitars, piano and drums supporting the concertina. Jack Malecha, Al Rezac, Charles Sticha and others maintained the Czech ethnicity along with their Bohemian melodies.[32] Strongly Czech, too, is the Wee Willie Band headed with expert concertina music supplied by William A. Makovsky. Born on the south side of Silver Lake, Minnesota June 11, 1940, he taught himself to play his father's concertina from the age of 10 onward. In 1961, he moved to Fergus Falls, where he played each Sunday night at a bar for $5.00 before founding his own band about 1970. Transferred to Minneapolis in 1986, Makovsky's Wee Willie Band has performed all over southern Minnesota, in neighboring and distant states, as well as in Germany. It has recorded 18 cassettes and was named Minnesota Ballroom Operators "Band of the Year" in 2000.[33] Late in 2003, the band's headquarters moved to Moorhead, Minnesota. Its recent staff includes Wally Kessler, Augie Makovsky, Bill "Wee Willie" Makovsky, and Jim Bartusek. From Lester Prairie, Minnesota come the Chuck Thiel Jolly Ramblers who also feature Czech and German music on Chuck's Wolfe concertina.

Sometimes the concertina gained preeminence through antics, such as the acrobatics readily displayed by the likes of Johnny Helget. In Traer, Iowa on July 13 and 15, 1978, with Franklin Lundak on his accordion, Helget entertained a large audience in the Traer Memorial Building. A career greenskeeper at the New Ulm Golf Course by day, Helget could sit, stand, roll, lie on his back, turn summersaults and never miss a note on the concertina by night. Often the crowds gathered not to dance but simply to watch the skilled frolics of Helget. They stared in amazement without much appreciation for the quality of the instrument but with great admiration for the showman's skill—which greatly popularized this intricate instrument. Others draw crowds readily in stunt-like dramatic performances, among them Gary Brueggen, Leon Olsen and Pulaski, Wisconsin stars like Chad Przybylski and his Polka Rythms Band.

One of the greatest players and promoters of the concertina during the 1970s and 1980s was Sylvester Liebl of Barre Mills, Wisconsin. The youngest of 12 children, he grew up in Willow Lake Township near Wanda, Minnesota. His parents, Joseph and Mary (Helget) Liebl, bought him his first concertina from the Vogel and Mueller Music Store in Springfield on February 22, 1929.[34] Born January 18, 1917, Liebl followed a line of ancestral musicians back to the Bischofteinitz region of western Bohemia.[35] One of his earliest performances occurred in 1929 on the Orange Crush float at Boxcar Days in Tracy, Minnesota. Following appearances at a dog circus, the Jackson County Fair in Windom and the school Christmas party near Wanda, Liebl played for 16 house parties in January, 1930, followed by Sauerkraut Days in Springfield where, for the first time, he got to witness Whoopee John Wilfahrt in action. Since Whoopee John was late arriving that evening, Liebl was invited to fill in with a few initial numbers, though not that evening with the full band. However, his performance at that venue led to a visit at Wilfahrt's home, where Liebl played a Silberhorn concertina for

The Wee Willie Band with leader Bill Makovsky on the Hengel's concertina. Steve Carlson, drums, Wally Kessler, guitar, Wee Willie, concertina, and Augie "Gus" Makovsky, bass horn. June 23, 2000.

Whoopee John.

With his sister already married to a man in the La Crosse area, and facing the worst of the Great Depression in southwestern Minnesota, Sylvester moved to the La Crosse area in 1934. In no time he found himself playing the concertina on local WKBH Radio. Here he met Ann Hohefeld and in 1938 married her, with whom he had nine children. Giving hundreds of appearances far and near, his endurance tests included the Yuba, Wisconsin Mardi Gras two-day dance annually for over 40 years. He was also heard on a raft of radio stations and programs until he finally retired in 1984. Thankfully his musical talents continued for local events and Sylvester Liebl Jr. took over the band, renaming it the New Jolly Swiss Boys. In the same time frame, his daughter Carol and husband Frank Seebauer founded a band called Daddy's Girls, featuring Amy Seebauer, Syl's granddaughter on concertina. Having merited the world's acknowledgements many times over, finally, on September 20, 1997, Liebl was inducted into the World Concertina Congress Hall of Fame. He had previously garnered other awards like "Best Polka Band in the Land" in 1972 and "Minnesota Music Hall of Fame" in November, 1993. By the time of his death in La Crosse on May 10, 2003 at the age of 86, he had been playing concertina for 73 years.[36]

Lesser known except in the Little Falls area of Minnesota were the Walzateers, headed by Jerry Biershbach on the concertina, supported by Bruce Austin, Don Girtz and Ervin Girtz.[37] Now and then Ernie Coopman and the Stagemen from Mankato came center stage. Ernie began playing the concertina at the age of 16 in 1949, going professional with Norm Wilke and the Little Fisherman Band from Le Sueur. In 1956 he joined Bruno Randles with the Jolly Brewers which he later took over.[38] Ernie Coopman died on December 12, 1998 and his Jolly Brewers, library was sold to Marvin "Cactus" Stoehr. Younger, but enthusiastic, was the Brad,

Ty Baden, Martin Gross, Dan Witucki, Claude Cashing and Neal Webb playing at EPCOT Center in Orlando, Florida.

Daniel M. Witucki of Winthrop, later of Orlando, Florida, playing his Hengel concertina at the Gibbon Polka Festival, July 24, 2003.

Brenda, Ricky, and Jeff Franta Band of rural Lafayette, Minnesota, both Jeff and Brad being concertinists. Their grandfather was John Fritsche, who also offered entertainment with his old time band.[39] Equally active was the Jolly Czechs Orchestra of Glencoe, Minnesota, led by Gene Streachek who had played previously with Jerry Dostal and with Babe Wagner.[40] Also of Czech heritage and from Glencoe was band leader Jerry Dostal with his orchestra, which produced many recorded albums during the 1950s and 1960s. Born August 8, 1908 in Hutchinson, Dostal started his own band in 1932, becoming known as "The King of Bohemian Music." Following service on D-Day and two bronze stars, in 1946, he reinitiated his band and in one season played every night for three consecutive months. His first recording, the "Pla-Mor Waltz," was made in 1948, and became a trademark for the band and ballroom. Other honors included recognition from the Minnesota Ballroom Operations Association for 50 years in the music and dance world in 1985, outstanding polka band, and induction to the Minnesota Music Hall of Fame in 1997. At the age of 92, Jerry Dostal of Glencoe, died April 3, 2001.[41] Then there was Art Fenske and the Jolly Coppersmiths, originally from New Ulm, but in 1980 in residence at 5913 Morgan Avenue South in Minneapolis. Some of his players included, in addition to Art Fenske on the concertina, Sue Johnson, Doug Johnson, Doug Dickover, also on concertina, as well as Chris Dickover and Rich Blomgren.[42]

A boy wonder with the concertina was the Winthrop, Minnesota farm youth, Dan Witucki, who learned the instrument from Ambrose Kodet instructing during the early 1970s for Christy Hengel in New Ulm. Because Dan's father was opposed to polka music in general, it was Dan's grandmother, Marie Kühn, who helped him acquire his first concertina. Beginning to play professionally at the age of 14, he soon organized his own Dan Witucki Band, then joined the Lester Schuft band. At a Gibbon Ballroom festival one summer he met and played subsequently for the Marv Herzog Band of Frankenmuth, Michigan. Later he again directed his own band called the Music Masters from Ohio. Following recovery from an automobile accident in Fort Wayne, Indiana, Witucki joined Disney World in Florida in 1987 where he appeared regularly at the Epcot Center.[43] He ceased employment with Disney in 2002 and continues

Performance on Mankato Television KEYC on October 20, 1980.
Front Row, L-R: Leander Dauer, Chicago; Christy Hengel, New Ulm; Wally Bauer, New Ulm; Marty Nachreiner, New Ulm at the age of eleven years standing out front; Allan Stueber, New Ulm; Johnny Gag, Mankato; Harold Loeffelmacher, who headed the Six Fat Dutchmen, New Ulm, in suit; Bill Brown Jr., New Ulm; Vince Sandhurst, Fulda; Mark Reibel, LeSueur; Paul Wendinger, New Ulm; Curt Orcherd, Madelia; Jerome Schmidt, Hanska. Second Row: Eddie Palmer, New Ulm; Allan Mohr, Mankato; Jeff Wendinger, the boy from St. George; Donnie Klossner, New Ulm; partially hidden is Tom Franta, New Ulm; Third Row: Ambrose Kodet, Mankato; Eddie Mathiowetz, Sleepy Eye; Paul Madsen, Albert Lea; Melvin Krzmarzick, Essig; Linus Kral, Sleepy Eye; Eddie Havemeiler, Nicollet; Herb Franta, Dennis Franta, Jeff Franta, Lafayette; Smiley "Whiskers" Weltscheck, New Ulm; Peter Wendinger, New Ulm and Leon Olson, New Ulm. Fourth Row: [Five players in back] Marv Nissel, New Ulm; Larry Olsen, Lake Benton; Walt Hansen, Canby; John Brown, New Ulm; Norbert Bandel, New Ulm.

playing the concertina and singing German folk songs while crafting church furniture by day.

Not as prominent but an example of another youthful concertina orchestra was the Thelemann family band from Le Sueur. Thelemann began in 1974 and continued with success at Gibbon and elsewhere, recording with the JBM Studio in New Prague.[44] Of comparable competence were the Northern Stars band, a family of five from Florenton near Virginia, Minnesota, where the parents, Ernest and Joan Aho of Finnish ancestry and playing style, were joined by their daughters Tina and Terri. Taippo, along with Teresa, played the concertina for the band.[45] The Northern Stars have performed at numerous Finnish celebrations and festivals throughout Minnesota, Wisconsin and Canada, as well as on the East Coast of the United States. They appeared on the Prairie Home Companion Radio Show, at the Finn-Fest in Duluth, and at the Grand Finnish Festival in Thunder Bay, Canada.

LaVerne Bzdok and her Starlites held prominence with concertinist Andy Stangler in Little Falls, recording and performing across the region.[46] However, Stangler died in a motorcycle accident in Colorado. From time to time he also performed with Jim Janochoski, with the Bob Brenny Band from St. Cloud, Minnesota, as well as for the Northside Dutchmen. The latter band is from New Ulm with members Tom Franta, Adeline Wiltscheck, Jerome Franta, Wally Bauer, Joyce Dauer, Eddie Palmer and Loren Schaeffler. Palmer plays a Hengel and a Pearl Queen while Schaeffler assists with a Patek.

Other concertina orchestras kept appearing steadily throughout the 1980s. A very fine example was the Larry Rysavy Concertina Band from Austin. Born in 1961, young Rysavy started at the age of five with a button accordion but switched to concertina when he turned 12 and went public with David Langer, Mark Kubat, and Dorothy Miller in 1977. His Czech heritage gave him the ability to sing original Bohemian folksongs and set them to music on his Hengel and Patek concertinas. In the mid-1980s his band consisted of Larry Rysavy, Michelle Rysavy, Dorothy Miller, Jason Dobrinz and Mark Kubat. Also fresh on the scene since 1969 was the Elmer Bartusek Band from Webster.[47] Besides Elmer on the concertina, players included Roland Snell, Gary Stepka, Dave Wondra and Mark Dvorak.

Sometimes large gatherings of concertina players appeared in concert over KEYC Television from Mankato, Minnesota, e. g. April 14, and October 20, 1980.

Performance on Mankato Television KEYC on November 7, 1983
Front Row (L-R): Arnie Milbrett, Melvin Krzmarzick, Christy Hengel, Harold Loeffelmacher in suit, Harold Tastel, Marv Nissel, Eddie Palmer, Smiley Wiltscheck, LeRoy Flor, Jerome Schmidt, Leonard Portner.
Second Row: Peter Wendinger, Paul Wendinger, Gilbert Saffert, Curt Orchard, Marty Nachreiner, Jerry Minar, Jeff Franta, Ernie Coopman, Herb Franta, Dennis Franta, Johnny Gag.

A number of those appearing in the photographs are Ambrose Kodet, Christy Hengel, Roger Kubes, Johnny Gag, Jeff Franta, Bill Brown, Jerry Schmidt, Jerry Minar, Norbert Brandel, Larry Rysavy, Gary Pikal, Tom Holm, Allan Wiltscheck, Dan Witucki, Art Fenske, Leonard Sticha, Larry Novotny, Donnie Klossner, Ernie Stumpf, and Eddie Palmer, at the April 14, 1980 sitting. On October 20 of the same year the players were mostly the same though there were a few new personages: Henry Dauer, Wally Bauer, Allan Stueber, Vince Sandhurst, Mark Reibel, Paul Wendinger, Eddie Mathiowetz, Millie Krzmarzick, Linus Kral, Leon Olsen, Norbert Bandel and others.[48]

The old time television show from Mankato, a few miles east of New Ulm, was the brain child of host Chuck Pasek on what he called the KEYC "Bandwagon Show." Begun in 1961, the Pasek spectacle changed little until his retirement in 1995 after 33 years at the microphone. In a newspaper interview on the occasion of his retirement, Pasek told of the many calls he had received from stations in Chicago and other cities wanting to duplicate the program because of its financial success. But when he explained that it was rich only in its concertina-played old time music, they would hang up. No doubt their behavior is indicative of the phenomenon that the music and its cherished instrument needed the right formula of a fine instrument played by top quality musicians in a territory housing the people who have always appreciated it—rural southern Minnesota, northern Iowa and western Wisconsin.[49] The television station beamed to the audiences for whom the area bands routinely played. Today the weekly broadcast continues

Leon Olsen of New Ulm and Klossner, Minnesota performs at the Gibbon Ballroom Polka Fest on July 22, 2004, using a Hengel concertina.

Johnny Gag of Mankato was born on a farm south of New Ulm in German-Bohemian territory and learned the concertina from his neighbor, Wenzel Fischer, a fine concertinist and instrument dealer. Johnny is pictured at left with an Echo and above with a double reed Pearl Queen concertina.

Gordon J. Prochaska of Montgomery, Ambrose Kodet of North Mankato and Alvin Chlan of New Prague, Minnesota, each playing a Hengel concertina.

On the left is Dwight Stang of Paynesville; in the foreground Carmen Lochner of Gibbon, at right is Harry Wojahn. Taken at the Cedar Mills, Minnesota Ballroom.

with announcer Dick Ginn [assisted from time to time by Tom Goetzinger of New Prague]. Working behind the scenes at the station since 1974, Ginn joined Pasek on the air in 1990, then took over in 1995. He also plays banjo for the Bruce Bradley accordion band.

Operating out of New Ulm is the Leon Olsen Band, Norwegian in name only. With a strongly German Dutchmen style of music, this Olsen band has always rendered numbers in the German tradition, though they are also proficient with modern and 1950s pieces. Although he started his own band first in 1971, Olsen had been playing his Hengel concertina since he was 11, when he began his career at the Checkerboard Café in Lake Benton earning $5.00 for the evening. As a high school student Olsen played trumpet, but as an adult he has taught concertina and guitar. After marriage his wife, Ann, convinced him to move to New Ulm where by day he restores and repairs tractors at Klossner. The leader of his own band, Olsen once performed as many as 40 sessions per month, including matinees.[50] Playing concertina with support from Gus Gottschalk on drums, Leon Olsen was joined by Paul Spencer on keyboard and doing vocals, both of whom have been with Olsen since 1971. In 2004 his band was honored by the Minnesota Ballroom Operators Association as "Band of the Year." At this time his band includes Gottschalk as well as Paul and Loretta Gerasch. Like Johnny Helget, Olsen used to play concertina while enacting various stunts though today he, like Gary Brueggen, is content with playing the concertina over his head.

Not to be confused with Leon Olsen is the Larry Olsen Band from Lake Benton, Minnesota. The Olsen brothers' sister, Carol Olsen, married Marv Nissel, thus linking them to the talented Marv Nissel concertina Band of New Ulm. Larry Olsen first created a band with his father, Arnold, on drums, sister Lisa on piano and himself playing a Hengel concertina. On his farm a half mile south of Lake Benton, Larry Olsen for years has offered a Music Fest every Memorial Day. He has played for many local festivities and appeared regularly at the Gibbon Ballroom in July.

Of more recent founding is the band called Adam and the Jolly Jammers from the city of Fairmont, south of New Ulm. Family-based in its composition are Adam Sandhurst playing the concertina with Brent, Randy and Ron Sandhurst, coupled with Myron Muehlbauer. As a three-year-old child, Adam admired his great uncle Vince, whom he mimicked with his little cardboard concertina. [Vince Sandhurst lived in New Ulm and created much of the engraving for the Brown concertinas being built in that city.] Playing with Vince since he was 10, but on the trumpet and not the concertina, Adam Sandhurst formed his own band in the year 2000 and has continued to play the concertina. Adam is distantly related to Delmar "Boots" Muehlbauer, Donnie Klossner, Maggie Ross, Peter and Paul Wendinger, all concertinists whose music he has always admired.[51]

Eastward of New Ulm at Mankato is the home of John E. Gag, the very alert and able concertinist who is a carpenter by trade, a German-Bohemian by birth, an old time musician by tradition, and a first rate concertinst. Born April 7, 1939 and growing up south of New Ulm, Gag was inspired by Wenzel Fischer whose artistry he could hear as the clear tones of a concertina wafted from Fischer's collection of them over to the Gag farmstead adjacent to Fischer's. Another spur to Gag's development of his own concertina skills was his uncle, Norbert Gag, who at times played concertina with Fezz Fritsche and at other times with the Six Fat Dutchmen. A dealer for concertinas, Norbert also enjoyed playing the concertina with his brother, John Gag, the father of the John E. Gag featured here. By age 12, John E. Gag had purchased his first concertina, a 76-key instrument, for $25. By the age of 17, before he could sample the beer himself, he was playing regularly for appreciative beer drinkers in the local taverns of New Ulm. Soon he graduated to regular dances with Norman Wilke's Little Fishermen Band of Le Sueur, followed by action with the Six Fat Dutchmen and the Katzenjammers. Older now, John Gag plays only for small affairs, usually solo or with minor combo units.

In the Bohemian tradition within the New Prague vicinity was the Little Fishermen band of LeSueur, headed from 1950-1968 by Norm Wilke. Susequently the band was piloted by Gordon Prochaska of Montgomery with Don Tupy, Don Kaisersatt, Harvey Dorn, Marvin Moravec with his Patek Deluxe concertina, Irvin Trcka, Joseph Klonne, and Bill Klabes. More recently the band acquired the expertise of local high school music teachers such as Leon Haefner, Mary Williams and John Henle with Ambrose Kodet replacing Moravec on the concertina.[52] Prochaska revitalized the band in 1997. It acquired some new blood with Frank Melmer, Neil Bohnack and Michael Budin, to create a band which continues its strong presence on the old time music scene. During a parallel time in the 1980s the Ivan Kahle Band was captured on recordings by JBM Sound, featuring powerful concertina players ever since 1946, among them, Wilmer Falk, Jerry Schuft, Lowell Schubert, Roger Kubes, Linda Schroeder, Ambrose Kodet and Jerry Minar.

During the 1980s, a top competitor on the concertina and producer of many recordings done at JBM Sound in New Prague was the Erwin Suess Hoolerie Dutchmen. Joined by band members from their own family, Erwin and Monica conducted tours to Germany and Italy and appeared frequently on Mankato KEYC Channel 12 Television.[53] Born August 2, 1927, Erwin Suess, for his Hoolerie Dutchmen, began playing the concertina in 1942 when he was 15 and in 1947, at the age of 20 commenced his long career performing for various local dance bands. His first assignment was with the Sellner Brothers Band in Sleepy Eye, then Frankie Breu's Little German Band. With his wife Monica (Spaeth of Morgan), and his sons, David and Duane, he started the Hoolerie Dutchmen Band in 1969. By this time, the Suess family band has ranged across the Midwest for nearly three quarters of a century. Son, David, before his early death, played concertina alongside his father and also ran his own dance band. In the early years, the Suess family owned and operated an 800-acre farm near Hanska, then Erwin hauled feed and kept books for Farmland Industries in Mankato before he retired to Eagle Lake near Mankato.[54] In August, 2003 Erwin Suess was inducted into the World Concertina Congress Hall of Fame.

The George Servatius Concertina Party—held every year at the V.F.W. Club in Melrose, Minnesota, this one on April 18, 2004. Here Richard Stang of St. Augusta plays concertina while Tom Gagnon of Glencoe drums. Gagnon is a multi-talented musician who plays concertina, button accordion and a variety of other instruments. Servatius is a dealer for concertinas and a multitude of musical paraphernalia and memorabilia.

Entertainment and the Concertina

Dolores and Cletus Goblirsch with their band members Jim Bartusek, Gary Schroeder, John Henle and Leon Haefner.

Roman Rezac, born August 9, 1917 in rural Webster, Minnesota, first bought a 76-key Pearl Queen in 1928 to perform with a seven-piece Smisek band. In 1933 he bought a Pearl Queen quad from Wenzel Fischer in New Ulm, creating his own band in 1937. Following World War II his band played for nearly a decade on KYSM Radio in Mankato and KDHL in Faribault. His band ceased performing in 1976. Photo taken August, 2004 at New Prague.

Karl Hartwich and Mollie Busta at Gibbon Ballroom, July 24, 2003.

From Cold Spring came to us the TNT Band, led by Todd and Terry Thielen, assisted by Grace Theisen and John Buerman, with young Terry Thielen playing the concertina.[55] Meanwhile, Ivan Plaggemeyer of Burnsville put together his Jolly Dutchmen with Roman Rezac on concertina and Glenn Wondra on either guitar or concertina, plus Ed Hruby, both from Montgomery. On his own later, Wondra started the band called Country Gentlemen for which Glenn has consistently performed as a fine concertinist and primary bearer of the melody. Roman Rezac with his concertina had been playing in his own band since 1937, at times averaging 26 nights per month, including ten years on a radio program and seven on television.[56] From Rochester in recent times comes the concertina band of young concertina player, Cory Miller. In Pierz the Polka Beats thrive under the leadership of concertinist, Dale Dahmen while Dwight Stang of Paynesville and Richard Stang of Augusta play equally competent Dutchman style concertinas. Dwight has also enjoyed the services of a female concertinist, Carmen Lochner of Gibbon.

Rudy Witthus of Arlington, Minnesota on April 13, 2004 at the New Prague Ballroom plays an Echo concertina built by Stan Uhlir. Born in 1914, Witthus played his first job at Hamburg, Minnesota using a Lange then progressed to a Black Beauty acquired from Silberhorn in Chicago, and later acquired a Patek, which was revamped for him by Stan Uhlir.

Over decades of time from northern Minnesota young players of the concertina appeared anew on the stages of dance halls. Joel Wahna, Ernie Mazurek and Joe Glowacki appeared as members of the White Eagle Concertina Band. Sometimes they performed under the name Northeast Five and then again as the Polka Playboys, although Glowacki more frequently played accordion.[57] From the south came the Vince Sandhurst Concertina Band from Fulda [succeeded by nephew Adam] with appearances at the Gibbon festival and on dance hall stages.[58] In the "Polish Brass" tradition was Ray Biernat on concertina, who backed up bandleader Roger Stigney together with Lloyd Huepenbecker, the drummer, and Dick Powell on brass joined by Bob Sierakowski on the guitar.[59] From Sauk Centre, Minnesota came Merle Felling and his Concertina Band, supported by Louie Schley on drums and Reuben Nathe on tuba and bass guitar. Bob Saulsbury and Dan Rassier also played with him.[60] Using Brown concertinas was Gary Zimanski with his Zimanski Brothers Polka Show Band from Courtland, Minnesota. Gary Zimanski benefited from Lynn on drums and John on bass when playing at weddings, anniversaries and regular public dances.[61] When Joe Czerniak of Duluth was inducted into the World Congress Hall of Fame, *Entertainment Bits* offered many photographs accompanied by a text concerning his successful output, covering 25 years prior to 1980.[62]

When the now-famous Karl Hartwich began playing his concertina for his Country Dutchmen, he lived at home in Orion, Illinois. Having embarked on the dance circuit with his concertina at age 12, Hartwich made trips to La Crosse to visit relatives where he became imbued with the concertina mastery of Sylvester Liebl and the Jolly Swiss Boys. To make his band sound complete in northwestern Illinois, Hartwich added Amy Sampson of Orion on trumpet and bass. Bernie Williams of Mount Joy, Iowa came aboard on trombone, Holly Hartwich handled the drums, Joyce Hartwich played piano with Norma Hartwich on tuba and vocals, and Gregg Serittsmeier of East Moline on bass. Mike Cielecki of Durant, Iowa played trumpet, fluegal horn, and did vocals while Tom Paulsen played trumpet. This band's first performance was for the Labor Day fall festival in Orion, Illinois. From there the band expanded all across the Midwest with regular appearances in all venues.[63] Karl has owned six concertinas since he first started playing. The concertina he currently uses is a Hengel produced in New Prague, known as the "Rosewood Hengel," which Karl has had for approximately three years. The instrument he plays today has a new look with all the old parts transferred from his 18-year-old Hengel. He has played in at least 30 states, the Caribbean, Europe, Mexico, and in 1998 the band was chosen to represent the State of Wisconsin at the Smithsonian Folklife Festival in Washington D.C. Karl with his band was also filmed for two television specials (River of Song and Wisconsin Folks) in 1997 and 1998. He has also played for Garrison Keillor.

Sometimes *Entertainment Bits* [alternatively, *Music and Dance News*] characterized a longtime favorite like Elmer Scheid, who in 1982, was featured for over 30 years playing the concertina. Having started with the Six Fat Dutchmen in 1936, Scheid was always especially proud of his Patek Deluxe concertina, purchased as his 16th birthday present when he was growing up in New Ulm.[64] Some consider this Chemnitzer concertina built by the Schlicht company in Chicago to be the finest one ever manufactured. Off stage, Elmer Scheid worked for a time at Minnesota Mining and Manufacturing in New Ulm, managed a New Ulm bar for Harold Loeffelmacher in New Ulm, and with Billie Tupy, another bar in New Prague. Scheid played for Babe Wagner, among others, before starting his own band. At the end of his career he sold his Patek Deluxe to Christy Hengel for $15,000 — it being considered still the finest model ever crafted.[65]

Famous today in the New Ulm region as well is the Cletus Goblirsch Band at home on Oakwood Heights adjacent to New Ulm. Sometimes Goblirsch performs on his own but more often appears with his five or six-piece support group. At other times specialty bands were starred in *Entertainment Bits*, such as Blanche Zellmer and the Waltz Kings, with top billing to Blanche in Montgomery, Minnesota. She was often supported by players such as Bill Busacker, Dale Korbel, Larry Novotny, Don Tupy and Ambrose Kodet on the concertina.[66] A similar Bohemian style is in evidence by the New Prague Czech Singers, who are accompanied by various concertina players, Ben Novotny in particular. Their record of 1982, produced by JBM Sound Production headed by Jerry Minar, depicts numerous Patek concertina models on the disk jacket.[67]

When a concertina party was held at New Prague's Park Ballroom February 27, 1983, retailers of the day were pictured, Jerry Minar and Bill Brown, for example, along with tables and tables of concertinas of old. Also pictured playing for the event were Ernie Coopman, Ernie Stumpf and others.[68] Also special was the Chesney Brothers Band[69] which used genuine Polish styles at northeast Minneapolis dance pavilions beginning in the 1940s with recordings for RCA and continuing from its University Avenue address in Minneapolis.[70] Also active in northeast Minneapolis in the mid 1980s was Dave Sowada and his Sheratons Band, consisting of Ed Jurek, Dave Sowada on concertina [at 509—84th Avenue N. E.], John Granda, Jim Schaefer, Art Schaefer, and Chet Gapinski.[71] Playing a Hengel and a Gem Deluxe, Dave Sowada used a threesome, consisting of Ed Jurek on guitar and John Granda on drums to make records, among them "A Concertina Mini-Album."[72] Off and on in the Twin Cities and on the Iron Range, both as a player of the Star concertina and as a disk jockey at varying radio stations, was Craig Ebel, a capable man on drums and varying instruments as well as on the concertina, Dutchman-style.[73] In 2003 Craig Ebel formed his own band called "Craig Ebel & DyVersa Co."[74] Craig Ebel continues prominently as host of "It's Polka Time!," a polka music radio program produced from the Twin Cities of Minneapolis and St. Paul, Minnesota, which is heard over 14 radio stations across the Midwest.

Perhaps the designation of finest concertina player in the Northeast Minneapolis Polish community would go to Raymond Arent, who was born May 22, 1915, one of five children. His father a blacksmith and welder, Ray

Raymond Rannow of Eden Prairie, Minnesota plays his Hengel concertina at the Glencoe Library-Community Center in June, 2004.

himself worked in the railroad heating business—even as one of his most admired mentors—Eddie Lash of Chicago—was also a boiler engineer. Already at Schiller grade school in Minneapolis, Arent mastered the violin and the concertina. He entertained often at school assemblies, in local taverns and while still in high school taught concertina technique to a constant pool of some 15 pupils. With his brothers he entertained initially at local northeast Minneapolis weddings for which he had bought a used 76-key Clarion concertina from Henry Silberhorn. Later he also acquired concertinas from Patek and the one that remains his favorite, a "Black Beauty" from Henry Silberhorn. An admirer of Eddie Chesney and other Polish style players, Arent resided at 2613 Armour Terrace, St. Anthony, Minnesota. Born May 22, 1915, Arent died on December 7, 2004. Another competent elderly Minnesota concertinist is Rudy Wittus of Glencoe who left the Minnesota scene and worked for 38 years in the Denver area managing a coop elevator. In his younger days he played concertina for the Garnett Schlottman Band and for Blue Gordon (Schlottman). Admirable, too, is the performance of Raymond Rannow

Mollie Busta is playing the keyboard as Marty Nachreiner, now of Sauk City, Wisconsin, but originally from New Ulm, plays a Hengel concertina at the Spillville, Iowa old time music celebration, July 19, 2003

Brian Brueggen of Brian's Mississippi Valley Dutchmen from Cashton, Wisconsin and Gary Brueggen of the Ridgeland Dutchmen Band - here playing keyboard for his cousin. Both are relatives of Sylvester Liebl, Sr. who lived at Barre Mills near La Crosse, Wisconsin, July 19, 2003.

Raymond Arent, distinguished concertina player and friend of Bob Novak of Lake Elmo, Minnesota, builder of the Echo. Here playing at the Concertina Superbowl on Saturday, January 31, 2004. Ray Arent died on December 7, 2004.

Marty Nachreiner (originally of New Ulm, now of Sauk City, Wisconsin) at Spillville Iowa, July 19, 2003, playing a concertina duet with Brian Brueggen — Brian's Mississippi Valley Dutchmen.

of Eden Prairie.

More in the German style also was the Bob Brenny Band of Albany, Minnesota with Bob [along with Andy Stangler] playing the concertina, Louie Dinndorf on saxophone, Bob Nathe on bass horn and Bob's sister, Mary Struzyk, on drums and banjo.[75] German as well were the Red Birds, led by George and Edna Schunk of rural Litchfield, who appeared frequently in parades with the concertina, drums and dancers.[76] Of comparable authentic German style was Lenny's Concertina Band from New Ulm, led by Linus "Lenny" Nachreiner playing drums and his son, Marty Nachreiner, on concertina, saxophone and a variety of other instruments. Early in its career, the band was supported by Jerry Olund, Dixie Frank, Amy Sampson, Keith Rees and, at times, Donnie Klossner, who spent 14 years with the Babe Wagner Band, and holds the Babe Wagner Band musical collection. They explicitly tried to be a band patterned on the Babe Wagner sound.[77]

Multi-talented Donald K. Klossner has been in and out of bands his entire adult life. He joined the Mel Storm Variety Band and played with the likes of Babe Wagner, the Six Fat Dutchmen, Jolly Brewers, Ray Dorschner, Elmer Scheid and others before creating his own electronic source for a full band sound produced by a computer, which he accompanies on the concertina. The owner of several concertinas and the musical library of the famed Babe Wagner band, he is pleased to perform on his two Midi concertinas, an A-Flat and a key of C. His "One Man Band," billed sometimes as "Musik mit Herz," operates from 63194 Fort Road, New Ulm, Minnesota. Likewise German in style with a large overlay of the Bohemian mixture typical of Minnesota bands is the Marc Frana Band of 301 South Iowa Street, Charles City, Iowa. Marc uses a Hengel concertina supported by Tim Howland on drums, Merlin Bartz on rotary valve bass horn and Nic Dunkel on trombone and trumpet. In addition to his Hengel, Frana uses a Gem Deluxe and a Patek concertina to achieve special tone quality.[78]

In neighboring Wisconsin was the Ray Konkol Band of 2311 Strange Street in the village of Whiting near Stevens Point, Wisconsin. Born in 1931, Konkol has been playing the concertina since the age of 12, first for the Melody Aces before joining the navy from 1951-1955. Returning in 1956, he formed the Jolly Doughboys, then

A great concertina player and admirerer of the Babe Wagner band is LeRoy Flor from New Ulm. Flor was born in the German-Bohemian Sigel township south of New Ulm not far from the John Wilfahrt family farm. Playing the concertina for him is as natural as speaking his local German dialect.

Donnie Klossner, famed for his role with the Babe Wagner Band, the Six Fat Dutchmen and many other fine bands, and for his role repairing the concertina for the Brown Music Store in New Ulm, here poses at the Czech Area Concertina Club in New Prague on September 14, 2004 with one of the relatively few concertinas built by Bill Brown.

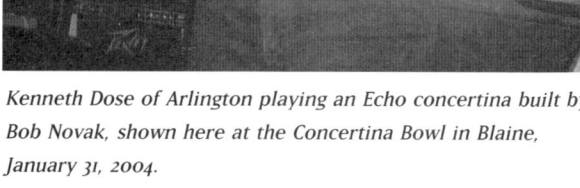

Kenneth Dose of Arlington playing an Echo concertina built by Bob Novak, shown here at the Concertina Bowl in Blaine, January 31, 2004.

Gilbert "Gilly" Maus of Pierz, Minnesota, born 1947. The self-taught Maus owns a 1972 Hengel, a Stradivarius and a 1936 Patek. He has played for Gene Retka on WYRQ Radio in Little Falls, Minnesota and is featured here at the January 31, 2004 Concertina Bowl in Blaine.

Annually since 1979 Art Ohotto, LeRoy Lewandowski, Chester Gapinski and Don Andersen, have staged a concertina party. At first it was to raise funds for the local Knights of Columbus organization in Coon Rapids, Minnesota. Too large for the original meeting hall, the Bowl moved in subsequent years to Fridley, then shifted to Brook Hall in the Blainebrook Entertainment Center in Blaine, Minnesota. Here it continues with about 800 concertinists and guests attending each year.

Ray Konkol exhibits his two Hengel concertinas at his home in Stevens Point, Wisconsin.

the Ray Konkol Band. From 1967 until 1985 he served the Rainbow Valley Dutchmen under Ray Dorschner but in 1986 reinitiated his own Ray Konkol Band. Although he liked his 1926 Patek triple, Konkol on a Hengel concertina was supported in the 1980s and 1990s by Kim Ristow, Lou Allen, Germaine Konkol, Linda Schroeder, and Ted Neveln creating a bright and lively musical style.[79] At Waupaca, near Stevens Point, was the Justmann Band, formerly the Andy Justmann Orchestra that began in 1947, known initially as Andy's Polka Boys. Now headed by Charlie Justmann of 230 Grand Seasons Drive in Waupaca, the band entertains all across Wisconsin, supported by fine musicians like Dan Marbes, Bill Sargent, Don Chesebro, and others. Recently, Charlie's father, Andrae Justmann, the owner of two Hengel concertinas, was inducted into the World Concertina Congress Hall of Fame.[80]

From Wisconsin, too, was Ray Dorschner, who founded the Rainbow Valley Dutchmen in 1950. Although he performed on saxophone, clarinet, and trumpet, his brother, Larry Dorschner, played the concertina while brother Theodore fingered the piano. Patterned after the New Ulm bands like Babe Wagner and Elmer Scheid, the Rainbow Valley Dutchmen Band was phased forward after Ray Konkol for a time took the place of Larry Dorschner on the concertina. When Ray Konkol returned to running his own band in 1985, the concertina slot for Dorschner was filled by Keith Zwack, a highly accomplished, technically skilled concertina player. At times, too, Randy Dorschner of Dorschner Music Service covered Ray Konkol's absence, as did Marty Nachreiner and Gary Brueggen until Brueggen organized his own band. The Dorschner father and son team live in Menasha and Appleton, where Randy Dorschner operates the Dorschner Music Service at 1721 West Wisconsin Avenue in Appleton.[81]

From Pulaski, Wisconsin for a 50-year-period stretching from 1945-1995 was concertinist Dick Rodgers. Born March 1, 1927 in Maple Grove township to Joseph Rodziczak and Stella (Gierczak), Rodgers led his own orchestra in dance halls, on local and syndicated television for 23 years, and fulfilling a ten-year contract with DECCA Records. A member of the Wisconsin Polka Hall of Fame and president for a time of the National Association of Orchestra Leaders, he was inducted into the World Concertina Congress Hall of Fame in 1996, even though his active career playing the instrument ended after suffering a stroke in 1995. From 1955 to 1978 his "Dick Rodgers TV Recording Orchestra" performed throughout the Midwest and on WMBV television in Marinette and subsequently on WLUK in Green Bay, Wisconsin. Before his retirement from the office in 1988, he had spent much of his career working at the Rodgers Insurance Agency founded by his father. At the age of 76, Dick Rodgers died January 22, 2004.

Also highly admired in Wisconsin and the upper Midwest is the Ridgeland Dutchmen Band fronted by Gary Brueggen of Ontario, Wisconsin. This is German-Bohemian country, within a circumference of Czech settlements like Hollsboro [called the Czech capital of Wisconsin], Yuba, and Mount Tabor. Initially the band consisted of Gary's grandfather, Herman Brueggen [now deceased] and Roger Brueggen, drummers. They were assisted by Shorty Brueggen with violin, Harry Brueggen with the guitar, cousin Steve Brueggen with banjo, Phillip Brueggen with trumpet, Willard Brueggen tuba and with both cousin Judy Brueggen Biever and Keith Larson playing the concertina. However, it has been Willard and Gary as father and son, who have shared the stage since 1982. Today the band consists of Gary playing several brands of concertina, Willard on the tuba, and Dennis Nadherny on drums. Nadherny originates from Omaha, where his father, Ronald Nadherny, operates his own band. Adding her vocals, piano rhythm

Edwartd T. Mathiowetz, Sleepy Eye, Minnesota

Darlene and John Lange of Clintonville, Wisconsin own Echo concertinas built by Bob Novak, playing here at the Gibbon festival on July 24, 2003.

Darwin J. Black, Fairfax, MN

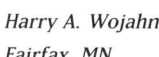

Harry A. Wojahn, Fairfax, MN

Eldred Doell, Greenville, WI. A carpenter by trade, Doell built the home for Rudy and Esther Patek when he moved to Weyauwega from Chicago in 1962. Here Doell holds a Patek B-Flat concertina.

Christy Hengel and Adrian Filipiak, Brooklyn Center, MN

Ed-Vern Black, Fairfax, MN

Gary Brueggen, of Ontario Wisconsin, playing his Wolfe concertina over his head at the Gibbon Ballroom, July 24, 2003.

Eric Malek of Malek's Fishermen Band from Duncan, Iowa, playing his Hengel concertina at Spillville, Iowa on July 17, 2004. Duncan is the Czech community a bit west of Garner, Iowa.

Jim Busta of Spring Grove, Minnesota taken October 12, 2004 at the Czech Area Concertina Club meeting. Born at Little Turkey near Spillville, Iowa, he has been the Superintendent of Schools at Spring Grove, since 1985.

and saxophone playing is Laurie Solberg. Playing banjo and singing is Robbin Becker. This band has won the Horizon Award from the Wisconsin Polka Hall of Fame. Part-time members of the band include Denny Anderson, Craig Ebel, Mike McIntyre, Chris Langen, Tom Schneider, Brian Barnetzke, Gary Hendrickson, Tanya Tauges, and Danny Jerabek, Jr.[82]

Another especially Czech-flavored family group is the Jim Busta Band of Spring Grove, Minnesota. In operation over 20 years, the band is under the guidance of concertinist Busta who serves by day as school superintendent in Spring Grove, Minnesota. Busta comes out of Bohemian upbringing at Little Turkey near Spillville, Iowa, where he with others organize an annual dance festival. With his Hengel concertina supported especially by his multi-talented daughter, Mollie, Busta has further support from Chad Busta, his son, of La Crosse, Wisconsin on drums. Jeff "Sparky" Biermann from rural Cascade Iowa plays the tuba and electric bass. Highly gifted Steve Kenny [of Irish background] from Anamosa, Iowa plays trumpet and trombone and also sings vocals with Mollie. Mollie plays several instruments at once, especially trumpet, saxophone, trombone, clarinet and keyboard (often two at a time) and handles a button box accordion with enthusiasm. Because of Mollie's admirable dexterity, Jim Busta's daughter in many respects "makes" the Busta band. When available, Mollie often plays for the Karl Hartwich Country

Dutchmen Band from Trempealeau, Wisconsin. She also teaches music at St. Mary's College in Winona, Minnesota. The Busta band is heavily booked throughout the Midwest.[83]

Also strong with its German-Bohemian style is Edward's Fishermen Band, now a third generation orchestra, from Garner, Iowa. This band started in 1932 under the initiative of Sylvester Malek in Duncan, Iowa, a hard core Bohemian settlement west of Garner, with Sylvester and brother Edward playing for house and barn dances. In 1934, they expanded to a four and eventually a six-piece Malek Accordion Band, averaging 200 jobs a year. After a time, Edward branched off to join Marvin Lackore in performing modern music. Sylvester continued his old time band until the 1960s when the elder Malek got tired of sometimes driving all hours of darkness 100 nights a year, arriving home just in time to milk his large herd of cows. But the band was resurrected under his son, Robert Malek, who in 1967 and in 1969 expanded its team of players. Since then it has played frequently as the six-piece Malek Fishermen Band. Starting in the 1990s, the children of Robert, Eric, and Crystal have joined in, making today's lineup the family, plus Ron Hrubes on keyboard and saxophone with Don Vandiepen on bass horn and vocals with [sometimes] Craig Ebel on drums.[84] Eric Malek remains the band's highly competent concertina player.

Similar in-the-family events have fostered the concertina as a valued, domestic, household instrument. In 1987, after Kevin J. Liss of Stevens Point, Wisconsin had bought a concertina from Sylvester Liebl of West Salem, Kevin married Lorie R. Liebl, the daughter of Sylvester Jr. and granddaughter of Sylvester Sr. Sylvester Jr. thus started the New Jolly Swiss Boys Concertina Orchestra to contrast with the original Jolly Swiss Boys organized and managed under the elder Sylvester.[85] We recall that Sylvester Liebl in the course of World War II was induced to shift the "German" out of his title and replace it with "Swiss." In a similar vein is the owner of Brueggen Oil Co. of Cashton, Wisconsin and band leader of the Mississippi Valley Dutchmen, Brian Brueggen, married Jodi Nissel, the daughter of concertinist Marv

Left to Right: Adolph A. Kodet [the father of Ambrose Kodet of North Mankato, Minnesota]; Alois E. Kodet, a drummer for the band and the brother of Adolph; Frank Senkyr, a brother-in-law, sibling of the wife of Adolph. They are playing a triple reed Pearl Queen or double Lange concertina. Adolph Kodet began playing concertina in 1915. Taken at a studio in Olivia, Minnesota, in 1917.

Nissel, in November, 2001 in New Ulm. For over 100 years, some 17 bands, including Polka Mass groups have consisted entirely of descendants of William Brueggen, Brian's great-great-grandfather. William came to the United States from Germany in 1857, was a drummer in the Civil War and farmed near Cashton, Wisconsin. Brian's first job was played at age 5 on a toy accordion where he earned 50 cents, and finished the job by falling asleep behind the stage. At age 9 he started playing concertina. For a number of years he played trumpet in his father's band. After a short experience playing with Danny Witucki and the Music Masters, Brian came back home to the Mississippi Valley and formed The Mississippi Valley Dutchmen which he leads with vast talent on his various Patek and Hengel concertinas.

Another Nissel daughter, Lori, in 1997 married Craig Ebel of the Twin Cities, who is a multiple musician capable of concertina, horns and drums, which allow him to go to bat for a host of dance bands. The balance of his time is taken by his syndicated radio shows.[86] Illustrating further this intra-family theme is the fact that Marv Nissel's wife is Leon and Larry Olsen's sister. Equally family-styled was the Bohemian Brothers Concertina Band of Owatonna, consisting of Ray and Marshall Miller on Hengel concertinas. They popularly sing the Czech vocals, supported at times by the elder Ray Valek on drums, who also sings. Tom Wencl and Marshall's wife, Dorothy, also play, Dorothy being the sister of Larry Rysavy.[87] Likewise family-related are such bands as Eddie Blazonczyk and the Versatones of Chicago, winner of the 1986 Grammy award plus a swarm of others. The Blazonczyk band has played more than 40 years with Eddie Blazonczyk, Sr. continuously from 1963 to 1997, when Eddie Blazonczyk, Jr. took over the operation.[88] Their highly energetic Polish style band travels widely to Florida, Arizona, and the Midwest, sometimes on cruise ships in the Caribbean, and regularly on Chicago radio.

Besides the major influence exercised by the ballroom operators in promoting use of the concertina, related venues have brought the concertina to the attention of audiences. A good example was, and remains, the so-called Concertina Bowl, which took its name from being scheduled close to football's Super Bowl in late January. The idea of a concertina bowl is due to the effort of Art Ohotto in Minnesota's Twin Cities. With LeRoy Lewandowski, Chester Gapinski and Don Andersen, Ohotto staged a concertina party in 1979 to raise funds for the local Knights of Columbus organization in Coon Rapids, Minnesota. Too large for the original meeting hall, the Bowl moved in subsequent years to Fridley, where it met annually for ten years. It then shifted to Brook Hall in the Blainebrook Entertainment Center on Central Avenue in Blaine, Minnesota. Here it continues past its 25th anniversary, with about 800 concertinists and guests attending each year. For his promotion of the instrument in this way, as well as for his skill as a concertina player, Ohotto was inducted into the World Concertina Congress Hall of Fame in 2001.[89]

Born in 1940 in Little Falls, Minnesota, Ohotto grew up on a farm near Elmdale and Bowlus north of St. Cloud, one of five children. He attended high school in Upsala, where he graduated in 1958, marrying his wife, Jeanette, from the same area in 1963. Ohotto's primary career was in the ceramic tile trade followed by real estate once he got his license in 1975. His first contact with the concertina came as a boy when a hired man was saving money to buy one and then spellbound the boy when he got it. However, Art Ohotto's father did not hear the tones as sweetly, with the result that Ohotto turned 23 before he could start to play the instrument. He launched his playing with a triple reed concertina from the Glass brothers and since has owned brands like Patek, Star, Lange, Pearl Queen, a Sitek [built by Star] and both a Hengel E-Flat and another in the key of C. With his band called "Concertina Power," supported by trumpet, clarinet and drums, concertinist Ohotto is well known on the Twin Cities entertainment circuit.

Success of the Concertina Bowl, now a registered

Art Ohotto, of northeast Minneapolis Polish descent, now lives in Fridley, Minnesota, here playing a Hengel key of C concertina.

Jerome Then of St. Cloud, Minnesota exhibits his four concertinas in his home on County Road 134. L-R: White Hengel C, Serial Number 116J71; Black Hengel B-Flat # 30A43, 1994; White Hengel E-Flat # 207A59; White Hengel B-Flat 227J61

trademark, was not automatic. During its first decade, achievement derived in part from the displays by Slim Maser, from his retail agency for the Star concertina in West St. Paul, an expert concertina player, builder and repairman, who in 1996 was inducted as a member into the Concertina Hall of Fame. In the next time frame, Joe and Bill Czerniak performed along with John Filipczak and the Classics, followed by Karl Hartwich and his Country Dutchmen, Craig Ebel and the Light Weights, as well as other fine orchestras. In essence, the Bowl is a 12-hour event, beginning at noon and lasting until midnight on the Saturday before the January Super Bowl. Showcasing the concertina at the Bowl is a concertina players' jamboree. As at Gibbon and concertina club sites in the upper Midwest, individuals or duos may sign up to perform from a platform equipped with a tuba player, saxophone and trumpet for accompaniment. Players arrive from eight states and Canada, all adding their enthusiasm for the entertainment available from the concertina.

Entertainment has also been the goal of traveling concertina players. Early in the 20th century there were the Peters Brothers who barnstormed the country. Max (1895-1983) and Helmut (1898-1994) were two of eight children born to Paul and Anna Hager Peters in Leipzig, a large city near Chemnitz. With their family, they came to the United States in 1912, where they settled in Henryetta, Kansas. Soon they headed north to concertina country, the upper Midwest—Illinois, Wisconsin, Michigan and Minnesota. Using primarily their Arnold concertinas and even more, Arnold bandonions, they either imported or brought them back on their many trips to and from Germany.[90]

Important, too, when considering the concertina's capacity for entertainment at home were the recordings, first on 78 rpm discs, then 45 rpm, followed by 33 rpm, then audio cassettes and now compact discs. Already in the 1920s, prominent concertinists like John Wilfahrt were able to break into the record scene on such labels as Okeh, Vocalian, and a bit later, Victor and Columbia.[91] During his prime recording years, Wilfahrt switched to DECCA recording from and for WCCO Radio, then advancing to WTCN television, which drew profits from his ability to attract advertisers while he entertained large audiences on the concertina.

Many other concertina players not only have no recordings but they also refuse to play in public. Such, for example, are John and Darlene Lange of Clintonville, Wisconsin. Born in Milwaukee, John Lange moved to the family farm with his parents at the age of five and attended Shawano schools. Darlene was born on a farm 12 miles distant and attended Clintonville school.

Having met at an old time dance, they married and ran the family farm for 33 years (with his father until 1976) and then as owner operator alone as Darlene worked at Metso in Clintonville for 36 years. John began playing the concertina when taking lessons from Casey Pszanka in Pulaski, Wisconsin and Darlene looked on but practiced diligently with John. In April, 2001 they purchased a new Echo concertina from Robert Novak in Lake Elmo, Minnesota and another one in the key of C in March, 2003, both with long plate reeds. In love with the instrument, they have since bought an E-Flat and have ordered a fourth. Members of the Northeast Wisconsin Concertina, Accordion and Button Box Club, they play well together and in sessions but rarely for public gatherings.

Hundreds of other concertina players fall into this category of the "individual" or private player, some of whom play for small events and home entertainment. Many play Hengel concertinas. Well known among them are such artists as David Czaja of Shakopee; Patrick Boulay of Minneapolis; Eugene DeMenge of Hutchinson; Marvin E. Bulau of Arlington; Edward I. Mathiowetz of Sleepy Eye; Butch E. Hermann of Belle Plaine; Marshall A. Miller of Rochester; Gene A. Eiden of Rochester; George V. Maha of New Ulm; Darwin J. Black and Edvern Black [the owner of the very first Hengel-built concertina] and Harry A. Wojahn all three of Fairfax; Bruce B. Libby of Roberts, and Eldred Doell of Greenville, Wisconsin; Melvin I. Bronstad of Chester, Iowa; Lauren A. Stueber of New Ulm; Roman E. Rezac of Webster; David J. Lukes of Lester Prairie; Melvin M. Weber of Cottage Grove; Robert B. Zeig of New Ulm; Leon J. Krzmarzick; Frederick T. Hunter of Oroville, California; Jerome A. Then of St. Cloud; Linus B. Kral of Sleepy Eye; Adrian Filipiak of Brooklyn Center; Dale Dahmen of Pierz; Anthony Lis of Stanley, Wisconsin; Irvin A. Geissler of Bloomington; Reverend Norbert J. Wilger of Altoona, Wisconsin, Scott Majeski [formerly Maciejewski] of Mosinee, Wisconsin, who both plays and does incidental repair, plus many others.

The role the concertina plays in the entertainment world is one that is mysterious, entangled and severely limited in audience appeal. It generates no rock concerts that draw screaming, passionately enthusiastic crowds. Nor are there concerts in symphonic halls anywhere featuring a bellows instrument, let alone a concertina. From its origins and its acceptance by the working class and the miners of eastern Germany to the stockyards of south Chicago and on to the expansive great plains of the upper Midwest, the concertina has

Allen J. Mohr of North Mankato, Minnesota showcases his two Hengel's concertinas, one a Key of C# 12, 58-0012 1958 and one a B-Flat # 17 59-0017.

Paul Wendinger of New Ulm, Minnesota, playing for one of his tour groups in Europe.

endured as a blue-collar, working man's instrument. Nevertheless, it is an instrument of mass appeal. Although it may be unwelcome on the concert stage, in the hands of today's craftsmen and performing artists, the visible and audible fact is self evident: that the outlook for the concertina has never been better! It has never been better built and certainly has never been so competently and artistically played.

While the concertina's presence on the entertainment scene remains confined virtually to the rural dance hall and the outdoor and weekend polka festivals of the Midwest, it has merited the highest praise for its tonal clarity. In the concertina today we still have what Hector Berlioz in 1860 described as "a small instrument with metal tongues which are vibrated by a stream of air.... The timbre of the concertina is penetrating and soft at the same time; in spite of its weakness it carries quite far."[92]

So expertly is the concertina being played by German, Bohemian and Polish ethnic artists in the 21st century, that enjoying the concertina is a rarified treat for those with a taste and appreciation for its artistry. In the Chemnitz area of Germany where the concertina was born, only a few players and a small number of builders are active. However, at Carlsfeld and a few other smaller cities, the bandonion is experiencing a modest rebirth. Since 1993 there has been the yearly Bandoneon Treffen [meeting of bandonion players worldwide] every September, meeting independently of each other at Carlsfeld, home of the Arno Arnold Factory, and at Chemnitz, where Uhlig and Lange were once the long distance builders.[93] The concertina, by contrast, has truly immigrated to America and finds itself at home, formerly but no longer in Chicago, but rather in the upper Midwest. As happened to many immigrants to Chicago, they tended to move on to the expanding frontier. In the same way, the concertina is most at home today in Minnesota, where it is built in largest numbers and with the highest quality, and in Wisconsin. Its future, while limited, is destined to prevail.

While the Whoopee John Band was inactive from 1966-1974, it was activated by Vern Steffel as to its musical library and its old time style. Sounding nearly identical to the old master's troupe, it reappeared in September, 1974 and continued until September, 2003. In this 1982 photograph, we see in the first row, Roger "Pinky" Norris on tuba, Alice Steffel on keyboard, and Vern Steffel on a Patek concertina. In the second row are Bob Seth on saxophone and clarinet, Doug Hougland on trombone, Jay Johnson on drums, Pat Dee on lead trumpet, Dave Vorgian on second trumpet, Dave Marvin on saxophone and clarinet and Bob Lake on saxophone and clarinet.

At the New Prague Ballroom meeting of the New Prague Area Concertina Club, high school student Timothy Chlan and Dale Pexa perform on December 9, 2003.

Entertainment and the Concertina

Below is a list of recent individual performers on the concertina at a January gathering in Fridley, Minnesota for the Concertina Bowl. Following this list are random photos of individual Midwest performers, concluding with noteworthy players with pictures and brief biographies.

PAST PERFORMERS AT THE FRIDLEY, MINNESOTA CONCERTINA BOWL

Alan Quade	Eddie Chock*	Lester Wiechman	Wally Kensey
Donny Roback*	Joe Czerniak ++	Rudy Witthus	Donald Joswiak
Kevin Ruprecht	Bill Czerniak* ++	Keith Zwack	Gene Keiffer*
Andy Stangler*	Art Fenski	Lori Rusin	John Mikla
Jerry Minar ++	Marc Frana	Dan Smieja	Clarence Ezuch
Adrian Filipiak	Dan Gruetzmacher ++	Craig Marsolek	Jim Wukawitz
Barney King* ++	Gary Maciej	Marysia Shudy	Marlene Gwost
Dick Klesk	Stan Marciniak	Bob Sibinski	Brandon Grebner
Verlee Klimek	Wee Willy Makovsky	Dave Sowada	Ernie Mazurek*
Bernie King ++	George Zezulka	Melinda Ruprecht	Christine Mazurek
Gayle White	George Benusa	Larry Rysavy	Riene Jutz
Lou Greub	Tom Gagnon	Don Artz	Dave Lukes
Bob Novak	Jerry Zelazny *	Michelle Kowalski	Karen Struzyk
Art Ohotto ++	Eddie Granda	Ray Kuchinski*	Mary Lou Czerniak
Jerry Pitzen	Dorothy Urbaniak	Gordon Lehrke ++	Duane Schulze
Carmen Lochner	Jim Dobosenski	Mrs. Pete Mrozinski, Jr.	Greg Lehrke
Donnie Klossner	Dale Dahman	Pete Mrozinski III	Jerry Krzmatzick
Jerry Schuft	Doug Dickover	Dave Novak	Hank Zelazny
Chris Christianson	Joe Biernat	Ron Achmann, Jr.	Richard Sauer
Delmar Cords	Gale Blohm	Marv Nissel	Bernice Sauer
Ralph Carlson*	Al Bohnen	Dick Toenyan	Dick Pugh
Dale Pexa	Joe Kaczmarczek	Roy Trojanowski	Ken Erickson
Arnie Checkalski	Robyn Jurek Mrozinski	Gene Welinski	Brian Brueggen
Joel Wanha	Todd Jurek	Lloyd Wasik*	Joe Carlson
Dennis Scheper*	John Deitz	Scott Dickover	Mark Sidla
Erwin Seuss ++	Ted Zawacki	Tony Dingman	Orris Ronsberg
Joe Shopek	3 Cs Bettis	Craig Ebel	George Palma
Don Anderson	John Filipczak	Ted Michurski	Adam Sandhurst
Ray Arent	Sid Fredrickson	Bruce Libby	Gilbert Maus
Augie Artwahl*	John Gag	Tim Maciej	Richard Raclawski
Dwight Stang	Karl Hartwich	Tom Miller	
Richard Stang	George Hebaus	Pete Mrozinski, Sr.*	++ World Concertina
Ernie Stumpf	John Hollerman*	Pete Mrozinski, Jr.	Congress Hall of Fame
Ed Garbasch	Len Strozinski	Vinny Lech	
John Shudy III	Stan Uhlir* ++	Galen Haas	* Deceased
Marlena Shudy	Slim Maser* ++	Jack Zimmerman ++	

The History of the Chemnitzer Concertina

George Maha of New Ulm playing at New Ulm's Minnesota Music Hall of Fame in Turner Hall February 13, 2005. Born at Lamberton in 1935, he started at about age 15 on a double-reed Lange concertina acquired from Wenzel Fischer. Here he plays Hengel No. 65, which he acquired in 1963.

Dain Moldan of New Ulm/Sleepy Eye, Minnesota was born in 1986, starting at the age of six with a Pearl Queen double reed before acquiring his Key of C Hengel. A student at Mankato State University, Dain plays in a family band consisting of his father, Fred and sisters Lisa and Lori Moldan.

Dennis Domeier of Fairfax, Minnesota plays concertina and sings Czech and German folk songs. February 13, 2005.

Adam Sandhurst plays the No. 1 New Prague B-Flat Hengel concertina built by Jerry Minar.

Jerry Minar of New Prague and Roman Rezac of Lonsdale pair with Hengel concertinas at the Minnesota Music Hall of Fame on February 13, 2005.

Charlie Braunreiter plays at New Ulm's Hall of Fame celebration February 13, 2005; formerly he played for the Billy Brown band.

Elmer Scheid plays a Hengel but is best known for his performances on his Patek, acquired in 1937 to play with the Six Fat Dutchmen until about 1946. In 1951 Scheid started his own band, which continued until about 2000 when arthritis reduced his skillful fingers to a lesser state of excellence. Taken February 13, 2005.

Leon Helget of Sleepy Eye, born in 1944, started playing by age seven, first on a Patek, next a Star, then a Pearl Queen, until he acquired his Key of C Hengel in 1971. His band performs about once a week now; in the past Helget also played for The Six Fat Dutchmen. February 13, 2005.

Gil Steil of Richmond, Minnesota was a longtime bandleader during the 1950s to the 1980s. A real estate associate by day, he was a dealer for Christy Hengel in the St. Cloud area of Minnesota.

Entertainment and the Concertina

At about the age of 15, Norbert Foegen of Arcadia, Wisconsin acquired a button accordion from Wilbur Heinz in Waumandee, Wisconsin, the village near where Foegen was born on June 9, 1930. A few years later he graduated to a piano accordion. Not until about the age of 45 did he switch to an Arno Arnold Bandonion triple reed instrument. A few years thereafter, with the aid of the Silberhorn instruction book, he switched to the concertina and bought a Hengel's from Herbert Beck, then living on the neighboring Fetting farm, next door to his own, near Waumandee. Norbert's first bout with a dance band included his brother Delbert on saxophone, Claremont Rotering on tuba and brother Marcel Rotering on drums. But that was with the piano accordion. Later he put the concertina to work with Delbert again, Harvey Lorenz on clarinet, David Bagnewski, tuba and his son Thomas, drums, for a time, succeeded then by Kathy Rumple. Three years ago in 2002 he sold the Hengel's to Gary Brueggen for use with his Ridgeland Dutchmen. Here Norbert plays for old time's sake at his 50th wedding anniversary held April 23, 2005 at the Hilltop Hall near Fountain City, Wisconsin, for which Gary Brueggen entertained.

Jerry Bierschbach, currently of Albany, Minnesota, was born April 21, 1953 at Long Prairie. By the age of 13, aided by lessons from George Servatius, he was playing the concertina at home on his father's farm. Coming of age, he took a job with Kraft in Melrose where he met his wife [Sherry Webb] in 1977 and by 1980 with support musicians was traveling in Germany. Playing frequently with Ervin Girtz and the Waltzeteers, Birerschbach owns two Hengel concertinas, two Brown-built concertinas and is proud of his 1938 Patek #5909 which is equipped with Friedl reeds. Taken in New Prague, April 12, 2005.

Born in 1958 at Minneapolis of a Swedish father, Ralph Carlson, and a German mother [Fuehling] from the Rollingstone area of Minnesota, Joseph Carlson, now resides in Sauk Centre. Employed today as a printer, Carlson took concertina lessons as a boy from George Servatius. His favorite concertina hero, however, was his own father who played a Glass-built quad. Soon the family moved to Little Falls where Ralph played for his Carlson Trio and Polka Jets Bands, but son, Joe, makes his mark with Stan Welle, of Stan's Country Dutchmen in Watkins, Minnesota. Joe likes best playing his 1974 Hengel B-Flat concertina although he is also proud of his Eagle C, one built by Walter Kadlubowski, Jr. after he had sold the Star Company in Chicago. Taken in New Prague, April 12, 2005.

Marlene Gettel Gwost [of Sauk Centre, Minnesota German heritage] is a mainstay [with her husband, Kevin, originally Gwosdz, a Little Falls Polish name] for the Nite Owls Band in Sauk Centre. Born in 1954, Marlene took lessons since the age of five from George Servatius in Melrose on an Arnold, which she liked. Soon she was helping out the family Gettel's Band headed by her father, Lawrence, when her sister, Karen, eight years her senior, needed a break on the concertina. A human services employee with her husband for Stearns County by day, Marlene loves the Arnold, has had a Stradivarius, as well as a 1937 Pearl Queen triple, and would like to own a Hengel. For a dozen years now she has been relying on her Star, played here at the annual April 3, 2005 party offered by George Servatius at the VFW club in Melrose.

Jon Dietz, originally of Montgomery, Minnesota now resides at West Bend, Wisconsin where by day he drives truck. Born in 1978, Jon learned the concertina from his father, Russell, who lent him his black Lange double reed. Soon Jon progressed to a 1938 Patek, still owned in the family. When a sophomore in high school, Jon acquired his own Star concertina from the Cliff Hermel music store in St. Peter. Three years later he traded it at Hermel's for a Brown, which he likes for its tone and its style of keyboard. In 1994, Jon started his own band called the "Twin Lakes Trio," which included Mike Budin and Ken Pavek, the latter being replaced now by Jon's brother, Matt Dietz. His group plays jobs about once a month though Jon also assists on bass horn for the Good Time Dutchmen from Kewaskum, Wisconsin. Here he plays his Brown concertina on March 19, 2005 at the Chandelier Hall in Hartford, Wisconsin.

Although Harvey Bergstrom is busy farming at Cayuga, North Dakota, he loves his new Hengel's concertina, one of the last crafted by New Ulm's Christy Hengel before finalization of the business transfer to Jerry Minar in New Prague. Bergstrom started playing in 1980 on a B-Flat Stradivarius and soon acquired a 1937 Patek C but then sold both until the late 1990s when his passion for the concertina was re-ignited. Here he plays at the George Servatius concertina party on April 3, 2005. It should be remembered that the concertinas built by Hengel bear the name "Hengel's;" those under the patent which was sold to Minar bear the name "Hengel" even though today both versions are authorized to Minar.

Inducted into the World Concertina Congress Hall of Fame in 1993, Adam Wanta of Hatley. Wisconsin plays a Stradivarius at the Chandelier Ballroom in Hartford, Wisconsin, March 20, 2005. Born at Wausau in 1937, Wanta is self-taught, starting about 1950 on a used Pearl Queen concertina from Vitak-Elsnic. He performs mostly with his wife on guitar at small parties. Following a career as quality controller for Weyerhaeuser, he retired in 2000 and likes his Star built about 1990 by John Bernhardt.

Footnotes

1 Among the many publications over the years, see *Entertainment Bits*, Vol. 19, No. 5 (October-November, 1991), p. 16. See also the websites sponsored by a variety of concertina enthusiasts.

2 The data for Kaminski and previously was gathered during interviews at performances, among them in Iowa, Wisconsin and at Gibbon, Minnesota during the course of 2003-05.

3 I am indebted for the newspaper clippings and telephone interviews granted by Hank Jacobs of Cudahy, Wisconsin.

4 *Business Journal* (September 5, 1988), p. 26.

5 *Entertainment Bits*, Vol. I, No. 1 (Spring, 1973) began and is still owned by the Minnesota Ballroom Operators Association, Inc. Its 2005 volume is 33. In about the year 2000 the name was changed to *Music & Dance News*. However, the title of *Entertainment Bits* remained in the subheading of the paper until recently. Thus, I have continued citations using the abbreviated title as EB, without italicization.

6 EB (Fall, 1973), p. 8. EB (August-September, 1983), p. 11B, has a photograph of the Wolf family band with two concertina players, Amby and his father, Tony Wolf. The Wolf recordings were listed in the 1990 "Minnesota Polka Recording" by the Minnesota Historical Society, No. C-004, St. Paul. The accompanying booklet by James Leary offers a summary of old time music in Minnesota, with mention of the salient concertina bands among them.

7 *Fairfax Standard-Gazette* (July 21, 2004).

8 EB (Summer, 1974), p. 12. Ibid. (June-July, 2001), p. 4.

9 EB (Summer, 1973).

10 EB (October-November, 1980), p. 20, reprint with photographs from *Minneapolis Tribune*, August 24, 1980. See also LaVern J. Rippley, *The German-Bohemian Roots of the Whoopee John Wilfahrt Orchestra* (Northfield: St. Olaf College Press, 1992).

11 EB (Fall, 1974), p. 16.

12 See in particular Chapter Eight in Rippley, German-Bohemians, the Quiet Immigrants, op. cit. pp. 213 ff.

13 EB (Spring, 1975), p. 5.

14 EB (September, 1977), p. 13.

15 EB (Summer, 1976), p. 16. The Dobosenski family players are highlighted also in EB (June, 1977), p. 23.

16 EB (August-September, 1983), p. 13B, with photographs. Also, EB (January, 1984), p. 12B. Later, Math Sladky was joined by Jim Kucera, who played for him on an Echo concertina.

17 EB (Winter, 1976), p. 2.

18 EB (September, 1977), p. 4.

19 For a full discussion of this tradition, see Kathleen Conzen, "Ethnicity and Musical Culture among the German Catholics of the Sauk, 1854-1920," in Philip V. Bohlman and Otto Holzapfel, *Land Without Nightingales: Music in the Making of German-America* (Madison: Max Kade Institute for German-American Studies, 2002), pp. 31-71. See the photograph and column in EB (June-July, 1988), p. 4. See also, Fred W. Peterson, *Building Community, Keeping the Faith. German Catholic Vernacular Architecture in a Rural Minnesota Parish* (St. Paul: Minnesota Historical Society Press, 1998).

20 EB (February-March, 1990), p. 13 and, in general, Kathleen Neils Conzen, *Germans in Minnesota* (St. Paul: Minnesota Historical Society, 2003).

21 EB (September, 1977), p. 2. Photo of Renata [Romanek] and Girls in EB (June-July, 1979), p. 8, also (December-January, 1980), p. 5, Renata holding her "Star" concertina. See also feature article and photograph, ibid., (February-March, 1980), p. 4. Another picture is available, ibid., (June-July, 1980), p. 17. Again, a photograph in EB (April-May, 1981), p. 4. A lengthy article about Renata and Girls appears in EB (August-September, 1982), p. 23. The Girls appear with their new bus in EB (June-July, 1984), p. 20A. The Renata and Girls summer feature 1985 is described in EB (January, 1986), p. 3.

22 Photograph in EB (February-March, 1981), p. 7.

23 EB (April-May, 1981, p. 31. Governor Quie with ballroom owners. See also EB (December, 1981-January 1982), p. 1, Quie proclaims June 20, 1982 Polka Day.

24 EB (December, 1977), pp. 13, 19.

25 EB [*Music and Dance News*] (August, September, 2004, p. 6.

26 *Hutchinson Leader*, (February 6, 2001), front page.

27 EB (April/May, 2004), p. 6.

28 EB (June-July, 1979), p. 9. Also multiple photographs in EB (December, 1980-January, 1981), p. 9.

29 EB (April-May, 1980), p. 26. See the photograph of Carol and Marv Nissel in EB (June-July, 1983), p. 6.

30 EB (April, 1978), pp. 27, 28. (April, May, 1979), p. 6 photo.

31 EB (April-May, 1981), p. 30. See also EB (June-July, 1981), p. 36, EB (October-November, 1982), p.23, and EB (October-November, 1990), p. 9.

32 EB (June, 19787), pp. 2, 6.

33 EB (June-July, 2001), front page, with picture.

34 EB (December, 1978), p. 12. The best overall biographical sketch of Syl Liebl is in *Music and Dance News*, i. e. EB (December, 1999-January, 2000), p. 6.

35 See LaVern J. Rippley with Robert Paulson, *German-Bohemians. The Quiet Immigrants* (Northfield: St. Olaf College Press, 1995), p. 230. The Liebl ancestry is from the village of Heiligenkreuz, northwest of Hostau, Bohemia.

36 EB (February-March, 1002), front page Hall of Fame achievements. Obituary in *La Crosse Tribune* (May 11, 2003), reprinted in EB (June-July, 2003), p. 6.

37 EB (April, May, 1979), p. 9.

38 EB (August- September, 1979), p. 12. Photograph with concertinas. in EB (February-March, 1981), p. 6.

39 EB (August- September, 1979). P. 25.

40 EB (October-November, 1979), p. 7.

41 *New Ulm Journal Obituaries*, 2001, online.

42 EB (October-November, 1979), p. 29. See photograph and story EB (December, 1980-January, 1981), p. 25. Art Fenske and band is highlighted in *ibid.* (October-November, 1984), p. 13. The band ceased operations in 1986. See article in EB (January, 1986), p. 8 with photograph.

43 EB (October-November, 1979), p. 30. Fine photographs in EB (October-November, 1980), p. 14. With his Music Masters Band from Ohio, see EB (October-November, 1983), p. 7B. A comprehensive Witucki biographical essay is in the special edition of the *Fairfax, Minnesota Standard-Gazette* (June 25, 2001), front page ff.

44 EB (February-March, 1980), p. 16, with photograph.

45 EB (February-March, 1980), p. 22. See also the photograph in EB (August-September, 1980), p. 20.

46 EB (April-May, 1980), p. 21. Concerning the Rysavy band, see also EB (December, 1983-January, 1984), p. 8B, with photograph.

47 EB (August-September, 1980), p. 6.

48 EB (December, 1980-January, 1981), pp. 4-5, two photographs.

49 *Mankato Free Press* (April 17, 1995), front page.

50 EB (June-July, 2004), p. 4, with photograph.

51 *Fairfax Standard-Gazette*, Minnesota "Polka Edition" (July 23, 2003), p. 5 with picture. Picture p. 13 of Larry Olsen band.
52 EB (February-March, 1981), p. 2, EB [Music and Dance News] (August-September 2004), p. 7 with photograph.
53 EB (February-March, 1981), p. 11.
54 EB (Summer, 1976), p. 17.
55 EB (February-March, 1981), p. 27.
56 Ibid., p. 28.
57 EB (February-March, 1981), p. 31.
58 EB (April-May, 1981), p. 18.
59 EB (August-September, 1981), p. 18.
60 Ibid., p. 11.
61 EB (October-November, 1981), p. 11.
62 EB (October-November, 1981), pp. 28-29.
63 EB (February-March, 1982). p. 15 with photograph.
64 EB (August-September, 1982), pp. 10-11, with photographs.
65 The "best" claim is made on the website of Loren Schaeffler, 1151 Lafayette Avenue Lafayette, Minnesota, but is supported by Christy Hengel as well.
66 EB (August-September, 1982), p. 25.
67 EB (December, 1982-January, 1983), p. 4.
68 EB (February-March, 1983), p. 27.
69 A photograph of Alex and Ed Chesney taken in 1919 in Minneapolis is featured in James Leary, *Minnesota Polka: Polka Music, American Music* (St. Paul: Minnesota Historical Society, 1990), p. 7 of the booklet to accompany the recording entitled *Minnesota Polka: Dance Music from Four Traditions*.
70 EB (June-July, 1983), p. 18, with photograph.
71 Ibid., p. 42, with photograph.
72 EB (June-July, 1981), p. 39.
73 EB (April-May, 1984), p. 17A, with photograph.
74 EB (October-November, 2003), front page.
75 EB (August-September, 1983), p. 15B.
76 EB (December-January, 1990), p. 24.
77 EB (October-November, 19984), p. 8A.
78 EB (February-March, 1985), p. 31, with photographs.
79 EB (June-July, 1988), p. 7, ibid. (December, January, 1991), p. 11.
80 Among other sources, see *Nord-Amerikanische Wochen-Post* (July 26, 2003), p. 10.
81 Letter from Randy Dorschner, September 30, 2003.
82 See Ridgeland Dutchmen website.
83 *Fairfax Standard-Gazette, Minnesota* (July 25, 2001), p. 5, and ibid., "Polka Edition" (July 23, 2003), p. 9, with picture. See also the Jim Busta website.
84 EB (December-January, 1990), p. 22. See also *Fairfax Standard-Gazette, Minnesota* (July 23, 2003), p. 9 with picture.
85 EB (February-March, 1987), p. 21. See also the article about Sylvester Liebl, Sr. in EB (February-March, 1990), p. 7.
86 http://www.itspolkatime.com/. It's Polka Time! is heard over eleven radio stations in five states across the Upper Midwest.
87 EB (October-November, 1989), p. 32. Interview with Glenn Wondra of Montgomery, July 27, 2003.
88 See their website and EB (August-September, 2003), p. 13.
89 Correspondence and interviews with Art Ohotto during July, 2003.
90 Leary, "The German Concertina in the Upper Midwest," op. cit., pp. 217-8. Helmut A. Peters of Belleville, Illinois and wife, Rose E. [Merod], operated the Concertina Klub on South Illinois Street in Belleville. He was buried in the Valhalla Mausoleum in Bellville. Cf. Obituary clipping with no date or newspaper title, in possession of the author.
91 LaVern J. Rippley, *The Whoopee John Wilfahrt Dance Band: His Bohemian-German Roots* (Northfield: St. Olaf College, 1992). Especially useful in tracking the early recording scene is Richard K. Spottswood, *Ethnic Music on Records: A Discography of Ethnic Recordings in the United States, 1893-1942*, 7 Vols. Esp. Vol. 1 on Western Europe and Vol. 2 Slavic (Urbana: University of Illinois, 1990).
92 Hector Berlioz, *Treatise on Instrumentation*, enlarged and revised by Richard Strauss, trans. Theodore Front (New York: Edwin F. Kalmus, 1948), p. 401.
93 http://www.chemnitz-concertina.de/de/index.htm

Appendix I
Hall of Fame

World Concertina Congress Hall of Fame.

The World Concertina Congress was begun in 1975 by a handful of Chemnitzer concertina musicians. Over the past thirty years it has grown to include thousands of musicians and enthusiasts from around the world, only a small percentage of whom have been inducted into the roster of honorees.

The founding members appointed the first officers as follows: Harold Zimmerman, President; Frank Stanczewski, 1st Vice President; George Hrica, 2nd Vice President; Earl Kops, 3rd Vice President; Nicky Nechanicky, 4th Vice President; Jack Zimmerman, Treasurer and Secretary; Pat Watters, Publicity.

The organization's Hall of Fame is not a place but rather a collective idea; a means by which the instrument's musicians honor their peers. The Hall of Fame recognizes international, national and regional Chemnitzer concertina musicians, as well as others who have supported this unique instrument. However, the majority of the Hall of Fame members are musicians who have kept the instrument alive at its grassroots level. Like few other halls of fame, the World Concertina Congress honors not only aficionados but also down-to-earth players whose contributions are important to the instrument's preservation.

In the succeeding lineup, inductees into the Hall of Fame are identified by primary location, each into one or more of the following categories: Bandleader, Composer, Innovator, Manufacturer, Musician and occasionally a category all its own.

The History of the Chemnitzer Concertina

— 1976 —

 Carl F. Uhlig
 Charles Wheatstone
 Henry Silberhorn
Ernest, Paul & Otto Glass (No Photo Available)
Joseph P. Elsnic (No Photo Available)

 Matt Pajakowski
 Arno Arnold
 Ed Teikowski
 Henry Schukert
 Andrew Karpek

 Pat Watters
 George Hrica
 Stan Nowicki
 Rudy Patek

1. Carl F. Uhlig — Germany, invented the Chemnitzer, concertina
2. Charles Wheatstone — England, invented the Wheatstone, English concertina
3. Henry Silberhorn — Chicago, author, composer, importer, "Clarion" concertina
4. Ernest, Paul & Otto Glass — Chicago, manufacturers, importers, builders
5. Joseph P. Elsnic — Chicago, player, composer, teamed with Louis Vitak
6. Matt Pajakowski — Buffalo, NY, composer, arranger, teacher
7. Arno Arnold — Germany, last of the Arnold builders, wholesaler
8. Ed Teikowski — Milwaukee, dealer, teacher, player
9. Henry Schukert — Chicago, teacher, arranger, repair, importer, builder
10. Andrew Karpek — Milwaukee, repair, retail, tuner, builder
11. Pat Watters — Minneapolis / Mosinee, WI, lifelong promoter
12. George Hrica — Chicago / FL, player, teacher, inventor
13. Stan Nowicki — Milwaukee, player, arranger, teacher
14. Rudy Patek — Chicago / Weyauwega, WI, importer, retailer, player

Appendix I — Hall of Fame

— 1977 —

Tony & Betty Wolf   Frank (Stann) Stanczewski   Jim Herda   John Wilfahrt

15. Tony and Betty Wolf   St. Joseph, MN, bandleaders, radio, teachers, players
16. Frank (Stann) Stanczewski   Buffalo, NY, "Crazy Fingers" player, composer
17. Jim Herda   Chicago, player, teacher, owned Concertina Lounge
18. John Wilfahrt   St. Paul, Whoopee John Band; pioneer player

— 1978 —

Irving Dewiz   Eddie Zima   Charles Blim   Edward A. Hermann

19. Irving Dewitz   Hustisford, WI, club organizer, player, teacher
20. Eddie Zima   Chicago, player, recording artist, composer "Circus"
21. Charles Blim   Chicago, exceptional player and recording artist
22. Edward A. Hermann   Chicago, player, condensed keyboard

— 1979 —

Dan Gruetzmacher   Harold "Zimmy" Zimmerman   Max Gajewski   Joseph Stacey

23. Dan Gruetzmacher   Wausau, WI, bandleader, composer, exceptional player
24. Harold Zimmerman   Union, MI, "Zimmy", sales, promoter, collector
25. Max Gajewski   Milwaukee, bandleader, artist
26. Joseph Stacey   Chicago, arranger, stylist, teacher

— 1980 —

Max Peters Helmut Peters Arthur Schmuldt

27. Max Peters   Milwaukee, Peters Brothers Band, bandonion specialist
28. Helmut Peters   Bellville, IL, Concertina-bandonion player, importer
29. Arthur Schmuldt   Ludington, MI, teacher, club organizer, player

— 1981 —

Joesph F. Czerniak Dr. John F. Check

30. Joseph F. Czerniak   Duluth, MN, artist, teacher, club organizer, repair, dealer
31. John F. Check   Oshkosh, WI, bandleader, composer, radio, recording

— 1982 —

Mildred Kaminski George Karpek

32. Mildred Kaminski   Milwaukee, WI, exceptional player, singer, "Concertina Millie"
33. George Karpek   Milwaukee, owned Karpek Music, innovator, builder

— 1983 —

Albert B. Nechanicky   Jack Zimmerman   Max [Ervin] King [Kusczynski]   Frank Kucera

34. Albert B. Nechanicky   Spokane, WA, composer, developed 130 key concertina
35. Jack Zimmerman   South Bend, IN, reed enthusiast, festival promoter, writer.
36. Max [Ervin] King [Kusczynski] Milwaukee, artist, player in harmony & duets
37. Frank Kucera   Elmonte, CA, player, promoter

— 1984 —

Lester Bondowski   Patti Grohek Wolfe   Andrew H. Roll   Paul Schroeder

38. Lester Bondowski [Bonde]   Milwaukee, player, stage performer with Groshek
39. Patti Grohek Wolfe   Milwaukee, duet player
40. Andrew H. Roll   St. Louis, MO, promoter, bandonion and Anglo concertina player
41. Paul Schroeder   Milwaukee, club organizer, promoter, player

— 1985 —

John Sienicki   Archie Maxim   Frank Klaman

42. John Sienicki   Mishawaka, IN, player, tuning, repair
43. Archie Maxim   Lowell, MI, player, vocalist, club organizer
44. Frank Klaman   Jackson, WI, composer, duet player with Max King

— 1986 —

William "Bill" Brown   George Servatius   Edward "Star" Starzynski   Henry Muench   John M. Bondowski

Joseph F. Ushman

45. William "Bill" Brown   New Ulm, MN, distributor, repair, builder, teacher
46. George Servatius   Melrose, MN, entertaining player, clown band, teacher
47. Edward "Star" Starzynski   West Dundee, IL, player, teacher
48. Henry Muench   Bloomer, WI, bandleader, player
49. John M. Bondowski   Oak Creek, WI, played on radio, sales for Teikowski store
50. Joseph F. Ushman   Springfield, IL, player, band leader, promoter

— 1987 —

Barney King   Bernie King   Leon "Leo Flowers" Kwiatkowski

51. Barney King   Schofield, WI, played concertina with his twin
52. Bernie King   Schofield, WI, with his twin, played for picnics, churches
53. Leon Kwiatkowski   Chicago, bandleader, teacher, aka "Leo Flowers"

Appendix I — Hall of Fame

— 1988 —

John Lowell Whalley

A. R. D. "Pat" Robson

Henry "Hank" Jacobs

Edward Rickert

Alvin R. Gostomski

Joseph F. Ushman

54. John Lowell Whalley — Milwaukee, Technician for Karpek, arranger, player
55. A. R. D. "Pat" Robson — London, England. Player, builder, researcher
56. Hank Jacobs [Jakubowski] — Fanklin, WI, Player, teacher, Karpek worker
57. Edward Rickert — Chicago, "Concertina Eddie" music store teacher
58. Alvin R. Gostomski — Milwaukee, "Al Roberts" bandleader, composer, teacher
59. Joseph F. Ushman — Spring Hill, FL, Player, promoter, club organizer

— 1989 —

Edward D. Radonski

Edmond Olshanski

Robert Storch

Walter "Wally" Stark

Harry Dolato

Elmer Stillman

Thomas "Smiley" Smigielski

60. Edward D. Radonski — Greenfield, WI, "Ed Donnie" bandleader, teacher player
61. Edmond Olshanski — Wausau, WI, player, promoter, club member.
62. Robert Storch — Muskegon, MI/Medford, WI, radio, performer, bandleader
63. Walter "Wally" Stark — Chicago/Garland, TX, player, repair, arranger, cousin to Patek
64. Harry Dolato — West Allis, WI, player from childhood to his 90s.
65. Elmer Stillman — Rockford, IL, Medford, WI, player, prolific arranger, radio
66. Thomas "Smiley" Smigielski — Milwaukee, WI, player, teacher, Karpek worker

— 1990 —

 Christy Hengel
 Aloisious (Tucker) Tucholski
 Leo Bartelt
 Happy Harold Jasicki
 Norman Carr

 Nicholas Kurszewski

67. Christy Hengel — New Ulm, MN, player, builder, lifelong promoter
68. Aloisious (Tucker) Tucholski — Buffalo, NY, teacher, composer, club organizer
69. Leo Bartelt — Chicago, player, promoter
70. Happy Harold Jasicki — Chicago, player
71. Norman Carr — Chicago, player
72. Nicholas Kurszewski — Chicago, player

— 1991 —

 John Benesh
 Benny Carter Dobiecki
 Milton Gruenwald
 Eddie Lash
 Irvin Kwas

73. John Benesh — Concertina and clarinet player, entertainer
74. Benny Carter Dobiecki — Milwaukee, player
75. Milton Gruenwald — Milwaukee, player
76. Eddie Lash — Chicago, salesman, player, expert Star player
77. Irvin Kwas — Chicago, player

Appendix I — Hall of Fame

— 1992 —

Albert O. Beelow   Harry A. Sonnentag   Larry Janke   Ervin Walenska

78. Albert O. Beelow — Algonquin, IL, teacher, writer, performer
79. Harry A. Sonnentag — Marathon, WI, player, composer, performer
80. Larry Janke — Milwaukee, WI, expert player
81. Ervin Walenska — Milwaukee, WI, truck driver, player, promoter, teacher

— 1993 —

Joseph Starck   Adam Wanta   Cliff Hermel   Katie Hermel   Ervin J. Lemanczyk

82. Joseph Starck — Hibbing, MN, barber, player, in Chicago, Minneapolis, Detroit
83. Adam Wanta — Hatley, WI, quality control technician, player, teacher
84. Cliff Hermel — St. Peter, MN, Gibbon Ballroom owner, drummer
85. Katie Hermel — Wife of Cliff, supporter, promoter
86. Ervin J. Lemanczyk — Glendale, IL, player, performer

— 1994 —

 John Bernhardt
 Barbara Bernhardt
 James P. Leary
 Ronald Buczko
 Mickey Stys

 Jerry Kramarczyk
 Walter Kadlubowski Sr.
 Walter Kadlubowski Jr.

87. John Bernhardt — Chicago, last owner-builder of Star, arranger
88. Barbara Bernhardt — Wife of John, promoter, supporter
89. James P. Leary — Madison, WI, wrote about concertina-*Land Without Nightingales*
90. Ronald Buczko — Joliet, IL, player, founder of Polka Club
91. Mickey Stys — Milwaukee, traffic manager, Old Timers Concertina Club
92. Jerry Kramarczyk — Harvard, IL, conservation officer, player, teacher, arranger
93. Walter Kadlubowski Sr. — Chicago, first to build Star concertina, promoter, builder
94. Walter Kadlubowski Jr. — Chicago, intermediate owner of Star, promoter, builder

— 1995 —

 Carl Neuman
 Alvin "Al" Czerniak
 Harry "Berg" Schwichtenberg
 Stanley F. Uhlir
 Charles S. Matulnik

95. Carl Neuman — Waupun, WI, director of Hustisford Concertina Club, player
96. Alvin "Al" Czerniak — Hot Springs, AZ, forest ranger, player, 1st Union Concertina Club
97. Harry "Berg" Schwichtenberg — Schaumburg, IL, player, tireless promoter
98. Stanley F. Uhlir — Minneapolis, designer, builder of Echo, player, promoter
99. Charles S. Matulnik — Westmont, IL, player, composer

Appendix I — Hall of Fame

— 1996 —

Jerry Minar · Marvin Spradau · John Gavlik · Frank Berent Sr. · Dick Rodgers

Slim Maser · Herman W. Yanke · Robert F. Nickel

100. Jerry Minar		New Prague, MN, dealer, player, teacher, builder of Hengel
101. Marvin Spradau		Mayville, WI, player
102. John Gavlik		Minneapolis/FL, fine player
103. Frank Berent Sr.		Chicago, fine player, entertainer
104. "Dick" Rodgers [Rodziczak]		Pulaski, WI, player, band leader, TV performer
105. Lavain "Slim" Maser		St. Paul, dealer for Star-built "Royal," tuner, player
106. Herman W. Yanke		Manistee, MI, player, "Yanke Waltz," shop
107. Robert F. Nickel		Chicago, player, promoter, expert drummer

— 1997 —

Stanley Paluszewski · Syl Liebl Sr. · Vernon Miller · Gordon Lehrke · Art Altenburg

108. Stanley Paluszewski — Chicago, player, promoter
109. Syl Liebl Sr. — La Crosse, WI excellent player, band leader
110. Vernon Miller — Milwaukee, player, band leader
111. Gordon Lehrke — Little Falls, MN, player, teacher
112. Art Altenburg — Milwaukee, owner of Concertina Bar, player

The History of the Chemnitzer Concertina

— 1998 —

Helen Brandon   Sue Gruetzmacher   Shannon Gunn   Earl Kops   Joseph A. Kujanik

Ron Lech   Karl Oriwohl   Ray Tabaczka   Eileen Sienicki   Betty Zimmerman

113. Helen Brandon — Union, MI, organizer with Harold Zimmermann of WCC
114. Sue Gruetzmacher — Wausau, WI, promoter, writer, organizer
115. Shannon Gunn — player, performer
116. Earl Kops — Muskegon, MI, player of B-Flat Stradivarius
117. Joseph A. Kujanik — Gary, IN, player TV entertainer
118. Ron Lech — Player, teacher, composer
119. Karl Oriwohl — Berlin, Germany, author of Bandonion history
120. Ray Tabaczka — Ludington, MI, player, band leader
121. Eileen Sienicki — St. Joseph, MI, founder of WCC and supporter
122. Betty Zimmerman — Wife of Jack Zimmerman, founder, organizer

— 1999 —

 Larry Dorschner
 Stanley Grabowski
 Robert Mathiowetz
 Leroy F. Reuter
 Anthony "Tony" Stimac
 Roger Terasek
 Lloyd Konrath
 Del Branz

123.	Larry Dorschner	Appleton, WI, player, had Hengel # 5 & # 9, played for brother Ray and his Rainbow Valley Dutchmen, built cases and reed blocks
124.	Stanley Grabowski	Kansas City, MO, player, instructor
125.	Robert Mathiowetz	Ashland, WI, player, brother of Cliff, who played for Babe Wagner
126.	Leroy F. Reuter	New England, ND/Woodstock, IL, player
127.	Anthony "Tony" Stimac	Wittenberg, WI, player
128.	Roger Terasek	Milwaukee, WI, promoter, player
129.	Lloyd Konrath	Germantown, WI, player, organizes Allenton, WI concertina festival
130.	Del Branz	Hartville, OH, player

— 2000 —

William "Bill" Landowski   Jerry Darlak   Ervin Behrend   Dan Niemczyk   Al Regner

Albert Giese

131. William "Bill" Landowski — Deceased, played with New Village Brass band
132. Jerry Darlak — Cheektowaga, NY, born Chicago, band leader, player
133. Ervin Behrend — Coleman, WI, player, teacher, promoter
134. Dan Niemczyk — Brookfield, WI player, teacher, entertainer
135. Al Regner — Chicago, 30 years band leader, player, promoter
136. Albert Giese — Milwaukee, player, band leader

— 2001 —

Joe Stulga   Leroy Deering   Bob Arthur   Cletus Goblirsch   Bill Czerniak

Walter (Wally) Fabisheck   Art Ohotto   Ed Suterko   Frank R. Stirrett

137. Joe Stulga — Lansing, IL, exceptional player, band leader
138. Leroy Deering — Milwaukee, band leader, Echo player, hymn singing
139. Bob Arthur Slawnikowski — Milwaukee, exceptiona player
140. Cletus Goblirsch — New Ulm, player, band leader
141. Bill Czerniak — Duluth/Minneapolis, player, band leader
142. Walter (Wally) Fabisheck — Chicago, player, arranger, composer
143. Art Ohotto — Minneapolis, player, promoter, Concertina Bowl
144. Ed Suterko — Reno, from IL, player, club organizer
145. Frank R. Stirrett — Ontario, CD, player, museum, Anglo concertina

Appendix I — Hall of Fame

— 2002 —

John Onak   Chuck Thies   Henry Holtz   Andy Justman   Bryan O'Donnell

Lloyd O'Donnell   Walter Piasek   Robert Novitzke

146. John Onak   Crete, IL, player since age 7, one man band
147. Chuck Thies   Muskegon, MI, player, Grand Rapids club
148. Henry Holtz   Muskegon, MI, player, radio
149. Andy Justman   Brownsville, WI, player, bandleader
150. Bryan O'Donnell   Milwaukee, player, son of Lloyd, bandleader
151. Lloyd O'Donnell   Milwaukee, player, bandleader
152. Walter Piasek   Muskegon, MI, tool maker, farmer, player
153. Robert Novitzke   Wausau, WI, player, promoter

The History of the Chemnitzer Concertina

— 2003 —

Greg Krawiec, Sr.　　Carl Penfil　　Ray Konkol　　Paul Kramas　　Gerrard Glysz

George Pauers　　Erwin Suess　　Thomas Sandel　　Stanley Yagelski　　Ken Yagelski

Friedrich Emil Lange

154. Greg Krawiec, Sr.　　South Bend, IN, concertina and accordion player
155. Carl Penfil　　Milwaukee, player, band leader, army entertainer
156. Ray Konkol　　Stevens Point, WI, played concertina for Konkol & Dorschner Bands
157. Paul Kramas　　Greenwood, WI, player on WCFW, Chippewa Falls
158. Gerrard Glysz　　Milwaukee, Polish style player and drummer
159. George Pauers　　Franklin, WI, player, band leader
160. Erwin Suess　　Mankato, MN, player, band leader
161. Thomas Sandel　　St. Joseph, MI, player, promoter, organizer
162. Stanley Yagelski　　Chicago, player, promoter, St. Joseph Concertina Club
163. Ken Yagelski　　Stafford, VA, player, tireless promoter, web site manager
164. Friedrich Lange　　Owner of Uhlig-Lange factory in Chemnitz 1892-1933

— 2004 —

 Raymond Arent
 C. E. Casey Bruzdzinski
 Dave Bruzdzinski
 Joseph Dylejko
 Paul Knoll

 Ambrose Kodet
 Steve Litwin
 Bob Novak
 John Janowski
 Maureen Harju

 Edward O. Peirick
 Peter D. Shudy
 Paul Vadovski
 Frank Waksmonski
 Joseph Zegarowicz

 Michael R. Smieja
 John Friedl
 Ernie A. Coopman

165. Raymond Arent — Minneapolis, player, all music, entertainer
166. C. E. Casey Bruzdzinski — Calumet City, IL, electronic technician, player
167. Dave Bruzdzinski — Calumet City, IL, player since age 12
168. Joseph Dylejko — Alabaster, AL, Polka Masters Band in South Bend, IN
169. Paul Knoll — Sarasota, FL, player, band leader, promoter
170. Ambrose Kodet — Mankato, MN, Computer scientist, player, engraver
171. Steve Litwin — Binghamton, NY, promoter, player, editor Polish-Am. Journal
172. Bob Novak — Lake Elmo, MN, promoter, player, builder of Echo concertinas

173. John Janowski	Grayslake, IL, player, founder Chicago Concertina Club
174. Maureen Harju	Freesoil, MI, player, teacher
175. Edward O. Peirick	Watertown, WI, player, composer
176. Peter D. Shudy	West Allis, WI, machinist, player
177. Paul Vadovski	Shelby Township, MI, player, promoter, writer
178. Frank Waksmonski	Hatley, WI, 60 years player, dancehall owner
179. Joseph Zegarowicz	Milwaukee, WI, player, composer
180. Michael R. Smieja	St. Paul, MN, player, assists Novak with Echo concertinas
181. John Friedl	Chicago, maker of reeds and plates
182. Ernie A. Coopman	Mankato, MN, player, band leader

— 2005 —

Main Category
John Filipczak
Karl Hartwich
Donald Klossner
William [Wee Willie] Makovsky
Marvin Nissel
Roman Rezac
Elmer Scheid
Paul Wendinger
Peter Wendinger
Daniel Witucki
Charles Rezepka
Vernon Tretow
John Pelczynski
Theresa Slipek

Deceased Category
Peter Mrozinski
Jerry Schuft
David Suess

Special Category
Leonard Rafalski
Gerald Zarling

Appendix II
Album Covers

Over a half century of time from 1950 to 2000, a plethora of concertina bands promoted their music, their styles and their brands of the Chemnitzer concertina on vinyl disks in 78, 45 and 33 rpm. Today they have shifted to cassettes, only to abandon them for the compact disk, the CD. Both of the latter vessels offer diminished space to explain the music and depict musicians on the cover. Presented below are samples of the thousands of album jackets that were created to promote musicians who played the concertina. They appear in no special order, nor is there any particular story to be told. It would be nice to have been able to date all of them but this proved elusive except in a few instances. Many of them no longer perform. Thus they should be viewed as representative of a cross-section of concertina bands and as informal pictorial evidence of concertina activities on the Midwest music scene.

"Zwack Old Tyme Band," July, 1979. Five brothers from Brooklyn Center, Minnesota began in 1976 and developed into a five-piece complement in 1977. Gary plays clarinet, sax and trumpet, Dave the tuba, Jim drums and Keith the Echo concertina while Paul plays trumpet.

"Peter and Paul Wendinger Band," posing with two Hengel concertinas, 1984. The band is supported by Wayne Wagner, Steve Moran, Mike Simon, Gary Gleisner and Doug Young.

"Wee Willie Makovsky Band," July 5, 1986 — Wayne Loebrich, Wee Willie, Marv Anderson and Augie Makovsky. Willie plays a variety of concertinas.

"Wee Willie Band," 1988 — Willie Makovsky, Marv Anderson, Augie Makovsky, Wayne Loebrick. Pictured is a Stradivarius concertina.

"Chuck Thiel and the Jolly Ramblers" of Lester Prairie, Minnesota. Gary Schmidt, Hilary Haag, Chuck Thiel — an English instructor at Lester Prairie High School — Matt Mohwinkel, and Ken Schmidt. Thiel is playing a Gem Deluxe concertina.

"TNT" Band of Cold Spring, Minnesota. Todd Thielen, Terry Thielen (holding a Stradivarius concertina with an electronic organ unit); Grace Theisen, John Bauerman and Dave Lohse.

Alvin Styczynski of Pulaski, Wisconsin playing a Star concertina.

"The Starlites" featuring LaVerne Bzdok of Little Falls, Minnesota holding a Hengel concertina — however, the concertina player is really Andy Stangler of St. Joseph, Minnesota. LaVerne plays drums, piano, guitar and banjo.

"Erwin Suess and the Hoolerie Dutchmen," with Hengel and Star concertinas. Support players include Monica Suess, his wife, John Henle, Richard Blomgren, Duane Suess and his wife, Denise Le Bert Suess.

"Lester Schuft and his Country Dutchmen." Don Petrick plays saxophone, Lester Schuft, trumpet, Marv Nissel, a Hengel. In back, Milton Klammer with trombone, Albert Schuft, drums, Leonard Sellner, bass horn and Ron Novotny, guitar.

"Larry's Concertina Band," — David Langer, bass horn, Mark Kubat, drums, Larry Rysavy with a Hengel and Dorothy Miller, guitar.

"Roman Rezac with his Old Time Czech Style Band." Front row — Joe Smisek, Ed Rezac, Roman Rezac with a Star. Back row — Dick Flicek, Germanus Kipp, William Kallal and Roy Valek.

Harvey Becker of Glencoe, Minnesota playing the Accordion-Tina, a rare creation by Christy Hengel to replicate the sound of the concertina with a piano keyboard. Most of the inner features and, in particular the reeds, are of concertina quality. His band is called the Riverside Dutchmen.

Donnie Klossner, playing a Star, and the Redbirds of New Ulm Minnesota, assembled here at the Zeiner Ballroom in Bixby, Minnesota. Don is accompanied by daughters, Shelly Jean and Debbie, along with Carolyn Klossner.

Dale Dahmen plays a Hengel with the "Polka Beats" of Pierz, Minnesota. Dale's concertina instructor was Gilbert Maus. He is accompanied by Kenny Faber of St. Joseph on drums, Adrian Sowada of Little Falls on saxophone and clarinet, and Kevin Brown from St. Cloud on trumpet, tuba and bass guitar.

Appendix II — Album Covers

Gordy Prochaska and the "Little Fishermen" Band of Montgomery. Playing a Patek concerina is Marvin Moravec of Montgomery. Front Row: Don Tupy, Gordon Prochaska, and Dan Kaisersatt. Back Row: Harvey Dorn, Moravec, Joe Klonne and Billy Kabes.

The Wally Pikal Band derives from Hutchinson, Minnesota, where it began in 1950. A master of the trumpet, three of which he can play at once, Pikal is supported by Marv Bulau on a Hengel concertina, Jerome Kadlec, saxophone, along with Cyril Vanyo, Marinus Fasching, Warren Will and Robert Busacker.

Dale Pexa and the "Country Girls" Band features Dale Pexa playing a Wolfe concertina. Front Row: Darcy Skluzacek, saxophone and Bridget Wagner, drums. Back Row: Fran Pexa, trombone, Dale Pexa Jr., trumpet and Christy Peters, guitar.

Leon Olsen Band. Leon started playing his Hengel with the help of his brother-in-law, Marv Nissel. Playing with Leon have been Paul Spencer, Paul Grasch and Dave Schaefer. The son of Arnold and Lorraine Olsen of Lake Benton, Minnesota, Leon is the brother of Larry Olsen who farms near Lake Benton.

Marv Nissel plays duets on a Hengel concertina accompanied by his wife, Carol on keyboard, seen here at the Glockenspiel in their hometown of New Ulm. Nissel's daughter, Jodi, is married to Brian Brueggen, leader of the "Mississippi Valley Dutchmen" of Cashton, Wisconsin. Daughter Lori is married to Craig Ebel, a concertina player.

Joe Novotny playing a Star. Begun in 1969, the Joe Novotny Dance Band operated from New Prague, Minnesota. He has written and arranged many old Czech folk songs and sings in Czech and English. Support is lent by Myles Skluzacek, trumpet, Richard Bartusek, bass horn, Joe Tupy, banjo or drums, and John Flicek, accordion.

The Novotny Brothers Band of Montgomery, Minnesota specialized in Czech singing, notably such fine numbers as the 'Lazy Farmer Waltz,' the 'Happy Joe Waltz' and the 'A Ja Sam Polka.' Larry Novotny played a Patek concertina while Dave, the bass horn, and John, drums.

Jerry Minar acquired some of the Anton Wolfe concertina production when the latter passed away. Although Wolfe made his own reeds from a spring steel company's raw materials, he later took over the remainder of the Rudy Patek concertina manufacture, which was subsquently bequeathed to Minar, who now builds the Hengel.

The "Mrozinski Brothers" Band of Minneapolis and St. Paul are actually Bill Czerniak and Jerry Zelazny playing Star concertinas and supported by John Keen on bass, Mike Wendolek, drums and Mary Czerniak, paino. The band is best known for its Polish style renditions.

The History of the Chemnitzer Concertina

"Malek's Fishermen" Band comes from Duncan, Iowa, a strong Czech community of 125 families, lying just west of Garner, Iowa. Originally it was Syl and Bob Malek, then they were joined by Joe Hrubes who played button accordion, then Dean Schilling from Clarksville, Iowa joined them with an A-Flat Hengel concertina. More recently son Eric joined, playing the concertina.

New Prague Czech Singers. Organized by Gladys (Novak) Tupy for the bicentennial in 1976, the singers included Adeline, Bill and Lorraine Bisek, Helen Bruzek, Ella and Eppie Kohout, Julie Krautkramer, Margie and Ben Novotny, Angie Simon, Clarence Smisek and Gladys Tupy. Jerry Minar and Larry Novotny played concertinas. Down in front are two Pearl Queen concertinas, three Patek models, a Stradivarius and an Anton Wolfe.

The Montgomery Czech Singers were organized by Blanche Havel Zellmer, who sings, arranges and writes the music. Singers standing: George Mucha, Juanita Factor, George Palma, Elmer Sticka, Doris Krenik, George Korbel, Babe Mucha, Quentin Scheonbauer, Irene Gaydon, Milton Korbel, Mary Bartusek, Joe Shimota, Glen Wondra (playing the concertina) Joe Budin and Ambrose Kodet (also playing the concertina). Seated: Rita Sticha, Ann Segna, Unice Wahsa, Sharon Kaisershut, Dorothy Peroutka, Glen Flicek, Joanie Kaderlik, Helen Keohen, Darlene Wondra, Janet Klebel, Cathy Oppegaard, Blanch Zellmer (director).

Don Klossner played Star and Stradivarius concertinas since the age of 13, and from 1955 until 1969 with the Babe Wagner Band of New Ulm. Here he plays a Star and a Stradivarius. He credits his learning about music to musicians like Swede Wagner, Lenny Wavrin, Spike Haskel and others. Shown here is also Al Maves of Hayfield, Minnesota who played for Kuhfuss Brothers and Babe Wagner as well as his own Swingin' Laendlers.

"Mel's Polka Stars" derive from Chester, Iowa. Mel Bronstad first learned of the concertina from Stanley Lozowski of Rice Lake, Wisconsin but drove to New Ulm for two years beginning in 1974 to take concertina lessons from Ambrose Kodet and formed his band in 1976. Here he plays a Hengel concertina.

Syl Liebl led the Jolly Swiss Boys for over a half century. Playing a Hengel concertina was Syl Liebl, supported by Ray Wuensch on saxophone, Tom Langen on bass, Rudy Langen on trumpet, Syl, Jr. on trumpet, and daughter Carol Seebauer on piano.

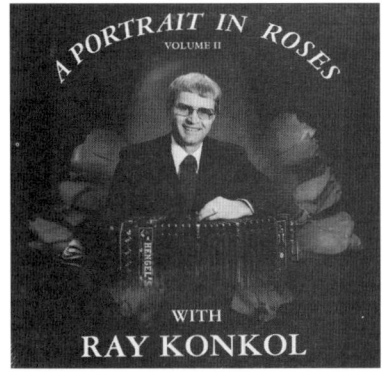

The "Ray Konkel Band" of Stevens Point, Wisconsin includes Ray playing his Hengel, Germaine Konkol, piano, Lou Allen, bass horn and Kim (Ristow) Pronschinske, drums. Ray sometimes plays a Wunderlich concertina featuring a mechanical tremolo. This instrument was made in Germany nearly a century ago.

Playing a Stadivarius concertina for the "Ivan Kahle Band" was Jerry Minar of New Prague, [though Ivan Kahle on trumpet before his death was based in Norwood, Minnesota]. Seated: Ivan Kahle, Jerry Kahle, saxophone, James Bartusek, drums. Standing: Ralph Littfin, bass horn, Minar, and Ray Dibbert.

The "Andy Justman Band" of Brownsville, Wisconsin in 1972 featured Frank Kempfer on saxophone, Tom Justman, saxophone and clarinet, Charlie Justman, tuba, Gary Zastrom, trumpet, Steve Speidel, trumpet, Dick Justman, drums and Andy Justman, a Hengel concertina.

Appendix II — Album Covers

The "Jolly Gentlemen Band" includes bandleader Eddie Adavickas, Dan Gruetzmacher on Stradivarius, Robert Schwartz, drums, Philip Gruetzmacher, banjo, young Keith Adavickas, 2nd trumpet, and Louis Zdrazil, lead trumpet.

Ivan and his "Jolly Dutchmen Band" features Roman Rezac of Webster, Minnesota on a Hengel, Ed Hruby of Lonsdale, bass horn, Glen Wondra of Montgomery, guitar, and Ivan Plaggemeyer of Burnsville, drums.

When it was active, the "James Gang" featured bandleader and concertina player Jim Horazdovsky, who used a Stradivarius, a Star, and an older Patek. Operating from Montgomery, Minnesota, Jim was supported by Linda Markl on bass guitar, Mel Storm, lead guitar and Bill Busacker, drums. Jerry Minar was Horazdovsky's teacher.

The "Jolly Coppersmiths Band." A regular feature of the band is its concertina trio consisting of Joel Wanha, Wally Kensy and Art Fenske, the bandleader from Minneapolis. Their support comes from Richard Blomgren on bass horn, Doug Johnson, trumpet, Sue Johnson, clarinet and saxophone, Wally Kensy, concertina and piano, Tim Mohrlant, drums, Wanha and Fenske play Hengel and Stradivarius concertinas.

Douglas Dickover and Art Fenske, both New Ulmers, played for the "Jolly Coppersmiths" of whom Fenske was the bandleader. Fenske plays a Patek and a Hengel concertina.

Heading the "Jolly Fishermen Orchestra" is Joyce Smieja of Royalton who plays trumpet and drums as well as vocals. Her husband, Benny, played concertina until his death on January 25, 1984. He was succeeded by Jerry Gwost from Flensburg, playing a Brown concertina. Terry Thelen plays tuba and Florence Magnan, keyboard.

The "Jolly Chaps Orchestra" of Stevens Point Wisconsin is headed by Tony Kaminski, bass horn. Ray Chojnacki, a Patek concertina while Gary Shirek and Don Zblewski play trumpets and Steve Grywacz, drums.

The "Johnny Helget Band" traces its origins to John Helget's birthplace, Sleepy Eye, Minnesota in 1939. At 13, his parents bought him a concertina but in 1956 he purchased his own Hengel at the age of 16. He is supported by Sarge Schroeder on drums, Leonard Hansen, bass horn and Dan Steenblock, trumpet.

Stunt-player of the concertina, Johnny Helget acquired the third concertina Hengel built. Here Frank Melmer supports him with trumpet and clarinet, Sarge Schroeder, dums and Leonard Hanson, bass horn.

Johnny Helget performs on two Hengels and one Pearl Queen concertina.

Karl Hartwich with a Star concertina at the age of 18 in his birthplace, Orion, Illinois, taken December 27, 1979.

The "Cliff Hermel Polka Party Band" features Marv Nissel with a Hengel. Richard Blomgren, tuba, Frank Melmer and Walt Siegmann, trumpets, Cliff Herml, drums, Carol Nissel, piano.

Cletus Schoen plays a Star with support from Carol Schoen, his wife, on banjo, and Butch and Cyril Schoen, percussion and banjo.

The "Dan Gruetzmacher Orchestra" of Wausau, Wisconsin features Dan's concertina performance with a Stradivarius, along with Jim Klinger on drums, Doug Bloom, bass horn, Don Artz, trumpet and Louis Zdrail, who excels on trumpet to render Bohemian style music.

The "Jeff Franta Band" featured Jeff with a variety of concertinas at age 16, though he began playing at the age of 8. The siblings in support include Brad Franta, 15, on bass, Brenda Franta, 17, drums, and Ricky Franta, 11, vocal. They work from home in Lafayette, Minnesota and draw inspiration from the talents of their grandfather, who played concertina with the John Fritschie Band, and their father, Dennis Franta, who also plays the concertina.

The "Merle Felling Band" of Sauk Centre, Minnesota, on a Hengel with support from Louie Schley on drums, Rueben Nathe, tuba, Bob Saulsbury, guitar and vocal and Dan Rassier, trumpet.

Dorine Hinnenkamp, known as the calm, cool princess of polkadom from Melrose, Minnesota, is one of the few female concertina players of note, here playing a Hengel concertina.

Tony and Betty Wolf with the "Deutschmeister Family Band" started in 1938 when Betty Arnold and Wolf were playing for other bands and decided to marry. Their own band was organized in 1958 with Tony playing concertina and Betty the piano. Soon it grew to include family members Arnold and Ambrose (Butch) on concertina, Michael, drums and Lisa, vocal. For years they relied on a Stradivarius concertina from the Bill Brown Distributing Company in New Ulm.

Appendix II — Album Covers

The "Revival Band" featuring Richard Hanzel, Guitar, Steven Skluzacek, trumpet, Mary Lynn Wolfe, Keyboard, Marty Weiers, Drums and Gary Pikal, a Hengel concertina. Pikal learned the concertina as a student of Jerry Minar.

John Check with a Patek concertina and The "Wisconsin Dutchmen" operated from 1547 Bismarck Avenue in Oshkosh, Wisconsin. Vocals were done by LeRoy Wolter, clarinet, David Marvin, reeds, Ray Wifler, baritone, Richart Altreuter and Don Hale, trumpet, and Neil Wilson, trombone. Tim Morrisey, played tuba, and Willie Zeamer, drums.

"Ernie Coopman and the Stagemen" of Mankato goes back to 1949 when at 16 Ernie Coopman started playing the concertina. In 1955 he joined Norm Wilke and the Little Fisherman Band, then in 1956 joined Bruno Randles and his Jolly Brewers, which he took over the next year. When his right hand was injured in 1967, he relinquished the concertina but was able to return in 1969. In 1973 he proceeded with the new Stagemen arrangement. Harvey Pagel plays bass and piano while Mike Sticha beats the drums. Stradivarius.

Ed Chesney played a Patek concertina with support from Bill Chesney on string bass. They offered Polish style, which they learned from their father, Alex Chesney, in northeast Minneapolis. For the most part they were popular in World War II and in the years following and played for the Polish National Convention when it was held in Minneapolis.

Brian Brueggen and the "Mississippi Valley Dutchmen" are based in Cashton, Wisconsin. In the Sylvester Liebl tradition, Brueggen plays a Hengel concertina supported by Phil Brueggen (his father) on trumpet, Nic Dunkel, trombone, Keith Reese, piano, Tony Kaminski, tuba, Bill Oelke, drums, and Tony Jorgenson, banjo.

Blanche Havel Zellmer plays the saxaphone for the "Waltz Kings" while Bill Busacker drums, Dale Korbel plays bass horn, Don Tupy, saxophone, Larry Novotny, vocals and Ambrose Kodet, a Hengel.

At Bill Brown Distributing Company, sometimes billed as the "World's Largest Concertina Company." A New Ulm mainstay for decades, the "Brown Boys" included not only the father by the name of Bill, but sons Billy, Jim, and John. They played Brown and Stradivarius concertinas.

Jim Busta with his Hengel and band thrive in a three-state area (Minnesota, Wisconsin and Iowa), fanning out from his base in Spring Grove, Minnesota where he is the superintendent of schools. His current talented asset is his daughter, Mollie, who plays a variety of instruments.

The "Bob Brenny Band" operated from Albany, Minnesota using a Stradivarius and support players Mary Struzyk, Louie Dinndorf and Bob Hathe.

→ 263

The Bill Bartusek Band began in 1968 with Bill using a Hengel supported by Jack Malecha, Al Rezac and Lenny Adamek.

Larry Olsen playing a Hengel, created a band with his father, Arnold, on drums, and his sister, Lisa, on piano.

Doug Dickover played his Hengel supported by Richard Blomgren on tuba, Roger Postal, banjo, and Carl Krueger, drums. On concertina duets Dickover was joined by Walter Kensy. On the wall behind the band are the words in German, "Lass doch die Sorgen zu Haus" — Leave your troubles at home.

The "Earl Schmidt Orchestra" shifted between Earl Schmidt of Cologne and Jerry Schuft [right] from Brownton, Minnesota. Thus at times it was the Jerry Schuft Band featuring Schuft on a Patek or a Hengel concertina.

Bill Czerniak and the Polka Soul Band usually featured the Star concertina. Bill's father, Joe Czerniak, taught him his Polish style, supported here by guest concertina players including his wife, Mary Lou Czerniak, Roger Juntunen and Jerry Zelazny, as well as Mike Nesgoda on drums, Jim Lampert, trumpet, Wayne Slowinski, and Paul Perfetti, trumpets, and Al Hansen, piano.

The five Zwack brothers feature Keith Zwack with his Echo concertina, Dave on tuba, Gary, saxophone, Paul, trumpet and Jim, drums. Keith composed "Marilyn's Waltz" for their mother and "Richard's Polka" for their father.

Roger Kubes of Montgomery, Minnesota played a Hengel for the songs recorded as "Polka Holiday," offering twelve original pieces witten by Father Robert E. Kapoun, the "Polka Padre," here playing the Wurlitzer 4300 organ.

Playing as the "Cliff Hermel Polka Party Band," Marv Nissel manipulates the Hengel concertina joined by Richard Blomgren on tuba, Frank Melmer, trumpet and sax, Walt Siegmann, trumpet, Cliff Hermal, drums and Carol Nissel, piano. For two decades the Hermels offered Gibbon Polka Days in Minnesota.

"Karl and the Country Dutchmen" offered this stunt photo of Karl Hartwich playing a Silberhorn (Lange) concertina, supported by Norma Hartwich with vocals, Joyce Cielecki, piano, Mike Cielecki, trumpet, Don Burghardt and Frank Melmer, trumpet, Bill Oekle, vocals, Kim Ristow, drums, and Rod Davies, tuba.

Appendix II — Album Covers

This album of "All-Star Concertina Solos" features Christy Hengel, who started his own band in 1947, playing from 1951-53 with the Six Fat Dutchmen, 1953-56 with Bruno Randles and from 1958-61 with the Sota Band. From 1965-73 he had his own band. Jerry Schuft played a Patek with Ivan Kahle and Earl Schmidt. Erwin Suess of Sleepy Eye operated his own band from 1969 to 2004 using a Hengel. Elmer Scheid started with John Fritsche, played with the Six Fat Dutchmen and Babe Wagner, and since 1951 with his own band. using a 1937 Patek.

The "Katzenjamers" of Madison Lake, Minnesota call this recording "Priming the Pump." Featured are Johnny Gag on a Patek concertina, Clete Frederick, drums, Der Cammack, tuba and Lowell Schreyer, banjo.

The "Marc Frana Band" from Charles City, Iowa features Marc with his Patek, Hengel and Gem Deluxe concertinas, and is supported by Nic Dunkel on trumpet, Tim Howland, drums and Merlin Bartz, tuba.

Featured on this Gibbon Ballroom No. 6 recording are New Ulm's Marv Nissel on a Hengel, Carol Nissel, keyboard and Cliff and Katie Hermel, then the ballroom owners.

Dale Pexa and the "Country Girls Band" features Dale Pexa on a Wolfe concertina, an instrument he has played since a teenager. Established in 1985, the band's recording jacket was created in 1986 in New Prague. His wife, Fran Pexa, plays keyboard and trombone, for which she won a state contest in her high school senior year. Assisting Pexa are his daughter, Fanny, on drums, son Dale, Jr., saxophone and piano, Bridget Wagner, drums and vocalist, Chris Peters, guitar, and Darcy Skluzacek, keyboard and saxophone.

The Six Fat Dutchmen band headed by Harold Loeffelmacher on the bass horn is supported here by Christy Hengel on a Patek concertina, LeRoy Dewanz, saxophone [glasses] and others.

Labeled "Concertina Holiday" by The Ray Dorschner "Rainbow Valley Dutchmen," are offerings by three concertina players: Ray Dorschner on the left, Ray Konkel, center and Randy Dorschner, right, all playing Hengel concertinas.

Bearing the title "Concertina Capers Plus Three," this album features from L-R: Gerald Kodet, Pat Fahey, Leo Johnson, Lowell Schreyer and Ambrose Kodet with a Hengel. The Kodet brothers came from Bechyn, Minnesota, having learned the concertina from their father, Adolph, who began playing a concertina in 1915. On this recording Gerald Kodet plays a Patek equipped with new reeds by Hengel in 1954.

Elmer Scheid appears on this jacket with his 1937 Patek concertina, rendering such numbers as Eddie's Waltz, Clairene Waltz and the Steirischer Ländler. Scheid has played for the Six Fat Dutchmen, Babe Wagner and with his own band since 1951.

Karl Hartwich offers this stunt photo entitled "Just Hangin' Around." On his album he plays the Policeman's Polka, Barre Mills Schottische and Libby's Ländler. He is playing a Hengel concertina.

Erwin Suess at the Glockenspiel in New Ulm is supported by his "Hoolerie Dutchmen." Playing a Stradivarius from his home in Eagle Lake, Minnesota, he was supported by his wife Monica on drums, Denise LeBert-Suess, piano, Duane Suess, vocals, Myron Muehlbauer, trumpet, Myron Wolf, saxophone and Jay Pattison, bass horn.

Christy Hengel offers a concertina concert including Elsie's Waltz, Ländler No. 20, and Old Man's Waltz, using Hengel three differently-keyed Hengels for this recording.

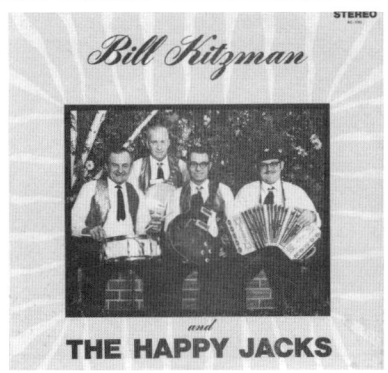
Bill Kitzman and "The Happy Jacks" from Moorhead, Minnesota feature Bill Kitzman on his Stradivarius supported by Herb Almer on guitar and vocals, Chet Bohn, banjo, Floyd Nelson, drums and Russ Paulson, saxophone.

Featuring all-time-great concertina players, this volume offers the likes of Elmer Scheid, Ray Konkol, Bill Brown, Dorine Hinnenkamp, Ray Dorschner, Ernie Coopmann and others.

Bill Brown of New Ulm offers Polka Town Favorites featuring Charlie Braunreiter on Star concertina.

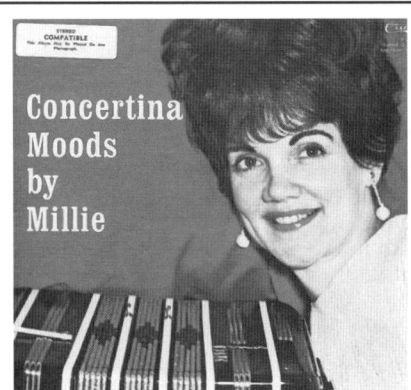
Concertina artist Millie Kaminski of Milwaukee started playing the concertina at the age of 15 and became adept at many styles for concertina, including Dutchman, due to her German descent. She nearly always played a Star.

This album contains a mixture of Polish, German and Bohemian styles played by 15 concertina artists. Pictured are Loren Huepenbecker, Jr., Hank Zelazny, Dale Benadek, Peter M. Mrozinski, Keith Zwack, Peter P. Mrozinski, Dave Sowada, Gordon Lehrke, Jerry Schuft, Billy Bartusek, Bruce Libby, Ernie Mazurek, Doug Dickover and Lavain "Slim" Maser.

The Dan Sturza Band comes from Owatonna, Minnesota. Playing since the mid-1970s, Dan is joined on his Hengel by sister Debbie Burnham on guitar, Verlin Nelson, drums, Paul Langer, tuba, and others.

Appendix II — Album Covers

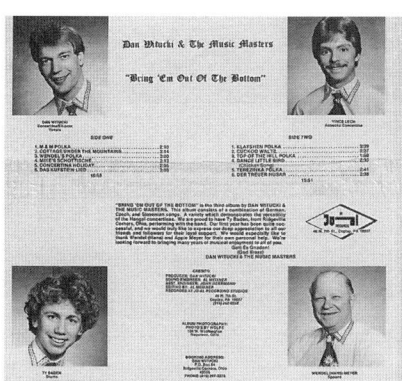

On this album, Dan Witucki and the "Music Masters Band" is featured by Dan, on a Hengel concertina and vocals, Vince Lech, concertina, Ty Baden, drums and Wendel Meyer. Witucki has played from Minnesota, Ohio, Disneyland in Orlando, and elsewhere.

Tony and Betty Wolf from St. Joseph, Minnesota led the Deutschmeisters Band, which began operations in 1954. He played the Arno Arnold concertina, she the piano with vocals broadcast over Radio Station KASM in Albany. Son Arnie joined them playing concertina, drums and bass. For a time they played as the "Magic Hearts" but later expanded to a 7-piece group and changed their name by means of a radio contest to "Deutschmeisters."

Playing an Arno Arnold concertina, Tony Wolf enjoys the assistance of wife Betty and five others to win the Minnesota Ballroom Operators award of 1963.

Booking at the time of this recording from his home on rural route 2, Hanska, Minnesota, Erwin Suess plays a Stradivarius. Born August 2, 1927, he organized the Hoolerie Dutchmen Band in April, 1969. His support musicians are his wife on drums, son Duane Suess on guitar and piano plus vocals, Arley Rolloff on clarinet and saxophone, Hilary Mohr on clarinet, John Henle on trumpet and Ron Baumbach on tuba.

Born at Sleepy Eye in 1927, Erwin married Monica Spaeth of Morgan in 1947. In 1949 they moved to their own farm near Hanska. From 1968-1976 Erwin hauled feed for Farmland Industries in Mankato and subsequently worked on their order desk. Of late they live in North Mankato. Here Myron Wolf plays the saxophone, Jay Pattison, bass horn, and Myron Muehlbauer, trumpet, Suess, a Hengel.

On this recording, Cliff Hermel drums while Johnny Helget plays the Hengel concertina for the Gibbon Polka Day festival at the Gibbon Ballroom. Helget taught the concertina for Christy Hengel and plays one for this recording.

Li'l Wally [Walter E. Jagiello] of Chicago plays the drums and the Star concertina. For this recording in the middle of the jacket is John Check who plays the concertina in a Bavarian hat, a style of music that honored Li'l Wally.

Randy Dorschner, the eldest son of Ray Dorschner and his Rainbow Valley Dutchmen, operates from his music store in Appleton, Wisconsin where he received his B.A. degree in music from UW-Oshkosh. He is supported playing his Castiglione concertina for this recording by Clayton Hopfensperger, Carl Lorens, and others.

Rick Gansen performs on a Star concertina procured from Brown's Music Store in New Ulm. He is assisted by his sisters, Debbie and Shelley, to make up the "Red Birds Band."

→ 267

Rodney Ristow from Alma, Wisconsin made up his "Swiss Girls Band" with the aid of Kathy Klevgard of Gilmanton playing trumpet, Heidi Heike from Mondovi also on trumpet, Susie Schmitt from Fountain City, saxophone, and Arlene Killian from Winona, Minnesota, drums. Daughter Kim soon became an all-around assistant. Ristow played a Hengel

Whoopee John Wilfahrt pioneered using the concertina for the old time bands of Minnesota. While he started as a child on the accordion, he early on switched to the concertina and never again took up an accordion. Seen here in a photo from 1937 playing for Radio WTCN in Minneapolis are L-R: Harold Anderson, Donald Rice, Ted Hofmeister, Otto Hofmeister, Hugo Hofmeister, Pat Wilfahrt, Whoopee John, with a Pearl Queen, and Edna Istel.

Butch Wolf, then of Cold Spring, Minnesota, playing a Stradivarius for which his parents, Toni and Betty Wolf, once were dealers in tandem with Pat Watters. Before his untimely death, Butch [Ambose] was also a concertina salesman. Supporting him were Kevin Motschke of St. Joseph and Mike Janey of St. Cloud.

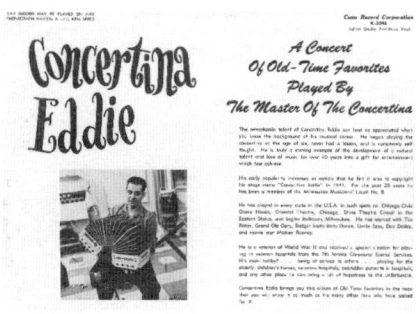

Concertina Eddie Rickert began playing the concertina at the age of six. Without ever taking a lession, he became so competent and popular that his name "Concertina Eddie" is copyrighted. A member of the Milwaukee Musicians Local No. 8, Eddie played concertina in every state in the Union. He is seen here with a Star.

The "Country Polkateers," headed by Gilly Maus, played at the Gibbon Polka Days in 1977 and immediately thereafter recorded this, their first album. Their Pierz, Minnesota musicians included Gilly and Joyce Maus who farm near Pierz. Gilly plays a Hengel, Kevin Gwost, clarinet, John Rauch, trumpet and tuba, and Gordy Austin, drums.

The Dick Rodgers [Richard Rodziczak] Band hailed from Pulaski, Wisconsin from whence Rodgers rendered his Polish style performances on the Stradivarius concertina for a half century. Playing the accordion in the upper left-hand corner is Dick Metko who from 1958 performed frequently with Rodgers. For 23 years, Rodgers' band performed on WBAY and on WLUK-TV, which for a time was carried by 17 stations in the Midwest.

Playing the concertina for the "Edel's Band" is Ray Edel, who was born and raised in Montgomery, Minnesota but moved later to Owatonna. He bought his first concertina at the age of 21 and by the age of 28 was running his own band, playing for weddings and anniversaries. Other members of the band for this recording include Margie Deml, Kurth Raichle, Leo Seykora, and Brian Raichle. With a Royal built by Slim Maser, Ray renders some of the numbers in their original Czech language.

Ernie Mazurek flexes his Gem Deluxe concertina for the "White Eagle Concertina Band," which operated from its Twin Cities base in Anoka, Minnesota. A Gem Deluxe is an Italian-built instrument in the family of Stradivarius, Grand, Castiglione and others. Supporting him are David Kile on saxophone, Frank Swaser, banjo, Dennis McDonough, drums, Jess Gordon, bass guitar, and Verlee Klimek, violin.

On this jacket Ernie Stumpf plays his Patek concertina. Born on a farm near Pierz, Minnesota, Stumpf loved old time music and dreamed of playing it on the concertina. In 1976 he purchased his first concertina from Jerry Minar and took a few lessons. Soon he formed his own band, which operated out of Belle Plaine, Minnesota. Support musicians included Donna Buckentine on drums, LaVerne McMillan, guitar and banjo, Gus Makovsky and Cliff Rasmussen, bass horn.

Appendix II — Album Covers

Gil Steil, by day a real estate agent in Richmond, Minnesota, evenings entertained dancers and partygoers in the wider St. Cloud region. At times with nine- and eleven-piece bands, he also played solo on his 1964 Hengel concertina. For several years Steil was a regional dealer for the Hengel concertina. Eventually he sold his band to Ray Drontel.

The Hayseeds band from Holdingford, Minnesota have entertained audiences all across Minnesota, using two concertinas played by Renee and Connie Fussy and supported by Diane Fussy on trumpet and Mark Fussy, drums.

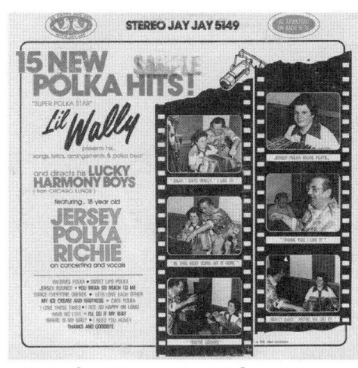

Lil Wally [Walter E. Jagiello], was born in Chicago August 1, 1930 to parents from near Zakopane in southern Poland. He recorded for Columbia Records beginning in 1949 and earned countless awards. He has rendered hundreds of numbers in Polish style but is versatile on related concertina numbers, using a Star concertina.

The "Nite Lites Band" features concertina artist Kevin Latzig of Winsted, Minnesota, using a Hengel. He is supported by Al Murphy and Ron Hlavka, on trumpets, Larry Dostal, drums and Mark Guggemos, bass guitar.

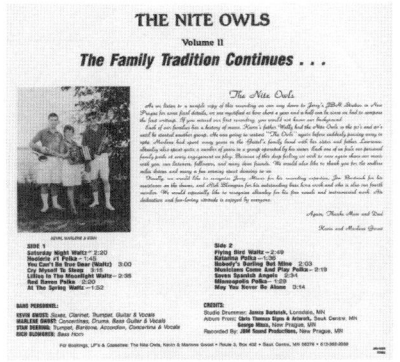

The "Nite Owls" are led by Kevin Gwost who plays saxophone and clarinet and Marlene Gwost, Star and Arnold concertinas. Supporting them are Stan Deering on trumpet and sometimes also the concertina, and Rich Blomgren, bass horn. They reside in Sauk Centre, Minnesota.

From St. Joseph, Minnesota came the Northern Lites, featuring especially Andy Stangler on one of his two Hengel and three Stradivarius concertinas, assisted by Jim Janochoski, drums and vocal and Phil Schreifels, bass guitar.

Renata Romanek plays a Star concertina for her band called "Girls, Girls, Girls," which is widely recognized as the polka band composed of an all-female staff. Supporting her are Cherie Ulovi on trumpet, Carmen Kubis, drums and vocals, Lisa Kloskowski, bass guitar and Heidi Drobnick, the fiddle. Their home base is Cloquet, Minnesota.

The Ridgeland Dutchmen are led today by Gary Brueggen. Begun in 1947 by Herman Brueggen, his father and the drummer, the band had members who were his children. When Herman died in 1971, the band passed to Philip and Willard Brueggen with support from Brueggen family members: Will on bass horn, Roger, drums, Harry, guitar and Philip, lead trumpet. Gary today ranks among the top living concertina players.

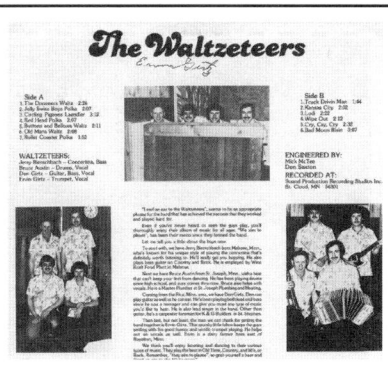

The Waltzeteers are managed by Jerry Bierschbach playing a Hengel or Stradivarius. Formerly from Long Prairie and then Melrose, Bierschbach now lives in Albany, Minnesota. Ervin Girtz helped bring the band together with Don Girtz on guitar and Bruce Austin, on drums.

→ 269

The History of the Chemnitzer Concertina

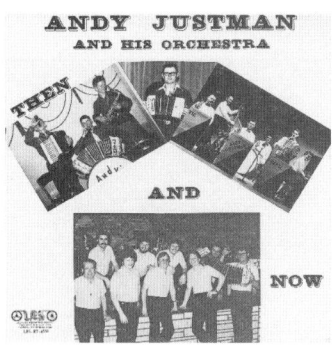

Andy Justmann and his Orchestra began playing in 1948 from his base in Waupaca, Wisconsin. At first, Carol Ehlers played piano accordion, Wilbert Beck, drums and Andy the concertina. By the 1980s, when this disk was recorded, it was an 8-piece band with Stephen Speidel on trumpet, Gary Zastrow on trumpet, Dick Justmann on drums, Charles Justmann on tuba, Francis Kempfer and Tom Justmann on saxophone, Dave Justmann on clarinet and Andy Justmann with Dwayne Fenske on Hengel concertinas.

Established in 1946 by two brothers, the Babe Wagner Band featured Ellsworth [Babe] and Virgil [Swede] Wagner, both brilliant musicians. Following the untimely death of "Babe" in 1949, the band carried on under "Swede." Don Klossner played Hengel #1 concertina with Swede Wagner on trumpet. The band always built its music around the concertina.

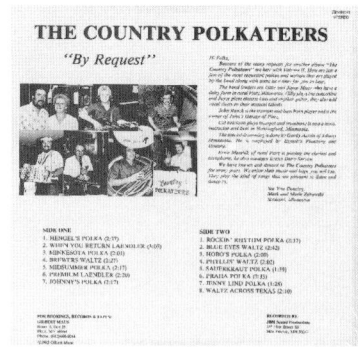

The Country Pollkateers are led by Gilly and Joyce Maus, dairy farmers from Pierz, Minnesota. Gilly plays the Hengel concertina, supported by his wife, Joyce on electric bass, John Rauch on trumpet and bass horn, Cal Erickson on trumpet and trombone, Gordy Austin on drums and Ernie Marshik on clarinet.

The "Czech Lites" of Montgomery, Minnesota feature Gary Korbel, a student of Jerry Minar, on a Hengel concertina, Jim Reeder on trumpet, Mark Trcka on drums and Lynn Storm on guitar.

Todd and Mark Dobesenski of Cloquet, Minnesota with their Cavaliers offer a Polka Portrait in Polish-style renderings. Todd plays a Star concertina, with Mark on bass and vocals, Chuck Burak on drums, Reg Lally on trumpet and Flügelhorn, Kevin Gran on trumpet and Lee Ruotsi on violin.

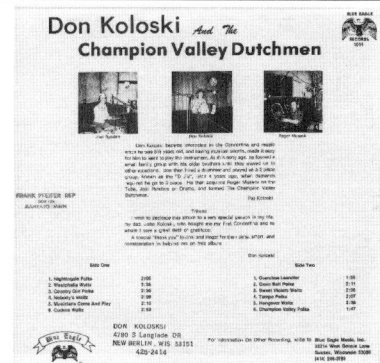

Don Koloski and the "Champion Valley Dutchmen" of New Berlin, Wisconsin feature Don on a Hengel concertina, Roger Musack on tuba, Joel Rynders on drums.

Don Morris and his Jolly Germans hail from New Ulm, Minnesota. Playing a Hengel concertina was Jerry Schmidt from New Ulm — Hanska, with John Henle on trumpet, Leonard Sellner on bass horn, Don Dewanz on clarinet and saxophone and Alfred Schroeder on drums.

The "Elmer Scheid Band" wished to be known as the King of Hoolerie. Elmer plays his Patek concertina in a live dance hall recording executed June 18, 1960 in the National Guard Armory, New Ulm, Minnesota.

From Belle Plaine, Minnesota Ernie Stumpf offers the album "Let's Dance Tonight" with a Hengel concertina, recorded in 1987.

Appendix II — Album Covers

The "Ivan Kahle Band" pictured here in 1971 offered these musicians — First Row: Ray Dibbert, Jerry Kahle, Ivan Kahle and Jerry Minar playing an Echo concertina. In the Back Row are Floyd Vikla and Frank Kubes, the father of Roger Kubes.

Walter [Lil Wally] Jagiello with his band offered expert Polish-style numbers on a Star Streamline concertina.

Jim Lovett and the Polka Stars offer the album "Let the Sun Shine In" with Lovett of Harrisburg, South Dakota on a Star concertina, Dan Slaba on drums, Gene Wingert on guitar, and Joan Olson on vocals.

Joe Tomaszewski and his Northeasterners offer Polish-style rhythms from their Twin Cities base, using a Star concertina.

Karl Hartwich, Brian Brueggen and Marty Nachreiner play Hengel concertinas on this album recorded when Karl was still booking jobs from Orion, Illinois or from Cochrane, Wisconsin. Additional players on the album include Keith Reese on piano, Kim Ristow on drums, Holly Verbeke also on drums and Doug Young on tuba. The cartoon figures depict Hartwich on the left and Brueggen on the right, distant blood cousins, close musical relatives.

The "Leon Helget Band" [Leon featured here with a Hengel concertina in caricature] books from Sleepy Eye, Minnesota. He is supported by Mike Moldan on trumpet, Bob Reid on trombone, Mark Isackson on saxophone, Jerry Haala on bass guitar, Lawrence Heiderscheidt on guitar and Clete Krzmarzick on drums.

The "Litt'l Fishermen" led by Roy Haag operated from Houston, Texas using a gathering of Bohemian and German musicians. Among them were Larry Schünemann on a Hengel concertina, Mark Voges on trombone, Roy Haag on trumpet, Russell Koehler on tenor saxophone, Alfred Pavlicek on trumpet, Victor Caka on clarinet and Theresa Bohac Haag on accordion and piano.

From Grafton, Wisconsin came the orchestra known as Little Johnny. Playing a Star concertina was John Wornardt with Ron Carr on saxophone, Jim Vollmer on clarinet and saxophone, Lou Allen on bass horn, Jim Martin on trumpet, Don Vosseteig on trumpet and Wayne Ohm on drums.

Marv Nissel of New Ulm has three Hengel concertinas and one Pearl Queen along with an A-Flat Patek with Friedl reeds. Carol Nissel, his wife, plays keyboard, Lori the concertina, Jodi Nissel the keyboard and piano. Dale Tolk plays trumpet, Richard Roepke, trumpet, Clarence Salaba, trumpet and Cliff Herman, drums.

→ 271

The History of the Chemnitzer Concertina

Math Sladky and his band of Waverly, Nebraska on this record plays a Stradivarius to enrich traditional Czech numbers. Support personnel include Emil Korbelik on trombone, Don Horacek on tuba, Leonard Chlup on trumpet and Flügelhorn, Gawaine Dvorak on accordion or concertina. Al Welsch plays the banjo and Bob Novotny the drums.

Ernie Mazurek and the "White Eagle Concertina Band" booked jobs from Anoka, Minnesota. A Polish-style entertainer, Mazurek here plays a Gem Deluxe concertina with support from Frank Swasser on banjo, Verlee Klimek on violin, Dale Gordon on guitar, Dave Kile on saxophone and Craig Ebel on drums. Norman Hall plays a Brown buttontina.

Brian and the Mississippi Valley Dutchmen of Cashton, Wisconsin feature Brian with his Hengel concertina, Phil Brueggen on trumpet, Nick Dunkel on trumpet and trombone, Laurie Solberg on piano, Bill Oelke on drums, Tony Kaminski on tuba and Tony Jorgenson on banjo.

"The New Jolly Swiss Boys" are the successors to Syl Liebl's band, which retired in 1984, resulting in this 1986 recording. Kevin Liss, originally from Stevens Point, Wisconsin, plays the concertina augmented by Syl Liebl, Sr. and Syl Liebl, Jr.'s wife, Marce, and Syl's daughter, Lorie. Support comes from Liebl daughter, Carol Seebauer, Bob Mitchel, Tom Langren, Bernice Celius and Frank Seebauer.

Bill Landowski from Brownsville, Wisconsin plays the Hengel concertina for the New Village Brass with support from players left to right: Ron Rusch, Scott Scheberl, Gary Kamrath, Karl Rusch, Ted Nevis, Jim Vollmer and Landowski on concertina.

Twin Concertinas -- means Peter and Paul Wendinger, today 40 years on stage, but here featured as young musicians with Hengel concertinas. Supporting musicians included at this time Francis Sellner on bass horn, Stan Draeger on drums and Frank Lindmeyer on banjo.

From Hatley, Wisconsin come the "Polka Sonics" led by Alan Budleski playing a Star concertina in a 1984 Polish-style recording. He is supported by Al Niewiadomski on trumpet, Mike Kubowski on guitar and vocals, Mike Szymkowiak on trumpet and Flügelhorn, Gary Soczka on drums and Ken Dunaj on piano accordion.

The "Ray Konkol Band" of Stevens Point, Wisconsin prided itself in offering many concertina solos by Ray Konkol, as shown in this early recording with a Hengel concertina.

Sylvester Liebl exhibits his Hengel concertina with performances by his Jolly Swiss Boys. Sometimes credited with inventing the "hobo style," Liebl signed a contract to play for Radio Station WKTY in La Crosse in 1961 and continued for a long run entertaining the Coulee region with his "Radio Favorites," the title of this record.

Index

Adam and the Jolly Jammers	217
Alex, Michael	96, 123
Photos of	94
Pineapple style of	122
Alfred Arnold Concertina and Bandonion Works	5, 197
Advertisement for (with picture)	9, 12
Distinguishing features of concertinas	12
Growth in popularity of	16
Logos	12
Map of geographical location	13
Photo of advertisement	5
Photo of concertina	13
Photos of (circa 1900 and 2002)	9
Publicity of Weltmeister (Pioneer Press)	98
South American distribution	16
Succession within family	15
Subdivision into different firms, dissolution	25
Altenburg, Art	
Photo of (also Art Altenburg's Concertina Bar)	95
Alinski, Saul	49
Arent, Raymond (1915-2004)	221-222
Photo of	222
Arnold, Alfred	22 ff., 157
Bandonion	175
French style	9
Pictures	9, 12, 175
Arnold, Arno (and company)	15, 99
Advertisement for	97
American distribution by	15
Photos of concertinas, etc.	28, 109, 198
Photo of Watters Distributing Co. ad	187
Slimline concertina, Photo of	201
Son of Ernst	15
Sonatone	155
Advertisement for	158
Arnold, Ernst	176
Scheller's *Symphonetta-Schule*	180
Avsenik, Slavko	193
Band, Alfred (1845-1923; son of Heinrich Band)	8
Band, Heinrich (1821-1860)	176
Death of	8
Inventor of Bandonion	3
Picture of	3
Bandonion Treffen	232
Bandwagon Show	
Photo from	162, 163
Bank, Vern C.	154
Barash, Don	
Photo of	115
Barta, Marion	
Photo of	104
Bässler, Ernst	7
Concertina distribution in U.S.	20
Christy Hengel and	85
Bässler, Karl	20
Becker, Harvey	205
Bergstrom, Harvey	
Photo of/biography	236
Berlioz, Hector	
Comment on concertina	232
Bernhardt, John	65, 66, 74
Photo of	73
Bertrand, Eugene	
Photo of	209
Bierschbach, Jerry	213
Photo of/biography	235
Bill Brown Music Store	
Brown Concertina Method	183
Frank J. Converse Deluxe Concertina Book	183
Birmingham, Merton	137
Birnstock, Gerhard	26
Black, Darwin J.	226
Black, Ed-Vern	92, 93
Photo of	226
Blazonczyk, Eddie	168, 229
Son Eddie Jr.	229
Blim, Charles J.	52
Father-son team	202
Bolster, John	160
John Bolster's Independent Accordion Service	99
Bondowski, John	184
Borgstahl, Wayne	94
Braunreiter, Charles (Charlie)	
Photo of	234
Brothers Dix	95

Brown, Richard		Importance to concertina market distribution	17
Photo of	172	Concertina Bowl	229
Brown, William W.	159, 184	Advertisement for	224
Assistants to	172	Founders	224, 229
Induction into Hall of Fame	172	List of performers for	233
Involvement in bands	172	Concertina clubs (bands, etc...)	27
Brown's Music and Distributing Company	100, 114, 116, 117, 124, 151, 159, 161, 163	43rd Street Concertina Club	167
		A.E. Boissoneault Band	137
Advertisements for	159	Alfred Schultz Band	135
Buttontina	120	Alpine Valley Concertina Club	166
Concertina promotion and	172	Andy Justmann Orchestra	225
Location	159	Babe Wagner Band	90
Brueggen, Brian	93, 101, 102	Klossner, Don and	90
Photos of	222	Sale of Hengel concertina to Butch Wolf	90
Brueggen, Gary	101, 212, 225	Billy Bartusek Band	212
Photo of	227	Blanche Zellmer and the Waltz Kings	221
Brueggen, Herman	225	Bob Brenny Band	215, 223
Brueggen, Roger	225	Bohemian-American Concertina Association of Chicago	125, 140, 166
Bush, George	102		
Business relations		Photo of	168
Bussmen, Harlan 167		Bohemian Brothers Concertina Band	229
Georgi/Vitak/Elsnic, Kodet/Minar	124	Brad, Brenda, Ricky, and Jeff Franta Band	213
Busta, Jim	227	Brian's Mississippi Valley Dutchmen	222, 228, 229
Photo of	227	Bruce Bradley Accordion Band	217
Busta, Mollie	227	Buffalo Concertina Club	167, 200-201
Photo of	219, 222	Central Wisconsin Concertina Club	166
Bzdok, LaVerne	215	Photo of	138
C.A. Wunderlich Company	165	Charles E. Scherzer group	133, 134
C.W. Meinel Company	7	Chemnitz Hilbersdorf Verein	26
Advertisement for	7	Chemnitz-Borna	26
Carlson, Joseph		Chicago Concertina Club	28, 61
Photo of/biography	235	Advertisement for	139
Check (Czech), John	93, 99, 162, 171	Photo of	200
Band members	165	Cicero Concertina Club	200
Donations by	171	Clarion Concertina Club	125, 140, 142, 166
Photo of	165, 208	Cletus Goblirsch Band	221
Chicago Stockyards	44, 46, 47	Concertina Youth Orchestra, Gelnau	23
Photos of	46	Country Gentlemen	220
Upton Sinclair's *The Jungle*	49	Craig Ebel and the Light Weights	230
Chlan, Alvin	93	Czech-American Concertina Band	28
Photo of (with Ambrose Kodet and Gordon J. Prochaska)	217	Czech Area Concertina Club	125
		Photo of	126
Chlan, Timothy		Dale Pexa Band	
Photo of	167, 232	Photo of	129
Chord chart	189	Des Plaines Concertina Club	164
Clinton, William Jefferson	113	Deutches Konzertina und Bandonion Bund	19
Columbian Exhibition, 1893	10, 42-43	Deutsche Tonkünstler-Zeitung	27

Index

Earl Schmidt and Jerry Schuft Orchestra	154, 211
Eddie Blazonczyk and the Versatones	229
Edward's Fishermen Band	228
Elmer Bartusek Band	215
Emil Berkhahn Concertina Band	135
Ernie Coopman Band	117, 213
Erwin Suess Hoolerie Band	218
Frank's Comedians	140
Frank Kinayski Band	212
Garnett Schlottman Band	222
German-Bohemian Whoopee John Band	209
Good Time Dutchmen	236
Good Times Concertina Club	166, 168
H. C. Germania Concertina Club	17
Henry Bobzien Band	140
Ivan Kahle Band	113, 114, 116, 153, 211, 218
Photo of	113
Jerry Schuft Orchestra	210
Jim Busta Band	227
Joe Tomaszewski Polka Band	99
John C. Scharbach Peppy Three Concertina Orchestra	137
Jolly Brewers	117, 213
Jolly Coppersmiths	214
Jolly Czechs Orchestra	214
Jolly Dutchmen	220
Jolly Gentlemen	160
Dan Gruetzmacher Orchestra	160
Jolly Germans Band	101, 104
Jolly Swiss Boys	101, 228
Jolly Jammers	217
Jolly Swiss Girls	153
Karl Hartwich Country Dutchmen Band	227-228
Kewaunee Federation of Musicians	154
Larry Olsen Band	217
Larry Rysavy Concertina Band	215
Lenny's Concertina Band	223
Leon Olsen Band	217
Lester Schuft Band	153
Little Fishermen Band	213, 218
Los Angeles Concertina Club	155
Malek's Fishermen Band	227-228
Marv Herzog Band	214
Marv Nissel Band	211, 217
Math Sladky Band	207
Melrose Clown Band	172
Michigan Concertina Association	166
Milwaukee Concertina Circle Club	28, 166
Advertisement for	139
Milwaukee Concertina Club (and members)	140
Photo of	138
Mitross Family Orchestra	133
Mrozinski Brothers "Aleatoric Ensemble"	99
Musik Verein Frohsinn	140
New Jolly Swiss Boys Orchestra	228
New Prague Concertina Club	
Photo of	116
Niclai Wekseth Band	135
Northern Stars Band	215
North Star Concertina Club	71
Otto C. Rettke S & R Concertina Orchestra	135
Photo of club in Chemnitz-Furth	18
Photo of Harmonikaklub, Chemnitz	19
Photo of Konzertina-Klub Chemnitz-Markersdorf	26
Photo of Patek Concertina Club of Chicago	53
Photos of	44
Photos of German Concertina Bands/Players	29 ff.
Picture of	17
Pittsburgh Concertina Club	164
Polka Beats	220
Polka Rhythms Band	212
Popularization of concertina through	21
Prochaska's Little Fisherman Band	93
Rainbow Valley Dutchmen	65, 225
Ray Dorschner Rainbow Valley Dutchmen	155
Ray Konkol Band	223, 225
Renata & Girls	171
Renata Romanek Band "Girls, Girls, Girls"	210
Reno Concertina Club	167
Ridgeland Dutchmen Band	225
Riverside Dutchmen	153
St. Joseph (Joe) Concertina Club	166, 169
Photo of	169
Sheratons Band	221
Silver Tone Melodians	140
Six Fat Dutchmen	85, 153, 156
Members	207
Slocum Lake Trio Concertina Orchestra	137
Star Concertina Club	166
TNT Band	220
The Classics	205, 230
Thelemann Family Band	215
Tony Wolf and the Deutschmeisters	154, 158

Village Concertina Band	112
Photo of and advertisement for	111
Vince Sandhurst Concertina Band	220
W. C. Oldenburg Concertina Orchestra	134
Waltzateers	213
Wee Willie Band	212
Photo of	211
Wisconsin Dutchmen	165
Youth group	37
Zims Novelty Concertina Orchestra	137
Concertina dealers	41 ff.
Pertinent maps	47, 48
Concertina export	5-6
C. G. Schuster, Jr. Company	6
Importance of Waldheim	17
Pertinent maps	10, 11
Problems for Germany	6
Rockhausen, Carl-Ernst Louis	6
To South America	5
To the United States	5
Importance of Carlsfeld to	26
Concertina fingering charts	180-181
Coopman, Ernie	117, 154, 221
Death of	213
Photo of	103
Czerniak, Joseph	99, 171, 184, 220, 230
Joe Czerniak's Duluth School of Music	100
List of students	206
Czerniak, William	99, 171, 184, 206, 207, 230
Bill Czerniak's Concertina Band	99-100
Death of	206
Dahmen, Dale	220
Dallape Accordion Company	93
DeWanz, LeRoy (Silvers)	155
DeWitz, Irving	164, 184
DeWitz Music Store	100, 164
Photo of (with daughter)	166
Dickover, Douglas	73, 78
Dietz, Jon	122
Photo of/biography	236
Dietzel, John	134
Dobozenski, Todd	206
Brothers Jeff and Jim	206
Doell, Eldred	
Photo of	151, 226
Dolge, Alfred	10
Dolge Company	12
Successor of Zimmermann	10
Domeier, Dennis	
Photo of	234
Domeier, Emil "Dumphy"	205
"Hoolerie"	205
Dorschner, Larry	65, 91
Building Hengel's house	124
Photo of	103
Dorschner, Randy	
Dorschner Music Service	225
Photo of	151, 210
Dorschner, Ray	65, 153, 225
Dose, Kenneth	
Photo of	224
Dostal, Jerry	214
Bio of	214
Doug's Music Shop	211
Durenberger, David (Dave)	102
Duane Pichelman Enterprises	162
Concertina Day	162
Dvorak, Gawaine	207
Ebel, Craig	221, 229
Elsnic, Joseph P.	45, 49, 97, 149
Engel, Herman	142
Entertainment Bits	202 ff.
Editor Doris Pease	204
President Lee Hens	202
Ewald, Paul	87, 88
Federated Teachers Service Corporation	159
Felling, Merle	220
Fenske, Art	214
Filipczak, John	206, 230
Photo of	205
Filipiak, Adrian	
Photo of	226
Fischer, Joseph	142
Graphic of manual	182
National Self Teacher for Concertina	180
Fischer, Paul	
Concertina of	24
Construction workshop of	24
Photo of	24
Fischer, Wenzel	145, 211, 217
Photo of	145

Index

Flor, LeRoy
    Photo of   223
Foegen, Norbert
    Photo of/biography   235
Friedl, John (1873-1948)   52, 87-88, 94, 97, 123, 124, 150
    Grandson John Schnittker   124
    Graphic of social security card for   86
    Photos of reed plates   87
    Photo of, with daughter Elsie   87
    Photo of, with wife   86, 87
G. S. (George Servatius) Music Service
Gag, John (Johnny)   217-218
    Photo of   216
Gagnon, Thomas (Tom)
    Photo of   218
Garroway, Dave   156
Georgi, Otto E.   41 ff., 142, 193
    Arrival in Chicago   41
    As supplier for Kadlubowski   62
    Columbia Records   193
    Death notice   45
    Graphic of business card for   54
    Gross Avenue (in Chicago)   44
    Name change to McDowell   45, 47, 48
    Whiskey Point   48, 49
    Photo of   41
    Photo of father   41
    Photos of "Pearl King" concertina and internal
        trademark   54
    Wife Anna S.   46
Georgi & Vitak   44
    Photo of Lange concertina   49
Gibbon Ballroom   152
    Photo of   152
Ginn, Richard (Dick)   217
Glass Brothers (of Brunndöbra)   58, 100
    Photos of nameplate and concertinas   63
Glass Family   62 ff.
Glier, J. W.   1
Goblirsch, Cletus and Dolores
    Photo of   219
    Photo of Cletus Goblirsch Band   221
Goetsch Music   100
Goetzinger, Thomas (Tom)   217
Gottfried, John   137
Graham-Lane Music   100
Griessbacher, Carl   162

Gruetzmacher, Daniel   96, 100, 184
    Gruetzmacher Concertina Sales   171
    Photos of   160, 199
    Photo with wife   157
Gut Ton Zeitung   19
    Retailers and distributors   19-20
Gwost, Marlene Gettel
    Photo of/biography   236
Handlung Musikalischer Instrumente von C. F. Uhlig   2
Hanson, Bernard   94
Hanson, Gordon   94
Harthenhauer, Uwe   26
Hartwich, Karl   92, 102, 220-221
    Karl Hartwich and his Country Dutchmen   101
    Photo of   219
    Photo with Pete Wendinger   206
    Rosewood frame concertina   122
    Smithsonian Folklife Festival   221
Havlicek, Edward   140
Hebaus, George   72
    Harrington, Helmich   72
    Picture of   71
Helget, John (Johnny)   93, 153, 207, 212
    Photo of   103
Helget, Leon
    Photo of   234
Helget, William   84
Hengel, Christian (Christy)   78, 80 ff., 119, 123
    Accordiontina   204-205
        Photo of   204, 205, 208
    Advertisements for   90, 95, 99, 150
    Contemporary Elmer Scheid   84, 100, 102, 153, 154, 221, 234
        Photo of   103
    Early contact with concertina   82
    Family of   80-81
        Brother-in-law Michael Grausam   89-90, 102
        Cousin Lawrence Turbes   82
        Photo of Mike Turbes   83
        Photos of   81, 85, 88, 90, 208
        Uncle Michael Macht   83
    Injury   83
    List of concertina owners (bands, etc...)   103
    Name change   86
    Name plates   101
    Nissel Brothers   86
    Photos of interview with Charles Kuralt   102

Photo with friends	82
Photos with Minars	121
Tuning work for Scheid	86
Kahle, Roman	86
Zwack, Patrick	86
Wife Valeria "Josie" Runnerstrom	94
Henrichs, Warren	143
Hermann, Butch E.	93
Hermann, Ed	192
Hermel, Cliff	204, 209
Photo of (with wife Katie)	152
Hernandy, John	140
Herzog, Marv	207
Hlavac, William (Bill)	122, 167
Photo of	121
Hohner, Mathias	1, 6, 43
Photo of concertina	198
Hölz, George	134
Höselbarth, Johann Gottlieb	16, 18
Hrica, George	163, 164, 181, 184, 200
Photo of	201
Prototypes for MIDI	182
Italian-American Accordion Company	148
Jacobs (Jakobowski), Henry (Hank)	69, 202
Photo of	69
Slide rule and	155, 194
Jagiello, Li'l Wally	
Famous concertina players and	200
Jilek, Brian	124
Photo with Minar	122
Jobst, Kurt	7
Photo of concertina	7, 20
John Deere Days	207
John Jastnski Music Company	50
Jugel, Siegfried	37
Kadlubowski, Walter, Jr.	
Photo of	64
Kadlubowski, Walter Sr.	61, 63, 64, 142, 148, 150, 162
Kalina, Roman	
Photo of	104
Kaminski, Mildred ("Concertina Millie")	201
Photo of	201
Karpek, Andrew	64, 95
Assistant George Pivnoff	67
Karpek Accordion Manufacturing Company	64, 67, 95, 100, 155, 202, 204
Photo of	68
Photo of former building site	68
Son George	202
Karrousel concertina	68
Photo of	68
Kesting Music Company	52, 96, 100, 116
Advertisement for	114
Royal concertinas	114, 115
King, Bernard and Barney	168
King, Max (Ervin Kuczynski)	202
Kreis, Ed	73
Klossner, Donald K. (Donnie)	223
Bio of	223
Photo of	104, 223
Kodet, Ambrose	93, 94, 100, 122, 123, 124, 151, 184, 192, 207, 218
Photo of	217
Photo of father and uncles	228
Kodet, Roger	153
Konkol, Ray	154
Bio of	223
Photo of	103, 225
Krulikoski, Leonard	109, 110, 154, 184, 207
Photo of	104
Krzmarzick, Melvin	86
Photo of (with Arlie Rolloff)	91
Work with Italian reeds	92
Kubes, Roger	113
Kuczynski, Paul	137
Kukacka, Louis	112
Kummer, John	52, 87, 88, 93, 123, 150
Photo of	84, 91
Kunz, Al J.	155
Kusserow, Ernst	17
Lamal, Prosper	43
Lange, Darlene and John	230-231
John, bio of	230
Photo of	226
Lange, Friedrich Anton	4 ff., 197
Death notice	22
Friedrich Lange Company	
(F. Lange vormals C. F. Uhlig)	6, 43
Bankruptcy	6
Graphic of business card	43
Majestic Concertina	4
As Wilfahrt's first concertina	78
Photo of	55, 198
Photo of Uhlig-Lange factory, Rosenplatz 2, Chemnitz	4
Photo(s) of Uhlig-Lange concertina	21, 34 ff., 164

Index

Successor of Uhlig	4 ff.
Lange, Friedrich Emil	17
Daughter Niemann, Martha Lange (husband Edward)	44
Death notice	22, 44
Photo	21, 42
Succession of firm from father	23
Wife Martha	44
Lash, Edward (Laszczak)	56, 150, 199
Death of	56
Photos of	56
Leder, Glen	143
Libby, Bruce	
Photo of	210
Liebl, Sylvester (1917-2003)	153, 212-213
Daughter and Son-in-law Carol and Frank Seebauer	213
"Daddy's Girls"	213
Photo of	100, 101, 104
Liebsch, Jerome	93
Lincoln House of Music	100
Lindstrom-Brown Publications	153
Lis, Tony	
Photo of	209
Liss, Kevin J.	228
Lochner, Carmen	220
Loeffelmacher, Harold	86, 156, 207
MacPhail School of Music	114
Maha, George	
Photo of, biography	234
Makovsky, William A.	212
Malecheski, Joe	
Photo of	92
Malek, Eric	
Photo of	227
Marek, Rudolph J.	140
Maser, Lavain Andrew (Slim)	115, 230
Photo of	116
Mathiowetz, Edward T.	
Photo of	226
Maus, Gilbert (Gilly)	
Photo of	224
McDowell, Mary	49
Mecca Music	100
Meidel Music Store	91
Menge, Alfred	85
Mertzacker, M.	140
Messner, Christian	1, 6
Micklitz, Fritz	17
Mid-American Music Association	205
Midwest Concertina Fans	166
Midwest locales	199
Mikla (Miklakiewicz), John	
Photo of	115
Milbret, Emil	156
Miller, Cory	220
Miller, Marshall and Ray	229
Minar, Jerry (Jaroslav)	107 ff., 167
Accordina	120, 205
Photo of	120
Army time	112
Careers	117
Concertina history exhibit	
German and American centers of production	127
Daughter Christy	114
Daughter Jenny	
Photo of	113
Daughter Tammy	114
Daughter Vicky	114
Father Jerry	107
Graphic of business agreements of	128
Graphic of purchase of Hengel trademark	127
Great-Uncle George	111
Induction into Concertina Hall of Fame	
Photo of	130
JBM Recording	117, 118, 167, 207, 215, 218, 221
Job with Stradivarius	117
Nameplates from Hengel	129
Photo of	107, 109, 116, 121, 234
Photo of early home	108
Photo of home/shop	112
Photo with Brian Jilek	122
Photo with Hengel	121
Photo with Kodet	123
Photo with son Jay	125
Photo with son Jay and Hlavac	123
Photo with wife	117, 125
Photo with Wolfe	120
Reworking Hohner accordions	112
Son Jay	
Photo of	110, 113
Photo with Hengel	121
Teacher Sister Imata	107

Tuning techniques	111
Wife Beverly Brunner	114
Minnesota Ballroom Operators Association	202 ff.
Minnesota Concertina Bowl (Fridley, MN)	233
Past performers at	233
Minnesota Music Hall of Fame	101
Minnesota State Polka Festival	171
Moening, Tony	172
Mohr, Allen J.	
Photo of	231
Moldan, Dain	
Photo of	234
Moore, Charlie	126
Moravec, Marvin	110, 112, 218
Morbidoni, Alberto	71
Morbidoni Accordion Company (Italy)	69
Sketches of Echo Double Reed concertina	69
Morris, James	125, 126
Mojsiewicz, Walter	65, 95, 150, 163
Mroczek, Walter M.	155
Mrozinski, Peter and Thomas	210
Mrozinski Brothers' Polka Super Sunday	212
Muehlbauer, Myron	
Famous relations	217
Music and Dance News	100, 155, 156, 160, 164, 168
Graphic of	161
Musilet, Joseph (Joe)	140
Nachreiner, Martin (Marty)	
Photos of	222
Nadherny, Ronald	225
National Concertina Convention	203
National Endowment for the Arts	
National Heritage Fellows	
National Geographic Magazine	102
Nebraska Record Company	169
Omaha Brass Band, etc...	169
Nechanicky, Albert G.	68
130-key system	68, 175
Graphic of instruction book	192
"Nicky's Instructor" for 130-key concertina	182
Photo of	68
Negrini & Borgonovi	94, 116
Neuman, Carl W.	208
Niemann, Carl Julius Ludwig	23
Niemeyer, William A.	144
Nienkark, Elmer	167
Nissel, Carol	212
Nissel, Jodi	
Wife of Brian Brueggen	228
Nissel, Marv	211–212
Novak, Robert	69 ff., 130
Photo of	70
Novotny, Larry	
Photo of	211
Novotny, Robert	
Photo of	209
Photo of concertinas	201
Nowicki, Stanley	56
Ohotto, Art	229
Bio of	229
Photo of	229
Olsen, Larry	217, 264
Olsen, Leon	
Photo of	216
Oriwohl, Karl	
Graphic of "Accordion" instruction	184
Oskar Seifert Publishing House	177
Papa, John	137
Pasek, Chuck	216
Paser, Roger	118
Patek, Rudy	46, 53 ff., 80, 95, 97, 110, 119, 124, 144, 145
Catalog page of	144
Concertina Self Instructor	147
Deluxe concertina	145
Graphics of various paraphernalia	146
Gravestone of	53
Pearl Queen dealer stamp	192
Photos of	52–53
Photo of concertina	166
Store of	46, 53, 74, 80, 100
Photo of envelope from	50
Photo of ID stamp of	193
Technical assistance offered	192
Perkowsky, Kajetan	65, 163
Wife Esther Annerson	53
Perpich, Rudy	102, 210
Peters, Helmut (1898-1994) and Max (1895-1983)	230
Pexa, Dale	
Photo of	232
Pieplow, Mark	212
Pikal, Gary	172
Pikal, Wally	204
Pillar, Richard (Dick)	168
Pirner, Christian Friedrich	16, 18

Index

Pleines, Roy Frank	
Graphic of "paid on account" form for Pearl Queen	141
Polka & Old Time News	66, 100, 153, 154, 155
Graphics of	153
Polka Day festival	91, 150, 152, 155
Advertisement for	203
Photo of	152
Polka Music Hall of Fame	168
Polonia Music House	50, 100
Owner, W. H. Sajewski	50, 51
Private players	
Listing of	231
Prochaska, Gordon	92
Photo of	217
Progressive Music Studios	100
Prohut, Lou	171
Promotion and Distribution	131 ff.
Concertina Players Magazine	131
Internet and	172-173
Photo of television appearance for	214, 215
Radio performances	154
Przybylski, Chad	212
Quie, Governor Albert	210
Raclawski, Richard S.	65, 72
Photo of	71
Randles, Bruno	213
Rannow, Raymond	
Photo of	221
Ratajczak, Floryjan	23
Prevalence in Poland	23
Ray Stolzenberg Enterprises	162
Reck, Ernie	167
Reichel, Christian Friedrich	16, 21, 176, 197
Emigration to Milwaukee	17
Reinhart, Hugo Steven	93
Photo of	207
Rezac, Roman	93, 220
Photo of	219, 234
Rickert, Eddie	166
Rindisbacher, Otto	140
Ristow, Rodney	153
Roback, Donald W. (1936-2004)	
Photos of	72
Roback (Chroback), Walter (father of Don) (1907-1980)	72, 205
Rodgers (Rodziczak), Richard (Dick)	99, 154, 225
Photo of grave of (with Rippley)	154
Roscianni, Pompillio	65
Sold Star brand in 1989 to Bernhardt and Cogana	65
Rostalsky, William	140
Rysavy, Larry	101
S. S. Gralak Music Store	50
Poster for	51
Sample melody charts (push/draw)	186
Sandhurst, Adam	217
Photo of	234
Schaefer, Fred	160
Scheffler, Max	
104-key system "Schefflersche"	179
Scheid, Elmer	
Bio of	221
Photo of	234
Scheller, Richard	
Patent for Symphonetta	25
Symphonetta-Schule für den Selbstunterricht	180
Schlicht, Otto (and factory)	44, 46, 52, 60, 74, 78, 80, 87, 88, 95, 96, 97, 100, 110, 114, 116, 121, 123, 152
Death notice of	57
Family	60
Patents for	58
Photo of	59
Schroeder, Linda	207
Schubert, Lowell	
Photo of	104
Schuckert, Henry, Sr. (1887-1967)	67, 84, 87, 96, 97, 143, 149, 184
Photo of	67, 144
Photo of "Queen"	67, 292
Schuckert Music Store	67, 143
Schuft, Gerald Erich (Jerry)	110, 153
Bio of	210 ff.
Photo of	209
Schunk, Alfred	143
Schutte, Francis	137
Senefelder Liederkranz	61
Sereika, Stanley	140
Serial numbers	
Graphics of Hengel configurations	101
Patek and Pearl Queen concertinas	73-74
"Jet Queen"	149
Star concertinas	74
Servatius, George	172, 184, 209

"Big Annual Concertina Party"	172
Photo of	218
Photo of	207
Photo of George Servatius Concertina Party	218
Wife Nellie	172
Scheffler, Max (1864-1930)	4, 8
Photo of	4
Photo of house/store	5
Store/home	4
Siewierski, Casey	171
Sig Manufacturing	123
Silberhorn, Henry (and company)	59, 95, 100, 131 ff., 199
128-key concertina	180
Advertisement for address change (with photo)	135
Bandonion music and	133
Beer Waltz Medley	
Beginners books in German	179
Brother Carl	131
Clarion concertina	137, 140
Photo of "Clarion" nameplate	60
Advertisement for	140, 143
Concertina methodology	177-181
Concertina Players Magazine	131
"Concertina specialist, Chicago"	178
Early life	60
Emigration to Chicago	61
Graphic of both hand exercises	183
Compositions by	135
Graphic of compositions by	133
Graphics of catalogues for	136
Graphic of Fingering chart for teachers of the concertina	181
Graphic of Fingering Chart	180
Graphic of Henry Silberhorn journal	132
Testimonials (various persons)	140
Graphic of instructional manuals	176
Graphic of instructional verbiage of music	179
Graphic of keyboard	194
Graphic of left hand exercises	182
Graphic of music theory rudiments	177
Graphic of receipt for Roy Frank Pleines	141
Graphic of chart for transposing keys of	193
"Hints, Helps and Advice"	193
Import problems for	134
Letter and used concertinas from	141
Library of	159
Loyola concertina	142
Advertisement for	142
Move from 516 to 519-21 Milwaukee Ave.	135
Photo of building	135
Orders from Czechoslovakia	137
Photo of building site	59
Photo of Rippley posing in T-Shirt for	137
Photo of store	131
Silberhorn's "Booster for the Advancement of the Concertina"	60-61, 133
Graphic for	134
Phil W. Beitel and	133
Sample page from	143
Teacher Frank Schmidt	134
Sister Valeria	210
Sitek, John	64
Sitek Concertina	64, 291
Smieja, Michael	71
Photo of	70
Wife Jeanne Goerrs	71
Solar, Louis	
Originated 124-key concertina	180
Sowada, David (Dave)	221
Spaeth, Felix	92, 94
Photo of	93
Stanczewski, Frank J.	70
Stang, Dwight	220
Photo of (with Carmen Lochner and Harry Wojahn)	217
Stang, Richard	
Photo of	104, 218
Star Concertina Manufacturing Company	61 ff., 124
Change of address	
Advertisement mentioning	148
Connection to International Accordion Company	61
Silberhorn and	95
End of	96
End of operations	66
Graphic of business card for	62
Photo of Kadlubowski, Walter, Jr.	64, 71
Photo of Kadlubowski, Walter, Sr.	61, 63, 64
Photo of Mojsiewicz, Walter	61, 65
Photo of Perkowaki, Carmen	61
Photo of Star concertina	62, 201
Photo of tuner Lucio Lorenzetti (1932-2003)	65, 66, 148

Index

Previous and current owners	65
Rate of production and CAD	66
Star-King concertina	66
Store site(s)	64, 150
Various concertinas	
Advertisements for	148
Stark, Walter M.	46, 184
Steffel, Vern	204, 209, 232
Steil, Gil	
Photo of	234
Sticha, Bohumil	112
Brother Leonard	112
Stoehr, Marvin "Cactus"	213
Stolzenberg, Ray	171
Streachek, Gene	214
Stumpf, Ernie	92, 221
Style of playing	
Immigrant influence on (regionality)	27
Divisions in Chicago and	46
Stypa, John	135
Suchan, Frank	140
Suess, Erwin	101, 153
Hall of Fame induction	218
Photo of	208
Suterko, Edwin P.	
Graphics of keyboard charts	184-185
Suess, Erwin	101, 153
Photo of	208
Switch types	189
Swoboda, William	140
Szymkowiak, Fritz	93
T. Kosatka & Company House of Music	52
Tango	21, 27
Tantow, Julius W.	140
Tanzbär	24
Advertisement for	170
Teikowski, Edward	56
Eddie Teikowski's Music Store	202
Terlikowski, Richard	94
Engraving and	122
Terlinde, Edward	107, 111
Terlinde Music Store	107
Advertisement for	110
Then, Jerome	
Photo of	230
Thielen, Terry	220
Thielen, Todd	220
Tucholski, Al	70
Uhlig, Carl Friedrich	1 ff., 163, 176, 197
Anzeiger Newspaper	7
Competitors in neighboring cities	7
Concertina inventor	1
Creation of Chemnitzer Concertina	2
Distinguishing features	3
Graphic of bass run	191
Graphic of slide rule	191
Keys of	
How to play in different keys	190-191
Maintenance	190
Melody side switches	189
Reeds—long plate, wax, pinned—and photos	187
Sound board and photos	187
Standardization of keyboard	8
Tips for practicing	189-190
Death notice	22
Early career	2
Handlung Musikalischer Instrumente von C. F. Uhlig	2
Picture of advertisement	6
Influence of Cyrillus Demian (1772-1847)	2
Music annotated and signed by	195
Picture	1
Picture of brochure	3
Prominence in Klingenthal region	2
Store site	2
Uhlir, Stan	69 ff., 112, 116, 154
Contributions of	70
Death of	71
Dobes, Edward	70
Photo of Dobes Krava Band	71
Echo concertina	70, 114, 116, 154
Photo of	114
United Music Company	100, 104, 109, 154
United Music Teachers of Hutchinson, MN	
Advertisement for	108
Uses in Entertainment	197 ff.
Dance halls	198, 202 ff.
Folk instrument	197
National location (nationalities)	197 ff.
"Majowka" (May Day celebration)	205
Playing styles	205
Rural instrument	199
VEB (Volkseigener Betrieb)	24, 97

Klingenthaler Harmonikawerke	98
Vierling, Nicky	90
Vicevich, John	289, 292
Vitak, Louis	44 ff., 80, 142
Home in Canton, Ohio	45
Raifanda, Antony (secretary)	45
Vitak-Elsnic Company	18, 46, 47, 52, 74, 95, 147, 149
Advertisements for	143, 149
Bohemian music	177
Buying Colonial Music Company	172
"Concertina News"	149
Different makes	149
Graphics of paraphernalia from	147
Photo of business envelope from	49
Photo of former store location	50
Photos of "Pearl Queen" nameplates	50
Purchases from William Brown	50, 77
Waller, Herman	140
Walles, Jack (Wally)	87
Italian Accordion Company and	89
Walles Music	90
Photo of building	89
Wallschläger, Klaus	
Photo of (with Symphonetta)	25
Wanta, Adam	
Photo of/biography	236
Watters, Pat	56, 96, 99, 128, 152, 155, 159, 167, 171, 181, 192, 199
All Star Concertina Vol. 1	157
Dance Bands started by	171
Photo of (receiving Hall of Fame award)	155
Graphic of letter/contract from Silberhorn	156
Weber, Janette	207
Wendinger brothers (Paul and Peter)	92, 153, 171, 207
Carving of	206
Photo of Paul	231
Weiss, Christian	1
Welk, Lawrence	156, 168
Wheatstone, Sir Charles	1, 3
Wilber Nebraska Czech Days	207
Wilfahrt, John Anthony, Jr. (Whoopee John)	
(1893-1961)	77 ff.
Acquisition of concertinas of	78
Brother Eddie	78
Advertisements for	80
Cousin Edward Kretsch	78
Cousin Otto Stueber	78
Photo of parents Barbara Portner and John Wilfahrt, Sr.	77
Photo of Whoopee John Band	78, 232
Son Patrick	79
Wife Bertha Gertrude Hillesheim	77
Wilfahrt's Concertina Club Orchestra	78, 133
Graphics of posters for	79
Okeh and Vocalion Recordings	79, 230
Wilger, Norbert	
Graphic of purchase order from Hengel	89
Wilke, Norman (Norm)	153, 155, 213
Witthus, Rudy	20, 222
Witucki, Daniel	101, 214-215
Bio of	214
Photos of	213
Wog, Orville	84
Wojahn, Harry A.	
Photo of	226
Wolf, Ambrose Butch	
Death of	210
Wolf, Betty	209
Graphic of instructional volume cover for	183
"Wolf's Concertina:" for self-taught player	182, 189
Wolf Concertina Studio	100
Wolf, Tony	99, 120, 171, 184, 209
Bio of	171
Photo with Servatius	158
Students of	164
Tony Wolf Deutschmeister Band	172, 182, 203, 210
Wolfe, Anton	54, 55, 118-120, 171, 205
Advertisement for	119
Brochure for	118, 119
Photo of concertina	127
Photo of workshop	119
Photo with Minar	120
Photo with Szymkowiak and Wydra	125
Wondra, Glenn	118, 220
World Concertina Congress	
(Hall of Fame)	126, 131, 160, 165, 169, 171, 200, 229, 239 ff.
Name register	170
World's Industrial Fair of 1893	4, 42 ff
Lange's success at	4, 43
Wünsch, Johann David (1814-1895)	16
Wydra, Alois L.	124, 166
Galaxy Concertina Manufacturing Company	124

Index

Advertisement for	124
Zadamek, Julius	17
Zelasko, John	
Photo of	63
Zelenka, Paul	100, 115
Zimanski, Gary	
Zimanski Brothers Polka Show	220
Zimmermann, Carl F.	7 ff., 176
Autoharp	
Advertisement for	8
Business in Carlsfeld	7
Emigration to Philadelphia	8
Expositions in London and Munich	7
Exposition in Paris	176
Naturalization of	10
Patent for concertina	14
Photo of	8
Wife Sophie	8
Zimmerman, Harold	165, 166, 199
Zimmerman, Jack	166, 169, 199
Zuehe, Merle	207
Zwack, Gary	212
Zwack Brothers Band	212
Zwack, Keith	212, 225
Photo of	151

Appendix III – A Photographic History of the Chemnitzer Concertina

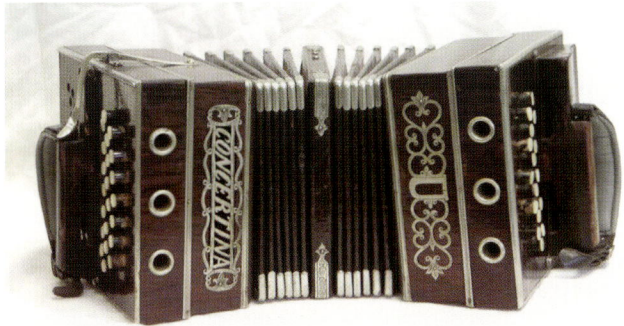

1. UHLIG (76 key / double reed). Carl Uhlig is credited with inventing the concertina in Chemnitz, Germany in 1834. Thus it is called the Chemnitzer concertina. The Uhlig was a low cost, simple instrument with only a few buttons per side. It was considered to serve in producing music for the "working class." As indicated a Uhlig nameplate has a large "U" in the center with scrollwork above and below.

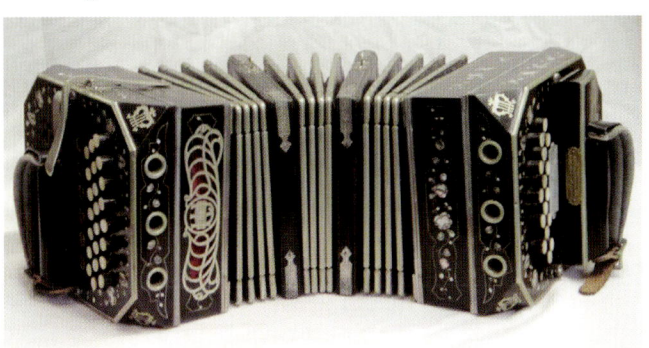

2. LANGE (78 key / double reed). This Lange has LU on the nameplate which indicates that Uhlig's son-in-law, Friedrich Anton Lange, has moved to the head of the Chemnitz company. This instrument has only 39 buttons, hence is a 78-key concertina. Note the ornate mother-of-pearl carefully fitted into the wooden frame.

3. LANGE (102 key / double reed). This is a Lange-Uhlig (LU) creation. However, the keyboard has grown to 52 buttons. As with all Chemnitzer concertinas, a different sound is achieved with each push and pull. This means that 52 buttons yield 104 notes or tones.

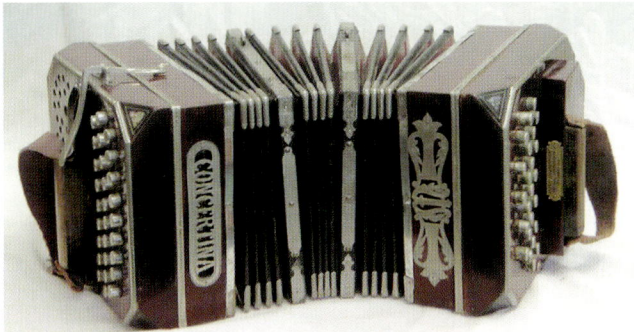

4. SILBERHORN (104 key / single reed). Henry Silberhorn came to Chicago in 1885 and was an early concertina importer, dealer, teacher and music writer. Although it appears he never actually built a concertina, he was influential in the process by which the concertina came to America. Silberhorn is one of the people who made Chicago the concertina hot spot of America.

5. LANGE (102 key / triple reed). The translation of the frontispiece "Lange vormals Uhlig" reads "Lange—formerly Uhlig." It is estimated that this instrument is from the late 19th century, thus over 100 years old. It has three reeds per key (two medium and one piccolo).

6. PEARL QUEEN (104 key / triple reed). Once it was believed that all Pearl Queens were produced and / or assembled in Chicago, often with German components. But this turn-of-the-century Pearl Queen was completely made in Germany! Notice the beautiful pearl and abalone workmanship.

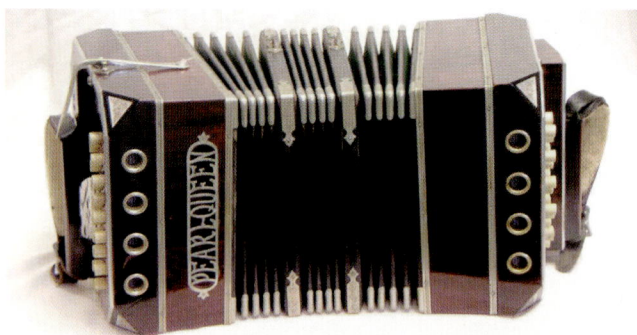

7. PEARL QUEEN (94 key/ triple reed). This concertina was factory-tuned almost a half tone flat in pitch. Hence, it is closer to a B rather than a C concertina. Why? Because the A:440 pitch had not yet been adopted as the world standard. It also has reed plates that appear to be made of zinc rather than the usual aluminum material.

10. SILBERHORN' CLARION (104 key / triple reed). The Clarion was a popular concertina in part because it had a deep sound in the bass section. Note the one-piece bellow stave and corner. *Silberhorn's Concertina Instructor* was published first in 1910 and re-issued many times, once in 1927, roughly the same year as this concertina was built, and is still in use today.

8. PEARL QUEEN (102 key / double reed). This concertina with the serial number 1494 was built in Chicago by the partnership company called Georgi-Vitak in 1916 and acquired by Jerry Minar in the early 1980s. Note the precise fittings of the irregular pieces of abalone. Selling originally for $140, it has the name of "Sweet 16." During this period, concertinas (Pearl Queen) were not furnished with frett plates (white grills on end caps). Was this a factory experiment or did someone add them later?

11. PEARL KING (104 key / double reed) with the serial number 29817. In 1924, the company once known as Georgi-Vitak became Vitak-Elsnic when Louis Vitak invited his nephew, Joseph Elsnic, to join him, and continued marketing the "Pearl Queen." On his own again, Otto Georgi introduced the "Pearl King" but imported the instruments from Germany. This one was finished in Germany on July 12, 1926.

9. PEARL QUEEN (102 key / double reed). When new, this concertina with the serial number 2069 sold for $50, below the fancy models like "Sweet 16" ($140-$90). This was the first concertina to arrive in New Prague and was played by Frank Vavra during the World War I period. Frank climbed the flour mill water tower to play for the whole town. Joseph Jiran was the seller, as indicated on the bellow.

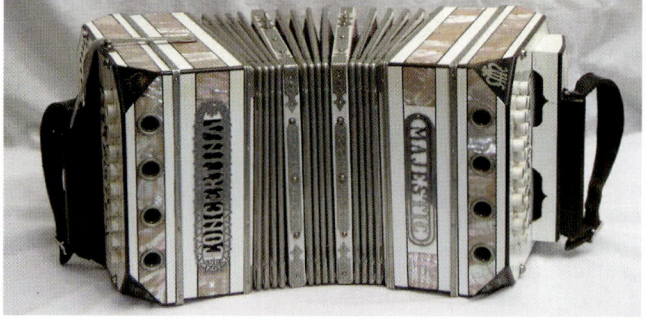

12. MAJESTIC (104 key / double reed) with the serial number 29818. It was built in the same factory and completed on the same day as the Pearl King, July 12, 1926. This indicates that the German factories were producing instruments which were sold under varying brand names. More information on this concertina and its twin (Pearl King) appears in chapter two.

Appendix III — A Photographic History of the Chemnitzer Concertina

13. PEARL QUEEN (102 key / triple reed) with the serial number 3667. This concertina is an early version of the Pearl Queen marketed by Vitak-Elsnic in 1925. The bass sound box is still in use, giving its bass section a deep, throaty reverberation. The pearl and abalone work with engraving is quite rare. The 1924 catalog indicates this concertina as a "Deluxe."

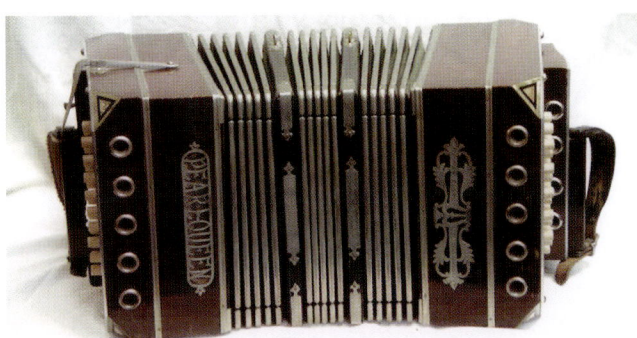

14. PEARL QUEEN (104 key / quadruple reed) with the serial number 4512. The instrument has one low reed, two mediums, and one piccolo. It is a 1920s quad, with a high/low switch on the treble side to shift the low reed in and out. However, the action mechanism is all wooden construction. It still has its original bass sound box.

15. PEARL QUEEN (104 key / double reed) with the serial number 4909. This is a 1930 model whose bass sound box has been replaced with frett plates by factory personnel. On this instrument the abalone was installed in rectangular pieces rather than in random and irregular shapes. The Frett plates (white grills) give the bass and treble keyboards a gentle, clean touch. Following its completion, John Vicevich first tuned this concertina on November 14, 1929. According to the 1920 and 1930 Federal Censuses, Vicevich was born in Croatia in 1878 and immigrated to Chicago in 1893 via Fiume [Rijeka] and labored as a railroad car inspector.

16. PEARL QUEEN (104 key / triple reed) with the serial number 5122. This concertina is an Otto Schlicht product. Its original catalog description reads: "No two concertinas have identical mother of pearl work. An owner can pick his Pearl Queen of a thousand." When new, it sold for $220. This concertina was completed on May 1, 1930 and tuned by J. Vicevich.

17. PATEK (104 key / double reed) with the serial number 5320. This is a 1932 model built at the Otto Schlicht factory which crafted many of the concertinas sold by Rudy Patek through 1946. Patek was a dealer, a distributor, a promoter, an importer and, only later, a manufacturer.

18. PATEK'S Special (104 key / triple reed). This concertina, built by the Otto Schlicht group, is one of Patek's best concertinas. It is the one played by Jerry Minar in the Fall, 1981 *Better Homes and Gardens Bride's Book*, featuring an "ethnic wedding" at Schumacher's Hotel in New Prague.

19. PATEK NONPAREIL (104 key / triple reed / key of C) with the serial number 5300. In 1932 Rudy Patek offered the Nonpareil, a word which in French means "unequaled" or "with no comparison." Inside is an aluminum action which replaced the wooden parts, offering better performance and greater durability.

20. PATEK EXCELSIOR (104 key / 1933 model / triple reed / key of C), with the serial number 5440. On request, Patek would engrave the owner's name on the bellow trim plate. Melvin Grewe of Gibbon, MN was the original owner. This concertina has aluminum action. However, many excelsior models were made with wooden actions.

21. PEARL QUEEN (104 key / triple, key of C) This immaculate specimen bearing the serial #5921 from the year 1939 appears to have never been played. It was acquired from someone in Colorado by Dan Gruetzmacher. Equipped with high triple sound only [no Hi-Lo switch], this concertina has reeds, half of which are Friedl-made, the other half "Dix" reeds from Germany.

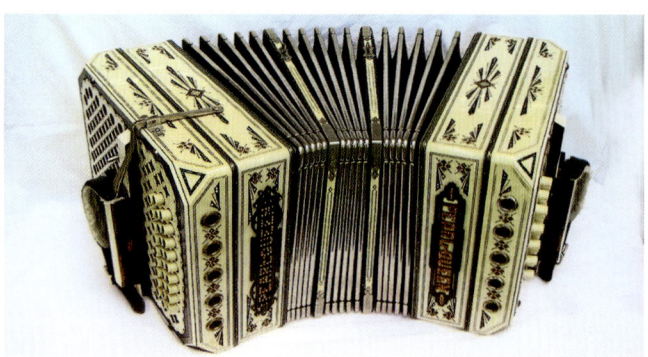

22. PEARL QUEEN (104 key / quadruple reed / Key of C) with the serial number 5847. The Otto Schlicht organization of Chicago produced these concertinas under the Pearl Queen name for the Vitak-Elsnic retailers. In 1937 this concertina was completed two digits ahead of Elmer Scheid's prized Patek, which has the serial number 5849.

23. PATEK (104 key / quadruple reed / Key of C) with the serial number 6158. It is believed that this is the last concertina built in the Otto Schlicht Factory (1946), Otto himself having died already in 1938. It has superb John Friedl reeds. At this time, due to the war effort, plastic had replaced metal on the bellows. Jerry Minar acquired this instrument from Christy Hengel in 2001.

24. PATEK (104 key / quadruple reed Key of B-Flat) An example of an Italian built Patek concertina with the serial number 019. These concertinas were produced during the early to mid-1950s after the Otto Schlicht factory ceased manufacturing concertinas. In the latter 1950s, Rudy Patek tooled up and built the "new style" Patek for several years, then decided to sell all inventory, parts, and equipment to Anton Wolfe in 1967.

Appendix III — A Photographic History of the Chemnitzer Concertina

25. PATEK New Style (104 key / quadruple reed / key of C / 1962 model)
This late model Patek with the serial number 566 was built by Rudy Patek himself after his move to Weyauwega, Wisconsin. However, the engraving was done by Mike Alex. Note that the concertina has no sound holes in the front and that its air lever is made of plastic rather than steel. This concertina is outfitted with waxed reeds, whereas the previous Otto Schlicht-built Patek concertinas all feature the long plate reeds installed with hook screws and not with wax.

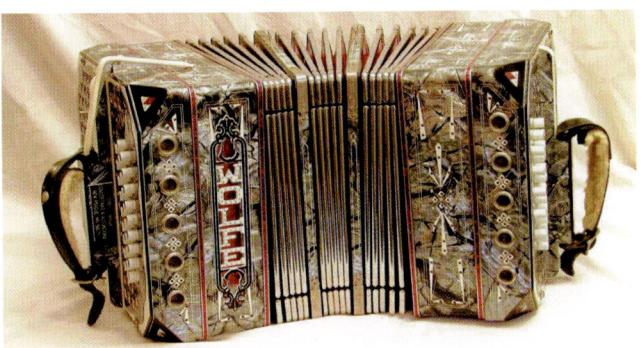

26. WOLFE (104 key / key of E-Flat), with the serial number 433 In 1967, Anton Wolfe of Stevens Point, Wisconsin purchased the equipment and stocks from Rudy Patek in Weyauwega, Wisconsin. A rather clever person, Wolfe hand-crafted the whole instrument from the exterior decoration to the reeds inside. Wolfe continued production until 1994, shortly before his death. His dealer from 1982-1994 was Jerry Minar.

27. GLASS (104 key / quadruple reed / key of A-Flat). Ernst Glass and his sons, Otto and Paul, had been producing concertinas in Chicago for many years and were probably the first to use aluminum action in their concertinas. Glass Brothers made their own reeds as well as the aluminum plates that hold the reeds. Note their typical "wagon wheel" style sound holes on each side. A Glass Brothers trademark is the six-pointed star on the beveled corners.

28. STAR (104 key / quadruple reed / key of C). The Star concertina with the serial number 263 originated from the International Accordion Company founded in 1917 by Walter Mojsiewicz, Walter Kadlubowski, Sr. and Kajetan Perkowski, making only accordions. In 1926 they began a separate division to create concertinas under the name Star. This endeavor continued with owners like Walter Kadlubowski, Jr., Pompillio Roscianni and his partner, Umberto Carroci, and finally Ed Cogana in partnership with John Bernhardt until 2000.

29. SITEK (106 key / triple reed / key of C), with the serial number 189. Note the extra button on the treble side, making it a 106 key instrument. John Sitek worked at the Star Company. In the 1930 federal census for Chicago, John Sitek is listed as having immigrated from Poland, 39 years old, born in 1890, having the occupation of "music teacher," and employed in "music."

30. STAR Special (triple reed / key of C). This early 1930s model illustrates today's preference for the famous "pineapple deluxe engraving. The New Prague Trivia Book by Greg Tikalsky features this instrument on the frontispiece. Christy Hengel states that Mike Alex decorated this concertina. It was built about the time Rudy Patek introduced the Patek Deluxe Concertina in his 1932 catalog.

31. Star (104 key / triple reed Key of B-Flat). The exterior of this concertina appears to be a Star manufacture. However, many internal parts more closely resemble the Pearl Queen. Croatian born John Vicevich [1878-1943], tuner for Vitak-Elsnic, was the likely owner of this concertina as indicated by the nameplate. The notation "tuned by J. Vicevich" appears inside numerous Pearl Queen concertinas built in the 1920s and 1930s, including numbers 14 and 15 in this section. This concertina was originally finished in white pearloid (now yellowing with age). When remodeling the instrument at a later date, large multi-colored rhinestones were added.

32. STAR BEAUTY (104 key / quadruple reed / key of B-Flat), with the serial number 1003. This is an example of the Star Beauty model which was produced from the 1960s until 2000, when Star officially ceased operations. During its 75-year history, Star passed through a half dozen owners. This instrument came originally with eight-tone change capability. Later someone converted it to a standard Hi-Lo setup, presumably to reduce the weight of the instrument.

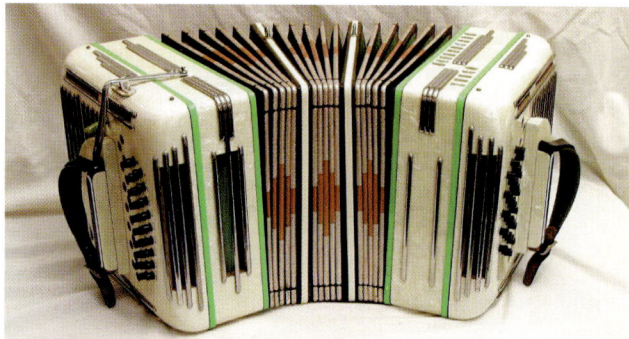

33. STAR "SCHUCKERT'S QUEEN" (104 key / quadruple reed / key of B-Flat), with the serial number 1259. The well-known concertina player, Henry Schuckert of Chicago, was also a tuner, music composer and dealer. Much like Silberhorn, he sometimes acquired concertinas from Star or Schlicht, did the reed work and tuning, and put his own name on the instrument for sale. Chicago players were fond of the condensed keyboard and the smaller buttons of these star models.

34. STAR "STREAMLINE" (104 key / quadruple reed / key of E-Flat). This design started approximately in 1950. This concertina with the serial number 1567 has a condensed keyboard and a design which seems to parallel the era's automobiles—shiny chrome and rounded corners. The last Streamline was built in 1979. Eddie Lash and Wally Jagiello among others in Chicago were promoters of Streamline models.

35. MORBIDONI (104 key / quadruple reed / key of C). Apparently dealers tried to produce a competitor to the "Streamline Star." Well-known Italian accordion builder, Morbidoni crafted this Star look-alike, probably at the request of a dealer-distributor in the United States. The Morbidoni trademark and logo is displayed on the back of the instrument. It is the only known Morbidoni quadruple reed.

36. NATIONAL (104 key / quadruple reed / key of C) with the serial number 166. A rare concertina built in Chicago by Walter Alex and son. The son was Mike Alex, the famous engraver for the Otto Schilcht factory. Mike Alex decorated Patek and Pearl Queen concertinas, the early Hengel concertinas, and some Star concertinas. In a recent visit with the widow of Mike Alex, Christy Hengel was told that this concertina was built in 1926.

Appendix III — A Photographic History of the Chemnitzer Concertina

37. Tanzbär (self-playing concertina). These concertinas were built in Germany to play from paper rolls drawn across tracker bars, much like a player piano. A 1927 brochure from a New England retailer offers descriptions, available rolls with American musical numbers and testimonials. This instrument appeared during the heyday of mechanical, self-playing musical devices.

40. ALFRED ARNOLD (104 key / triple reed key of C) with the serial number B109022, completed March 28, 1938. This concertina has a beautiful wood finish, however, with a plain front and no sound holes or air valve and no front nameplate. In player parlance, its rear air valve makes this concertina a "shirt sucker." Its rear air valve has a nameplate with the letters AA [Alfred Arnold]. The popular assumption is that Alfred Arnold made as many if not more bandonions than concertinas. The bandonion remains a prized instrument in Argentina for tango music.

38. HOHNER "ECHO" (102 key / triple reed / key of C). Hohner, the harmonica and accordion giant in Germany, produced a few Chemnitzer concertinas, apparently to test the market. Note the initials M-H (Matt Hohner) in the beveled corners and the M. Hohner insignia on the right side hand rail. All indications are that actual manufacture was by one of the established factories (Lange, Arnold, etc.) and not by Hohner at Trossingen.

41. ARNO ARNOLD (104 key / quadruple reed / key of E-Flat), with the serial number D5782, completed on March 4, 1958. The Arno Arnold factory in Germany produced 17 different models for beginners, learners and professionals, but production ended in the mid-1960s at a time when Pat Watters of Minneapolis was their main distributor in the United States. John Bolster in Minneapolis tuned this one. This 1958 model features aluminum action parts. Most Arnold concertinas had wooden actions, which were prone to breakdowns.

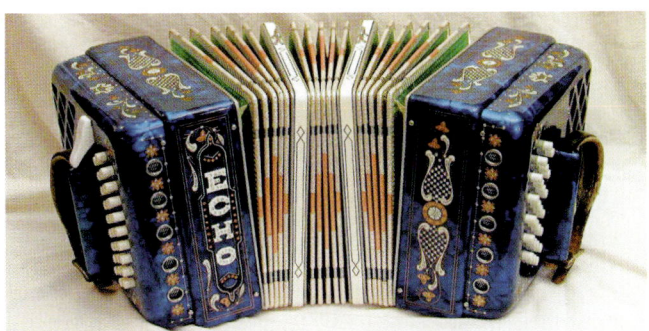

39. ECHO (104 key double reed / key of B-Flat). Stan Uhlir, originally of Montgomery/Heidelberg Minnesota, but later of Minneapolis, imported these concertinas from Italy as beginner models in the 1960s and 1970s. However the most popular Echo instruments are quadruple reeds. Upon the death of Uhlir in 1996, Robert Novak of Lake Elmo took over production of the Echo. Uhlir perfected a clever method of tooling for producing concertina buttons which he sold to Jerry Minar in 1996, shortly before his death.

42. ARNO ARNOLD "Slim Line"(104 key / quadruple reed / key of B-Flat), with the serial number D6532, completed on August 5, 1960. The Arno Arnold factory at Obertshausen near Frankfurt produced many varied models of concertinas. Some have the usual characteristics such as the "Slim Line" model shown here. This concertina is so slim that, when played, one feels one's two hands will almost touch. Tony Wolf of the Deutschmeisters Band played an E-Flat "Slim Line" most of his life, as did his son, Ambrose "Butch" Wolfe.

43. RC LEPPERT (78 key / double reed / key of C) Once in a while a person finds a "one of a kind" concertina. RC Leppert was a tuner in the Chicago area (Jerry Minar owns a Pearl Queen with stamping inside: tuned by RC Leppert). Leppert apparently built this concertina which also features his "patent pending" mechanical tremolo (vibrato) mechanism which is engaged by pressing on a lever next to the air lever on the right side of the concertina.

44. SILBERHORN (104 key / triple reed / key of B-Flat). From the 1920s era, this concertina is rare because it was factory-tuned to B-Flat. Thus it is perfect for playing with a trumpet, for both these instruments transpose C music into B-Flat. This concertina was built for Silberhorn by a factory in Germany. In his *Booster* for concertinas (1927-1932), Silberhorn made strong statements in favor of bass sound boxes, however the majority ruled and soon these models disappeared.

45. STRADIVARIUS (104 key / quadruple reed / key of E-Flat mussette, Model 45M, built about 1975). When the Arnold Factory of Carlsfeld and later of Obertshausen in Germany ceased production, Pat Watters went to Italy with drawings to have an Italian company produce the Stradivarius for the United States market. Several Italian brands followed later. In the late 1960s Bill Brown in New Ulm took on sales for the Stradivarius and also built his own Brown brand. From 1975-1982 Jerry Minar was a Stradivarius dealer, as was Dan Gruetzmacher in Wausau, Wisconsin and Ambrose "Butch Wolf", in St. Cloud, MN.

46. HENGEL'S (104 key / quadruple reed / key of C), with the serial number 61-0046 was produced as number 46, completed December 11, 1961. In 1953, Christy Hengel purchased the remainder of the equipment and stocks of Otto Schlicht in Chicago. Hengel Manufacturing started in Sleepy Eye, then moved to Waseca and since 1965 has operated in New Ulm, Minnesota. Hengel has received numerous awards for his fine concertinas. Approximately the first 100 Hengel concertinas were equipped with Hengel hand-filed reeds. Jerry Minar plans to reintroduce hand-filed reeds with the tooling and equipment now in his possession.

47. HENGEL'S (104 key / quadruple reed / key of B-Flat / 1978 model), with the serial number 227A78, completed August 15, 1977, his 228th concertina. Originally owned by Roman Rezac of Webster/Lonsdale, it features a double switch 1) usual Hi-lo and 2) mussette reed in and out. It also features an electronic organ unit which was installed by Loren Schaeffler of Klossner, Minnesota. By this date the reeds were Hengel-shaped which means Italian-produced reeds with Hengel modifications.

48. HENGEL (104 key / quadruple reed / key of E-Flat mussette), with the serial number 20237, bearing the number 27, was built in New Prague, completed February 8, 2003. In 1995, Jerry and his son, Jay Minar, having made many trips for training purposes to the Hengel shop in New Ulm, produced the New Prague Hengel No. 1. This concertina being number 27 was engraved by Ambrose Kodet and then painted and decorated with rhinestones by Minar's wife, Beverly Minar. All parts are authentic Hengel-acquired materials. The brand names Hengel and Hengel's are registered trademarks now owned by JBM Sound Inc. of New Prague, Minnesota.

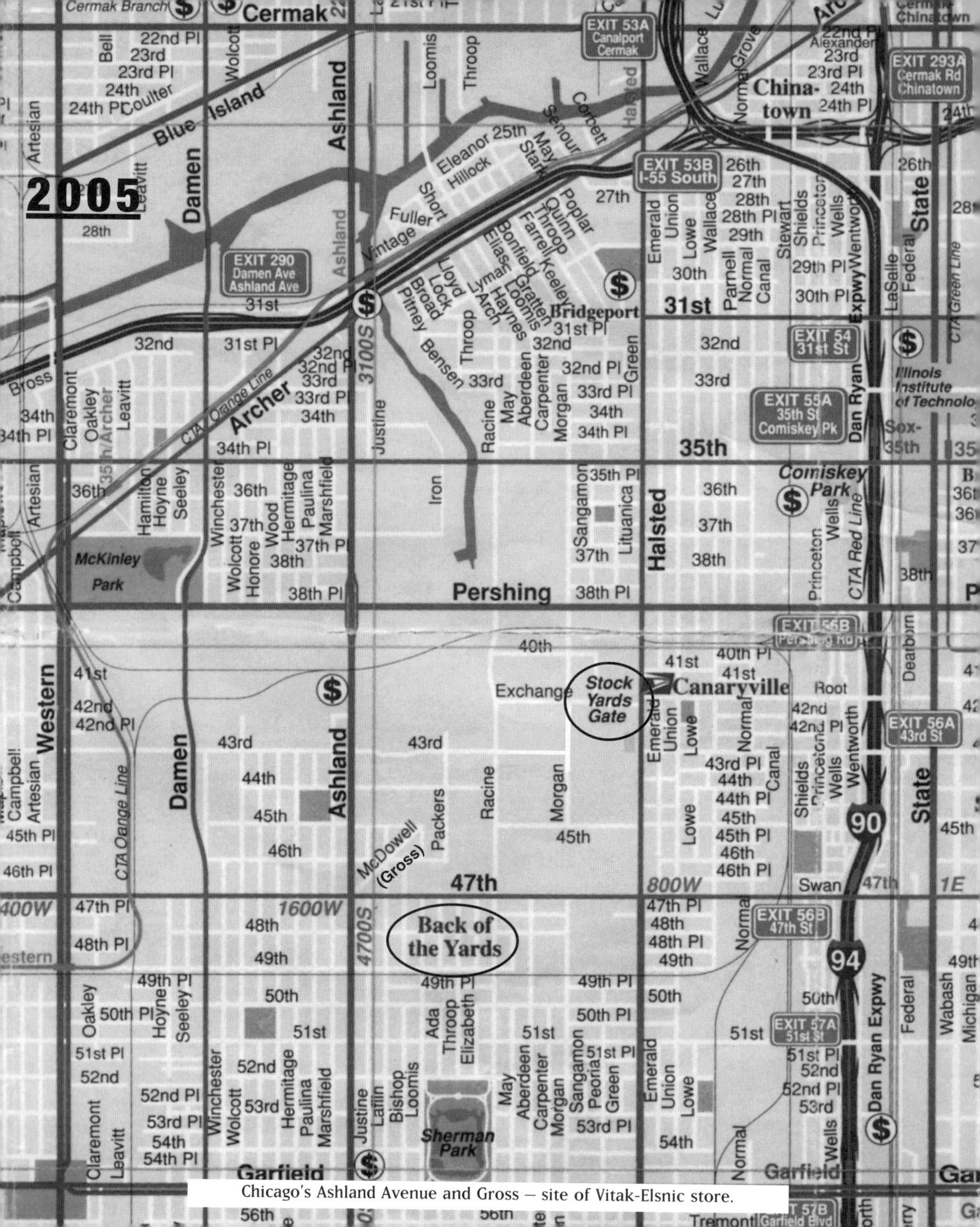

Chicago's Ashland Avenue and Gross — site of Vitak-Elsnic store.